Your Soul's Navigational GPS

Daily Encouragement for Your Journey through
*G*od's Word, *P*ersonal Testimonies and *S*ongs

Brandi N. Jefferson-Motley

Published By Mr. Alexander M. Jefferson

Your Soul's Navigational GPS
©2017 by Brandi N. Jefferson-Motley

All rights reserved. No part of this publication may be reproduced, stored in a retrieval system, or transmitted in any form or by any means—electronic, mechanical, photocopy, recording, or any other-except for brief quotations in printed reviews, without the prior permission of the publisher.

Published 2017, by Mr. Alexander M. Jefferson
East Meadow, New York, U.S.A.

ISBN 978-0-9978332-2-5
Library of Congress Control Number: 2017936228
This book is printed on acid-free paper

All scripture quotations, unless otherwise indicated, are taken from the New King James Version. Used by permission. All rights reserved.

Cover Illustration: Christopher B. Motley
Cover design: August Pride, LLC
Interior design: Adina Cucicov

Printed in the United States of America

To my husband, Christopher, your love and support have been the wind beneath my wings, when I didn't even know that it was time to take flight.

Alexander, Ariana and Amina, you three are my reminders each and every day of just how much the Lord loves me. Out of all the mothers, past, present and those who still have yet to be born, He chose ME for YOU.

Each of you constantly inspire me to be all that God has created me to be.

Encouragement for Your Journey Prayer

As you walk along the path that is set before you, here is my personal prayer for each of you:

I pray that you always know the importance of making time for the Lord first...
(Seek first the kingdom of God and His righteousness, and then all these things will be given to you too... Matthew 6:33)

I pray that you will align yourself with God's will for your life and watch how He will work on your behalf...
(The Lord makes secure the footsteps, of the person who delights in him... Psalm 37:23)

I pray that you never lose sight of how special you are...
(I will give thanks to you because I have been so amazingly and miraculously made. Your works are miraculous, and my soul is fully aware of this... Psalm 139:14)

I pray that while in the midst of a storm you always remember to rejoice and praise His name...
(In this you greatly rejoice, even though now, if for a little while, you have had to suffer various trials... 1 Peter 1:6)

I pray that you will not allow yourself to be burdened or bound by your past....
(Brothers and sisters, I know that I still have a long way to go. But there is one thing I do: I forget what is in the past and try as hard as I can to reach the goal before me... Philippians 3:13)

I pray that just as God blesses you, you will be a blessing unto others...
(Let your light so shine before men that they may see your moral excellence and your praiseworthy, noble, and good deeds and recognize and honor and praise and glorify your Father Who is in heaven... Matthew 5:16)

And lastly, I pray that you never forget that the sky is not the limit, when God is the one navigating your path...
(Now to the One being able to do super-abundantly beyond all of the things which we ask or think according to the power being at work in us... Ephesians 3:20)

This prayer I submit in the most holy and precious name of Jesus... Amen

Contents

Forsaking All I Trust Him (Faith) 1

   James 1:6 (Worldwide English (New Testament)/WE) 2
   Philippians 4:19 (The Message /MSG) 4
   Lamentations 3:25 (New International Reader's Version/NIRV) 5
   Isaiah 8:12-13 (Easy-to-Read Version/ERV) 7
   1 Corinthians 2:9 (Amplified Bible/AMP) 8
   Philippians 4:13 (Amplified Bible/AMP) 9
   Luke 1:37 (Amplified Bible/AMP) 10
   Philippians 1:6 (The Living Bible/TLB) 12
   Deuteronomy 31:8 (Amplified Bible/AMP) 13
   Ephesians 3:20 (Amplified Bible/AMP) 15
   Job 42:2 (World English Bible/WEB) 17
   Hebrews 11:8 (New International Reader's Version/NIRV) 19
   Philippians 3:12 (J.B. Phillips New Testament/PHILLIPS) 20
   2 Corinthians 4:13 (The Living Bible/TLB) 22
   Jeremiah 17:7 (Expanded Bible/EXB) 23
   Habakkuk 2:3 (Contemporary English Version/CEV) 24
   1 Timothy 6:12 (Easy-to-Read Version/ERV) 25
   Hebrews 10:23 (Complete Jewish Bible/CJB) 26
   Psalm 31:24 (New International Reader's Version/NIRV) 28
   Psalm 119:11 (Contemporary English Version/CEV) 29
   Luke 18:27 (The Message/MSG) 30
   Hebrews 13:8 (Lexham English Bible/LEB) 31
   Job 23:14 (International Standard Version/ISV) 33
   1 Samuel 17:45 (New International Reader's Version/NIRV) 34
   1 Peter 2:2 (New Life Version/NLV) 36
   2 Peter 1:4 (GOD'S WORD Translation/GW) 37
   Philippians 4:12 (The Living Bible/TLB) 38
   Philippians 4:6 (GOD'S WORD Translation/GW) 39
   John 15:7 (Young's Literal Translation/YLT) 40
   Proverbs 23:18 (The Voice/VOICE) 41

Matthew 14: 28-29 (Lexham English Bible/LEB) ... 42
Isaiah 55:9 (Holman Christian Standard Bible/HCSB) ... 44
Genesis 28:15 (Lexham English Bible/LEB) ... 45
1 Corinthians 15:57 (New Revised Standard Version/NRSV) ... 46
Proverbs 3:5-6 (Contemporary English Version/CEV) ... 47
Proverbs 19:21 (English Standard Version/ESV) ... 48
Revelation 3:8 (Easy-to-Read Version/ERV) ... 49
Psalm 9:10 (New Life Version/NLV) ... 51
Hebrews 4:16 (Contemporary English Version/CEV) ... 53
1 Timothy 1:19 (Amplified Bible/AMP) ... 54
1 Corinthians 2:5 (The Message/MSG) ... 56
Isaiah 14:24 (New International Reader's Version/NIRV) ... 57
2 Samuel 22:33 (New English Translation/NET Bible) ... 58
Deuteronomy 30:16 (The Message/MSG) ... 59
Deuteronomy 15:5 (New American Bible (Revised Edition)/NABRE) ... 61
Ephesians 6:16 (New Life Version/NLV) ... 62
John 7:38 (Amplified Bible/AMP) ... 63
Romans 10:10 (Complete Jewish Bible/CJB) ... 65
Acts 13:47 (New American Bible (Revised Edition)/NABRE) ... 66
Psalm 119:66 (Amplified Bible, Classic Edition/AMPC) ... 68
2 Timothy 2:7 (New American Bible (Revised Edition)/NABRE) ... 69
Revelation 14:12 (New English Translation/NET Bible) ... 70
Lamentations 3:24 (The Voice/VOICE) ... 71
1 Thessalonians 5:24 (New Life Version/NLV) ... 72
2 Corinthians 5:7 (The Voice/VOICE) ... 73
Numbers 23:19 (New English Translation/NET Bible) ... 75
Romans 10:17 (English Standard Version/ESV) ... 76
Psalm 118:6 (The Voice/VOICE) ... 77
Matthew 6:34 (The Message/MSG) ... 78
Proverbs 4:25 (Expanded Bible/EXB) ... 79
Hebrews 11:1 (J.B. Phillips New Testament/ PHILLIPS) ... 81
Romans 4:20-21 (Easy-to-Read Version/ERV) ... 83
2 Timothy 4:7 (The Voice/VOICE) ... 84
Psalm 112:7 (The Living Bible/TLB) ... 85
Isaiah 55:11 (Names of God Bible/NOG) ... 87
Hebrews 6:11-12 (The Message/MSG) ... 89
Job 9:27 (Darby Translation/DARBY) ... 92
2 Corinthians 1:10 (New International Reader's Version/NIRV) ... 94
Hebrews 6:1 (The Message/MSG) ... 96
Hebrews 12:1 (The Voice/VOICE) ... 97

Isaiah 50:7 (The Living Bible/TLB) 98
Colossians 2:7 (Contemporary English Version/CEV) 99
John 20:29 (Worldwide English (New Testament)/WE) 101
Psalm 27:13-14 (Amplified Bible, Classic Edition/AMPC) 103
Hebrews 11:6 (New Life Version/NLV) 105
Galatians 6:9 (Amplified Bible, Classic Edition/AMPC) 107
Isaiah 40:8 (The Voice/VOICE) 109
Deuteronomy 13:4 (Holman Christian Standard Bible/HCSB) 111
Psalm 119:30 (New International Version/NIV) 113
Deuteronomy 31:6 (New Life Version/NLV) 115
Genesis 15:6 (Amplified Bible/AMP) 116
1 Timothy 3:9 (New International Reader's Version/NIRV) 118
Psalm 143:8 (The Message/MSG) 120
Hebrews 11:3 (New International Reader's Version/NIRV) 122
Proverbs 16:20 (Amplified Bible, Classic Edition/AMPC) 123
Isaiah 45:2 (Amplified Bible, Classic Edition/AMPC) 125
Romans 4:21 (Amplified Bible, Classic Edition/AMPC) 127
Romans 12:12 (Expanded Bible/EXB) 129

God's Word is Complete, His Love is Unconditional and His Power is Inexhaustible 131

Malachi 3:6 (The Living Bible/TLB) 132
Psalm 32:7 (The Message/MSG) 133
Isaiah 45:8 (Good News Translation/GNT) 134
1 John 4:10 (The Message/MSG) 135
2 Corinthians 5:17 (J.B. Phillips New Testament/PHILLIPS) 136
Matthew 10:29-31 (Names of God Bible/NOG) 137
1 Peter 5:10 (New International Reader's Version/NIRV) 138
Isaiah 11:2 (The Message/MSG) 139
Luke 5:26 (New Living Translation/NLT) 140
Zephaniah 3:17 (Good News Translation/GNT) 141
Hebrews 6:18 (Contemporary English Version/CEV) 143
John 4:13-14 (The Message/MSG) 145
Proverbs 16:24 (Names of God Bible/NOG) 147
2 Thessalonians 3:3 (Amplified Bible/AMP) 149
Romans 8:37 (Amplified Bible /AMP) 151
Isaiah 58:12 (The Message/MSG) 153
2 Corinthians 2:14 (New American Standard Bible/NASB) 155
Revelation 1:8 (Amplified Bible/AMP) 156
Isaiah 12:2 (New English Translation/NET Bible) 157
Deuteronomy 31:8 (International Standard Version/ISV) 159

Colossians 3:23 (Amplified Bible/AMP) 161
Proverbs 16:9 (GOD'S WORD Translation/GW) 163
Psalm 18:35 (Amplified Bible/AMP) 165
Lamentations 3:22 (New American Bible (Revised Edition/NABRE) 166
Psalm 138:7 (New Century Version/NCV) 167
Isaiah 41:10 (Easy-to-Read Version/ERV) 168
Isaiah 64:8 (The Voice/VOICE) 169
Psalm 55:22 (Easy-to-Read Version/ERV) 171
Romans 8:28 (Contemporary English Version/CEV) 173
1 Chronicles 29:11 (New Life Version/NLV) 174
Psalm 146:5 (GOD'S WORD Translation/GW) 175
Jeremiah 31:3 (English Standard Version Anglicised/ESVUK) 176
Psalm 27:1 (Holman Christian Standard Bible/HCSB) 177
Jeremiah 33:3 (Amplified Bible/AMP) 178
Proverbs 3:13 (Amplified Bible/AMP) 179
Psalm 41:11 (Modern English Version/MEV) 180
2 Timothy 1:9 (International Standard Version/ISV) 182
Psalm 52:8 (Lexham English Bible/LEB) 183
Psalm 34:18 (The Voice/VOICE) 185
2 Peter 1:3 (International Children's Bible/ICB) 186
2 Corinthians 12:9 (The Voice/VOICE) 188
Romans 5:8 (The Voice/VOICE) 190
Job 5:9 (New Living Translation/NLT) 191
Isaiah 60:1 (New Life Version/NLV) 192
Titus 3:5 (Easy-to-Read Version/ERV) 194
Isaiah 43:1 (The Voice/VOICE) 196
Psalm 86:15 (International Standard Version/ISV) 197
Isaiah 61:3 (International Standard Version/ISV) 198
Psalm 5:12 (New King James Version/NKJV) 200
John 1:16 (New International Version—UK/NIVUK) 201
Isaiah 42:16 (International Children's Bible/ICB) 202
Ephesians 1:11 (The Living Bible/TLB) 203
Psalm 147:5 (The Message/MSG) 204
Psalm 139:5 (Complete Jewish Bible/CJB) 205
Nehemiah 9:6 (Easy-to-Read Version/ERV) 206
John 15:16 (Worldwide English (New Testament)/WE) 207
Isaiah 58:11 (New International Version—UK/NIVUK) 208
Philippians 4:7 (J.B. Phillips New Testament/PHILLIPS) 210
Jeremiah 10:6 (New Century Version/NCV) 211
Exodus 34:6 (1599 Geneva Bible/GNV) 212

Psalm 56:8 (The Living Bible/TLB) 213
Isaiah 40:28 (Modern English Version/MEV) 215
Isaiah 26:4 (The Voice/VOICE) 217
Psalm 36:5 (The Message/MSG) 218
Ephesians 4:6 (Expanded Bible/EXB) 220
Psalm 103:10 (International Standard Version/ISV) 222
Isaiah 30:18 (The Voice/VOICE) 223
Psalm 31:19 (New English Translation/NET Bible) 224
Ephesians 1:4 (Good News Translation/GNT) 226
Jeremiah 32:27 (New American Bible (Revised Edition)/NABRE) 228
Joshua 1:5 (Names of God Bible/NOG) 229
Matthew 10:31 (The Voice/VOICE) 230
Romans 5:5 (Amplified Bible, Classic Edition/AMPC) 232
Hebrews 10:14 (Amplified Bible/AMP) 233
Isaiah 59:1 (New American Standard Bible/NASB) 235
Matthew 11:29 (Revised Standard Version Catholic Edition/RSVCE) 237
2 Timothy 4:22 (New Life Version/NLV) 238
Matthew 19:26 (Disciples' Literal New Testament/DLNT) 239
Revelation 3:16 (J.B. Phillips New Testament/PHILLIPS) 240
Malachi 4:2 (Easy-to-Read Version/ERV) 242
Acts 20:24 (New Living Translation/NLT) 244
Psalm 86:5 (New Revised Standard Version/NRSV) 245
Proverbs 19:23 (New English Translation/NET Bible) 246
John 10:14 (Amplified Bible/AMP) 248
Acts 17:28 (J.B. Phillips New Testament/PHILLIPS) 249
1 Corinthians 8:6 (Contemporary English Version/CEV) 251
Psalm 34:19 (The Voice/VOICE) 252
2 Samuel 22:2 (Easy-to-Read Version/ERV) 253
Psalm 33:18 (New International Version/NIV) 254
2 Peter 3:18 (Amplified Bible, Classic Edition/AMPC) 255
Proverbs 15:3 (International Children's Bible/ICB) 257
2 Timothy 2:1 (Mounce Reverse-Interlinear New Testament/MOUNCE) ... 259
Mark 8:36 (The Voice/VOICE) 260
Amos 3:3 (Modern English Version/MEV) 262
Psalm 107:14 (New English Translation/NET Bible) 265
Daniel 4:3 (The Message/MSG) 266
Psalm 108:4 (Amplified Bible, Classic Edition/AMPC) 267
John 1:29 (Disciples' Literal New Testament/DLNT) 268
1 John 4:11 (The Voice/VOICE) 270
1 John 4:16 (J.B. Phillips New Testament/PHILLIPS) 271

Romans 6:17-18 (Modern English Version/MEV) 273
Genesis 50:20 (New International Reader's Version/NIRV) 275
Jeremiah 32:17 (Amplified Bible/AMP) 277
2 Thessalonians 3:16 (The Voice/VOICE) 279
Psalm 91:14-15 (The Voice/VOICE) 280
1 Chronicles 29:12 (Holman Christian Standard Bible/HCSB) 282
Ephesians 2:8 (Worldwide English (New Testament)/WE) 283
Nehemiah 1:5 (New Living Translation/NLT) 284
John 6:35 (Lexham English Bible/LEB) 285
Psalm 126:5 (Lexham English Bible/LEB) 287
Job 12:10 (The Voice/VOICE) 288
Psalm 103:13 (The Voice/VOICE) 289
Jeremiah 1:5 (New Life Version/NLV) 291
1 Thessalonians 5:11 (New International Reader's Version/NIRV) 293
Deuteronomy 32:4 (International Standard Version/ISV) 296

Praise And Worship Are How I Express My Gratitude 297

Psalm 113:3 (Amplified Bible/AMP) 298
1 Corinthians 1:4 (The Living Bible/TLB) 299
Hebrews 4:16 (Worldwide English (New Testament)/WE) 301
1 Thessalonians 5:16-17 (Expanded Bible/EXB) 302
Colossians 1:11 (Complete Jewish Bible/CJB) 304
Psalm 103:2 (Expanded Bible/EXB) 306
Ephesians 5:20 (International Standard Version/ISV) 308
Hebrews 13:15 (Complete Jewish Bible/CJB) 309
Hebrews 12:28 (English Standard Version/ESV) 310
Exodus 15:2 (Common English Bible/CEB) 312
Psalm 139:14 (Authorized (King James) Version/AKJV) 313
Psalm 146:2 (International Children's Bible/ICB) 315
1 Thessalonians 3:9 (New Living Translation/NLT) 316
Deuteronomy 10:21 (New International Version/NIV) 317
Psalm 63:3 (The Message/MSG) 318
Isaiah 12:5 (Contemporary English Version/CEV) 320
Hebrews 13:16 (The Message/MSG) 321
Psalm 35:28 (Amplified Bible/AMP) 323
1 Thessalonians 5:18 (The Voice/VOICE) 324
Psalm 71:14 (Wycliffe Bible/WYC) 325
Psalm 150:2 (The Living Bible/TLB) 326
Psalm 103:1 (Amplified Bible, Classic Edition/AMPC) 328
Isaiah 43:21 (The Voice/VOICE) 329

    Psalm 118:21 (International Standard Version/ISV) 330
    Psalm 136:26 (The Voice/VOICE) 331
    Isaiah 42:12 (Amplified Bible, Classic Edition/AMPC) 332
    2 Corinthians 4:15 (GOD'S WORD Translation/GW) 333
    1 Chronicles 16:8 (New Living Translation/NLT) 334
    John 4:24 (The Voice/VOICE) 335
    Psalm 34:1 (Common English Bible/CEB) 336
    Psalm 100:2 (Modern English Version/MEV) 337
    Jeremiah 17:14 (Expanded Bible/EXB) 338
    Psalm 30:12 (The Voice/VOICE) 339
    Psalm 71:8 (Wycliffe Bible/WYC) 341
    Psalm 63:4 (The Message/MSG) 342

Life Is Fragile, Handle It With Prayer 345

    Psalm 5:3 (Common English Bible/CEB) 346
    1 Peter 5:7 (The Living Bible/TLB) 347
    Luke 18:1 (The Living Bible/TLB) 349
    1 Kings 8:28 (Easy-to-Read Version/ERV) 350
    Matthew 6:6 (The Message/MSG) 351
    Psalm 145:18 (Expanded Bible/EXB) 352
    Colossians 4:2 (Amplified Bible/AMP) 353
    Exodus 33:14 (Complete Jewish Bible/CJB) 355
    Psalm 141:2 (Names of God Bible/NOG) 356
    Psalm 138:3 (The Voice/VOICE) 358
    Jeremiah 29:12 (Amplified Bible/AMP) 360
    Mark 11:24 (Amplified Bible/AMP) 361

Surrendering Must Be Adopted As A Lifestyle 363

    Matthew 6:33 (The Message/MSG) 364
    Romans 12:2 (The Voice/VOICE) 365
    John 15:5 (J.B. Phillips New Testament/PHILLIPS) 367
    1 Peter 2:9 (The Living Bible/TLB) 368
    Isaiah 9:4 (Names of God Bible/NOG) 370
    Galatians 2:20 (New Living Translation/NLT) 372
    2 Timothy 1:7 (New International Reader's Version/NIRV) 373
    Revelation 21:5 (Disciples' Literal New Testament/DLNT) 374
    Psalm 139:16 (The Message/MSG) 376
    2 Corinthians 4:7 (The Voice/VOICE) 378
    Psalm 90:12 (New Living Translation/NLT) 380
    Galatians 5:1 (World English Bible/WEB) 381

Isaiah 26:3 (Amplified Bible/AMP)	383
John 15:4 (The Message/MSG)	385
Ephesians 4:31-32 (New Life Version/NLV)	386
Colossians 3:10 (International Children's Bible/ICB)	388
Jeremiah 31:19 (Common English Bible/CEB)	390
Luke 11:28 (The Living Bible/TLB)	392
Philippians 3:13 (Expanded Bible/EXB)	393
Matthew 5:16 (New Century Version/NCV)	395
Jeremiah 29:13 (Amplified Bible/AMP)	397
Matthew 5:14-15 (J.B. Phillips New Testament/PHILLIPS)	398
Philippians 2:13 (International Standard Version/ISV)	399
Isaiah 43:19 (The Living Bible (TLB)	400
Psalm 119:105 (Easy-to-Read Version/ERV)	401
John 8:36 (Amplified Bible/AMP)	402
Psalm 37:5 (The Voice/VOICE)	403
Proverbs 18:21 (International Standard Version/ISV)	404
Psalm 32:8 (New International Version/NIV)	406
Psalm 33:4 (Easy-to-Read Version/ERV)	407
Psalm 66:9 (New English Translation/NET Bible)	408
Colossians 1:10 (Amplified Bible/AMP)	409
Psalm 18:30 (GOD'S WORD Translation/GW)	410
Psalm 16:2 (The Message/MSG)	411
Proverbs 16:3 (Expanded Bible/EXB)	412
Romans 8:15 (Common English Bible/CEB)	414
Matthew 7:14 (Easy-to-Read Version/ERV)	416
Ephesians 5:8 (New Century Version/NCV)	417
Psalm 73:28 (The Living Bible/TLB)	419
Psalm 40:8 (New Living Translation/NLT)	421
1 Peter 3:15 (Contemporary English Version/CEV)	422
Ephesians 5:17 (The Message/MSG)	423
Proverbs 26:17 (New English Translation/NET Bible)	424
Luke 6:46 (Disciples' Literal New Testament/DLNT)	426
Luke 9:23 (New Century Version/NCV)	427
1 Thessalonians 5:19 (Amplified Bible/AMP)	428
2 Corinthians 2:9 (Amplified Bible/AMP)	429
Psalm 119:32 (World English Bible/WEB)	431
John 3:30 (The Message/MSG)	433
Ezekiel 36:26 (Expanded Bible/EXB)	435
Mark 11:25 (Amplified Bible, Classic Edition/AMPC)	437
2 Timothy 2:15 (The Living Bible/TLB)	439

Galatians 5:25 (The Voice/VOICE) 441
Psalm 18:6 (Modern English Version/MEV) 443
1 Peter 3:4 (The Voice/VOICE) 444
Psalm 119:133 (Amplified Bible/AMP) 446
Proverbs 19:8 (Complete Jewish Bible/CJB) 447
Psalm 118:5 (Expanded Bible/EXB) 449
Matthew 18:21-22 (Amplified Bible, Classic Edition/AMPC) 451
Luke 7:47 (New International Reader's Version/NIRV) 454
1 Corinthians 13:5 (Easy-to-Read Version/ERV) 456
2 Corinthians 3:17 (Amplified Bible/AMP) 458
Hebrews 4:12 (Complete Jewish Bible/CJB) 460
Psalm 62:1 (New International Version/NIV) 462
Psalm 139:23-24 (Complete Jewish Bible/CJB) 463
1 Timothy 4:16 (Contemporary English Version/CEV) 464
Psalm 46:10 (Amplified Bible, Classic Edition/AMPC) 466
James 4:8 (New Life Version/NLV) 468
John 17:3 (Contemporary English Version/CEV) 469
Philippians 4:8 (Tree of Life Version/TLV) 471
Jeremiah 10:23 (Lexham English Bible/LEB) 473
Luke 9:62 (Disciples' Literal New Testament/DLNT) 474
1 Thessalonians 4:1 (Tree of Life Version/TLV) 476
Psalm 28:7 (New English Translation/NET Bible) 478
Ezekiel 36:27 (Lexham English Bible/LEB) 480
Proverbs 31:27-28 (GOD'S WORD Translation/GW) 481
Ephesians 4:24 (The Voice/VOICE) 483
Psalm 86:11 (The Living Bible/TLB) 485
Romans 6:14 (The Living Bible/TLB) 487

Tests And Trials Come To Make Us Better, Wiser and Stronger 489

Isaiah 64:8 (The Voice/VOICE) 490
Ecclesiastes 7:8 (New Life Version/NLV) 491
Psalm 46:1 (New Century Version/NCV) 492
Isaiah 40:29 (Amplified Bible, Classic Edition/AMPC) 493
Isaiah 38:17 (The Voice/VOICE) 494
Joel 2:25-26 (The Voice/VOICE) 496
John 16:33 (The Living Bible/TLB) 498
2 Corinthians 4:8-9 (Amplified Bible/AMP) 499
James 1:3 (Amplified Bible/AMP) 500
James 1:12 (Good News Translation/GNT) 501
Habakkuk 3:19 (Amplified Bible/AMP) 503

1 Corinthians 10:13 (The Message/MSG) 505
Deuteronomy 20:4 (The Living Bible/TLB) 506
James 1:2 (Expanded Bible/EXB) 507
James 5:11 (Easy-to-Read Version/ERV) 509
John 14:27 (Jubilee Bible 2000/JUB) 511
Job 23:10 (Amplified Bible/AMP) 512
2 Corinthians 12:10 (Lexham English Bible/LEB) 514
Isaiah 43:2 (The Living Bible/TLB) 516
1 Peter 4:12-13 (Easy-to-Read Version/ERV) 517
Isaiah 54:17 (Good News Translation/GNT) 518
Psalm 66:10 Expanded Bible/EXB 519
Psalm 119:50 (International Children's Bible/ICB) 520
Proverbs 24:10 (Contemporary English Version/CEV) 521
Job 8:7 (New American Bible (Revised Edition)/NABRE) 523
1 Peter 1:6-7 (J.B. Phillips New Testament/PHILLIPS) 525
Luke 8:39 (J.B. Phillips New Testament/PHILLIPS) 527
Philippians 2:14 (Amplified Bible, Classic Edition/AMPC) 530
Isaiah 48:10 (New International Reader's Version/NIRV) 532
2 Chronicles 20:17 (New Living Translation/NLT) 535
James 1:4 (The Living Bible/TLB) 537
Psalm 71:20 (New International Version/NIV) 538
Psalm 61:2-3 (New Life Version/NLV) 539
Psalm 119:111 (Lexham English Bible/LEB) 540
Isaiah 41:13 (The Voice/VOICE) 541

FORSAKING ALL
I TRUST HIM
(FAITH)

James 1:6 (Worldwide English (New Testament)/WE)

⁶ But when you ask, you must believe that God will do it. You must not doubt and think, 'Perhaps God will not do it.' A person who doubts is like a wave on the sea. The wind drives it this way and that way.

In every circumstance, we have to believe that the Lord will come through and make a way, with a boldness that doesn't even invite the opportunity for second thoughts or inward reservations to surface.

When you believe and have faith, it doesn't matter if God's plans for your life haven't come to fruition yet. You will have made the commitment and conscious decision to plant your feet firmly on the foundation of God's Word; not allowing anyone or anything to sway you left or right.

It is so important that we are in alignment with God's will for our lives, so that we can be in tune with what God has for us. Even if we are not 100% sure as to where our path is leading, we know who to trust to lead us along the way. As we take that personal, one-on-one time, to not only converse with the Lord, but to patiently wait to hear a word from Him, we are given the opportunity to allow His Word to be that daily bread; which nurtures and sustains us.

God's Word is like a universal, all-in-one vaccination. By injecting God's Word into your life, you will possess within yourself the answers and remedies to ward off any attack that may come up against you, because God's Word is true.

When our faith and trust is in the Lord, we can say, with assurance, that whatever we ask for in prayer, we shall receive. How important it is that we know what to petition the Lord for. If we don't keep our minds on God and on what He desires for us, we could end up making requests that have nothing to do with the destiny that God has written specifically for us.

Our loyalty cannot be divided. Our faith must be in God and God alone. We do not want to find ourselves in an unsettling place; tossed to and fro because we pray and say we have faith in the Lord, but our actions reflect something completely different.

Remember, believing in the Lord means trusting that He'll come through even when the enemy is attacking you from all sides. Believing in the Lord also means that when you don't know and can't see what is ahead, you are still singing, dancing, rejoicing, celebrating and honoring the name of the Lord because you know that we serve a God who supplies all of our needs and who promises to never leave us nor forsake us.

We serve a God whose limitless love for us, gives us the confidence to expect and believe in the impossible, having not one doubt that it will ALL work together for our good.

Suggested Song of Meditation: "I Believe" by Marvin Sapp

Philippians 4:19 (The Message /MSG)

> *¹⁹ You can be sure that God will take care of everything you need, his generosity exceeding even yours in the glory that pours from Jesus.*

Lately, I have truly come to recognize how imperative it is that we transform our mindset from what the enemy would like to make us believe, to what God has confirmed and promised in His Word for us. When I can recall the countless times and ways that God has delivered and set me free from my circumstances, trials and obstacles don't get the opportunity to burden and weigh me down as they have in the past.

I am expecting nothing but the greatest things from the Lord. I know that by walking according to His plan, I cannot miss out on what God has for me. Even when there are still so many details unknown and connections yet to be established, with assurance, I can declare that my situations are already getting better and that God is moving on my behalf.

There is a definition of fear that I heard one time, that I haven't ever forgotten. Fear was defined as not trusting in the integrity of God's Word.

The thought that anything that I say or do could be perceived as me not trusting in the integrity of God or His Word, was so profound and eye-opening. I don't want even a drop of fear to contaminate the trust, confidence and belief that I have in the Lord. I can speak and declare that it's already getting better and easier and that God is already moving on my behalf because of the marvelous works that He has already accomplished in my life.

Each situation that I am believing God for is an opportunity for me to activate my faith in a way that it hasn't ever been done before.

I have no doubt that it's already getting better, when we serve a God that will supply every last one of our needs. I don't need to see the expected outcome or resolution to begin thanking the Lord in advance for it. Because I have learned that God meets us at the level of our expectations, you can best believe that I have placed the highest of high expectations on the Lord.

Suggested Song of Meditation: "Already Getting Better" by William Murphy

Lamentations 3:25 (New International Reader's Version/NIRV)

²⁵ The LORD is good to those who put their hope in him. He is good to those who look to him.

Rejoice in the Lord always. I will say it again: Rejoice!

No matter where you may find yourself, there is always a reason to rejoice. If for no other reason, sing songs of praise and thanksgiving knowing that it wasn't an alarm clock or rooster that woke you up this morning, but the Lord, himself.

So many times we get caught up in the hustle and bustle of our day-to-day activities or overwhelmed by current trials or tests that time passes right before our eyes.

Regardless of who we are, we are all in need of and are expecting God for something in our lives. One of the hardest things for us to do is wait. When we are going through, we want the pain or obstacle removed right away. When it doesn't feel or look good, we do not want it in any way, shape, fashion or form. What I have learned is that it is how you wait that is most important.

If you are looking to God for answers or direction, but harbor doubt that He will indeed answer or turn your situation around, then you are working against yourself. The Lord is good to those who wait on Him, good to the soul that seeks Him. When we wait, we should always be seeking the Lord.

How do we seek you say? Well, I am glad you asked.

By spending time in the Word, studying what God has said, we can find the answers that in turn put us in the position to claim what God has promised. Prayer is another imperative component during seasons of waiting and expectancy. Prayer allows you that one-on-one time with our Heavenly Father, where you can bring your problems to Him and pray over all the issues that you are concerned with. Seeking the wisdom and discernment to know what is truly of God should be part of your prayer time as well.

If we patiently wait on the Lord, regardless of how long our troubles may be extended, and seek out God with our souls, He WILL show us his astounding lovingkindness. To patiently wait at times sounds like an oxymoron because people don't like to wait for much of anything for any amount of time. We get frustrated if we are in the drive-thru at a fast food restaurant and the wait to request and receive our food is too long. So imagine our impatience when we are really going through a situation that we KNOW if God doesn't lay His hands upon it, there is no other way it can be improved or turned around.

Well, unlike that quick value meal that you may get going through the drive-thru that satisfies a temporary hunger, the sustenance (by way of reading the Word, praying and meditating on who the Lord is) that is fed to your soul, through waiting patiently and seeking Him, will more than sustain you and keep you full in the knowledge that if you believe and trust in the Lord, you will receive what He has promised.

God always comes through. He may not come through on your time or my time, but I shout telling you that I know and He has shown me every time that He is an on-time God.

So whatever you are believing Him for today, no matter how long you have been in the midst of your situation, do not give up and do not stop waiting and believing. More importantly, wait on Him with the assurance that there is no need to worry, because God would not allow you to be where you are if He didn't already know that you could handle it AND hadn't already made the provisions to help you through it.

Trust in the Lord, do not be discouraged or dismayed, because God always keeps His Word.

Suggested Song of Meditation: "Wait on the Lord" by Donnie McClurkin

Isaiah 8:12-13 (Easy-to-Read Version/ERV)

¹² "Don't think there is a plan against you just because the people say there is. Don't be afraid of what they fear. Don't let them frighten you!"
¹³ The Lord All-Powerful is the one you should fear. He is the one you should respect. He is the one who should frighten you.

I am as much of an auditory learner as I am a visual learner; which is why, in recent days, I have had to keep my exposure to social media and the news to a minimum.

It seems like no matter where I look or what I see being displayed on TV, everyone has an opinion or theory about the conspiracies or plots that we need to be fearful of. I've seen very few take the initiative to be that light and to encourage others to get back to what has been lost; and that is God being at the center of it all.

Although the times we are living in currently are dark and disheartening, my faith in the Lord is stronger. I am able to be fearless, bold and brave in the name of my Lord and Savior because I recognize that when I walk in the light of His Word, the utter darkness can't grab hold of me.

It is not what man is capable of doing that I fear. And no matter how news commentators, politicians, celebrities or other public figures may attempt to incite fear and terror in us, their words do not frighten me.

Contrary to the beliefs of some, man does not have the final say; God does. And that is why it is the Lord All-Powerful, whom I hold sacred, whom I fear, whom I respect and whom I hold in awe.

Fear keeps us bound; the Lord has brought me way too far and has shown me way too much for me to be re-shackled.

Instead of being afraid, I will continue to trust in the Lord and do as 1 Corinthians 16:13 instructs. I will be watchful, stand firm in faith and be mature, courageous and strong. It's through my faith in God's Word that my fearlessness automatically activates.

So beware of those conspiracy theories. Being fearful will cause you to lose your mind if you let it. But our God reminds us in 2 Timothy 1:7 that He did not give us a spirit of fear, but of power, love and a sound mind.

Suggested Song of Meditation: "Fearless" by Jonathan Nelson

1 Corinthians 2:9 (Amplified Bible/AMP)

⁹ But, on the contrary, as the Scripture says, What eye has not seen and ear has not heard and has not entered into the heart of man, [all that] God has prepared (made and keeps ready) for those who love Him [who hold Him in affectionate reverence, promptly obeying Him and gratefully recognizing the benefits He has bestowed].

I personally am not one for making resolutions at the end of each year. I made a decision long ago and resolved to make God the head of my life and to strive to live according to His principles each and every day. That doesn't mean that I don't sometimes fall, that it's always easy or that I always understand everything that is happening around me.

What it does mean is that I have chosen to trust the One who knows me better than I know myself; the One who knows the thoughts and the plans that He has for my life. And since my eyes haven't seen, my ears haven't heard, nor am I able to imagine, ALL that God has prepared for me, I am excited about what lies ahead in my future because I know who is in control of it.

I am also one who believes that reflection is good; not to just look over the past 12 months but over one's life in general. It's in those instances when you recall countless times where you encountered situations and obstacles that you know you could not rectify yourself and that it was only because God did it, that you got through it.

Those recollections aid in increasing our faith because we know firsthand what it means to be on the receiving end of God's infinite grace, mercy and favor. As it has been sung time and time again in one of my favorite songs by Tye Tribbett, "If He did it before, He'll do it again. Same God right now, same God back then."

Given all that God has already done in each area of my life, if He chose not to do anything else, He has already far exceeded all that I could have ever imagined. When I think about where I started and where I am currently, I have no doubt that God is still doing His best work in my life.

Suggested Song of Meditation: "The Best is Yet to Come" by Donald Lawrence

Philippians 4:13 (Amplified Bible/AMP)

> *¹³ I have strength for all things in Christ Who empowers me [I am ready for anything and equal to anything through Him Who infuses inner strength into me; I am self-sufficient in Christ's sufficiency].*

One of my absolute favorite verses in the Bible is Philippians 4:13.

We have the assurance that we are able to accomplish all things through who Christ empowers us. Instead of allowing our thoughts to make us feel defeated, we look to the Word of God to build us up. In order to live out our lives according to God's principles and ordinances, it's imperative that we submit our thought life over to Christ.

In the verse that precedes, Paul says, "I know how to live on almost nothing or with everything. I have learned the secret of contentment in every situation, whether it be a full stomach or hunger, plenty or want (Philippians 4:12)."

And the reason all of that is possible is because we have strength for all things through Christ.

As I think about that verse, I remember something that my pastor in Maryland shared with the congregation a couple of years ago. He said, "Life is not about our happiness but about our conformity and God shaping us into who He requires us to be." That resonated so deeply with me because I know that happiness is subjective and influenced by our external circumstances.

When we are conforming and seeking out what is God's will for our lives, we put ourselves in the position to be shaped and molded into who God says we should be. All that molding and shaping by God allows us to declare boldly and encourage not only ourselves but others knowing the empowerment and contentment that can be found, throughout all we face in life, because of Christ.

Suggested Song of Meditation: "All Things Through Christ" by Earnest Pugh featuring Bishop Rance Allen

Luke 1:37 (Amplified Bible/AMP)

37 For with God nothing is ever impossible and no word from God shall be without power or impossible of fulfillment.

I have always loved the state of sunny Florida. I love being surrounded by so many of the marvelous works that God has created. It is so uplifting to look up at the sky, the clouds, the sun, the sand and ocean knowing that the same God that called all of that into existence, also called us into existence with a specific purpose. Nothing is impossible for God.

One of the most beautiful elements of Florida's scenery to me are the palm trees. As beautiful as palm trees are, they are generally located in states and countries with tropical climate. And no matter how hard it rains or how far the palm trees may bend from one side to another, when the storm has come and gone, they are still left standing.

That is the kind of faith I have in God. I know that no matter where I am placed in life, when I have God directing my path, it doesn't matter how strong or impossible the storm may appear to be, not only will I not be broken, but that same storm will be turned around for my good, because nothing is impossible for God.

How do I know that nothing is impossible for God?

Because, I have seen God do what others claimed was impossible. I have seen Him bring restoration, renewal and rejuvenation in areas that seemed so dismal and to be lost causes. Even when we are led astray, God covers us with His grace in a way that erases our past and makes us white as snow. No matter how hard the trial may appear, like the palm trees that we were surrounded by this weekend, you may be bent and tried to the extent to where you feel you cannot handle it anymore; but hold on, because our God never fails. He has never lost a battle, nor has He ever lost a victory.

In the midst of the storm, through our natural sight we are unable to see all that is working in the background for our favor. Sometimes we need to be in a place where we rely on more than what we can see with our naked eye. We need to be in a place where we believe God for what we can't see.

How can our faith grow if we don't utilize it?

No matter what it is, give it to God. We serve the God of the underdog. God has and will use people whom others have counted out, rejected, looked past and cast aside. He will take your mess and turn it into a message, your test and turn it into a testimony and change your victim mentality to that of a victor! Since we have seen the countless ways that He has worked in our lives already, we can boldly profess that our God can do the impossible.

Suggested Song of Meditation: "I've Seen Him Do It" by Kurt Carr and the Kurt Carr Singers

Philippians 1:6 (The Living Bible/TLB)

> *⁶ And I am sure that God who began the good work within you will keep right on helping you grow in his grace until his task within you is finally finished on that day when Jesus Christ returns.*

When I was younger and in the choir, we used to sing a song called "Please Be Patient with Me." The chorus to that song stated, *"Please be patient with me, God is not through with me yet. When God gets through me, I will come forth as pure gold."* Back in my youth, I thought that was a song that needed to be directed at others; the naysayers, criticizers and unbelievers who were on the sidelines observing you as you tried to navigate through this course called life. But as I have gotten older, I feel like a lot of times the one who is the most impatient and judgmental about where we are or aren't, is ourselves.

We can have it made up in our mind the completion date we have established for situations to be resolved and reconciled; losing sight of the fact that, Our Creator, who has begun a great work in us, will not stop in mid-design or halfway through. He will keep perfecting us and helping us grow in His grace until His task within us is finally finished.

We may find ourselves discouraged, disappointed, confused, cast down and alone at times. But we must continue to remind ourselves to stand strong and remain confident in the Lord. God is not like man. His thoughts are not our thoughts; nor His ways our ways. The Lord does not lie and He finishes everything He begins.

When we are patient and can recognize that no matter what our situations may reflect, God is not through with us yet; we can make that proclamation that the Lord is working it out and turning our situations around for us. The Lord's timing is perfect. He doesn't make mistakes and cannot fail. Therefore, whoever you are and wherever you find yourself today, praise and rejoice in the name of the Lord because it won't always be like this. Those tests and trials are tools utilized for our growth and betterment, so that the end result will be us being everything the Lord desires us to be.

Suggested Song of Meditation: "Turning Around for Me" by VaShawn Mitchell

Deuteronomy 31:8 (Amplified Bible/AMP)

⁸ It is the Lord Who goes before you; He will [march] with you; He will not fail you or let you go or forsake you; [let there be no cowardice or flinching, but] fear not, neither become broken [in spirit—depressed, dismayed, and unnerved with alarm].

This book has been birthed from a motivational and inspirational ministry that began on July 29, 2013, as a weekly Monday encouragement email to family and friends.

I have to tell you that I was so nervous because the enemy had me second-guessing whether I was qualified or even able to take on such a responsibility. I have always known that I had a love for people. With words being a huge part of who I am, I felt a desire to do more. Singing, finding the meaning to the lyrics in songs, public speaking and writing have always been passions of mine.

With God's Word, guidance and through transparency and encouragement, I hoped that by sharing who God has been, is and continues to be in my life, I would be able to reach the hearts and minds of others, thus, driving them closer to the Lord.

But, being someone who has always looked for validation and approval from others, the thought of just giving it all to God and allowing Him to lead me, although it was what I definitely needed to do, was also outside of my comfort zone and a little bit scary.

I was reminded that not only did God not give me a spirit of fear, but that He chose me for a specific reason. And throughout my life, He was preparing me for a time such as this. I also knew that what may seem impossible in its natural form was completely possible with God's supernatural blessing and covering over me. God was challenging me and, in turn, would take me to places I hadn't yet visited or even imagined.

Starting this journey was one way of saying "Yes" to God's will for my life. Being stretched out of my comfort zone meant that I was coming into my destiny.

But, what if I chose the wrong song and/or scripture? What if I typed the wrong message?

Just as those thoughts came, they fled. It was as if God was saying, "Hush child; this is not about you, but about what I intend to do through you." When that happened, a peace set in, because I knew that anything that I placed in any email (when then transitioned into daily blog posts), would come from Him. I was just the vessel being used.

It is my desire to be used by God over and over again. And that can only happen when I take myself out of the equation and focus solely on the One who has gone and will continue to go before me in all things. God has been and always will be faithful to me and never leave me alone. Knowing these truths, I welcome coming out of my comfort zone, as long as I know it's what God has called me to do. It's also a lot easier to step out on faith, even when it's not comfortable, because God has commanded us to be strong and courageous; to not be afraid or discouraged because the Lord our God, is with us wherever we go (Joshua 1:9).

Please do not shy away from coming out of your own comfort zone, in the name of Our Heavenly Father. He knows the thoughts and the plans that He has for us. When God challenges us it is indeed for our betterment. There is a specific destiny that He has for each of us. By saying "Yes" to His will and His way each and every day, God will get the glory and we shall be victorious.

Suggested Song of Meditation: "Comfort Zone" by Marvin Sapp

Ephesians 3:20 (Amplified Bible/AMP)

²⁰ Now to Him Who, by (in consequence of) the [action of His] power that is at work within us, is able to [carry out His purpose and] do superabundantly, far over and above all that we [dare] ask or think [infinitely beyond our highest prayers, desires, thoughts, hopes, or dreams]—

Ephesians 3:20 is another one of my favorite verses. I need you to understand why, over time, it has come to be one of my favorite verses for encouragement. Growing up, I always loved to push my imagination to the limit. When I was younger and was tasked with a project or assignment that required any form of creativity, I made it my duty to take everything to the next level. I have never been one to think on a small scale; it's always been on the largest scale possible and those practices have spilled over into my adulthood.

Ephesians 3:20 serves as a reality check for me. Ephesians 3:20 reminds me that no matter which grandiose plan or thought I could have for myself or my life, we serve a God that is able to do "exceedingly and abundantly" or as the Amplified Bible version says "superabundantly, far over and above all" that we could ever dare ask or think according to His power that works in us.

If we are faithful to believe that whatever God has spoken, He will be faithful to perform, we shall see the tables turn in our favor. But we have to be willing to believe that God is able, in spite of what our current circumstances may be reflecting. We have to trust in the Lord with all our hearts, faithfully believe in His Word, wait with expectancy for that which shall come to us and not allow any room for doubt to enter.

Knowing that we serve a God who is able to surpass the highest prayer, desire, thought, hope or dream that we could ever conjure up, fills me with more than just encouragement; it fills me with excitement as well. There aren't any limits to what God is able to do, if we just believe. And while we are believing and waiting on the Lord to move in the midst of our situations, we should be praising and thanking God through it all. I was reminded that when we praise and thank God in the midst of our plight, we are shutting the door to the enemy.

Don't put God in a box. He is able to move in ways that are so profound that when it's all said and done there can be no question about who made it all possible. I know this firsthand because I have seen God do so many things in my life that exceeded every last word that I uttered to Him in each of my prayers. And please understand, being the resident optimist, my expectations on the Lord are set so high, or so I think, until He brings resolution to my situations and I see that I wasn't even scratching the surface on what God had in store for me.

I know, not only what God is capable of but that if He has done far more than I could ever dare to ask before, He will do it again. In the midst of my struggles, I will be faithful to believe and I will praise Him throughout the entire process, knowing that what is on the other side of it will leave me blessed and blessed "superabundantly".

What we believe determines how we proceed and what we shall receive.

Suggested Song of Meditation: "Faithful to Believe", by Byron Cage

Job 42:2 (World English Bible/WEB)

² "I know that you can do all things, and that no purpose of yours can be restrained.

Each year that I am blessed to see, always holds a specific meaning for me, as I recall them. In 2014, I saw the marvelous works that could have only been orchestrated by the hands of God in my life. Strongholds and years of generational bondage were broken and I was reminded that it doesn't matter what man says "No" to, or how others may reject or deny you, when God's approval and "Yes" are over you and your situation, there's no way that man's "No" can override God's "Yes!"

I was also reminded that nothing is impossible with God (Luke 1:37). I am only human, but I am a human with a purpose and a destiny. I know that in my natural state I am limited, but I can do ALL things through Christ who strengthens me (Philippians 4:13).

I have recognized the importance of getting to the root of the strongholds in my life and letting go of all the weight that I have been carrying which has gotten in the way of me being everything God desires me to be. That weight has been in the form of some people, situations and ways of thinking.

Being someone who is very analytical and who desires for it all to balance out in the end, I have realized that it doesn't always need to add up for it all to work together. I know wholeheartedly that man does not have the final say, because I belong to God and greater is He that is in me than he that is in the world (1 John 4:4).

Even though I have no idea what lies ahead, I know that I have the power to endure, because we have the greatest example of enduring that was set by Christ. When I lived in Maryland, our pastor shared with us that Christ did not put the focus on His current circumstances as He was preparing to be crucified. Jesus focused on the joy on the other side of what He was about to face. Our pastor then followed up by saying, "You can handle a crucifixion when you know a resurrection is coming." We just need to endure the tests and trials for a little while longer.

And so with all the ups and downs and highs and lows, I can confidently say that my spiritual endurance, my staying power, to run this race (which is more like a marathon) that God has set before me has truly been developed. I know that regardless of the hurdles or pits I may have to leap over or the metaphorical walls I may hit, I will have a strong finish because of the strong faith that I possess that continues to grow. Because I am a child of God, I know that victory is mine!!

I approach each day with a resilience that I haven't ever known before and I thank God for the life lessons that have helped to mold and change me thus far in my journey. I put all my trust in the Lord, who can and has the ability and power to do anything! It is He who has the final say in our lives!!!

Suggested Song of Meditation: "God Can" by Andrea McClurkin-Mellini

Hebrews 11:8 (New International Reader's Version/NIRV)

⁸ Abraham had faith. So he obeyed God. God called him to go to a place he would later receive as his own. So he went. He did it even though he didn't know where he was going.

I love Hebrews 11:8 because it is a clear illustration of what, not just faith, but what radical faith looks like. That is the kind of faith I desire to exercise every day. Whether a change or move is coming in the form of a physical relocation to areas unknown, a new employment opportunity or business venture, expansion to one's ministry, etc., we need to remember that, at times, God will guide us in ways that are unbeknownst to us but completely known inside and out to Him. And that is where radical faith comes in; knowing that when you consult God in every area and aspect of your life and allow Him to direct the moves and changes that are to occur, you don't need to see the way or the completion of things to know that His ways are always right and will be for your advancement.

Where will our paths lead ultimately? We haven't the slightest idea. But, who we do know, is the God we serve. Nothing is greater than Him nor is anything impossible with Him. Stand firm and strong in your faith because God already knows who and what will be awaiting you in each season of your life and He has already equipped you to not just make it but be victorious along the way.

Don't get caught up in the semantics, because those are just some antics used by the enemy to get you distracted and off course from the destiny and inheritance that God hand-picked and created specifically for you!

Suggested Song of Meditation: "Find Us Faithful" by Steve Green

Philippians 3:12 (J.B. Phillips New Testament/PHILLIPS)

¹² Yet, my brothers, I do not consider myself to have "arrived", spiritually, nor do I consider myself already perfect. But I keep going on, grasping ever more firmly that purpose for which Christ grasped me.

Good gracious, the past week, it has been so cold here in Maryland. It became reminiscent of the brutal cold days that I had to walk to school in when I was younger. It was so funny because a couple of my family members actually made reference to the same thing on Facebook. As my two oldest children were leaving to go to school this morning, the wind sounded like a serious force to be reckoned with.

It reminded me of when I was younger and the weather conditions were so much worse than they are now, but we didn't get the option of schools being delayed or closed. We had to walk in the blistery cold with that unsympathetic wind hitting us with every step. Sometimes, the winds would be so strong we would turn around and walk backwards, as the tears froze on our cheeks, hoping to counter the impact of the force of the wind. Regardless of the conditions that we were subjected to, we pressed on and moved forward until we reached our goal; which was shelter from the elements and warmth from the school building. Giving up was not an option, because no one was going to turn back around and tell their parents they didn't go to school because it was too cold. Our two options were to press through it or face our parents. I think we all know which one we opted for.

All of that got me thinking about our walk as Christians. I will tell you that I rejoice in knowing that I am nowhere near where I used to be, but in no way have I arrived yet. I am still a work in progress and my growth is contingent on me getting out there and walking (sometimes running) that course that God has for me. That course will be met with challenges and adversity at times, but when we have the proper mindset we are able to persevere and make it through. The proper mindset means persevering with a smile still on your face and a presence still wrapped in joy; so much so that people have no idea that you are even going through. In no way can we progress on our path without putting forth the proper effort. Faith alone without works is dead (James 2:17).

We are blazing through and grasping for that purpose that God has for our lives because He seized and specifically chose us for the paths that have been laid before us. We have to have longevity and recognize that what is ahead for us cannot be accomplished by sprinting; we have to view our journey and train ourselves with a marathon-like mindset, knowing that speedy fixes and effortless resolutions are not the answer.

Never forget that Christ has taken hold of you, so that you can reach the goals that are ahead of you. Keep pressing on to reach them.

Suggested Song of Meditation: "Pressing On" by Chicago Mass Choir

2 Corinthians 4:13 (The Living Bible/TLB)

¹³ We boldly say what we believe, trusting God to care for us, just as the psalm writer did when he said, "I believe and therefore I speak."

Today I woke up very excited thinking about what the Lord is doing in my life. I find confidence in knowing that He who has begun a good work in me will carry it on to completion, until the day of Christ Jesus (Philippians 1:6).

I have learned the importance of speaking what we believe into existence. When we hope and trust in the Lord we are not just reminded that the Lord is our all in all but that He is our impenetrable defense.

When we equip and arm ourselves with the Lord's words and promises, we can boldly proclaim the declarations that God has spoken over our lives.

Trusting in the Lord means that we can see, receive and believe, before anything ever happens. It means being able to speak victory over yourself, regardless of what the battle may look or feel like right now.

We have that assurance that God will make a way for us out of the wilderness; and for those areas that have been dry and unfruitful; God will put a river in our deserts. He will restore to us all that the locusts have eaten, if we believe and have faith in Him.

What is spoken comes from within. What we believe influences every last word that comes from our mouths and each of our actions. When the source and foundation of our beliefs are rooted in the Lord and His promises, we will purposefully and enthusiastically speak what God has pronounced over us.

My question to you is, "What will you speak?" Will you declare that you are the lender or the borrower, above or beneath, the head or the tail? Will you proclaim a prosperity or poverty mindset, restoration or continuous depletion?

Activate your faith and speak all that you know will happen through Christ Jesus.

Suggested Song of Meditation: "It's Gonna Happen" by Jekalyn Carr

Jeremiah 17:7 (Expanded Bible/EXB)

⁷ "But the person who trusts [has confidence] in the Lord will be blessed. The Lord will show him that he can be trusted [...whose trust/confidence is in him]

I remember having a conversation with someone regarding confidence. I was explaining that no matter what is going on in my life, I refuse to allow that to be reflected externally or for me to take it out on others, because the details and resolution to my circumstances in my life are in God's hands. All of my confidence is in the Lord. No matter what, my hope is in the Lord. That is why while in the midst of a storm, my countenance and posture will remain positive and I will continue to strive to encourage others because it is the Lord who holds the master plan in each of our lives.

I don't know about you, but I am forever appreciative that the Lord's thoughts are not our thoughts, nor are His ways our ways (Isaiah 55:8). God's ways are higher and deeper than we could ever begin to comprehend. Even though how the Lord does what He does remains a mystery, we just need to remember that He is capable of doing it.

Because of the faith that I have in the Lord and the trust that I have in His Word, I am able to have all my confidence in Him, regardless of what my current situation could be indicating. I know that if God said that He will perform it, then it will be accomplished and that is why I will continue to stand on His Word.

We are reminded in 2 Corinthians 1:20, "For as many as there are promises of God, in Him is the Yes! Therefore, also through Him is [spoken] the Amen to God for His glory, through us."

It is my desire that all that I say and do reflects the confidence that I have in our Lord and Savior. None of what you see is about me, but about God obtaining the glory.

Suggested Song of Meditation: "Confidence" by Tasha Cobbs

Habakkuk 2:3 (Contemporary English Version/CEV)

³At the time I have decided, my words will come true. You can trust what I say about the future. It may take a long time, but keep on waiting—it will happen!

I was reminded that each trial and obstacle is preparing me for my destiny. The Lord knows who and what we need; along with when we need it. I know that with each step I am brought that much closer to that vision that the Lord handcrafted specifically for me.

The vision that God has given me doesn't mean that the road will be without bumps, dips and trips. On this journey, I don't need to be an eagle-eyed prophet to know all that I have and will endure are tools of preparation for what God has for me. These obstacles that were intended for evil; even with the pain and trouble they may cause, I thank God and am filled with such gratefulness for what I am called to endure because it's pushing me into my destiny.

The difference between a victor and a victim is the mentality one possesses. Because I know my identity and that I am victorious through Christ Jesus, tests and hurdles do nothing but fuel my desire and drive to do what is pleasing in the Lord's eyes even more. I only want what God has for my family and me and in His time.

My patience, trust and faith in the Lord strengthens as I wait. I remember Victoria Osteen saying once that, "Sometimes, the word "wait" can feel like a "weight." But I will continue to wait on God and I recognize that tests and trials are a part of His plan and because I am pushed by them, I am made stronger and end up learning just how to trust in the Lord.

Suggested Song of Meditation: "It Pushed Me" by J.J. Hairston and Youthful Praise

1 Timothy 6:12 (Easy-to-Read Version/ERV)

¹² We have to fight to keep our faith. Try as hard as you can to win that fight. Take hold of eternal life. It is the life you were chosen to have when you confessed your faith in Jesus—that wonderful truth that you spoke so openly and that so many people heard.

In my past, I have fought for relationships that either the season had passed on them and it was time to release them or they never meant me any good, but in my head, if I did everything in my power, I would have the ability to change the situation around. Like I said, my perspective was all out of whack as you can see, because that statement was so grammatically incorrect.

Once I woke up and came to my senses, I realized that the main relationship that was/is worth fighting for was my relationship with the Lord. God is the best friend we could ever ask for, one that we can always depend on and who sticks closer to us than a brother (Proverbs 18:24). He sits so high and looks so low. He meets us where we are and shows us, time and time again, that we are worth fighting for. Not one thing can prevent the Lord from getting to us. Because of the life that we chose when we professed our faith in Jesus, we have that reassurance that each of us, the calling over our lives, our families, our peace, our joy and our walk with the Lord are all worth fighting for.

We are able to run our best race of faith when we establish that relationship with God and make the commitment to surrender it all to Him. As His children, we were made for so much more and that is definitely worth going toe-to-toe for. As our faith strengthens, walking by faith and not by sight becomes second nature to us.

God has some really extraordinary things in store for those who are committed to Him. Eyes have not seen, nor ears heard, nor the heart of man imagined, what God has prepared for those who love him (1 Corinthians 2:9). There isn't a truer love or friendship than that which can only be found in the Lord. I was always told to choose my battles wisely and believe me I do. When it comes to my faith, I am in it to win it; no other options will be entertained!!

Suggested Song of Meditation: "Worth Fighting For" by Brian Courtney Wilson

Hebrews 10:23 (Complete Jewish Bible/CJB)

²³ Let us continue holding fast to the hope we acknowledge, without wavering; for the One who made the promise is trustworthy.

Oh, how I love waking up to the sound of rain tap dancing against the roof and my windows. To many rain may seem like an inconvenience. I believe that what I truly love about rain is what it represents. When rain falls, soil thirsts no longer, crops are re-hydrated and flowers, trees and the rest of nature's inhabitants are provided that liquid substance needed to survive and grow. Each is so dependent on rain to survive and has absolutely no control over when and how much rainfall will depart from the sky.

Looking up at darkened clouds in the sky, which have assisted in paving the way for the rainfall, I rejoice in knowing that a breakthrough in the clouds, for the sun to appear and then do its part, is on its way.

I continue to learn so much about myself and the undisputed power of surrendering. Making the decision to surrender, means that we are believing God for the changes that we are seeking in our lives. It means that we are voluntarily making the stand that we want any behaviors, actions, ways of living or mindsets that have been a hindrance in us living victoriously, to be removed.

The process is one that can be very trying and that is where we have to have the stamina to hold on. Don't sleep; the enemy will try to pound us with one attack after another to get us to give up or at least get distracted from the finished place God has brought us to and hinder the preparation that is occurring as God gets ready to springboard us into our new season.

During this purging process, I have shed some tears and that is what the rain reminds me of. Tears hold two distinct meanings for me. In one manner, the tears that I shed are a release of the despair, anxiety and worry that the enemy has attempted to keep me consumed with. In the other manner, when I have been brought to such a place of elation and hope, allowing tears to fall from my ducts is the way that I express the joy from within. Just like roses that grow in a bed full of lilies, I too, need water to grow.

Whatever we are believing God for, know that tests will come and that the enemy is going to try any- and everything to discourage us. Regardless of the futile attacks that the enemy may attempt to conjure up, we have to hold on because we have come too far and our breakthrough is on its way.

Suggested Song of Meditation: "Hold On" by James Fortune & FIYA featuring Monica and Fred Hammond.

Psalm 31:24 (New International Reader's Version/NIRV)

²⁴ Be strong, all you who put your hope in the Lord. Never give up.

I have always been one who loved to read. Reading, singing and dancing was where it was for me. In my preteen years, I discovered a passion for writing and during my adolescent years, I began to write poems and songs. Writing was very therapeutic for me and served as an escape from so many things; especially the hurt and pain that I harbored. One of my favorite authors has always been acclaimed American poet, storyteller and activist, Maya Angelou. I was thrilled to learn that the United States Postal Service released a "forever" stamp in her honor.

As I began to reflect on some of her literary work, a couple of stanzas from "Still I Rise" came to mind. I definitely could relate to the sentiments conveyed by Ms. Angelou when she wrote, "Does my sassiness upset you? Why are you beset with gloom? 'Cause I walk like I've got oil wells pumping in my living room. Just like moons and like suns, with the certainty of tides, just like hopes springing high, Still I'll rise."

Yes, life throws many curve balls and unexpected twists and turns in our direction. Sometimes what we are experiencing can be so overwhelming, but giving up shouldn't ever be an option. We have to find that courage that only comes from knowing who our protector is and whose love is able to strengthen us and be our guide even when we can't tell our right from our left.

My courage and confidence comes from the Lord. And that means that, yes, I can be getting attacked from all sides, but I'm going to stand tall, walk upright, with a smile and a stride that says, "In spite of everything that is currently in front of me and against all odds, I won't ever give in." We know that trials and tests come to strengthen us; therefore, holding on and persevering is what must occur. Like hopes springing high, the sky is not the limit for us because we serve a God who is able to do the impossible. Our God will go infinitely beyond our highest prayers, thoughts, hopes or dreams.

As you wait on the Lord, don't lose faith or give up. The same God who had the power to raise Jesus from the dead is the same God who is able to ensure that we rise above any problem or circumstance that we are facing.

Suggested Song of Meditation: "Still I Rise" by Yolanda Adams

Psalm 119:11 (Contemporary English Version/CEV)

¹¹ I treasure your word above all else; it keeps me from sinning against you.

Over the past few days, I have gained an even greater appreciation for the Word of God that is nestled and hidden in my heart. God's Word is holy and in His Word we have at our disposal all the instructions that we could ever need to live the life the Lord desires for us.

There isn't one situation or circumstance that could arise that the steps to being victorious haven't already been provided. When we study His teachings and treasure every word that He has spoken and commanded, the truth is then able to abide in us. God's Word is alive, active and lasts forever and ever. It never fails.

It's in His Word that along with the truth, I am able to obtain a peace that surpasses all understanding. His Word provides me with direction when I am lost; and trust me, there have been many times when I felt like I was in the middle of the wilderness without any form of light, compass or anything to push me in the right direction. But then I remembered that the Lord's Word is a lamp unto my feet and a light unto my path (Psalm 119:105). To resist going down the wrong road or making the wrong decisions, I have turned to the Word of God and all that I have known the Lord to be in my life.

Through the Word of God, I have also come to understand what it truly means to be loved, filled with joy and strength and on the receiving end of His everlasting grace and mercy. Whatever answers I am searching for can be found in the Bible. When the Bible is where I seek the truth, I am then better able to discern when it is God who is speaking to me and when it isn't. I recognize how holy God's Word is. It has been with me from the beginning and it shouldn't ever be ignored. I will continue to spend time reading and meditating on His Word and I will cherish all that I learn and reference it as I continue down this path of mine.

Suggested Song of Meditation: "Holy is Your Word" by J. Moss

Luke 18:27 (The Message/MSG)

²⁷ "No chance at all," Jesus said, "if you think you can pull it off by yourself. Every chance in the world if you trust God to do it."

No matter who you are, where you are or what you have done, I am here to remind each of you that we can and will make it and will observe the impossible done in our lives, if we just trust in the Lord and wait on Him to turn our situations around.

By participating in Dr. Celeste Owens' The 40-Day Surrender Fast (numerous times in fact), I have witnessed and learned what truly happens when you surrender control of every area of your life to the Lord and allow Him to work in the midst of it.

Relinquishing control has brought me so much closer to the Lord. I have been challenged to not only believe and have faith but to declare those things that were not, as if they already were. That has been monumental for me. I have always had faith in the Lord. But it's something else to have that blind faith in the Lord and to not only believe what you are hearing, but to proclaim it, not just privately, but to others. I have been able to hear Him without any confusion; knowing that it is indeed Him and not the enemy. I have been able to see some of His promises for my life already come to fruition.

God instructed me to do my part and trust Him to do the rest. I realized that by standing on the promises that He had spoken, I would make it through, if I placed and kept my trust in Him.

I don't know what you are believing Him for, but I'm here to tell you that if you stay obedient, trust in the Lord and say yes to His will, you will make it!!! What is impossible for man to accomplish is absolutely possible if you trust and believe God to do it.

Suggested Song of Meditation: "I Can Make It" by Bryan Popin

Hebrews 13:8 (Lexham English Bible/LEB)

⁸ Jesus Christ is the same yesterday and today and forever.

We can speak about so many things that are honestly insignificant. We have to be even more adamant about speaking the Lord's promises into the atmosphere. We have to be able to speak it, even when we don't see it; that my friend is faith at its best.

We have to be bold and courageous in the name of the Lord. There was a time when I would have been hesitant in making my declarations known. What has changed from then to now, you may ask? It definitely has not been the Lord, but me. I have realized that through it all Jesus has been the same. That brought me back to something I shared back when my blog was still in its infancy.

When a person applies for a new job, one of the inquiries that is made pertains to their past work history/experience. The potential employer desires to know which skills and abilities one has acquired, performed and mastered that would make them qualified for the position. That consistency in their work reflects someone who can be depended upon to fulfill the requirements of the position and thus, be a true asset to the company.

That same principle applies to our spiritual walk. Take a moment to reflect on your life thus far. Think about the circumstances and situations that were so overwhelming. You had no idea how you would make it through. While we were in the midst of our troubles, we just knew it was the worst thing we'd ever encountered. Although the challenges we face day-to-day may change, we serve a God who is the same. There isn't one single thing that is a surprise to the Lord or that He cannot fix. How do we know that? Because not only does His Word tell us so, but so does God's past work history in our lives.

No matter the problem, if we believe and trust in the Lord, we will see that if God did it before, He'll do it again. Instead of being anxious, nervous or worrying what the outcome will be, we must remember that the Lord doesn't change. I promise that you could search all over and won't ever find anyone with a track record like God's. There isn't enough time to write all that God is able to do; but one thing I know He can't do, and that's fail.

That is why we should rejoice, because each of us has our own story. That story is filled with nothing but reminders of how God's grace and mercy has kept us. We have countless examples of all the ways that Jehovah Jireh—Our Provider, has brought us out of our troubles. We should be quick to give God the honor, glory and praise because we have that confirmation that He's the same yesterday, today and forever.

The Lord is so faithful. Open your heart to receive, and your mouth to declare, everything that He has in store for you.

Suggested Song of Meditation: "Same God (If He Did It Before)" by Tye Tribbett

Job 23:14 (International Standard Version/ISV)

[14] He'll complete what he has planned for me; he has many things in mind for me!

To be all that God desires for me to be, I have to keep my mind right. It's also imperative that anything that can be used as a distraction or as a tool to negatively infiltrate my thought life be removed.

I don't have the time, space or inclination to harbor or believe anything that is not of God. I know that what I believe directly affects what I say and what I do. That is why I am so thankful for the relationship that I have with the Lord, because He is the ultimate educator. In those times, when I wasn't utilizing the proper method or technique to solve my problems, in His Word I was given the correct solution. When everything around me was in disarray, He provided me with countless examples of how He was able to connect the dots in my favor.

I am in a place in my life where I truly comprehend, have accepted and rest in the knowledge that it is God who controls my destiny and nobody else. It is God who doesn't need any time at all to turn our circumstances around. Therefore, I have the reassurance that regardless of whatever hiccups or setbacks that I may encounter, they are actually high-five's and setups that the Lord is preparing me for.

I have faith and trust and believe that everything that the Lord has for me, I shall receive. I know that He will fulfill what He has planned for me.

I can make the declaration that I shall leap into my destiny because I know that the words that go forth from the Lord's mouth shall not return to Him empty. They shall make the things happen that the Lord wants to happen; and they shall succeed in doing what God sent them to do (Isaiah 55:11). Your blessings are just around the corner. Are you ready to leap into your destiny?

Suggested Song of Meditation: "I Shall Leap" by Le'Andria Johnson

1 Samuel 17:45 (New International Reader's Version/NIRV)

⁴⁵ David said to Goliath, "You are coming to fight against me with a sword, a spear and a javelin. But I'm coming against you in the name of the Lord who rules over all. He is the God of the armies of Israel. He's the one you have dared to fight against.

There is so much power in our praise. I think that a lot of times we understate all that can be accomplished on our behalf through the praise we offer up to the Lord.

When we are obedient and take the time to not just pray and release our situations to the Lord, but to also praise His name while in the midst of our struggle or conflict we will see miracles occur that we never thought were possible.

When we praise and worship the Lord, we will see strongholds come down. We will have front row seats to the mighty battles that are won when we insert praise into our lives. One of the things that I love about the Lord and the immeasurable love, grace and mercy that He has for us is that no matter how big our problems, generational curses or setbacks may appear to us, nothing that we experience is greater than the God we serve.

I have been taught and have learned not to be moved by what I see, but instead by what God has declared and promised. One amazing example of this premise can be found in the story of David and Goliath.

David was just a boy, chosen by God to defeat a physical giant who had no problem defying God and taunting His soldiers. Where David appeared to be the most unlikely candidate and as if he was making a death wish, by volunteering to fight Goliath, David was confident because of the faith he had in God. Because of the victories David had already obtained over a lion and a bear, he praised the name of the Lord and believed that the same God who had delivered him from the paws of those two animals, would also render him victorious once again; and this time against Goliath. And he was absolutely right.

God had already given David all he needed to defeat his giant (literally). David didn't require the armor or the weapons that the other soldiers utilized. David was a shepherd and was prepared to face Goliath in that role and with the tools the Lord had allowed David to gain experience and victory with.

Sometimes what we are facing in front of us, can feel and appear to be of a "Goliathesque" nature. We can't see how to get over, under or around it. But when we learn that the battles we face are not ours but the Lord's and we can praise His name, we are able to claim our victory before it even comes because we recognize that what we are encountering has created an opportunity for God to display His power. Everything that we need to be victorious, God has already placed within us; the provisions have already been made.

When we believe and trust in the Lord, we are able to sing and shout praises because we know that God will deliver His children from overwhelming and unspeakable odds. God will show His glory and regardless of what form our particular giant may take, it will come down.

Something that I constantly hear is, "Stop telling God how big your problems are; start telling your problems how big your God is!!"

Our praise is part of the equation in conquering our giants. I praise the Lord in knowing that the bigger they are, the harder they'll fall.

Suggested Song of Meditation: "Giants" by Donald Lawrence

1 Peter 2:2 (New Life Version/NLV)

> ² *As new babies want milk, you should want to drink the pure milk which is God's Word so you will grow up and be saved from the punishment of sin.*

With so many people I know recently giving birth, it really got me thinking about when my children were babies and the importance of them having the proper nourishment to thrive, grow strong and be healthy.

All of that also made me start to reflect on the daily nourishment or spiritual milk that we require to thrive and grow in our salvation. The sustenance that can only be found in God's Word is what I desire. Each day I hunger for it, just as newborn babies desire physical milk. God's Word is the truth and we need it to survive. It is the compass and our source of direction both day-to-day and in those seasons when we lose our way. We can always depend on God's Word to keep us.

When we first come into contact with God's Word, it is something brand new and we are enlivened and intrigued by what each page holds. In just living, I understand the importance of constantly grabbing hold of God's Word as a source of motivation, guidance and encouragement.

I recognize that by studying, meditating and being a doer of God's Word, I am given the fundamentals and the staying power to be victorious and to continue maturing in my spiritual walk.

Suggested Song of Meditation: "The Word" by Deitrick Haddon

2 Peter 1:4 (GOD'S WORD Translation/GW)

⁴ Through his glory and integrity he has given us his promises that are of the highest value. Through these promises you will share in the divine nature because you have escaped the corruption that sinful desires cause in the world.

I am wonderfully overwhelmed!! There have been so many amazing milestones taking place within the same time frame and if you think the enemy hasn't been busy, you are sadly mistaken. But let me tell you why I don't have time to focus on the enemy's shenanigans; because I am holding onto and resting on every promise that the Lord has made on behalf of my family and me.

The Lord never said I wouldn't be tried or that I wouldn't experience trials or hardships. What He did promise is that I wouldn't ever endure more than I could bear. He promised to never leave me nor forsake me and that everything that the enemy has intended for evil, He would turn it around for my good.

I don't have the time to be tripped up or distracted by the enemy. My faith is so strong and continues to grow stronger each and every day. My heart is focused on the goals that are set before me and that is another reason why I am holding onto every promise.

Not only do we serve a God who does infinitely beyond all that we could ever ask or think, but that same God has given us His promises that are of the highest value. We have been given an inheritance that is imperishable. God cannot lie and therefore, if He has declared it, it will happen (point…blank…period).

We must do our part and turn our backs on those selfish and worldly desires that can corrupt and lead us down the wrong path. We have to hold onto His unchanging hand, so that we are able to receive the rich and wonderful blessings that God has promised us.

Suggested Song of Meditation: "Every Promise" by Zacardi Cortez featuring Lalah Hathaway

Philippians 4:12 (The Living Bible/TLB)

¹² I know how to live on almost nothing or with everything. I have learned the secret of contentment in every situation, whether it be a full stomach or hunger, plenty or want;

Even with it being such a celebratory time for my family and me, I can't help but think about the chapters that are closing and the ones that are opening before us. For many, the unknown causes fear and worry. These days, my response is different. In any and every circumstance, I don't need to know the specifics as to how things are going to work out; I just need to know that, through God, my family and I will make it.

The secret of being content in every situation is knowing that I can do all things through Christ who strengthens me (Philippians 4:13).

From my oldest who is in college, to my middle child who is in high school, down to my youngest who is in kindergarten, I pray that my children never forget that. I always want them to have that same feeling of contentment while waiting on the Lord.

We will have mountain high and valley low seasons, but when the Lord is the conductor and navigator that is charting our courses, we will not only have contentment but joy as well!!

Our God gives hope to the hopeless, life to the lifeless, will be a friend to the friendless and will mend every area of our brokenness.

Because nothing is impossible with God, this is neither the time nor the place to give up or throw in the towel. Your best days are still ahead of you, if you just hold on and keep trusting in the Lord.

Suggested Song of Meditation: "Not The Time Not the Place" by Marvin Sapp

Philippians 4:6 (GOD'S WORD Translation/GW)

⁶ Never worry about anything. But in every situation let God know what you need in prayers and requests while giving thanks.

I have heard it said time and time again that "prayer changes things". What I have come to learn is that prayer changes me and that positions me to make the necessary changes in my life with the assistance and guidance of the Lord.

I give God all the thanks, honor and praise. I know that in every situation, when I pray and make my petitions known before Him, I do not have to worry about what the outcome will be because what God has for me is far better than anything I could ever dream of asking for. I also recognize that the Lord knows the desires of my heart.

Even when faced with what seems like the most impossible and challenging of circumstances, I have come to understand why it is so important not to fret or become anxious as I wait on the Lord to work in the midst of my situations. When worry is introduced into the equation, with it comes the appearance and perception of doubt in the Lord and what He has promised He will do in our lives.

I cannot allow one second to go by with there being a chance of it appearing as though I do not believe or trust in the Lord. In every situation, I know that the Lord is always present. I can hear His sweet voice telling me not to worry because He loves me, He knows and sees it all, He won't ever abandon me and desires only the best for me.

No matter the hurt, pain, disappointment or obstacles we may experience, we cannot be anxious, nor should we fret. Honor, cherish and give thanks for that one-on-one time with the Lord where you are able to connect directly to Him and just release and surrender it all.

Worrying is not an option when we know who is in control of our lives. Obstacles no longer have the power to leave me feeling weak and disadvantaged. I now draw courage and strength from them, knowing that God's grace is sufficient for me. His strength is made perfect in my weaknesses.

Praying and worrying at the same time is counterproductive. It can only be one or the other and I have chosen not to worry.

Suggested Song of Meditation: "Don't Worry" by Kirk Franklin

John 15:7 (Young's Literal Translation/YLT)

⁷ If ye may remain in me, and my sayings in you may remain, whatever ye may wish ye shall ask, and it shall be done to you.

Lately, there has been the same underlying theme for me. That theme has been the importance of not just establishing our faith, but exercising radical faith in ways that we never have before. In speaking to various individuals, it is evident that all of us are resting on God's promises.

Therefore, we should not be surprised when we assert our faith and demonstrate such a level of belief and trust in the Lord that the enemy is not so happy and thus, he comes out with guns blazing, just hoping to chip away at the forcefield of faith that has been constructed.

It has been stirred up in my spirit to really drill in on the importance of believing in the Lord and standing on His Word, no matter what. Regardless of our situations or circumstances, we are to confidently stand on the Word of God.

The only way to have the kind of faith that can keep you persevering even when what you are believing the Lord for has yet to come to fruition, is by abiding in Him. When we follow the Lord's teachings and His Word remains within us, anything that we ask of the Lord, shall be done for us.

By standing on God's Word, we are able to fill ourselves up with the truth, which prevents opportunities for the enemy to get us distracted.

Stay divinely connected to the Lord and His Word, believe and abide in Him and you will see that in His perfect timing, the Lord will answer.

Suggested Song of Meditation: "I Stand On Your Word" by Jonathan Butler

Proverbs 23:18 (The Voice/VOICE)

¹⁸ Your future with Him will be certain, and you will not have hoped in vain.

Even though I love the gospel music that current artists are releasing, there are times when I need to hear that old school gospel. It's the kind that I remember seeing my grandmother rock back and forth and sway to in church, as she waved her fan to the beat of the song. Today was definitely an old school gospel day for me.

It seems these days, as if everything I think or do is connected to the future plans that my family and I have. I'm in a place I haven't ever been before and with a mindset and level of faith I haven't ever known before. I recognize that I am believing that God will move in ways I haven't ever expected or needed Him to before.

In another season of my life, my response to all of this would have been filled with anxiety, fear and worry. But in this moment and in this season, I am empowered and confident because my trust in is the Lord and Him alone.

I can look for my miracles, expect the impossible, feel the intangible and see the invisible when I know that my future with the Lord is certain and that my hope will not be in vain or disappointed. There is no limit to what the Lord can do. When we believe and receive that truth, God will begin to perform the unimaginable in our lives. He works in ways that we cannot see and will make a way where there appears not to be one in sight.

As I wait on the Lord and stand on His promises, it is through the power of the Holy Spirit, that a confident hope overflows from me (Romans 15:13).

Suggested Song of Meditation: "Expect Your Miracle" by The Clark Sisters

Matthew 14: 28-29 (Lexham English Bible/LEB)

²⁸ And Peter answered him and said, "Lord, if it is you, command me to come to you on the water!"
²⁹ So he said, "Come!" And getting out of the boat, Peter walked on the water and came toward Jesus.

I am here to tell you that there is nothing like knowing that you have people that will pray with and for you. Yesterday, that was exactly what I needed and the Lord knew that.

When it comes to engaging in spiritual warfare you can become so weary. For me, I become both weary and restless. And just like Moses needed his brother, Aaron, and his friend, Hur, to hold his hands up in times of battle to remain victorious, there are times when I too need some assistance. And I thank the Lord for those who help keep me lifted up in times of spiritual battle.

So much of what is ahead for my family and me is unknown, I feel like I am having a "Peter" moment.

Yes, we know that nothing is impossible with God. And so it has been my resolve for a while now that if what I am embarking upon is of the Lord for Him to just reveal that to me and without any questions and upon His instruction, I will move. It doesn't matter how frightening or fearful it may appear or how outside my comfort zone it may be. If it is what the Lord desires, then that is the direction that I will move in. God has never failed and I know that He's not going to begin now.

It took a while for me to fully grasp that concept. I am someone who is very meticulous and who tries to plan for everything. I ask all the questions possible, make all the necessary moves and strive to be proactive in all things, but have learned that none of that matters if God is requiring me to do something, be something or go somewhere else.

But that is where my faith must stand. I call upon His name and wait for Him to answer me. No matter how the waters rise or the activity of the waves increase, I will keep my eyes from being distracted by the water and will not be concerned about my feet failing. I will stay focused on the One whose sovereign hand will guide me.

These are new and different times that I am facing. Because I recognize that, I know that I need the Spirit to lead me where my trust is not confined nor within any type of borders. I'm ready to go wherever it is the Lord desires me to be. I'm ready to walk upon the waters and to go further and deeper than my feet could ever naturally take me; knowing that when God's super meets my natural my faith is made stronger; because I am in His presence.

Preparing for this move to Long Island has been anything but uneventful. And the journey getting there has not been as smooth-sailing as I hoped it would be. Ironically, we have chosen to live in a place that is surrounded by water. No matter the depth of the waters that encompass the island, in the deepest oceans, I will not fear my feet failing because my faith will stand knowing that the Lord's grace proliferates in the deepest waters.

Suggested Song of Meditation: "Oceans (Where Feet May Fail)" by Hillsong United

Isaiah 55:9 (Holman Christian Standard Bible/HCSB)

⁹ "For as heaven is higher than earth, so My ways are higher than your ways, and My thoughts than your thoughts.

As my family and I prepared to relocate back to NY from MD, we were taken on such an emotional rollercoaster ride. At the end of the whole process, I was reminded that we can have hundreds of ideas of how things are going to work out in our lives, but it is so true that the Lord's ways are so much higher than ours; as are His thoughts. With this situation, there was so much I was trying to figure out and get answers to. But I remembered that with God, I don't have to have it all figured out. It's about trusting and believing in Him and His ways. I know that He is working behind the scenes on my family's behalf and that the right house is coming. I know that the Lord will make a way for us somehow. And more importantly, when it all happens, everyone will know that it wasn't because of us or our realtor, loan officer or anybody else. It will be because of **God** and **God alone!!**

At church, our pastor was talking about facing our giants. And a part of facing our giants is knowing how to overcome rejection. That spoke so loudly to me today, because at the beginning of this week we knew we had an accepted offer, which by the end of the week became a rejected offer. But as our pastor stated, "If we're going to get to where God wants us to be, we have to learn to overcome rejection. And more importantly, rejoice as you overcome that rejection because when you're rejected that means that God has something special for you."

I only want the house that God has for us. Therefore, I am grateful for the roller coaster ride that we were taken on this week, because the decision to ultimately reject our offer, released us to be ready for where we're supposed to be. I don't need to know how it's going to happen, because I know that God is already where I need Him to be and that He's working it all out for the good of my family.

The Lord has never let me down before and I'm not throwing in the towel now. I have the kind of faith that can move mountains and I have no doubts that God's going to come through and make a way, as He has countless times before in my life.

Suggested Song of Meditation: "The Lord Will Make a Way Somehow" by Kim Burrell and Hezekiah Walker

Genesis 28:15 (Lexham English Bible/LEB)

15 Now behold, I am with you, and I will keep you wherever you go. And I will bring you to this land, for I will not leave you until I have done what I have promised to you."

Man oh man, the blog post that I was working on today could have gone in about 50,000 different directions, but a brief thunderstorm and some quiet time reeled it all in for me. There have been so many instances in my life where the enemy attempted to stop me and plant me in nothing but sinking sand, but because of the Lord's love for me, I was protected. I was neither overtaken nor was I ever left alone.

When I read the above verse, it made me think about my current voyage back to NY. What a journey it has been; filled with tears, fears and disappointments. And through it all, the Lord has always been there to protect and keep me.

Moving back to NY was never a thought for me, until my husband suggested it a few years back. I knew that a lot would have to be worked on, within me, for me to be ready and prepared to go back. Upon hearing from the Lord and realizing that returning to NY was part of God's plan for my life, I began to lean on the Lord in ways I hadn't ever thought to before, because I was in a very vulnerable and pivotal point in my life.

As I began to journey down the path of healing and restoration, I knew that the Lord was with me. I knew that all the areas where I needed Him to step in and make me whole, He would. And even when unexpected situations surfaced, I began thanking the Lord because each situation peeled back another layer of the onion that needed to be acknowledged and then surrendered to Him.

I have learned that it's so much easier to go through trials and tribulations when you know you are not by yourself and that the Lord is right there to protect you. It's also comforting and encouraging to know that the Lord will not stop or leave our side. Each day, I rest on those promises, knowing that the Lord is there to answer my call. While in the midst of it all, it is because of God's limitless love that I am protected and kept, as I travel the road that has been set before me.

Suggested Song of Meditation: "In The Midst of It All' by Yolanda Adams

1 Corinthians 15:57 (New Revised Standard Version/NRSV)

⁵⁷ But thanks be to God, who gives us the victory through our Lord Jesus Christ.

What an amazing service our church had during the 12 o'clock service. I am a creature of habit and when it comes time to receive the word that the Lord has placed within my pastor or any guest pastor that visits our church, I have my Bible, my notebook and my pen ready.

There are times, though, when God will interrupt the natural flow of things so that His will is accomplished and not what we may expect to occur. It is on those days, that I feel that my soul is ministered to in ways that surpasses my own understanding. I guess that's one of the reasons why the Lord instructs us to "lean not unto our own understanding."

Today, between the praise and worship that was performed and conducted, the example of the woman with the issue of blood that was utilized and the notes that I transcribed, I really gained new insight into what victory truly is and why, each day that I live, I can say, "I win!!"

I have learned that victory does not always look the way we expect it to with our naked/natural eye. It is when our spiritual senses are finely tuned and our lenses are corrected through the faith that we have in the Lord that we are able to see ourselves the way God sees us. When we are able to do that, our perspective changes, we begin to see the victory that is right in front of us and realize that there is absolutely no way that we can fail.

Because of Jesus Christ and through the example of the woman who had the issue of blood; but who also had the faith and believed that if she could just get close enough to touch Jesus, her situation could change, I am reminded that whoever has the faith to believe that God can change their situation, will be made whole. I win, because I have no doubt that God is who he says He is. Victory is mine and I am declaring that the Lord will bring a change to my circumstances.

Suggested Song of Meditation: "I Win" by Marvin Sapp

Proverbs 3:5-6 (Contemporary English Version/CEV)

⁵ With all your heart you must trust the Lord and not your own judgment. 6 Always let him lead you, and he will clear the road for you to follow.

Yesterday in church, one song that ministered to me both at the beginning and at the end of the service was, "I Won't Go Back." For those who have never heard the song, the first verse speaks to being changed, healed, freed and delivered; while finding joy, peace, grace and favor. The chorus of the song states, "I won't go back, to the way it used to be, before your presence came and changed me." In the second verse the psalmist speaks to the sins, shame and guilt that have been forgiven and that there are no more chains, no more fear and that their past is over.

Even after leaving church, I kept humming that song. Thank you Jesus!!

As I pray and meditate over where I currently am, I realize more than ever, that even when so much makes absolutely no sense to me, I am not about to rely on my own insight or understanding. I will lean on, trust in and be confident solely in the Lord; with all that is within me.

If I ponder on something for too long, I may be inclined to go backwards. But when I take the time to stop and be still, I end up reassured, because of what the Lord has already declared in His Word.

There was a time when I was so misguided and going every which way but the right way. But oh happy day!! When I learned the importance of recognizing and acknowledging the Lord in everything that I do, He straightened my paths and cleared the roads that I was meant to follow.

Regardless of the mountains that I must climb or the battles that I must fight, giving up is not an option. I have come way too far and the Lord's presence in my life has changed me far too deeply for me to allow the temporal tests and obstacles that are brought before me to get me sidetracked.

I have peace because I'm aware that in this world trials and tribulations are a part of life. But I remain encouraged because the Lord has overcome the world.

I don't believe for one nanosecond that the Lord has led and directed me this far to leave me. And so, on days when it's a little rough and I feel my back is against the wall, I look to the hills because that is where my help, strength and direction comes from.

Suggested Song of Meditation: "Can't Give Up Now" by Mary Mary

Proverbs 19:21 (English Standard Version/ESV)

²¹ Many are the plans in the mind of a man, but it is the purpose of the Lord that will stand.

One song that I have been singing throughout the day is, "I just can't give up now, come too far from where I started from. Nobody told me the road would be easy, but I don't believe He brought me this far to leave me." I went from that song to Anita Wilson's, "Jesus Will" before taking a nap. When I woke up from my nap, my youngest daughter asked to see my phone so she could look at Nick Jr. and some family pictures that we had taken.

As I was looking out the window, my youngest daughter placed my phone down next to me and said, "Mommy you need to hear this song that you like." I looked down to see that she had gone in and pulled up, "Jesus Will" for me to hear. Once again, that song was right on time.

How surreal it has been for me, in regards to our home-buying process; so much so that I couldn't even sleep. With all that the Lord had just done for my family and me, I expected the attacks from the enemy to soon surface. And just as I thought, determined to get me distracted from what the Lord is doing in my life and with the hopes of placing me in a state of fear and worry about what is to come, potential obstacles seemed to be on the horizon before our relocation and placement in our new residence could occur.

When I lived in Maryland, I remember our pastor saying that God will put us through character tests. He will allow us to encounter a situation that is similar to a previous one to see what our response will be. A situation that would automatically cause us to be afraid and concerned; had we learned to stand fast on His Word and believe that He is working it all out for our good?

I know that no matter how I plan things in my head or expect them to turn out, it is God's plan and purpose for my life that will stand and succeed. We serve a strategic God, who plans everything in our lives down to the microsecond. He orchestrates and directs our steps, which results in us being in the right place at the right time and meeting the right people.

Regardless of how the situation looks or what the enemy may try to get us to believe, we must always remember that the Lord is working out every aspect of our lives for our good. God is concerned about everything that concerns us. Whatever the test may be and no matter what we are struggling with, we must continue to stand on the promise that the Lord's decree and counsel shall be established and will prevail in our lives.

Suggested Song of Meditation: "Working It Out" by Chicago Mass Choir

Revelation 3:8 (Easy-to-Read Version/ERV)

⁸ "I know what you do. I have put before you an open door that no one can close. I know you are weak, but you have followed my teaching. You were not afraid to speak my name.

I have absolutely no doubt that everything that the Lord declares and promises shall come to pass. That is not something that we ever have to lose hope in or be concerned with.

It's funny because in the beginning of June we knew we had found the house and put in an offer that was accepted "with conditions" because my VA home loan was not a conventional loan that required a down payment. And then, in the beginning of July 2015, after switching realtors, we came across another house that was even better than the first and, once again, we knew hands down this house was the one. When our realtor made the offer, she explained it was a VA home loan and therefore didn't require a down payment or any "good faith" or earnest money deposit. The seller stated that they had no problem with that and we even moved the closing date up to July 20, 2015, since the house was vacant. Lo and behold, while composing the contract, the seller's attorney suggested that a $10,000 "down payment" should be provided since my VA home loan didn't require a down payment and to basically "keep me honest" and less apt to back out of the contract.

We then encountered unexpected turns that neither my realtor, my attorney, my loan officer, my husband, nor I saw coming from the seller's side. With that being said, I stood my ground. I know countless of veterans who when they purchased their homes, their VA home loan and the privileges associated with it were honored. If they were asked to provide a "good faith" or earnest money deposit, it wasn't ever for more than $1,000. And it shouldn't be for me either.

I served my country, and not only met the qualifications to be eligible to use my VA home loan, but I also went through the whole process of having an underwriter go through all my financials to sign off and pre-approve me for a particular mortgage amount. In both these instances, the amount I offered was enough, but there were some things going on in the background that were not in my favor.

Because it wasn't what God had for me, those doors were closed. And I am indescribably grateful. I have said numerous times that I don't want my family and me anywhere that God hadn't chosen for us to be. Those who have known about what transpired during this timeframe thought that I was sounding good and being strong for my family. And I had to let them know that this wasn't a facade. In spite of it all, I was still rejoicing and being thankful.

The Lord is constantly watching me and how I conduct myself on a day-to-day basis. When it comes to this home-buying process, I know that I have done all that I am supposed to do. In my natural state, I am weak, but it has been through the Lord's teachings and by paying attention to His Word, that through Him, I have been made strong. And I know that in His time, we will be blessed in ways infinitely beyond anything we could have ever thought or dared to think or ask for.

I find joy and peace in realizing that the Lord is not finished with me yet. He will bring me out. I continue to ask that His blessings and favor overflow in my life so that I can be a blessing to others and continue to do what is pleasing in His sight.

Therefore, a pity party is not on the agenda. We are having a praise party, because when the Lord opens that door that leads to what will be our new home, no man will be able to close it; and that is because what God has for me is truly for me!!

What is ironic is that everyone keeps getting caught up in these "good faith" deposits they feel I should provide. When in all actuality it is because of what the Lord has revealed and deposited into me, that I am able to lean on the better than good, more like amazing faith that I have in Him, which has no problem waiting until I receive what He has selected specifically for me. Nothing else will be accepted.

Suggested Song of Meditation: "It Is for Me" by the Miami Mass Choir

Psalm 9:10 (New Life Version/NLV)

¹⁰ Those who know Your name will put their trust in You. For You, O Lord, have never left alone those who look for You.

Something that I have discovered as I continue to grow and mature in my spiritual walk is that when the Lord wakes me up and instructs me to do something, that is not the time to be sluggish or lethargic; I am expected to make haste and get it done right at that moment.

That occurred recently. As I was laying in bed, trying to go back to sleep, the Holy Spirit led me to get up and grab the laptop because there was a word I needed to hear at that particular moment. God is so awesome, because there were endless choices of videos to choose from and I needed direction. I prayed for the one that I should click on and once I found the title, I thought I was preparing to hear a message delivered by Bishop T.D. Jakes, but to my surprise and enjoyment, God's Word was provided by way of the amazing, Pastor Sheryl Brady. What a powerful and life-changing message I heard that morning.

One thing that most people know about me is that I love to learn. I love uncovering the facts and methods that will assist in my decision-making processes. When it comes to my spiritual walk, it is that much more imperative that I know where to go to gain the knowledge and instruction which then transforms into the wisdom required to live the life, have the victory and walk into the destiny that God has for me.

In this season of transition, I have found myself asking God, "Why" a few times. This particular period of transitioning has been more challenging than I ever imagined it would be. As Pastor Sheryl Brady pointed out, it can be very taxing to be going somewhere and not know exactly where that somewhere is, how you're going to get there or when you're going to get there. Much of what was expressed in that statement was exactly where I found myself. Although there is a lot that is unanswered, what I do know is that I have been instructed to get ready.

As Bishop T.D. Jakes had stated previously and Pastor Sheryl Brady reiterated, in this transition season that I am in, I am caught somewhere between a caterpillar and a butterfly. Something insightful that she expressed, which resonated so deep in my soul, was when she said, "I can't fly yet, but I refuse to crawl another day in this life."

I know that my prayer life has become that much more fervent; with there being so many questions I have had. During much of this time, I honestly have felt like God has been so inaudible and silent. I have sought Him out for clarification and answers and because He's been so quiet, I have begun to question myself and if I have missed what the Lord has for me.

But today, Pastor Sheryl Brady said something so profound and it spoke right to where I am as a child of God in transition and one who is always so quick to say that school is in session every day and there is always something else to learn.

What Pastor Sheryl Brady said was, "Have you ever noticed how quiet God is while you are in the middle of your testing?" She followed that up by saying that God is a teacher and teachers do not talk during the test; they talk before the test; and if we are good students, anything that the Lord told us before the test is what will come out in the middle of the test." She concluded by reminding us that God knows that we have what it takes to pass the test, or else He would have never put us in it in the first place." I almost ran around the building on that one!!

God's love, grace and mercy has revealed to me all that I need to get through and be victorious. Through His Word, I am fed and given the fuel that is required for me to endure and persevere.

I must trust the Lord, who is my teacher, and in doing so, I have the reassurance that everything will work together for God's glory and for my good. I believe Him and won't ever doubt Him because I know that God won't ever put more on me than I can handle. He does everything in His perfect timing.

My soul has been filled with such an indescribable joy and peace from the message I watched this morning. It was right on time. I sing praises and exalt His name because He may not come when you want Him, but He's always right on time!!!

Suggested Song of Meditation: "Trust Him" by Tamela Mann

Hebrews 4:16 (Contemporary English Version/CEV)

¹⁶ So whenever we are in need, we should come bravely before the throne of our merciful God. There we will be treated with undeserved kindness, and we will find help.

Although it is pretty hot outside with temperatures in the 90's, it's less humid and the elements have ushered in a pretty nice breeze. No matter how hard the wind blows or the trees may lean in one direction or another, there they are, still standing.

That is quite reminiscent of my life. I have been flipped upside-down by so many unexpected circumstances and situations. When I look back from then to now and on all things that probably should have defeated me, I know that it has been because of God's grace and mercy that I am still here standing. Early on in my spiritual walk, the significance of fearlessly and courageously approaching God in prayer was made clearly evident. Going before the throne of our merciful God means I am guaranteed to be treated with undeserved kindness, along with finding well-timed help; coming just when I need it.

It is God who has the final say in our lives, and nobody else. In the presence of our Heavenly Father, I am able to stand, as a testimony and representative of His grace and goodness. I am so grateful that even when it appeared as if the pain was too much to bear or that the road blocks and obstacles were too hard to push through, the Lord was right there all the time covering me with His grace and keeping me from being consumed.

Having a history with the Lord means that I have a confidence in Him, which prevents me from becoming easily discouraged or agitated when troubles and difficulties arise because I have the promise that His grace and mercies are renewed each day and will provide me with everything I could possibly need to make it through. I have heard it said, "You may end up getting knocked down, but not knocked out." I thank the Lord for His everlasting mercy and loving-kindness towards us. Through every trial and every test, the enemy is defeated because Jesus, Our High Priest with ready access to God, intercedes on our behalf. Therefore, here we are, still standing.

Suggested Song of Meditation: "Here I Am" by Marvin Sapp

1 Timothy 1:19 (Amplified Bible/AMP)

¹⁹ Holding fast to faith (that leaning of the entire human personality on God in absolute trust and confidence) and having a good (clear) conscience. By rejecting and thrusting from them [their conscience], some individuals have made shipwreck of their faith.

When you are a child of God, you never know when God will present you with an opportunity to be a witness to others about His steadfast and faithful love, mercy and grace. And that was what occurred for me earlier today in the commissary. The tool that was actually utilized today was the shirt I had on.

My son graduated from high school in May 2015. During his senior year, I was tasked with coming up with a design for the Class of 2015 parent t-shirts. Something that I thought would be really nice, was if our family's mantra was placed on the shirts. My husband and I always tell our children and each other that, "The sky is not the limit." I know that most people say, "The sky is the limit." But for us, we always felt that with God navigating our course, even the sky wasn't the limit, because there aren't any limits to what the Lord can do in our lives or to the grace and mercies that we have access to.

The person in the grocery store stopped to ask me about my shirt and what I took it to mean. As I explained to them the premise behind it, we began talking about being spiritual and our faith. The person asked me, "How do you keep holding on and believing, especially when you really desire to do so, but everything around you makes it so difficult?"

I responded that my faith is my lifeline and what I need to survive. I shared that in no way did I get to where I am today in my spiritual walk overnight. And even though I am not where I used to be, I have so much further to go. I expressed that I know what it's like to be hanging on by a thread, but it's because of my trust and faith in the Lord that I have been able to hold on and press through until the Lord delivers me from my circumstances.

I have had seasons in my life when my conscience was compromised and I couldn't tell right from wrong. Instead of holding on, I couldn't hold out any longer and not having that endurance and patience severely impacted the condition of my faith. It most definitely was comparable to a ship that had sunk.

That sinking feeling took me to such a low place. I needed the Lord to remove everything that had been a hindrance to me trusting and seeking Him out daily the way I needed to, for Him to get the glory in my life and for His will to be done.

If we're honest, even when we say, "I'm trusting and believing you Lord," doubt tries to creep in and get us off course. That is why reading and meditating on the Word and having a serious one-on-one relationship with the Lord are so imperative. When those things are in place, you can speak and believe (without any doubts) in those promises that the Lord has for you and tap into that reserve tank of faith, when you feel yourself getting close to running on "E."

I am able to hold on because I have a heart that believes in His Word and so I am able to stand on His promises as well. I have chosen not to be fearful because He is with me. I will not be dismayed or anxiously look about, because He is my God. He has promised to strengthen me, help me and uphold me with His righteous right hand (Isaiah 41:10).

I have discovered what it takes to keep holding on and I thanked the Lord for the opportunity to share what I have learned with others.

Suggested Song of Meditation: "Holding On" by Jamie Grace

1 Corinthians 2:5 (The Message/MSG)

> *⁵ Your life of faith is a response to God's power, not to some fancy mental or emotional footwork by me or anyone else.*

There is so much going on around me and on a level that if I allowed myself to get distracted, it would cause me to come tumbling down and that is not what I want. To ward off and prevent that from happening, I have dedicated my time to creating an atmosphere of faith that is rooted in and is a response to the power of God and not some fancy mental or emotional footwork performed by me or anyone else.

What that means is that God doesn't need my assistance for His will to be done nor does He need me to seek out the assistance of others to help move His plan along. Regardless of the time frame we believe we are operating under, God's timing is perfect and when I am navigating within that atmosphere of faith, I can continue to press forward with my head up.

When my focus is on God's unlimited power, I am able to remain encouraged because of the belief that I have in the Lord and His ability to make changes in my circumstances and me. That same power provides the opportunity for miracles, breakthroughs, healing and deliverance to take place.

How easy it is to say you believe and that you have faith when everything is going your way. But what about when you get that call back from the doctor, or when you get summoned into your supervisor's office and are given that unexpected pink slip or when you find yourself displaced and no longer with a place to call your own?

It is during these times, and all others, that having an atmosphere of faith is most definitely required. In those moments, you realize all that is completely out of your control and that the only way it can be transformed is by believing in the power of our Lord and Savior.

I know it's hard. All you desire to do is believe and keep holding on and it seems as if, as soon you think you have made it past one hurdle, ten more pop up, falling right in line after the first one. But I want to encourage and remind you (and myself) that no matter what the problem, situation or circumstance is, it's never too late if you have the faith. It will work out, if you just keep trusting and believing and do not doubt.

What kind of atmosphere are you operating in right now? I am operating in an atmosphere of faith.

Suggested Song of Meditation: "Atmosphere of Faith" by Kevin Levar

Isaiah 14:24 (New International Reader's Version/NIRV)

²⁴ The Lord who rules overall has made a promise. He has said, "You can be sure that what I have planned will happen. What I have decided will take place.

During my prayer and private time, something that I have become more and more appreciative and grateful for, is that the Lord's thoughts are not my thoughts, neither are His ways my ways (Isaiah 55:8).

I am one who likes to have things in order, organized and for it all to make sense. I love researching and uncovering the answer and root to the problems in front of me. That probably has been one of my greatest challenges because how and when I think things should occur, rarely happen in that manner.

As I go deeper in my relationship with the Lord, I am recognizing the importance of not leaning unto my own understanding; because that does nothing but hinder my progress and get in the way of me receiving what the Lord has for me.

Something that has become clearly evident is that no matter how I try to plan or arrange things to happen in a certain order, what God has planned is what will happen. It is what He decides, and not I, that will take place.

That is why every single aspect of my life has to be released and turned over to the Lord because when His way and His will is being done in my life, I know that I am moving in the right direction and that victory is mine; because the Lord can't and won't fail. I used to hear people use the phrase, "It's my way or the highway." That's a very unhealthy and unproductive way of thinking.

For me, there is only one way and that is God's way. It's not about me, but completely about Him and the thoughts and plans that He has already decided for me.

Because I know that what the Lord thinks shall come to pass and what He has purposed shall stand; it's His will and way that I seek.

When I allow the Lord to have His way in every facet and component of my life, I can only succeed because failure is not an option for Him.

Suggested Song of Meditation: "He Won't Fail" by Marvin Sapp

2 Samuel 22:33 (New English Translation/NET Bible)

³³ The one true God is my mighty refuge; he removes the obstacles in my way.

I love reading inspirational quotes and motivational phrases. My words of affirmation and encouragement tank can't ever be too full. I desire for it to be constantly overflowing. I meditate on those words and phrases and recall them to help assist me during my journey.

Earlier today, I read a phrase that stated, *"If God is all you have, then you already have everything that you need."* That resonated so deep within my soul because in this season of transition that my family and I are in, one thing that I have consistently proclaimed with all the unexpected circumstances that we have encountered is that, "All of this is out of our control and we must surrender it to God because He is all we have and the only one who can turn our situation around."

How encouraging and invigorating it is to know that the One who we put all of our dependency and trust in, is more than enough and possesses everything we could ever need.

Because of the Lord, we are provided with new mercies each and every day. He is our strength and our power and He removes the obstacles that are in our way. We are cloaked in a garment of love that prevents the enemy from having victory because God is the one who fights our battles for us. We serve such a faithful and intentional God.

Each morning I am reminded that I don't have to have it all figured it out because it's not for me to figure out. My role is to be obedient and to continue operating in the faith that I have in the Lord. I am to stand on His Word and His promises and never forget that God is most definitely my all in all.

Whatever I need, God is. The Lord is my savior, my deliverer, my healer, my peace, my hope, my joy, my strength, my friend, my keeper, my way maker and so much more. He is our God and with Him we have everything we could possibly require.

Suggested Song of Meditation: "God Is" by Patrick Dopson

Deuteronomy 30:16 (The Message/MSG)

> *16 And I command you today: Love God, your God. Walk in his ways. Keep his commandments, regulations, and rules so that you will live, really live, live exuberantly, blessed by God, your God, in the land you are about to enter and possess.*

I am here to remind you that God has not forgotten you. The Lord is working behind the scenes on your behalf. What He has for you is tailor-made specifically for you and not anyone else.

If we commit to loving the Lord, walking in His ways and keeping His commandments, rules and principles, our blessings, breakthroughs and miracles will be unlocked and released before we know it.

Today's verse ministers to me on so many levels because of all that the Lord has performed on behalf of my family in a matter of seconds and minutes. For a while it appeared to my natural eye as if we were not progressing forward in any way. But through my spiritual senses, I knew better than to allow what was being reflected in front of my face to outweigh what I knew about my God and what happens when His super meets my natural.

I am still weeping and leaping with joy over the home that God has blessed us with. A home that places us further ahead than any other home that we had toured or viewed as a potential online. It is a home that has brought a dream to reality that I had so long ago and had forgotten that I had ever spoken, to a select few, into existence.

Every area where we needed a breakthrough, God provided it and infinitely beyond anything that we could have ever thought or dare to think of.

As a parent, to know that we have been placed within an area that has an outstanding public school district is beyond words. And the blessings haven't stopped with the house and the school district.

Today the Lord blessed me to experience another first. Since leaving to go to college at the age of 17, I have lived in numerous apartments and when it came to furnishing them, I had to do it room by room most of the time. Especially when I became a mom at the age of 20. I didn't have the funds or credit established to furnish an apartment all at once. But today, the Lord showed us unbelievable favor and released blessings in such a way that we were able to purchase everything that we needed for every room in our whole house.

All I could do was continue to thank the Lord. I have been so humbled and at the same time my faith has been skyrocketed and elevated to a whole 'nother level. I didn't know what the Lord was going to do or how, but I believed and trusted that He was going to do it.

I kept my faith in the power of the Most High God and sought to follow His commandments and rules in every situation I have encountered. I am here to remind and encourage each of you that when those things are done, without any complaints or doubts in the Lord, you will see the miracles, blessings and breakthroughs that you are expecting released and unlocked right before your eyes.

Our God is still in the blessing business and your blessing is closer than you think.

Suggested Song of Meditation: "God Is Blessing" by Jonathan Nelson

Deuteronomy 15:5 (New American Bible (Revised Edition)/NABRE)

⁵ If you but listen to the voice of the Lord, your God, and carefully observe this entire commandment which I enjoin on you today.

Just to be in the presence of the Lord; to have all distractions removed and making the choice to take the time to carefully listen to the voice of the Lord and hear a word from Him has ways of bringing changes, not just to our circumstances, but to us as well.

In those times when we are going through and feel all alone, if we seek out the Lord, we will uncover the importance of listening obediently to God and diligently observing the commands that He gives us. When we are able to do this, we will see the Lord bless us in the ways that He has promised.

I pray for discernment each and every day. I know that there is a war that is taking place constantly and I must be prepared for that spiritual warfare. The only way to do that is by diligently seeking out and waiting to hear from the One who is the source of my faith and speaks victory.

I am well aware that there is another voice that attempts to steer me down another path; one filled with destruction and defeat. But since we are the Lord's sheep, we hear His voice; He knows us and we follow Him.

Hearing a word from the Lord is undoubtedly life-changing. Our strength is renewed because we know that our battles are not our own and are being fought by our Heavenly Father. We can find our confidence in Him and, therefore, should not accept or entertain a victim or defeatist mentality. Remember that nothing is impossible with God. If we have faith, just the miniscule size of a mustard seed we are able to move mountains.

I am here to tell you that through my faith in the Lord, I have seen those mountains removed and watched giants be obliterated. It is His Word that is the fuel for my soul and which electrifies the neurons that transports messages within my brain. Those messages consist of relaying the truth that the Lord speaks and not the lies and deceit that the enemy operates in.

The Lord is the reason that I am here today. You will not find any friend greater or better than Him. With everything that God has done for me and all the special ways that He has cared for me, I bless and honor His name.

In all that I experience I know that I will be better than alright, because I have heard the voice of the Lord and His Word tells me so.

Suggested Song of Meditation: "The Word" by Brian Courtney Wilson

Ephesians 6:16 (New Life Version/NLV)

16 Most important of all, you need a covering of faith in front of you. This is to put out the fire-arrows of the devil.

When I think about where I was a week ago and all the flaming spears that the enemy was on a mission to hurl at me compared to where I am at this present moment, I am still left feeling wonderstruck. We serve such an amazing and wonderful God. My faith in Him continues to strengthen and grow deeper in ways I couldn't even fathom before. And with each twist and turn that I encounter, one thing that I know is that with the Lord we are more than conquerors.

Throughout this season of transition, I have had to continue to remind myself that I wasn't battling flesh and blood. And the reason I had to tell myself that was because, everywhere I turned, someone was trying to make me question what I knew God had spoken to me and over my life. Many tried to make me believe their role in my life was the deciding factor in how things would play out for me; and not what the Lord had already declared.

There were times when I was mocked because of the shield of faith I was placing in front of me. In those darkest hours and when I was in dire need of a miracle, I kept that shield positioned before me, held high and even when I didn't have the energy to press forward, God stepped in and I was made stronger and found the endurance to keep going; praising Him all along the way. Where my natural state was running on "E", God's supernatural met me right where I was and gave me all that I needed to overcome my situation and see the victory that He had spelled out for me.

There isn't one situation that we can't overcome when we have God guiding us every step of the way. Because we are His believers and followers, that positions us to be overcomers. The devil is defeated and no plan nor plot of his shall ever be able to prosper. It's when we are in the midst of fiery trials that we see the power that our faith truly possesses. With God, all things are possible and when you have trust and believe in the Lord and cover yourself in the faith that you have in Him, you have no choice but to be victorious.

Suggested Song of Meditation: "Overcomers" by Jekalyn Carr featuring Shana Wilson

John 7:38 (Amplified Bible/AMP)

³⁸ He who believes in Me [who adheres to, trusts in, and relies on Me], as the Scripture has said, 'From his innermost being will flow continually rivers of living water.'

One of the stories that I enjoy reading in the Bible is about the Samaritan woman at the well that Jesus encounters in the 4th chapter of the book of John.

In so many ways in the past, I could relate to the Samaritan woman. The lifestyle she lived was one that was frowned upon and so she was mocked, ridiculed and judged. To avoid the least amount of public interaction and sarcasm, she would choose the hottest time of the day to retrieve water from the well, knowing few people would be out and about at that time.

I definitely could relate to that. I had made decisions and sinned in ways I was not proud of. Because I always felt under the microscope, I would attempt to make moves and take care of errands and other responsibilities at times when others didn't, to avoid the questions and the judgments that seemed automatic when it came to me. In my own way, I was just trying to make it, because I knew that the questions would cause me to have to address things I wasn't ready to. Honestly, I was just trying to make it through living day-to-day like the Samaritan woman and Jesus was desiring to reveal truths to me as well.

Jesus wasn't concerned with the rules on that day, but was more concerned about the opportunity for grace to be shown. Where the Samaritan woman thought choosing the hottest and most uncomfortable time of the day was the best time for her to go to the well to get water, it actually proved to be the perfect time for her to have an encounter with the One who mattered the most.

Just like the Samaritan woman, I had to have my "at the well" moment too. I thank God that I was in a place where I had a thirst for the truth; something that is able to do far more than natural water; which is a necessity for everyday living. In believing, adhering, relying and trusting in the Lord, I now possess the key that unlocks the living waters that are associated with everlasting life, to overflow from my heart. It has been God's amazing grace that has saved and kept me.

Throughout the ages, the physical and man-made wells that have been used as a water source, have always had a possibility of running dry. It could be in abundance one day and then the next time water is needed, retrieval is not possible. But because of Jesus, we are given access to a well that never runs dry.

When we believe in the Lord, we are able to face and confront who are and upon doing so, we will see God's grace at work in our lives and we will want to share all that we have learned and received from the Lord with others. His love, peace, joy, grace and mercy is a never-ending well. I am so thankful and grateful that no matter what we are in need of nor how many times we may stumble or fall, we can always go back to the well!! It's a well that never runs dry!!!

Suggested Song of Meditation: "Never Run Dry" by Casey J

Romans 10:10 (Complete Jewish Bible/CJB)

¹⁰ For with the heart one goes on trusting and thus continues toward righteousness, while with the mouth one keeps on making public acknowledgement and thus continues toward deliverance.

A conversation that my children and I had quite some time ago, was in reference to the importance of us choosing our words wisely in all situations. I wanted them to know that what we speak has the power to be the greatest source of encouragement or our greatest source of hindrance; it just depended on which side they chose for themselves.

I also began explaining to them that the words we speak come from what we believe and that is connected to what is stored up in our hearts. I have heard all my life that, "words have the power to breathe life and to destroy." It wasn't until those instances when I was on the receiving end of the most hurtful and toxic verbal exchanges that I really began to comprehend what that truly meant.

Negativity has the potential to create a gray cloud of gloom that follows you throughout all that you strive to accomplish. That is why, around the same time, I also made the commitment to be my own source of encouragement and not allow all that was happening around me to get in the way of all that I was believing and trusting the Lord for in my life.

Part of that commitment meant that not only would my heart continue trusting in the Lord, but my mouth would continue to speak into the atmosphere and make public acknowledgement of all that the Lord has decreed over my life. In my heart and in my spirit, there is much that I am believing God for.

This is not the time to be discouraged or to let doubt or worry speak on my behalf. I recognize the power that our words possess and that is why I choose to speak God's love, His grace, His mercy and His favor into every facet of my life.

By believing in our hearts, we are made right with God. It is when we open up our mouths and openly declare our faith, that our salvation is confirmed. And to me, that is a very beautiful thing.

Suggested Song of Meditation: "Speak" by Myron Butler

Acts 13:47 (New American Bible (Revised Edition)/NABRE)

⁴⁷ For so the Lord has commanded us, 'I have made you a light to the Gentiles, that you may be an instrument of salvation to the ends of the earth.'

Since I have been under the weather for a few days now, being able to rest really hasn't been possible. Not even an hour after being able to finally fall asleep, I was awakened in the wee hours of the morning today by the sound of raindrops that were so loud hitting the window pane, it sounded like someone had taken a set of drumsticks and had commenced to initiating a drum roll.

I have always loved the sound of rain, but at first, I was startled this morning until I realized what it was. The rain subsided by early afternoon but for most of the day, there were just these heavy and ominous darkish-gray (nearly black) colored clouds hovering low in the sky.

But as I was driving my son to the campus for his evening class, the sun began breaking through the clouds. It was like the gloomy and dreary illustration that was painted in the sky just hours earlier, hadn't ever occurred. As we were looking at the sky my son said, "Mom, you know what I have noticed since we moved to Long Island?" And I asked him what had he observed. He replied, "I have noticed that no matter how dark the clouds may get, the sun always shines; that sunlight always appears before the day is over.

After reflecting on what my son had said, I told him that was a great observation that he had made and that it had caused me to drill a little bit deeper in a way that I wanted to share in my blog that evening.

In thinking about the dark cumulus storm clouds, that at times, seem to appear out of nowhere and the sun's ability to still shine through, it got me to thinking about the storms that have raged in my life and how I had to learn how not to allow those temporal storm clouds to block the light that the Lord placed within me to share with others.

I know that each storm has led to restoration, renewal, rejuvenation and breakthroughs in my life. Those storms have also been used to sharpen and mold me. I'm not the same person that I was and I owe it all to the Lord. That is why each day, I pray that when people look at me, they see the God that is in me.

I want to be His representative on those days when the sun is shining so bright that you need a parasol to prevent the sun rays from damaging your skin. But I also want to be His representative when the storm clouds are so thick that it looks downright impossible that the sun could ever find a little break in the sky to shine through.

Whether I'm opening my mouth to initiate a conversation, lifting my voice to sing songs of praise or letting my fingers do the walking to publish another blog post, I hope that it is the Lord in me that you see. May His Son shine in and through me, just as the physical sun does in the skies set before us. God made us a light to the nations, so that we could be an instrument of salvation. That is a role that I take very seriously, because He didn't have to choose me.

It was indeed, His amazing grace, that saved a wretch like me; therefore, working for the advancement of His kingdom is how I show my gratitude.

The song for today's blog was a gift from one of my sisters in Christ today. I thank God for placing the right people in my life, at the right time and for being in a place where I openly welcome and receive what they desire to share with me.

Suggested Song of Meditation: "Let Them See You" by Lauren Daigle

Psalm 119:66 (Amplified Bible, Classic Edition/AMPC)

⁶⁶ Teach me good judgment, wise and right discernment, and knowledge, for I have believed (trusted, relied on, and clung to) Your commandments.

"It depends on who is giving you the promise and it depends on who is signing their name on that check you are receiving."

What a profound statement that was. I heard it just a few moments ago on the YouTube video that I found for the vocalist whose song I am using this evening.

In my life, I have been in situations where I have accepted checks that didn't always have sufficient funds in the appropriate accounts to cover them. I have also believed promises and made life decisions based on those same promises; which when spoken were never intended to be carried through or upheld. In both those instances, I was the one left feeling empty and overdrawn.

When you are broken, the decisions you make come from a place of brokenness. Therefore, your ability to discern right from wrong, good from bad and sometimes even left from right are significantly impaired. Trust, I have been there and know that it took seeking the Lord and requesting guidance and instruction from Him for me to realize where I was, where I needed to be and where I never needed to go again.

By reading the Word and gaining a better understanding of God's commandments, I was given the tools required to obtain wise and right discernment, good judgment and the knowledge needed to live my life on purpose and according to God's will. What I believed was no longer attached to or driven by the opinions or actions of man, but instead by what I believed in the Lord.

With God, we are able to not just believe but rest on the promises that He has made because God cannot lie and in Him we have everything that we could ever possibly need. Jesus paid it all when He bled and died for our sins.

Because of my belief in the Lord and because I choose to cling to what I have found in His Word, I don't ever have to wonder if I'm forgiven, if I'm loved, if I have been set free or if I will receive all that God has for me.

He is my Savior and I don't just believe in every word that the Lord has spoken, but in every thought and plan that He has for my life as well. The best thing about believing in the Lord is that I don't have to see it happening right in front of me for me to trust that it's still going to happen for me.

Suggested Song of Meditation: "I Believe" by Tinika Wyatt

2 Timothy 2:7 (New American Bible (Revised Edition)/NABRE)

⁷ Reflect on what I am saying, for the Lord will give you understanding in everything.

Each day I look at my three children, at the ages of 19, 15 and six years old and I reflect on who and where I was at each of those ages. I think about all that didn't make sense to me at those specific ages and then throughout various seasons of my life.

There were so many times when I felt so alone and clueless. I knew what I believed and who I believed in, but what was playing out in front of me was the complete opposite of all that I expected. And that was due largely to the fact that my expectations were placed on man instead of where they belonged; and that was on the Lord.

My days were filled with silence, as I just waited for understanding. My faith was all I had and with each twist and turn, I was reminded that the Lord knows my breaking point and how much I can bear. So, if the Lord gave permission for me to endure my current situation, then He also had already made the provisions for me to make it through whatever obstacle I was facing.

What I have endured each day and each step that I have taken has been preparing me to be the person that God called me to be. And in those times when I couldn't hear His voice and needed guidance, I rested on the promises and plans that I knew the Lord had declared over my life, because I know that the God we serve is omniscient and always right by my side.

In retrospect, I can tell you that the Lord has provided me with understanding to the questions that have burned inside of me for so long and I have even been given insight to the ones that I wasn't even aware that I needed answers to.

As I get older and my relationship with the Lord grows deeper, my faith grows stronger and I am given the ability to understand things that I couldn't even begin to comprehend before.

Suggested Song of Meditation: "I Understand" by Smokie Norful

Revelation 14:12 (New English Translation/NET Bible)

¹² This requires the steadfast endurance of the saints—those who obey God's commandments and hold to their faith in Jesus.

One of the hardest things for us to do is hold on and be patient. That is especially true when we are experiencing trials, tests or persecution. It also holds true as we wait on the dreams and aspirations that we have been clinging to, to come to fruition.

I have come to realize that the key to having the steadfast endurance that is needed for us to succeed in accomplishing the goals and achieving the promises that the Lord has for us is our ability to habitually keep the Lord's commandments and remaining faithful to Jesus.

When we encounter negativity or adversity, it can become so easy to allow hopelessness to get us distracted from the plan that the Lord has for our lives.

I think that we can all agree that trials are a part of life that no one is particularly thrilled about, but when we change our mindset about the tests that we face, we recognize that we should count it all joy; because we know that each test produces steadfast endurance, serves a purpose in the journey to our betterment and is working together for our good.

It's imperative that we hold on to our dreams and never lose hope. It's so much easier to have that assurance in ourselves when we have acquired the knowledge of who God says we are and the thoughts that He has for each of us.

By keeping and leaning on God's Word and His commandments, we can find the peace and the passion to pursue our purpose while we are waiting for everything to fall into place in our lives.

Earlier today, I read a post from Bishop T.D. Jakes that stated, "Don't let your condition distract you from your position. Pursue your purpose with passion."

I really began to meditate on those words because I know it's human nature for us to become so consumed with the temporal conditions that are before us that we allow them to hinder our progress towards the goals we are striving to achieve.

But that is where remaining faithful to Jesus comes into play. In doing so, discouragement is replaced by determination and drive, moping is replaced by motivation and we are able to hold on because of the faith that we have in the Lord.

Suggested Song of Meditation: "Hold On" by Yolanda Adams

Lamentations 3:24 (The Voice/VOICE)

²⁴ Have courage, for the Eternal is all that I will need. My soul boasts, "Hope in God; just wait."

If there is one thing that I am sure of, it is this—that the Lord is everything that I will ever need; therefore, I place my hope in Him and my mind is put at ease as I wait on Him.

Something that I spend a lot of time doing is thinking. I realize that can be both a good thing and a bad thing. But lately many of my thoughts have pertained to all that the Lord has done in my life and all the areas in which He has made ways when there didn't seem to be any in sight. I have come to recognize, embrace and rejoice in the fact that neither the thoughts nor the ways of the Lord are like mine. He works in ways that are invisible to the human eye and incomprehensible to the human mind; and that is just fine with me. I have witnessed and experienced the miracles, breakthroughs and the freedom that can only come from living a life surrendered to Christ.

I believe in a God who will make walls come tumbling down, who parts seas; along with causing giants and strongholds to collapse and be forever destroyed. He's a God who is able to accomplish immeasurably more than I could ever conjure up in this head of mine.

The Lord is a way-maker. I have tried Him and can testify that nothing is impossible for Him. When challenges arise and it appears to be the worst thing that I have encountered to date, I rejoice and get excited to see how the Lord is going to make a way and bring me through.

In each situation, I have come to depend on God. As I wait, I watch closely, because as it states in Isaiah 43:19, "I am preparing something new; it's happening now, even as I speak, and you're about to see it. I am preparing a way through the desert; Waters will flow where there had been none." Knowing that the Lord is my portion and my way maker, fuels me with the hope that I need to keep me encouraged, joyful and ever so thankful as I wait on the Lord.

Suggested Song of Meditation: "Way Maker" by Jason Nelson

1 Thessalonians 5:24 (New Life Version/NLV)

²⁴ The One Who called you is faithful and will do what He promised.

One thing that we can't ever lose sight of is that the love of the Lord never fails. It doesn't give up nor does it ever run out on us. It is very important to remember that, not just when everything is going our way, but especially during those times when we are encountering obstacles and various forms of trials in our lives.

Our prayer lives are critical to our relationship with the Lord. I learned early on that I couldn't be one who just prayed to the Lord when I was in trouble or when it seemed as if all else had failed. Communicating with the Lord has to be a daily commitment. For me, it seems as if I need to commune with the Lord more on an hourly or minute-by-minute basis.

Now, I'm not one for heights, although I will make my way to the top of the Empire State Building or Statue of Liberty (those are the two exceptions). But I am not one that you will ever catch on anyone's roller coaster or apparatus similar to that.

So as those seasons arise when mountains are placed before me that I have no clue as to how I will climb or make my way over them or when the woes associated with the emotional roller coaster ride I now find myself on start to become overbearing, I fall back on the knowledge of who is in charge of my life; of who is faithful and will do what He has promised.

As a child of God, there is no room for disbelief. Disbelief creates barriers between the Lord and us, which can result in us not arriving at our land of milk and honey.

Because of the countless ways the Lord continues to show His faithfulness to us and all the times previously that He has come through for us, we shouldn't dare question or doubt that He will deliver us again. In His Word, we have endless examples of what God will do, if we just believe and trust in Him.

He's the same God yesterday, today and forevermore. And because He does not change, we are not consumed nor are we separated from Him.

It's not a question of if the Lord will move; we should get excited wondering how He will do it and already be praising Him in advance for the victory that has already been won.

Suggested Song of Meditation: "Same God" by Richard Smallwood

2 Corinthians 5:7 (The Voice/VOICE)

⁷ The path we walk is charted by faith, not by what we see with our eyes.

Have you ever had one of those weeks when you just had to declare and decree what you were not going to give the enemy power over your life to accomplish? Well this was one of those weeks for me and I needed the enemy to know that no matter the "jedi" mind tricks he tried to perform or the attempts to make me go backwards and stay there, my faith supersedes anything I could ever face.

Lately I have felt like I was running on fumes. You know how your car can be on "E" and the low fuel light will come on, but you will drive those last few miles before stopping to fill it up? Well, spiritually, I was in need of a "fill up" and I hoped that the word I would receive would minister to me exactly where I was. And as always, the Lord knew just what I needed to hear and the guest preacher who delivered the word, illustrated what I needed to hear in a way that I could relate to undoubtedly.

The message that was shared spoke to how we should behave and what we should remember when we find ourselves living in our own "Egypt", a foreign land where we are encountering obstacles, trials and tests.

Our faith is the key to being victorious. It's through our faith that we are reminded that God is omnipresent and always with us. Whatever roads we travel, the Lord is already there.

It is our faith that will keep us trusting and believing in the Lord; even when everything else around us would suggest we worry and be afraid. Our faith reminds us that even when we are not immediately removed from a trying situation, it's all working together for our good.

The troubles we face are used to train us and the trials we endure are used to teach us. And while we are pressing through, we can rejoice in knowing that God is in the midst and right there with us to comfort, console and strengthen us.

We have to be able to believe and call those things that are not as if they already are. We have to live and walk confidently with our belief in the promises that God has made.

As the guest preacher so wonderfully illustrated, "Faith is not "A la carte"; it is "Table d'hôte." That analogy took me back to the training I received as I was obtaining my Culinary Arts degree. "A la carte" means you can pick and choose off the menu what you want and what you don't want. In comparison, "Table d'hôte" means that you are entrusting the culinary expertise, knowledge, skill and portfolio of the head chef; with little to no input from you, in creating the meal you are expected to enjoy.

That is some serious food for thought. When I know that my faith in the Lord is all I need, the Executive Chef who I am entrusting to bring together all the ingredients in my life is no one but the Lord!!!

Having an unwavering faith and diligently seeking the Lord grants me access to receive wisdom, favor, restoration, strength and healing. Because I walk by faith and I live by that faith, I know that when I seek the Lord, I will find Him. There is no question that I believe in what He says He'll do.

Suggested Song of Meditation: "Faith" by J. Moss

Numbers 23:19 (New English Translation/NET Bible)

¹⁹ God is not a man, that he should lie, nor a human being, that he should change his mind. Has he said, and will he not do it? Or has he spoken, and will he not make it happen?

Over the past couple of weeks, I have been tending to the emotional jambalaya that has been simmering over here. It would be wonderful if right when we are able to catch our breath and things seem to be going great, all we would have to focus on are all those positive feelings and experiences. But as most know, when breakthroughs and strongholds are broken and promises are brought to fruition, the enemy gets upset and the attacks that come right behind all that are stronger and packed with more heat.

Even when the intensity has been kicked up a notch, I am grateful for God being who He is. He is too big for error and too wise for mistakes. Unlike man, the Lord does not lie nor does He change His mind.

Because of who the Lord is, I am eternally thankful because I know that when tests and trials come my way, they are being used by the Lord to make me better. When situations arise that have me feeling a little bit of everything, I know that there is more that the Lord is desiring to reveal to me; and more that I need to pay attention to, so that I can surrender it all to Him and be free.

We serve a mighty God who is perfect in all His ways. He knew us before we ever entered this world and took our first breath. He has consistently loved and kept us when others wouldn't and in spite of our shortcomings and imperfections.

I rejoice knowing that while in the midst of my challenges and as I wait on the Lord to instruct me which way to go, He holds me close and provides the protection that I need to make it through.

For the tests and trials that come to make me strong, along with the reassurance that I have that what the Lord says He will do, will get done and what He has spoken, will come to pass; I give thanks to the Lord and thank Him for being God.

Suggested Song of Meditation: "Thank you for Being God" by Travis Greene

Romans 10:17 (English Standard Version/ESV)

¹⁷ So faith comes from hearing, and hearing through the word of Christ.

As I was beginning to type the salutations for one of my blog posts, I chuckled after typing the words, "encouragement for your journey." I haven't ever denied for one moment that the posts that I share each day are probably more for me than anybody else.

In the past couple of years, since giving birth to the concept associated with my blog, I have recognized the importance of being able to encourage myself, even if no one else does.

Speaking of birthing, just as a baby requires the proper nourishment to be healthy, to grow and to survive, so does our faith. It is extremely imperative that my faith receives the proper nourishment for me to have that divine connection with the Lord, for me to grow in my spiritual walk and survive is this unpredictable world that we live in.

My faith obtains the nourishment it requires from the Word of God.

We have to hear the Word over and over so that it has the opportunity to penetrate our hearts and take hold of the perspective and manners to which we think and respond to situations. In God's Word we find the truth that is needed for transformations and breakthroughs to occur. That truth, which is nestled in His Word, gives us the confidence to petition the Holy Spirit to speak to our hearts and provide us with a message of love that will encourage us.

Just like the lyrics from Donald Lawrence's song, "Encourage Yourself" reminds us, "Sometimes you have to encourage yourself. Sometimes you have to speak victory during the test. And no matter how you feel, speak the Word and you will be healed. Speak over yourself, encourage yourself in the Lord."

I don't make a move without hearing from the Lord first. It is the Spirit that guides me and His Word that I abide by. In every situation and through every circumstance, I will request that the Spirit keep on talking to me.

Suggested Song of Meditation: "Speak to My Heart" by Donnie McClurkin

Psalm 118:6 (The Voice/VOICE)

⁶ The Eternal is with me, so I will not be afraid of anything. If God is on my side, how can anyone hurt me?

These past couple of days, the confirmation of what the Lord has spoken to my heart and stirred up in my soul has appeared in the most unexpected places.

It is so important that we not only read the Word, but know the Word. God's Word is the truth and the greatest defense we have against the lies, inaccuracies and manipulations that the enemy utilizes. When we have the Word of God stored up in the treasure chest of our hearts, fear doesn't get the opportunity to affect us the way it normally would.

While at church, the message we received came from Luke 2 (in its entirety) and it provided insight into the events leading up to Jesus' birth and afterwards. It also gave us a deeper understanding into the obedience that Mary and Joseph demonstrated.

As I listened to the message, I also noticed that in the second chapter of Luke, twice it was mentioned (in Luke 2:19 and Luke 2:51) that Mary recognized the importance of treasuring God's Word and pondering them in her heart.

Words are very important to me and it is the truth that I require all day, every day. My primary love language is "words of affirmation" and so for me, storing up verses and stories from the Bible that I can recall and call out in my times of need, is major.

What the enemy or the world has for me doesn't get to impact me like it used to because I am continuously seeking the Word; seeking to be guarded with the truth.

Jesus' birth constantly reminds me of just how much the Lord loves me. And His love outweighs any attack, plot or scheme that the enemy could devise against me. If God is on our side, how can anyone hurt us?

Suggested Song of Meditation: "By Your Side" by Antwaun Stanley

Matthew 6:34 (The Message/MSG)

³⁴ "Give your entire attention to what God is doing right now, and don't get worked up about what may or may not happen tomorrow. God will help you deal with whatever hard things come up when the time comes.

I am a person who is very analytical and who likes to plan things out, with backup plans being a part of my contingency strategy. I believe those are beneficial attributes to possess, but I have also come to recognize that although being proactive is definitely in my favor, I cannot worry or be anxious about what is to come in the days ahead.

Because the Lord is in control, I have come to appreciate the importance of giving God my entire attention toward all that He is doing right now in my life. Only the Lord is all-knowing and I am sure that anything that I am in need of; He will more than provide for. Therefore, I cannot get worked up about what may or may not happen tomorrow.

No matter what each day may bring, I'm not worried. In His Word, God has promised to help see me through any trials that may come my way. In life, we can make the mistake of being so preoccupied with trying to see what is coming next, that we don't take the time to just live and treasure all that the Lord is doing for us at that very moment. Time is so precious and tomorrow is not promised. Instead of worrying today about the "shoulda", "coulda", "wouldas" and "what ifs" of tomorrow, I am truly learning to value all the little things throughout each day that represent God and symbolize the love that He has for me.

Losing sleep over what the next day will bring doesn't help me. Whatever tomorrow has for me, I will be ready. I cling to the fact that the Lord's steadfast love never ceases and that His mercies never come to an end and begin afresh each morning. Great is the Lord's faithfulness and through His Word, we are given all that we need to succeed right where we are.

Suggested Song of Meditation: "Watching...The Moment" by Vashawn Mitchell

Proverbs 4:25 (Expanded Bible/EXB)

> ²⁵ *Keep your eyes focused on what is right [or straight ahead], and look straight ahead to what is good [your eyelids on what is in front].*

Wow, what a year 2015 was. Although I strive to adhere to the Lord's instructions at all times, there had been those instances where the Lord was calling me to do something and because it took me outside of my comfort zone, I became hesitant in moving forward.

December 31, 2015 marked a whole year, 365 days, in which I published blog posts each and every day. It was exactly on December 31, 2014, that I decided to stop running in the opposite direction of where the Lord wanted to guide me.

Little did I know that these daily motivational and inspirational blog posts would be one of the main tools of communication between the Lord and myself, providing me with the encouragement that I needed to face what was ahead of me each day.

2015 was a year of incredible highs. We rejoiced at our son's graduation from high school as we reflected on the amazing young man he had always been and the remarkable young adult he had grown into. We sought God's guidance to help prepare him for his next chapter in college. We celebrated the strength, excellence, independence and individuality that our oldest daughter uncovered within herself and vowed to assist her in making sure that nothing nor no one would ever have the opportunity to block the light that shines so radiantly from within her. We continue to marvel at our youngest daughter, "The Prophetess" as we call her, who is the best parts of all of us, and always finds a way to make everything that we experience an opportunity to pray and thank the Lord.

My family and I watched as the Lord opened doors for us that no one could close. Every step of the way as we prepared to relocate back to New York, we were covered by God's steadfast love and unmerited favor.

Even though we had some awesome memories, we also encountered some heartbreaking lows too. My oldest two children's grandmother, who was a second mom to me and a very special woman whom we loved very much, passed away unexpectedly. It was as if time had just stopped and the only sense that we could make of it all was that, even in the midst of unexpected tragedy, God is still in control and we have to keep trusting and believing in Him as we move ahead.

Relationships and connections that appeared to be promising and heading in one direction, veered off course and down a path that I did not agree to follow. And even then, with a heavy heart, I found peace in knowing that trouble doesn't last always.

I'm not the same Brandi that I was back on December 31, 2014. I know I've been changed. All in all, I came through 2015 stronger than I ever thought possible, wiser because of the knowledge I possess about the Lord and, in turn, myself; and more spiritually mature because of the purpose-driven life I am focused on living.

I'm not looking back; I'm moving forward. My pastor told us last Sunday that we cannot win the race that is before us if while we are running we're constantly looking behind us.

Suggested Song of Meditation: "Moving Forward" by Israel Houghton

Hebrews 11:1 (J.B. Phillips New Testament/ PHILLIPS)

^{11 1} Now faith means putting our full confidence in the things we hope for, it means being certain of things we cannot see.

What a blessing it is to have the opportunity to be in the house of the Lord each Sunday. It made me think of one of the lines from a praise and worship song that I used to sing when I was younger. That particular line from the song says, "I'm glad to be in the service one more time."

After being fed by the Word of God that my pastor shared with our congregation, I came home and began to study the devotional content for the Bible plans that I have started on my YouVersion Bible App.

I would definitely suggest that everyone take some time out and review the various lists of Bible plans that are available. Every day there is so much that I continue to learn about the Lord and the plans He has for my life. These Bible plans help to provide that supplemental spiritual nourishment that I require if I desire to live my life to its utmost potential for Christ.

As I was reading my Bible plan pertaining to God's closeness, a sentence regarding faith really stuck out to me. The sentence stated that, "Faith is not knowing the details of what the future holds, but trusting that the Lord will be with you in it."

That was so profound and encouraging to me at the same time. Honestly, although I would love to know what I can expect in the seconds, minutes, hours, days, weeks, months and years that are ahead of me, I know that is not how it works.

I recognize that the Lord goes before me and walks this journey alongside me; therefore, I do not hesitate to trust and have confidence in His Words and promises.

Faith is a mandatory and vital part of our relationship with the Lord. Without faith it is impossible to please God (Hebrews 11:6).

Because of who the Lord is and has shown Himself to be, time and time again, my faith has been established and continues to increase. It is rooted in God's Word and provides me with the encouragement, insight and strength needed to walk the path that has been prepared specifically for me by our Heavenly Father.

It's through faith that I am able to call those things which are not, as if they already were (Romans 4:17).

Faith is a gift from God. It comprehends as fact that which cannot be experienced by the physical senses. It means believing in God's promises and that He is faithful to fulfill them, long before those promises ever come to fruition.

May the faith that we have in the Lord continue to grow and intensify.

Suggested Song of Meditation: "Faith Come Alive" *by Tasha Page-Lockhart*

Romans 4:20-21 (Easy-to-Read Version/ERV)

20 He never doubted that God would do what he promised. He never stopped believing. In fact, he grew stronger in his faith and just praised God. 21 Abraham felt sure that God was able to do what he promised.

A few days ago, I shared about faith being a gift from God. Since then, I have had a few conversations about the importance of faith; which got me thinking.

Last night, when my husband and I were at bible study, our pastor was doing a review of what had been discussed prior to the New Year being ushered in. I was asked to read Romans 4:20-21 and those two verses regarding the unwavering faith that Abraham had stuck with me all throughout the night and into the day.

Even though he was much past the age of having children, Abraham's faith did not weaken when he thought about his own body, which was already good as dead now that he was about 100 years old, or about Sarah's inability to have children.

Abraham never doubted that God would do what He promised. Abraham never stopped believing. In fact, he grew stronger in his faith and just praised God. Abraham, by his faith, acknowledged that God was faithful and powerful enough to keep His promise.

That's the kind of faith that I desire to have and that I pray is observed by others every day. A faith that no matter how unlikely, regardless of the amount of time it takes for the promise to be realized, or even how absurd it may sound to others, I won't ever doubt or stop believing that God will do what He has promised to do. He's able!!

My faithfulness to God is not just demonstrated by the words I speak or type but also in my actions on a day-to-day basis. Through the faith that I have in the Lord, I desire to be a vessel used to draw others unto Him; instead of a deterrent that hinders another's possible spiritual awakening or further growth.

Abraham provides us with an excellent example of the kind of faith we should possess and the posture we should maintain as we wait on the Lord. He didn't stagger or waver in unbelief at the promises made by God. His faith and trust grew stronger and he praised the Lord for his blessing even before it happened.

Faith is the key. I am encouraged because I know that kind of unswerving, unyielding and blind faith is possible, because I have examples like Abraham to follow in the Word of God.

Suggested Song of Meditation: "Faith is the Key" by Alvin Slaughter

2 Timothy 4:7 (The Voice/VOICE)

> *⁷ I have fought the good fight, I have stayed on course and finished the race, and through it all, I have kept believing.*

It is through the faith that we firmly take hold of, both during those mountaintop seasons and when we find ourselves encountering those valley experiences, that we are able to press forward, stay on course and finish the race that is before us.

This morning as I was reading my "Living On Purpose" Bible plan, Jim Daly made a statement that spoke to that inner track and field girl I will always be and the mindset we must maintain as we run our own individual races. He stated, "Nobody runs a race to get to the middle; it's finishing strong that counts."

I had such an a-ha moment because there was a time in my life, in my junior high and high school years, when track and field was everything. I intended on being the next Flo Jo. Jim Daly's statement caused me to recall some of the races I took part in back in my youth and how giving up wasn't ever an option. I wasn't a long distance runner, but no matter how short or long the distance was, I was expected to run my best race and to have the endurance (with some on reserve), to keep pushing and finish strong.

All of that caused me to reflect on the spiritual race that each of us is running. Unlike the races I have been used to, what we are running is not a quick 50-, 100- or 200-meter dash; it is a marathon. Therefore, we must possess that spiritual endurance needed to stay on course and finish our races. I read a quote online regarding endurance that stated, "There are no shortcuts to endurance, you have to train yourself to make peace with the long route, every day, and do it, and love where it is taking you." As we keep believing and trusting in the Lord, we have to make peace with the journey that lies ahead of us and love where this race that we are running takes us.

Suggested Song of Meditation: "Run "Til I Finish" by Smokie Norful

Psalm 112:7 (The Living Bible/TLB)

⁷ He does not fear bad news, nor live in dread of what may happen. For he is settled in his mind that Jehovah will take care of him.

Over the past few weeks, I have observed many sharing the word or mantra that the Spirit has spoken to them in regards to the particular season they are in as they continue in their spiritual walk.

For me, that word has been trust. As thorough and detailed-oriented as I am and regardless of the years of wedding and event planning that I have under my belt, the one thing I have learned over time is that you can think you have your day planned and organized down to the smallest detail and in the blink of an eye, everything can change.

As a matter of fact, everything has changed. That has been the central theme of my life lately. Relationships and connections that I thought were unbreakable and everlasting seemed to dissolve like sugar crystals in a cup of liquid within a matter of seconds. New beginnings and restoration that appeared to be on the horizon in other relationships that have occupied the deepest corners of my heart, took an unexpected turn that left me so devastated my tear ducts couldn't even produce anymore tears to fall from my eyes.

I could hear the Lord saying through the words of the suggested song of meditation, "In those times when you don't feel me near, when the pain is so severe, when your world is flipped upside down and those you thought were closest are nowhere to be found, will you trust me? What about when I instruct you to release, the very thing that you have been clinging for dear life to, will you trust me?"

And my answer is, "Yes, I'll trust you Lord!!"

I have come to a place where I don't live in fear of bad news, nor do I live in dread of what may happen. My heart is steadfast and prepared because I trust and am confident that the Lord will take care of me.

I may not understand why things occur in the manner to which they do, but I believe that is why we are instructed in Proverbs 3:5 to, "Trust in the Lord with all your heart and do not lean on your own understanding." It's the minute we begin to analyze and break down things through our own filters and thought processes, instead of through the Word of God and the promises that He has made, that we begin to veer off course.

Something else that I have learned is that if something (whether that is a situation or relationship) that I have prayed and petitioned the Lord about doesn't come to fruition, it's for one of two reasons; either it's not the appointed time or it's not part of God's plan for my life.

Either way, we must rely on the trust that we have in the Lord because we don't want anything before God desires for us to have it; nor do we want anything that is not according to His will.

Suggested Song of Meditation: "I'll Trust You, Lord" by Donnie McClurkin

Isaiah 55:11 (Names of God Bible/NOG)

¹¹ My word, which comes from my mouth, is like the rain and snow. It will not come back to me without results. It will accomplish whatever I want and achieve whatever I send it to do."

I have to tell you that it never ceases to amaze me how one word from the meteorologists about a potential storm front, will cause people to run out and stock up, leaving the shelves at every store completely meager and desolate. Before a single raindrop or snowflake has the opportunity to form and cause any degree of accumulation, just the prediction of what may be on the horizon will cause us to want to be proactive and ready.

Now, I am definitely one who prefers to be proactive rather than reactive and so I understand the thought process in making sure that you are well-prepared for all that meteorologists alert us to. We rely on the education, training and resources that they have obtained and utilize. Sometimes they are accurate, but sometimes the information they receive does not come to fruition the way they predicted.

All of that got me to thinking. If just a prediction from the meteorologists can cause us to do all we can to prepare for what they say is ahead for us, why don't we exercise that same diligence; speaking, moving and being ready in a way that shows that our faith is so strong that we believe the Word that God has spoken over our lives, even before it accomplishes all that the Lord said it would?

I love the "Names of God/NOG" translation of the verse for today's blog. In this translation, the Lord declares, "My word, which comes from my mouth, is like the rain and snow. It will not come back to me without results. It will accomplish whatever I want and achieve whatever I send it to do."

When we hope and trust in the Lord, we are not just reminded that the Lord is our all in all but that His Word never fails and He is our impenetrable defense. It's when we equip and arm ourselves with the Lord's promises, that we are able to boldly proclaim the declarations that God has spoken over our lives. Trusting in the Lord means that we believe, see and receive long before anything ever happens.

Just as 2 Corinthians 4:13 reminds us, "But having the same spirit of faith, according to that which is written, "'I believed, and therefore I spoke. We also believe, and therefore also we speak.'"

God's Word always produces fruit, accomplishes what God intended it to and prospers everywhere He sends it. Therefore, we have that assurance that God will make a way for us out of the wilderness and for those areas that have been dry and unfruitful, God will put a river in our deserts. He will restore to us all that the locusts have eaten, if we believe and have faith in Him.

When the source and foundation of our beliefs are rooted in the Lord and His promises, with no hesitation, we will eagerly and purposefully speak what God has declared over us; and our actions will reflect our belief that God's promises will happen!!

Suggested Song of Meditation: "It's Gonna Happen" by Jekalyn Carr

Hebrews 6:11-12 (The Message/MSG)

¹¹⁻¹² And now I want each of you to extend that same intensity toward a full-bodied hope, and keep at it till the finish. Don't drag your feet. Be like those who stay the course with committed faith and then get everything promised to them.

I continuously stand in awe of the Lord. Before heading out with my oldest daughter earlier today, I sat at the laptop and had already picked out a song, verse and message for the blog that I intended to have finished before 5:00 p.m. I had every intention of completing my post once we arrived at our location, because I knew that I had an hour and a half window, which was more than enough time.

Well, because we were located on the lower level of the building we were in, I didn't have any Internet connection so that meant that I would have to wait until we traveled back from Brooklyn to finish what I had already started.

But after coming home, eating dinner with the family and taking a look at what I had done thus far; I wasn't feeling led to continue with what I had and just as that thought came across my mind, the song that is listed below as the suggested song of meditation, began to play on Pandora; which led to new verses and a new message being shared.

During most of my adolescence, early college and military years, I constantly wondered what God's purpose was for my life. I have heard it said that the area where you have the most passion and are inspired to do more and incited to try and make a change; that is where you'll find your divine purpose.

I have always been one who has always taken joy in being a source of encouragement for others. As I got older and because of the life experiences I had already encountered, that drive led me to focus specifically on women and young girls. I realized that not knowing my self-worth and allowing the world to be the deciding factor in how I was defined; instead of that definition coming from the Lord and what He had spoken in His Word, was a huge part of the reason why I found myself in the situations that I did.

Recognizing how the wrong mindset can significantly impact the words that we speak over ourselves, I decided to create a women's clothing line, exactly 10 years ago. The line displayed encouraging phrases across the apparel with the hopes of inspiring other women to change their outlook on the journey they had been chosen for; along with motivating young girls to truly think about their view of themselves and the life choices they could possibly end up making.

I was so excited and everyone that I shared my dream of starting this clothing business with stated it seemed like a great idea, but once I got everything in order and launched the business, the support from those who I thought were closest to me, became non-existent. That was an extremely difficult pill for me to swallow and it actually made me begin to second guess what I knew I had been called to do.

I haven't ever been one to give up, but in this particular season in my life, I was in such a vulnerable place. I was also stepping outside of my comfort zone because although I wanted to sell this line of inspiring apparel, I didn't like to ask people for anything; especially anything having to do with money.

It was so bad that when my children would have school fundraisers, I wouldn't even bother anyone for orders, I would just look and see how many items needed to be sold for them to get a prize and I would make sure that at least that many items were on their order forms.

So, having to promote and sell my clothing line made me very nervous and ready to throw in the towel; even though I had received God's approval and possessed a Bachelor's degree in Business Management; acquiring all the instruction I needed to be successful. But this was something very near and dear to my heart and it was about more than a clothing sale.

It was about hoping that the words that were stirred up in me to have placed on my items would inspire and speak to others.

I prayed and prayed and just asked the Lord to give me the discernment, courage and diligence that I needed to follow through with this venture and all that He had purposed for my life. It hurt significantly not to have that understanding and support of my vision by those I knew and thought I was close to. But God's favor caused groups of absolute strangers, whom I wouldn't have had the opportunity to even cross paths with if it hadn't been for the clothing line, to take interest and purchase apparel from it.

From colleges to domestic violence shelters to AIDS Awareness groups and to everyday people, who just desired to have a piece of inspiration to wear from time to time, each step that I was taking was bringing me closer and closer to my destination.

It wasn't the time to get sluggish or to drag my feet, because I knew that my desire to encourage women and young girls was connected to God's purpose for my life. From that moment, I have been determined to stay the course and never give up.

My desire to encourage other women and young girls is far more than a passion. God is woven in and out of every aspect of it; therefore, I don't ever have to question whether it's my purpose. All that I have learned about the Lord and myself by just living life and through the committed and daring faith that I have in Him, has helped to shape me into the woman of God that I am today.

Over the past 10 years, the platforms that I have utilized to answer my calling have evolved but as I continue to gain a deeper understanding of the Lord's will for my life, my drive to be a conduit and vessel of encouragement intensifies. I live to serve the Lord and for His will and not mine to be done.

Giving up is not an option. There is still more left for me to do. I embrace and am excited about what lies ahead, especially when I know that everything that I need to minister to others, the Lord has already imparted inside of me. It's all for His glory and I will keep working until the end because I believe that what I hope for will happen.

Suggested Song of Meditation: "Never Give Up" by Yolanda Adams

Job 9:27 (Darby Translation/DARBY)

²⁷ If I say, I will forget my complaint, I will leave off my [sad] countenance, and brighten up

Yesterday, as I was responding to a message on social media, I came across and was truly blessed by the following quote by Dr. Tony Evans, "Smile by faith, when you can't smile by feelings."

I love to smile and to be in the position to make others smile. I have been like that since I was a young girl going to the kiddie discos each week in NYC. No matter what was going on around me or how I felt internally, externally when I walked out the door all everyone ever saw was a smile on my face.

By no means was it a fake or disingenuous facial expression that I was sharing with others. Even back in my youth, I never liked attention and so I felt that if my countenance ever reflected the pain and hurt I was actually feeling it would have caused people to take notice; which in turn would have meant a whole lot of questions being asked that I didn't want or wasn't ready to answer.

I have always believed that smiling was contagious and so regardless of what I was going through, I knew that if I was smiling and laughing in spite of it all, I could also help to bring a smile and laughter to someone else.

That way of thinking stuck with me into my adolescent and adult years, but it evolved and took on a different meaning. When I was younger, I smiled with the hopes that what I was really feeling wasn't being observed and that in time things would change and get better.

As I got older, learned more about the Lord and the importance of my faith in Him, the smile that people saw every day when our paths exchanged in the streets, in the workplace, in learning environments or anywhere else, was connected and rooted in my faith and not in the temporal issues or feelings I was dealing with or harboring at that time.

There's a testimony even in that because when I am given the opportunity to share just some of what the Lord has done in my life and where He has brought and delivered me from, it surprises so many people who knew me during those various seasons because they didn't have the slightest inkling or clue that I was dealing with all that I was.

And my response to them has always been, "You weren't supposed to. Even though I was hurting, sometimes depressed and so confused, I smiled, because I knew that the Lord was working it all out on my behalf and that when it was all said and done, I would be better for it."

It's not a coincidence that it takes fewer muscles to smile than it does to frown. Not only do we look better when we smile, but when we can smile while in the midst of storms and trials, we are showing the enemy and those around us (who may be watching) that even though our days may not be perfect, our God is and there is a purpose for each and everything.

Smile, even though it hurts. Smile, when there seems to be no way out. Smile, when it feels like you don't have the strength to do anything else. Smile, when it appears all hope is lost. Smile, even in those times when you feel all alone.

Smile, because you know that God is working on your behalf.

Suggested Song of Meditation: "I Smile" by Kirk Franklin

2 Corinthians 1:10 (New International Reader's Version/NIRV)

¹⁰ God has saved us from deadly dangers. And he will continue to do it. We have put our hope in him. He will continue to save us.

As I was lying down and getting a couple more hours of sleep in before I had to head out this afternoon, I was looking at the island and palm trees that my daughter had made for me out of Lego toys and it made me think about how much I love the Caribbean and the opportunity to gaze upon hundreds and hundreds of palm trees.

I absolutely love palm trees so much that my husband actually researched the various types of palm trees we could purchase and plant here at home that would be able to thrive in the weather here in Long Island.

I have always believed that there were qualities about palm trees that I could relate to. Despite the elements or circumstances that palm trees encounter, they have been constructed in a way that provides them that staying power; under the most severe situations.

I can apply that observation with the kind of faith I have in God. I know that regardless of the season I may find myself in or how I may be going through the fire; when I have God directing my path, it doesn't matter if I am tried from every side or if the situation looks impossible, not only will I not be broken or destroyed, but that same storm will be turned around for my good, because nothing is impossible for God. His record is flawless.

How do I know that?

Because I have seen for myself (time and time again), God do the phenomenal and what others claimed was impossible. I have seen Him bring restoration, renewal and rejuvenation in areas that seemed so dismal and to be lost causes.

Regardless of how hard the trial may appear; even in those instances when you may be bent to the degree that you resemble a contortionist and tried to the extent where you feel you cannot handle it anymore, hold on, because our God never fails. He has never lost a battle and if we look back over our lives we will be reminded of the deadly dangers and doom that He has and continues to save us from.

We are eyewitnesses to the Lord's greatness, faithfulness and all the ways He has provided and made a way out of no way for us.

And that is why we must put our hope in Him because as Luke 1:37 reminds us, "With God nothing is ever impossible and no word from God shall be without power or impossible of fulfillment."

In the midst of the storm, through our natural sight we are unable to see all that is working in the background on our behalf. Sometimes we need to get to a place where we rely on more than what we can see with our naked eye. That is where our faith is activated.

Suggested Song of Meditation: "I've Seen Him Work" by Anita Wilson

Hebrews 6:1 (The Message/MSG)

> ⁶¹ *So come on, let's leave the preschool finger-painting exercises on Christ and get on with the grand work of art. Grow up in Christ. The basic foundational truths are in place: turning your back on "salvation by self-help" and turning in trust toward God.*

As I was looking at my Google calendar for 2016 and placing future appointments and events on the various dates throughout the year, I began to think about the milestone that this year will represent for our family.

In 2016, all three of my children will be enrolled in an educational institution; my son in his second year of college, my oldest daughter in her first year of high school and my youngest daughter in her first year of elementary school.

Ever since each of my children were little, the importance of seeking academic excellence and going beyond has always been emphasized.

All of that got me thinking about my spiritual growth. I can't stay in the elementary setting and think that just having the basic foundational truths will be enough to sustain me in my day-to-day Christian walk.

There is no way my son could have entered college or my daughter into middle school and soon high school if all they had to rely on was the knowledge they obtained in kindergarten and those first years.

The same principle holds true for us. We have to move on from the initial lessons about Jesus, so that we can press on in our maturity and go beyond. We should be finished with those beginning lessons about Christ and not have to keep circling back around to where we started.

When we move beyond the basic teachings and drill deeper for a more perfect understanding of the Anointed One, we are able to move beyond what we used to do, beyond where we used to be and beyond those situations that left us filled with so much hurt and pain.

Because of Jesus' blood that was shed for us, our yesterdays have been washed away and we are given the opportunity to go beyond by gaining the more detailed and advanced teachings of Jesus that are key to our spiritual maturity.

Therefore, here is my declaration.

There is so much for me to learn about Jesus and that is what I intend to do. I'm no longer in elementary school and therefore my knowledge of Him shouldn't be on an elementary school level either. I'm moving beyond and won't be stopped.

Suggested Song of Meditation: "Beyond (The Declaration)" by Anthony Brown and group therAPy

Hebrews 12:1 (The Voice/VOICE)

¹² So since we stand surrounded by all those who have gone before, an enormous cloud of witnesses, let us drop every extra weight, every sin that clings to us and slackens our pace, and let us run with endurance the long race set before us.

It is such a beautifully sunny day today. Even if it's rainy or overcast, I am still able to find something encouraging in my surroundings.

When it's sunny, it puts me in such a great mood. The sunshine makes me smile a little harder and hum a little louder. The reason for that is because I can't ever say the word sunshine without visualizing it spelled "Son-Shine"; which automatically causes my mind to shift from whatever I was thinking about to thoughts of God and His faithfulness.

Each of us has obstacles that we are facing and that is where our faith takes center stage and provides us with the encouragement that we need to have that active persistence to press forward.

Faith means holding tight to the hope that God will triumph, when we can't see the outcome or what lies ahead. My faith reaches out to the Lord because I know He is able. Not only do I know because of what He has done and continues to do in my life, but I have been given countless examples of witnesses, who have gone before me and by faith have testified to the truth of God's absolute faithfulness.

Whether it's Mary, Noah, Esther, Daniel, Leah, Moses, Ruth, David, Rahab, Job, Sarah, Abraham or the other countless heroes of faith that are located throughout the pages of the Bible; upon realizing the commonality that we share, we can find that motivation when we are encountering those storms of life. At some point in their lives, each of them (like us) found themselves in places they never dreamed or expected they would be and it was because of their faith in God's strength, faithfulness and promises that they clung to that hope in Him and found that strength required to endure.

Don't get tripped up!! We have to strip ourselves of every unnecessary weight and the sin that so easily entangles us and cloak ourselves in a garment of hope and encouragement that is rooted in the faith and trust that we have in the Lord. During those times when you need a little boost of endurance to run the appointed course that is set before you, reach for the Word of God and find your inspiration in the stories of hope associated with all the pioneers and veterans of faith who obeyed the Lord and blazed the way for us.

Suggested Song of Meditation: "Be Encouraged" by William Becton

Isaiah 50:7 (The Living Bible/TLB)

⁷ Because the Lord God helps me, I will not be dismayed; therefore, I have set my face like flint to do his will, and I know that I will triumph.

It seems like every weekend for my family is jam-packed in one way or another. Sometimes it's like we're all going in separate directions with the various activities, appointments or engagements that we're involved in. But then there are weekends like this one, that I truly cherish when the five of us are all in the same place at the same time; just enjoying what God has brought together for us individually and collectively as a family.

More than ever, the importance of doing God's will has been the central theme for all the decisions that I make. Even though I have many questions and there is much I still don't understand, I am able to walk with confidence and with a countenance that expresses my determination to make the necessary moves to go forward without wavering or second-guessing what the Lord says.

The resolve that I have comes from knowing that when I trust in the Lord, He will lead me through the doors I am supposed to walk through and down the paths I'm supposed to travel. No matter what issues I may encounter, the Lord is there to help me address them and I won't be left feeling disgraced or put to shame.

By making God's will the focal point of my decision-making process, there is no room for doubt and fear. My family and those I come into contact with observe a boldness in me that is only possible because I seek the Lord in all things.

Left to my own devices, I have encountered seasons where I have stumbled and veered off course from what God had purposed for me. But, in learning from those trials, I have acquired invaluable knowledge and wisdom. Now I take what others would view as a risk, chance or gamble and do what God has called me to do, with confidence. I recognize that when it is the Lord's will and not my own that is being accomplished, I can only win. Because the Lord helps me every step of the way, my circumstances are not met with consternation or distress.

Suggested Song of Meditation: "Your Will" by Darius Brooks

Colossians 2:7 (Contemporary English Version/CEV)

⁷ Plant your roots in Christ and let him be the foundation for your life. Be strong in your faith, just as you were taught. And be grateful.

After just completing registering my youngest daughter for kindergarten, I don't know who was more excited as we turned in all of her necessary forms and documentation. We then commenced to dance back down the hallway laughing and discussing all that she had to look forward to in a few months.

After getting my daughter secured in her booster seat, as I stood by my van, my eyes started to water and my soul was overwhelmed with so much gratefulness for all that God has been, is currently being and will be to my family and me.

In that moment, it really hit me that while my son begins his sophomore year in college and his younger sister begins her first year in high school, their baby sister would be starting her first year in elementary school.

There has not been one day in any of their lives, when I have not expressed the importance of God being first, knowing their value and worth and seeking excellence in all they do. In order to assist them in grasping and taking hold of all that I was chosen to share with them about the Lord, themselves and just living; I have to lead by example first.

As much as I stay on them about studying and knowing the material that will help catapult them into their destiny, I too, am required to do the same.

They know that without God we are nothing and that when we must have faith in Christ, and I'm talking about a faith that is so firmly and deeply planted in Him; that when the storms of life come raging, the roots don't break. Instead, those roots attach themselves even deeper to Christ as their foundation and we, in turn, are able to be continuously built up by God.

It's because of the teachings and promises of the Lord that my faith is as strong as it is. But there is still so much more for me to learn, more knowledge for me to gain; which in turn becomes more wisdom for me to share with those whom God entrusted to me and whose paths He has aligned with mine to intersect.

There is so much gratefulness overflowing from my heart, not just on this day, but every day. Today was a reminder of all the victories, blessings, favor and provisions that God provided us with in order to arrive at this very moment. It also adds more fuel to that "reserve tank of faith" I have.

Tests and trials are guaranteed to come, but when you can look back and see where God has brought you from time and time again because of the faith you had in Him; you can tap into that reserve tank and obtain that extra encouragement and spirit of thankfulness that you need to press forward.

We need to have palm tree-like faith!!! That means that we will have to go through some uncomfortably warm temperatures and situations as part of our growth in the Lord. And with that also comes times when the storms of life will be present. But because we remain deeply rooted in Jesus and the Word of God, we will have the assurance that once that obstacle or test is over, we will be standing because our foundation is not built on sinking sand, but in the Lord Himself. And for that, we should be forever grateful.

Suggested Song of Meditation: "Grateful" by Hezekiah Walker

John 20:29 (Worldwide English (New Testament)/WE)

²⁹ Jesus said to him, `You yourself have seen me. Is that why you now believe? God will bless people who believe though they have not seen me.'

I have always believed that a relationship isn't defined by the "warm and fuzzy" moments or when everything is going in your favor. It's when you encounter tests and trials and nothing seems to be going your way, that you really learn where the foundation of your beliefs lie and in turn, you gain a deeper insight into yourself.

It's so easy for us to believe, trust and praise the Lord when prayers are being answered in the way we hope they will or when God shows up in a manner that is greater than we ever knew was possible.

But what about those times when we don't feel the Lord near, or our petitions seem to be falling on deaf ears and the resolution to our circumstances is not arriving in the time frame we have set?

I still believe.

I will tell you that I have put my trust and faith in people that I have seen on a day-to-day basis, with my own natural eyes, and have suffered the most heartbreaking and disappointing situations.

With Jesus, it doesn't take me having to see Him for myself to know that He is real.

At church, we have a replica of the crown of thorns that Jesus wore and the nails that were hammered into Him when He was crucified for our sins. When I attempted to touch the crown, without injuring myself and saw the length, along with feeling the weight of the nails that were hammered into His hands and feet; it was such an indescribable moment. My eyes began to well up with tears at just the thought of all He endured for us.

I don't need to physically lay my eyes on Jesus to get a glimpse into just how much I am loved. And that is why I am able to still believe, even though I cannot see Him and even when things temporarily appear to not be in my favor.

What I do see is how, if I continue to trust and believe in Him, ways are made out of no way and what is deemed as impossible is accomplished effortlessly and within moments.

There is a confidence that grows, because it is through my faith that I realize just how intentional the Lord's relationship with me is.

The path that I have and am traveling has been a very contorted, and yet, very rewarding one. I have learned how to bend to the left, right, front and back, as I press forward and praise my Lord Jesus Christ all along the way.

I don't rely on what I can see naturally because I have been fooled numerous times by my natural senses. But my spiritual senses are connected to my relationship with the Lord and it is through them that I have learned and continue to gain knowledge about Jesus and all that His life, death and resurrection means for me.

Suggested Song of Meditation: "I Still Believe" by Crystal Lewis

Psalm 27:13-14 (Amplified Bible, Classic Edition/AMPC)

¹³ [What, what would have become of me] had I not believed that I would see the Lord's goodness in the land of the living!
¹⁴ Wait and hope for and expect the Lord; be brave and of good courage and let your heart be stout and enduring. Yes, wait for and hope for and expect the Lord.

Lately, various situations have caused me to reflect on how important it has been that I have learned to wait on the Lord.

When I am going through and waiting on the Lord's promises, it's in those instances that my strength is renewed by the trust that I have in the Lord's faithfulness and goodness. I am able to remain encouraged and to encourage others because I wholeheartedly believe that He will work each and every situation out for me.

I have that belief in the Lord because I have innumerable examples of the miracles, breakthroughs and favor that will occur if we just wait on Him.

We serve an on-time God and I have always said even if it takes longer than I would like for my situation to turn around, I know that God's timing is perfect and I don't want anything any sooner or later than when God declares I should have it. And because He is the author and finisher of my faith and the giver of life, I rest and find peace in the fact that even when I can't see it, He's working behind the scenes on my behalf.

Isaiah 40:31 is one of my favorite verses and it states, "But they that hope in the Lord, shall change strength, they shall take feathers as eagles; they shall run, and shall not travail; they shall go, and shall not fail. (But they who hope in the Lord shall renew their strength, they shall grow wings like eagles; they shall run, and shall not labour, or struggle; they shall go, and shall not faint.)

As we welcomed our loved ones into our home this weekend, I was reminded that we obtained the home that we have this very evening because we learned to wait on the Lord.

As we took part in the celebration of our church's anniversary, gratefulness continued to flow from the deepest corners of my heart, because finding a church home is a task to never take lightly; especially when you are thinking about the spiritual journey for not just yourself, but your entire family. And to see how our church has been such a blessing to every member of my family, in just the few months we have been members; that's God.

Waiting on the Lord has allowed things to happen in our lives that cannot be connected to anyone other than the Lord our God.

Because our hope is in the Lord, He renews our strength.

Wait on the Lord, please. Your greater is coming. The things that God will do for you, will render you speechless, but will give you the endurance to run and not be weary, to walk and not faint. When the promises that God has made over your life start coming to fruition and in ways you cannot even mentally comprehend, you will realize that by learning how to wait, your obedience paved the way for God to do the unimaginable.

Suggested Song of Meditation "They That Wait" by Fred Hammond

Hebrews 11:6 (New Life Version/NLV)

⁶ A man cannot please God unless he has faith. Anyone who comes to God must believe that He is. That one must also know that God gives what is promised to the one who keeps on looking for Him.

Often there are times when I would become agitated if I did not publish my blog within the time frame that I have set for each weekday. On the weekends, we are involved in so much and within locations where I am not able to work on my blog, which is why the weekend posts are normally published later in the evening.

Then there are days like today, when even though I had all intentions of posting my blog hours earlier, the Lord will call me to rest and just be still. While retreating to that secret place, I no longer become concerned about the time on the clock; but rather by what the Lord is desiring to reveal to me.

Now more than ever, I have become even more cognizant of all that I say and do. Not that it wasn't ever a priority before, but making sure that who I am is in alignment with the Lord and His Word is of the utmost importance.

Lord willing, I will be 40 years old at the end of this year. And I will tell you that for the first three decades of my life, I was so broken, misguided and confused. I spent more time trying to decipher and uncover what it took to please man than I did anything else.

There was so much I didn't know. And the answers, the truth, were just a page turn away; in the bibles I had in possession. But that was then and this is now. I'm here for the sole purpose of living my life according to God's will.

Because of the relationship that I now have with Christ, it is evidently clear, that in order to be victorious and to live the life that God has purposed for me, I have to believe that He exists, that He is who He says He is and that He will give what is promised to those who diligently seek Him.

I can't expect victory without an unwavering faith being present. Not only is faith mandatory, but it's also quite a privilege to be able to draw near to the Lord.

Because of His love that resides within me, I know that I can win. Even before the race is over, I can already see myself at the finish line. I believe that I will make it and that everything will fall into place. And just as one of the lines in the song states, "I am able to visualize the land, while riding through the storm," because of the faith that I have in the Lord.

By believing in the Lord, being obedient and keeping our focus on Him, we will be rewarded. We are walking right into our victory.

Suggested Song of Meditation: "I Gotta Believe" by Yolanda Adams

Galatians 6:9 (Amplified Bible, Classic Edition/AMPC)

⁹ And let us not lose heart and grow weary and faint in acting nobly and doing right, for in due time and at the appointed season we shall reap, if we do not loosen and relax our courage and faint.

As my youngest daughter and I have been observing various plants and flowers breaking through the soil and sprouting up into the air, it has caused me to think about the harvest I am anticipating from the seeds I have sown.

Because I am a new creation in Christ and no longer tied to that old way of thinking and doing things, I am waiting with expectancy for that harvest I will reap because I have not grown weary or tired in doing what is good and right.

There was a time when I would get so frustrated because, honestly, I got tired of being the "bigger person" all the time. But that was my flesh speaking and the old mindset that I used to possess. I was struggling to move past a lot of the disappointments, hurt and pain that I was harboring.

I was trying to do what was right, but for all the wrong reasons; and that was creating many obstacles and roadblocks in my spiritual walk with the Lord.

But God....

In studying His Word and gaining a deeper knowledge of the Lord, I began to understand that I couldn't keep sifting my decisions through the "Brandi filter". I had to deny myself (taking the focus off of me) and anything that was not God's will for me so that I could walk and have a life of faith that was modeled after the attributes associated with the fruit of the Spirit.

Those attributes include love, joy, peace, long-suffering, kindness, goodness, faithfulness, gentleness and self-control.

The fruit of the Spirit is not a buffet. You don't get to pick or choose which attitudes and actions you would like to abide by. Because our life is now hidden in Christ, when we are constantly doing those things that are pleasing in God's sight, it is the Christ in us that the world will see and not us, ourselves.

I have come to realize that when we make the decision to do the right thing, even when it's not always the easiest, most comfortable or popular thing to do, the seeds that we are sowing will bless us tremendously, in due season, if we do not faint or give up.

We can't operate in the flesh and expect to reap blessings. A farmer doesn't plant apple tree seeds, expecting orange trees at harvest time. We will most definitely reap what we sow.

I thank God for a changed mindset and His Word, which is that light that chases away all the darkness, inaccuracies and confusion that the enemy attempts to utilize to keep me from obtaining all that the Lord has for me.

This is indeed my season and I know that all that I have been striving to do for the Lord and all that I have encountered is working for my good. I will reap that harvest because I have not thrown in the towel nor have I become faint in doing what is right along the way.

Suggested Song of Meditation: "It's Working" by William Murphy

Isaiah 40:8 (The Voice/VOICE)

⁸ The grass withers, the flower fades; nothing lasts except the word of our God. It will stand forever.

As one gospel song says, "I'm standing on the promises that cannot fail. When the howling storms of doubt and fear assail, by the Living Word of God, I shall prevail. I'm standing on the promises of God."

There is not one day in my life where the words that were spoken, heard and read didn't play a vital role in the thoughts that I harbored toward myself; which in turn significantly impacted the life choices I ended up making.

I have always been fascinated with words. I was (and still am) that proud nerdy girl, who always desired to learn more. I wanted to uncover the origin, meaning, synonym and antonym for each new word. I was instructed to always use the Thesaurus and Encyclopedias that we had, with each assignment I was given that included a written component.

I have always listened to the words and meanings of every song that has come into contact with my ears and even uncovered a passion for writing songs, poetry and short stories.

So, when I tell you that I am a "words" person, you can believe it.

I have always chosen my words very carefully. I am a 70's baby, who was raised in the church and learned early on that words have the power to breathe life and destroy. Those sentiments were also reiterated in school because we recited The Golden Rule every day before class started. I took, "Treat others the way you want to be treated," to heart; therefore, I never desired to say or do anything to anyone that I didn't want them to say or do to me. In so many ways, it was a gift and yet a curse at the same time.

The downfall to putting so much emphasis on words is that if your trust is not in the right place, meaning with the Lord, allowing so much value and expectation to be placed on the words of man can lead to some very unfortunate and even heartbreaking situations.

I truly had to learn that the hard way. But I am thankful for the faithful and promise-keeping God that we serve. In putting my trust in the wrong individuals and places, the result was me eventually ending up in the only place where I knew I didn't have to worry about the authenticity of the words and plans that I was hearing regarding the path I needed to take for my life.

It is the Word of the Lord that I rely on and find stability in. His divine Word and promises will stand forever. God is not man, that He should lie. It's not man who is responsible for determining our destiny; it is the Lord.

Because we were chosen and handpicked by God, man doesn't get to determine or say how much we are worth or valued. The direction my life takes is no longer navigated by the words of man, but by the never failing and always prevailing Word of the Lord.

In Isaiah 55:11 God reminds us, "The words I speak are like that. They will not return to me without producing results. They will accomplish what I want them to. They will do exactly what I sent them to do." And in Joshua 21:45 we are also reminded, "Not a single one of all the good promises the Lord had given to the family of Israel was left unfulfilled; everything he had spoken came true."

The same God who didn't leave one single promise that was made to the Israelites unfulfilled, is the same God whose word I choose to trust and believe in each day that I live. Although, in some ways, my needs may be different, our God is the Alpha and the Omega; the same yesterday, today and forever. Blessed are those who hear the Word of God and obey it (Luke 11:28).

I truly have come to love the way that the Lord has intricately woven me and the importance that words do have in my life. Therefore, it is His Word that I seek, trust, stand on and put into practice. His Word gives me life and leaves no doubt about its reliability. God's Word will stand and prevail forever.

Suggested Song of Meditation: "Your Word" by Tonex and The Peculiar People

Deuteronomy 13:4 (Holman Christian Standard Bible/HCSB)

⁴ You must follow the Lord your God and fear Him. You must keep His commands and listen to His voice; you must worship Him and remain faithful to Him.

When I was younger, there was a song that one of our choirs would sing. The lyrics for that song were as follows, "Gain the world, give me Jesus. You can have fortune or fame. You can have worldly acclaim, but I'm happy with Jesus alone. You can have this old world, but I'll take Jesus for mine."

I used to love that song. Because I love to sing, there wasn't a song at church that I didn't enjoy belting out. Even when I was too young to understand the full meaning of what I was singing, I just knew that the songs made me feel good and it was something that I felt deep within me; in such a way, it didn't parallel to anything else.

Now that I am older, I will tell you that there isn't anything of this world that is worth placing before the Lord. Every day that I am blessed to awaken, with absolute gratitude flowing from my heart, I rejoice that I have been adopted back in my Heavenly Father's family.

I am so grateful for the eternal life that I have access to because of the divine bloodline that I am connected to through Christ Jesus. I choose light over darkness and know that it is the Lord my God, and Him alone, that I must imitate and revere. I choose to follow His commandments, to obey His voice, to be faithful to Him and to worship and cling to Him and no one else.

It's amazing how the enemy will try to make us think that by choosing the Lord, we have to give up everything. He's even tried to use those closest to me, to make me question my decision to follow the Lord.

I won't ever play myself and say I know everything, but let me share just a little of what I've learned. Satan is a LIAR. His native tongue is lying. John 8:44 reminds us of this very thing, "He has never been truthful. He doesn't know what the truth is. Whenever he tells a lie, he's doing what comes naturally to him. He's a liar and the father of lies."

And contrary to what the enemy would like to make us think, we gain more than we could ever imagine by putting God first, seeking Him out and obeying His commandments.

We can't be lukewarm nor can we be ashamed or hesitant on taking a stand.

Without the Lord, I am and can do nothing. But with Him, all things are possible. I choose the Lord, because there is no one greater. He is the Alpha and the Omega. He knows all, sees all, is everywhere and is concerned about every last thing that concerns me. He has the final say in all things. He's faithful and His love knows no boundaries.

For these reasons and countless others, if you ask me, I will always choose the Lord.

Suggested Song of Meditation: "I Choose You" by Brandon Camphor & OneWay

Psalm 119:30 (New International Version/NIV)

³⁰ I have chosen the way of faithfulness; I have set my heart on your laws.

As I continue to read Pat Layton's book, *Life Unstuck*, I am convinced more than ever that it was written specifically for me. I am so thankful that, through my children's request to go to Barnes and Noble; I was led to find the very last copy.

Being someone who is very much influenced by words and the thoughts that I possess; this book was right on time for me.

As I acknowledge the areas of my life where I need the Lord to set me free, I am truly beginning to comprehend just how everything that has been happening over the past few months has been leading to this very moment.

As I shared in the beginning of January, because of personal situations that I was overwhelmed by and thought I had pushed far back into the corners of my psyche, the condition of my heart and my mind were affected negatively. I was walking around, every day, with a blood pressure higher than I ever knew it could go and found myself enveloped with such a sadness and heaviness that I just couldn't shake.

I have always said that the greatest and most tumultuous trials I have ever encountered have always pertained to affairs of the heart. But it was the thoughts that I had during those circumstances that had the most impact on my heart and the decisions that I, in turn, made.

I was reminded of that when I was reading the chapter entitled, *"Unstuck Thoughts"* and Pat Layton stated:

"You see, who we are, what we do, how we behave and what we say all generate from deep inside of us, a process that starts in the heart and comes to life in a thought. The heart always represents—physically, spiritually and emotionally—the very center of our being."

It appears as if I have every page of this book underlined and highlighted thus far. But there was such a wake-up call and dose of clarity that I extracted from the sentiments shared above.

So much of what I have been, what I have done, how I have behaved and what I have said has been linked to what I believed everyone expected from me. It wasn't necessarily what was right or what was true; but what I believed I was supposed to do. But being someone who is not lukewarm or ever on the fence about anything, there lay my internal conflict.

And that is why I have chosen and will continue to choose the way of truth; God's Word. When what I believe about myself and what I know to be true are based on what I have read and studied in His Word, that's when transformations occur.

I am able to speak that truth over myself and any situation that arises because I know the power that can come from only believing in the Lord.

As I embrace all that the Lord is disclosing to me, I couldn't help but think about one of my favorite verses. Romans 12:2 tells us:

"Don't change yourselves to be like the people of this world, but let God change you inside with a new way of thinking. Then you will be able to understand and accept what God wants for you. You will be able to know what is good and pleasing to him and what is perfect."—(Easy-to-Read Version/ERV)."

Because I believe that God's Word is true, I have set my heart upon it, so that my thoughts can be aligned with God's promises.

Suggested Song of Meditation: "I Believe" by Micah Stampley

Deuteronomy 31:6 (New Life Version/NLV)

⁶ Be strong and have strength of heart. Do not be afraid or shake with fear because of them. For the Lord your God is the One Who goes with you. He will be faithful to you. He will not leave you alone."

What a tiring but very wonderful and productive day I just had with my family. I totally understand why for so long, I used to hear those older than me say, "There just aren't enough hours in the day." Today was one of those days.

I will be the first to tell you that I don't ever like to disappoint anyone or feel like I have failed at anything. For so long, the enemy had access to and manipulated my way of thinking.

I would believe that if my circumstances did not improve in the manner to which I thought they should or if prayers that I had submitted to the Lord went unanswered; that meant I had failed and was a disappointment to the Lord and others.

That is why I love Deuteronomy 31:6, because in this verse I am constantly reminded that God has promised to remain with me, to protect me, fight for me and bless me; therefore, I am destined to prevail because God won't let me fail.

By trusting and believing in the Lord, through faith, I have also realized that if a prayer I have submitted hasn't been answered yet, that is for one of two reasons. Those two reasons are, either it's not the season for that which I am seeking the Lord to happen or it's not going to happen because what I'm asking for is outside of God's will and what He has purposed for my life.

In both instances, unlike the failure that the enemy would like to make me believe I am, I win on both fronts. God knows everything. He knows what is best for us and when the best time is for all things to come together for us. Therefore, let me just say that I don't want anything before God says the time is right nor do I want anything that does not fall in line with His will.

Since God's love never fails, we can rejoice in knowing that He won't let us fail.

No matter who or what you may find yourself up against or how hard the road may get, you have to keep believing, dreaming and hoping. Have faith in the One who promises to finish the good work that He has begun in you and who showers you with a steadfast and boundless love that can't and won't ever let you fail.

Be strong and fearless and don't ever stop depending or relying on the Lord. He will take care of you and won't ever fail you.

Suggested Song of Meditation: "God Won't Let Me Fail" by Tamika Patton

Genesis 15:6 (Amplified Bible/AMP)

> *⁶ Then Abram believed in (affirmed, trusted in, relied on, remained steadfast to) the Lord; and He counted (credited) it to him as righteousness (doing right in regard to God and man).*

Now faith is the substance of things hoped for and the evidence of things not seen. One of the greatest examples of faith was displayed by Abram, who later was renamed Abraham by the Lord as He declared that as long as Abraham walked blameless before the Lord, he would be extremely fruitful and the father of a multitude of nations (where kings would descend from).

I love the story of Abram and Sarai (Abraham and Sarah), because it shows the transformation that occurs when we take our hands off the situation and trust in the Lord and His promises; which in turn, allows our faith to rise over our own thoughts and the circumstances that may be before us.

I personally can relate to Abram and Sarai. I know that there have been seasons in my life when the Lord spoke promises over my life; but because it was in complete contrast of where I currently was and what the Lord had spoken wasn't happening fast enough for me, I then decided to take things in my own hands and attempt to "help the Lord out".

That didn't fare too well for Abram and Sarai, nor did it fare well for me thousands of years later.

But once Abram made that vow to walk blameless, to believe wholeheartedly in the Lord and obey His every command, he began to see what God had promised come to fruition in his life.

When God commanded Abram, he obeyed and that faith made him right with God. That is the kind of obedience and faith that we need to have in the Lord.

Once the son, Isaac, that God promised Abram (who was now called Abraham) was born, Abraham's faith only grew stronger. Abraham trusted that God would fulfill every promise He had made.

The evidence of that faith was undeniable as God tested Abraham and instructed Him to offer the son that he waited 100 years for as a burnt offering.

As many times as I have read Chapter 22 in Genesis, the verse that has become the focal point for me has been Genesis 22:5, where Abraham told the two servants that had accompanied him and Isaac to the land of Moriah to, "Stay here with the donkey; the lad and I will go yonder and worship, and we will come back to you."

Abraham didn't say, "I will" but "we will" come back to you. Abraham had a faith in the Lord that I don't know if most of us today, would exercise.

Abraham didn't know that the Lord was going to provide a ram in the bush that would be substituted as the burnt offering instead of Isaac. He had no clue what was going to happen, but he was obedient and exercised his faith no matter what.

That's the kind of faith I desire to have. As I thought about Abraham's faith, it led me to some scriptures that my husband shared with me this evening from the book of James. In James 1:2-8 (via The Message/MSG translation) we are reminded to:

"Consider it a sheer gift, friends, when tests and challenges come at you from all sides. You know that under pressure, your faith-life is forced into the open and shows its true colors. So don't try to get out of anything prematurely. Let it do its work so you become mature and well-developed, not deficient in any way. If you don't know what you're doing, pray to the Father. He loves to help. You'll get His help, and won't be condescended to when you ask for it. Ask boldly, believingly, without a second thought. People who "worry their prayers" are like wind-whipped waves. Don't think you're going to get anything from the Master that way, adrift at sea, keeping all your options open."

Stand firm on God's Word and let faith arise!!

Suggested Song of Meditation: "Let Faith Arise" by BridgeCity

1 Timothy 3:9 (New International Reader's Version/NIRV)

⁹ They must hold on to the deep truths of the faith. Even their own minds tell them to do that.

One of my favorite songs by Donnie McClurkin is, "I'll Trust You Lord." It's the beginning lines to that song that I have been repeating over and over in my head, as of late. Those lyrics say:

"I know that faith is easy when everything is going well, but can you still believe in Me when your life's a living hell? And when all the things around you seem to quickly fade away, there's just one thing I really want to know. Will you let go? Will you stand on My Word? Against all odds will you believe what I have said? What seems impossible, will you believe? Every promise that I made will you receive?"

My answer to each of those questions is, "YES, I trust you Lord. I'll still believe even if I don't see how it will all work out."

So many situations in my life have changed without a moment's notice. There is so much I don't understand and so many tears that have been shed, but it is because of the faith that I have in the Lord that I am able to hold firmly to the deep truths of the faith that God has made known to me with a clear and pure conscience.

The testing of our faith doesn't come when everything is going our way. It's when we're blindsided or left feeling like we have been sucker-punched, without any prior warning, that we are to activate our faith and keep our eyes fixed on the Lord, knowing that His Word is true and that He is our refuge in every situation.

I've also come to learn that it's really easy to say that we only want what God has for us, when it is packaged the way we expect or in a more favorable manner.

But what happens when, what God has for us, is in complete opposition to what we expected for ourselves?

That is where I find myself today. I've been trying to hold on in certain situations, but that voice inside me has been telling me to let go and to place all my energy and focus into grasping tightly to the Lord and His Word; as I wait on Him.

Through faith, 2 Timothy 3:16-17 reminds me that, "Every part of Scripture is God-breathed and useful one way or another—showing us truth, exposing our rebellion, correcting our mistakes, training us to live God's way. Through the Word, we are put together and shaped up for the tasks God has for us."

I don't need to see how the circumstances in my life will work together for my good, to believe and have faith that they will. No matter how long it takes, I will keep holding on.

Suggested Song of Meditation: "I'll Hold On" by Tamela Mann

Psalm 143:8 (The Message/MSG)

⁸ If you wake me each morning with the sound of your loving voice, I'll go to sleep each night trusting in you. Point out the road I must travel; I'm all ears, all eyes before you.

I am here to testify to the truth that, "Weeping may endure for a night, but joy comes in the morning (Psalm 30:5).

Over the past few days, I have found myself in such unfamiliar territory, which brought out an anxiousness and concern that I hadn't ever experienced before. Because of the fear of possible devastation and disappointment that could be on the horizon, I just wanted the Lord to give me a sign right then when I felt I needed the confirmation, so I would know in which manner to proceed.

I have no right nor the authority to put the Lord in a box, in any way, shape, fashion or form. I was so ashamed when I realized that I had allowed fear to tip the scales, where my faith had always outweighed.

I fell to my knees, weeping and asking the Lord for forgiveness for allowing, what appeared to be His distance and non-communication, to incite worry and fear; instead of trusting and standing on that same faith that I have had in Him, when all other tests and trials have come my way.

I was reminded last night that trusting and having faith in the Lord means also trusting in His timing. Just because things are not happening in the way or within the time-frame I desire does NOT mean that things are not happening in the background; which will bring everything together according to His plan and for my good.

I needed music to minister to my soul so that the garment of heaviness I was carrying could be eliminated. The two songs that I chose were, Donnie McClurkin's, "I'll Trust You, Lord" and the suggested song of meditation that is listed below.

As I listened to the words of the two songs, my entire frame of mind and posture changed as I thought about the importance of the Lord knowing that in those times when I call on Him and He doesn't seem near or if He instructs me to let go of the very thing that I think I am to cling to—I will continue to trust Him.

Even when I don't know the outcome, the Lord has shown me that I am able to go to sleep each night trusting Him because of His unfailing love, promises, grace and mercy that I have to greet me with the dawning of each new day.

The enemy would like to make me think there is no way that I'll get through this or that the past will repeat itself. But another truth that I hold tight to is that the enemy's native tongue is lying (John 8:44).

The lengths and tactics that he would utilize, with the hopes of my heart being utterly divided, just goes to show me how much more diligent and determined I must be to keep trusting in the One who has and will never fail me.

This is a testing period for me and my instructor is my Heavenly Father. And what I learned a while ago is, just like the teachers that we have encountered throughout our educational journey, when it came time for a test, they didn't talk while the test was being administered. They had already provided their pupils with all they needed to pass the test.

Just because the Lord is quiet doesn't mean He's not present. To the contrary, the Lord is always there by our side. It's just that He's already imparted and given us all that we need to pass the test if we just trust in Him and His Word, which is the lamp unto our feet and the light unto our path.

I am kept in perfect peace because my mind is staying on the Lord. I choose to trust Him in all circumstances and not be sidetracked by what is or isn't seen with my natural eye.

Suggested Song of Meditation: "I Trust You" by James Fortune and FIYA

Hebrews 11:3 (New International Reader's Version/NIRV)

³ We have faith. So we understand that everything was made when God commanded it. That's why we believe that what we see was not made out of what could be seen.

There have been certain seasons in my life, when one word remained the underlying theme for me. Depending on where I found myself at that time, the word has changed from forgiveness to love to grace to mercy to patience and as of late that word has been, "faith."

It is because I am well aware that, "Without faith it is impossible to please God (Hebrews 11:6)," that I reach out to the Lord and seek a deeper understanding of Him and His purpose for my life; so that thoughts of abandonment, shame, regret and fear don't have the opportunity to re-attach themselves to me; thus hindering my walk with Christ.

Hebrews 11:1 clearly defines faith as the substance of things hoped for, the evidence of things not seen. I have memorized and sang that verse more times than I can remember.

As many times as I have read Hebrews 11, tonight it was Hebrews 11:3 that stuck with me and I kept reading it over and over. When I think about the universe and everything that has been created, I recognize that the reason its ALL in existence is because God commanded it to be. Since what is seen has not been made out of things which are visible; how could I ever be concerned about those things that I am trusting and believing the Lord for?

If He commanded it, it will happen and through faith I am given the assurance about things that I cannot see.

I came across an acronym for the word faith and it read: Forsaking, All, I, Trust Him.

And that is the place where I have arrived. I am abandoning and deserting any and everything that would hinder me from trusting the Lord completely and living the life that He has purposed for me.

I am forsaking it all and embracing every ounce of faith that I have because I know that nothing is impossible for the Lord.

When it comes to exercising my faith, I desire to stand with the likes of Abel, Noah, Enoch, Abraham, Sarah, Jacob, Joseph, Moses, the people of Israel (as they went right through the Red Sea as though they were on dry ground and when they marched around Jericho for seven days, and the walls came crashing down), Rahab, Gideon, Barak, Samson, Jephthah, David, Samuel and many others.

By faith we understand and Hebrews 11 is a clear depiction of faith in action.

Suggested Song of Meditation: "Hebrews 11" by Richard Smallwood

Proverbs 16:20 (Amplified Bible, Classic Edition/AMPC)

²⁰ He who deals wisely and heeds [God's] word and counsel shall find good, and whoever leans on, trusts in, and is confident in the Lord—happy, blessed, and fortunate is he.

During a week when it seems as if every time you turn on the TV or gain access to the Internet, another heartbreaking and tragic event is occurring; I have needed scriptures and songs of praise and worship to serve as sources of encouragement to deter me from remaining saddened or with a heavy heart.

The key to my mood and outlook changing was tied to me taking my focus off the things that are currently happening and instead, remaining focused on the Lord and His instruction that we have within our grasp.

When I think about Proverbs 16:20, I also begin to reflect on Proverbs 3:13 which states, "Happy (blessed, fortunate, enviable) is the man who finds skillful and godly Wisdom, and the man who gets understanding [drawing it forth from God's Word and life's experiences]."

While journeying the path that God has established specifically for me, I feel so fortunate for the opportunities to obtain godly wisdom. The path of wisdom leads to a full and fruitful life. Oh, how I desire to live life to the fullest extent, until it overflows, constantly gaining wisdom as I travel along the way.

Everything about the Lord is right. I have always heard it said that we should strive for joy in our lives because happiness is determined by our external circumstances, whereas joy comes from seeing and knowing the Lord.

In the translation of the verse listed above, the word happy is synonymous with the word blessed.

I recognize that only the Lord can provide us with the wisdom to live righteously; which in turn, gives us the ability to endure trials optimistically.

Therefore, in instances when I use the word happy, it is in reference to feeling fortunate. We are so blessed to be connected to the Lord. The love and gratitude that I feel, along with the eagerness that I have to worship Him, is rooted in the realization that Jesus' life saved my life.

I choose to deal wisely and heed God's Word and counsel when it comes to making decisions in my life. It is the LORD that I lean on, trust and am confident in.

As I gain greater understanding from both God's Word and life experiences, the Lord positions me to obtain a deeper insight into His desire for my existence. And that leaves me feeling so happy (blessed and fortunate).

Suggested Song of Meditation: "Happy" by Tasha Cobbs

Isaiah 45:2 (Amplified Bible, Classic Edition/AMPC)

*² I will go before you and level the mountains [to make the crooked places straight];
I will break in pieces the doors of bronze and cut asunder the bars of iron.*

A couple of days ago, one of my sisters in Christ reminded me that we serve a "way-making" God.

These past few months have clearly shown me, that no matter how far-fetched it may seem for a potential resolution or outcome to be accomplished, the God we serve loves us so much that He goes before us, clearing and paving the way. Mountains are leveled, walls begin to fall and barriers are knocked down.

Because of the power that the Lord possesses, miracles are performed that cause the crooked places in our lives to become straight.

Regardless of the obstructions, impediments, hindrances or obstacles that are positioned to make it appear as if our backs are against the wall or that we can't move forward or win, we must never forget that nothing is too difficult for our God.

When I think about who I am and where I find myself today, I know that the Lord has brought me from a mighty long way.

His grace has carried me and the only reason I am able to sit at my laptop and share my thoughts is because the Lord continues to make a way for me.

I know that none of that would be possible if I relied on my own understanding and analysis of the situations that I have had to face.

But before I even get tempted to try to decipher or guess what lies ahead for me, my thoughts automatically go to Proverbs 3:5-6, which instructs us to "Trust in and rely confidently on the Lord with all your heart and do not rely on your own insight or understanding. In all your ways know and acknowledge and recognize Him, and He will make your paths straight and smooth [removing obstacles that block your way]."

I don't need to know how the Lord orchestrates all that He does, but I know that He does it. I also don't know why He has chosen to do all that He does for me, but I am forever grateful that He does.

He moves mountains, slays giants, destroys yokes and quiets storms.

Our Heavenly Father knows exactly what He is doing. He is well aware of our past, our present and what each of our end results will be.

We may not see a way in front of us; but as long as we trust in the Lord and keep pressing forward in the faith that we have in Him, we can be confident that the same God who provided a way for us before, will do it again!!

Suggested Song of Meditation: "Made A Way" by Travis Greene

Romans 4:21 (Amplified Bible, Classic Edition/AMPC)

²¹ Fully satisfied and assured that God was able and mighty to keep His Word and to do what He had promised.

As I think about holding onto every promise that the Lord has made, I think about the lyrics that say, "Standing on the promises I cannot fall, listening every moment to the Spirit's call, resting in my Savior as my all in all and standing on the promises of God."

There are days when it seems like not much at all makes sense. But I am so grateful that there is one thing that I can always hold on and cling to; that being the promises that the Lord has made.

The only way to have the kind of faith that can keep you persevering, even when what you are believing the Lord for has yet to come to fruition, is by abiding in the Lord and His Word.

When we follow the Lord's teachings and His Word remains within us, we become fully convinced that what the Lord has promised, He has the ability to perform.

I am here to tell you that there is not one thing that any of us has faced, are facing or will face that the Lord has not already provided the solution for and the steps that should be taken as we are going through.

If we don't take the time to know His Word, then we won't have the slightest idea of which principles should govern our lives.

No matter what our external circumstances may reflect, when we have that unwavering faith and trust in the Lord, our belief in Him will cause our focus to be diverted from the problems themselves, because of the assurance that we have in God and all that He is able and capable of accomplishing.

God is able. He won't fail. Don't give up or give in. our God will be there until the end.

2 Peter 1:4 reminds us of this when it says, "Through His glory and integrity He has given us His promises that are of the highest value. Through these promises you will share in the divine nature because you have escaped the corruption that sinful desires cause in the world."

It's through our faith in the Most High, that we are able to reach the unreachable and conquer that which would appear to be unbeatable.

Regardless of the strongholds and obstacles we may encounter, we can claim that freedom and victory in advance because we have the confidence and certainty that there is nothing too hard, too great or too powerful for our Lord and Savior.

I won't stop holding on because I know that, when we abide, vitally united with the Lord and His Word remains in us and continues to live in our hearts, whatever we ask, it shall be done for us (John 15:7).

Suggested Song of Meditation: "Every Promise" by Earnest Pugh featuring Lalah Hathaway

Romans 12:12 (Expanded Bible/EXB)

> ¹² *Be joyful because you have hope [Rejoice in hope]. Be patient [Endure] when trouble comes [in suffering/tribulation], and pray·at all times [faithfully; with persistence/perseverance].*

One Sunday, when we attended our church in Maryland, we had a guest pastor deliver the word. He delivered such a profound message that I couldn't even digest it all at once. I knew that what he was saying was speaking directly to me and so it had to be broken down and ingested in smaller parts to truly appreciate and receive what the Lord was conveying through him.

The beginning part of the message spoke to how when God makes us a promise, it's always, "Yes." God's promises don't mean "Maybe" or "We'll see." More importantly, when God says, "Yes," we have to be able to just say, "Amen." When we say, "Amen" we have to be able to do it without any negativity or conditions attached to it. Saying, "Amen" means that we affirm and agree that the promises God has for us will happen. We must walk by faith and not by sight. If we can't do that, we will miss out and not redeem the blessings that God has for us. That spoke in volumes to me, because I have said many times that I do not ever want to be the one getting in the way of my own blessings.

From there, we learned the importance of staying positive despite haters and heartbreak. If you don't know by now, being the resident optimist is something I do and have always done. I try at all times to spin the situation and look at it in a positive light. I will not say that is always an easy feat. It's even more difficult when striving to be who God calls you to be, causes opposition to come from people you would least expect. In the past, as a people-pleaser, I would truly internalize and beat myself up when being attacked by others; especially when I knew that either (a) I hadn't done anything to them for the response I was receiving or (b) the particular individual didn't even know me, which left me in a serious state of confusion.

My confusion led to clarity when I realized that each person God has utilized to mold and shape me into the individual I am today. It definitely hasn't been an uneventful and smooth-sailing journey. This path of mine has been met with much heartache and disappointment, because I am one who loves hard. I graduated from the school of, "You go hard or you go home." So many times, loving hard severely impaired my vision.

I have made the disclaimer that while others are trying to juggle the balls in their lives, I'm the one ball they didn't want to drop because where those other ones were rubber and can bounce back, I was the one glass ball in the mix and if I was dropped, I would break.

Forsaking All I Trust Him (Faith) | 129

Yesterday, we were charged to stop allowing people to take residence in our mind, because then we end up becoming consumed by them and their negative ways. We were told if we are going to allow people to take residence, at least make them pay rent. Even though I found that statement to be amusing, it was also so true. I have been so guilty of getting pulled in and then becoming consumed and overwhelmed by the other people's situations; but not anymore.

I don't have any more heartbreaks to give out or blessings to give away. My heart has been shattered many times, but God has been right there to cover and protect me. What the enemy believed would lead to my demise and take me out, God turned it around and breathed new life into me and my circumstances. His love fused every single piece of me back together. God shows us His kindness in that after we have suffered for a little while, He restores, strengthens and establishes us (1 Peter 5:10).

Through it all, I'm still here. Because I have learned to rejoice in hope, to be patient when trouble arises and to pray faithfully, God has kept me. And that is why when you see me, you're going to see me smiling and staying positive because my faith is stronger than anything I may face.

Suggested Song of Meditation: "I'm Still Here" by Jessica Reedy featuring The Soul Seekers

GOD'S WORD IS COMPLETE,
HIS LOVE IS UNCONDITIONAL
AND HIS POWER IS
INEXHAUSTIBLE

Malachi 3:6 (The Living Bible/TLB)

⁶ "For I am the Lord—I do not change. That is why you are not already utterly destroyed, for my mercy endures forever.

When a person applies for a new job, one of the inquiries that is made pertains to their past work experience. The potential employer desires to know which skills and abilities one has acquired, performed and mastered that would make them qualified for the position. That consistency in their work reflects someone who can be depended upon to fulfill the requirements of the position and be a true asset to the company.

Here is what I want each of you to do. Take a moment to reflect on your life thus far. Think about the circumstances and situations that were so overwhelming. You had no idea how you would make it through. While we were in the midst of our troubles, you just knew it was the worst thing you'd ever encountered. Please know that we are not the reason our circumstances and situations have been overcome. Although the challenges we face on a day-to-day may change, we serve a God who is the same. There isn't one single thing that our God can't fix. How do we know that? Because of His résumé of accomplishments in our lives.

No matter the problem, if we believe, we will see that if God did it before, He'll do it again. Instead of being anxious, nervous or worrying what the outcome will be, we must remember that the Lord doesn't change. I promise that you could search all over and won't ever find anyone with a track record like God's. There isn't enough time to write all that God is able to do, but one thing I know He can't do is fail.

That is why we should rejoice, because we possess countless examples of all the ways that our Heavenly Father has brought us out of our troubles. We should be quick to give God the honor, glory and praise because we have that reassurance that He's not only omniscient, but the same yesterday, today and forever.

He continues in His purpose for our lives and is not turned here and there. I hope each of you finds encouragement and confidence in knowing that the Lord does not change and His mercy endures forever.

Suggested Song of Meditation: "Same God (If He Did It Before)" by Tye Tribbett

Psalm 32:7 (The Message/MSG)

⁷ God's my island hideaway, keeps danger far from the shore, throws garlands of hosannas around my neck.

Each night when it is time for me to begin the process of completing my blogs, I always utilize Biblegateway.com, to see the various translations of the verses that I am led to select.

I love to see how each translation goes about capturing and illustrating God's Word. Tonight wasn't any different. With my family and I just returning from our vacation in Puerto Rico six days ago, I believe that is why The Message/MSG translation of Psalm 32:7 resonated so much with me.

Puerto Rico has always been my children's and my favorite vacation destination. No matter what goes on in our lives, as soon as the plane lands and I see the palm trees and begin to hear the sound of salsa music playing and Spanish being spoken, I know that I have found my escape; even if only temporarily.

In The Message translation of Psalm 32:7, God is compared to an island hideaway; where He keeps danger far from the shore and throws garlands of hosannas around our necks.

When I think about the Caribbean islands, I instantly think of serenity and rest. Those two words also describe what I am able to obtain through Christ.

Because Jesus watches over us, is our hiding place from every storm of life and keeps us from getting into trouble; it is so much easier to go through trials and tribulations when you know you are not by yourself and that the Lord is right there to protect you. Jesus is my refuge and through Him, I am able to obtain that peace, serenity and rest.

Each day, it's His promises that I choose to trust and believe in, knowing that the Lord is there to answer my call. It's not because I have always obeyed Him or been that faithful, but oh, how grateful I am that He chose me to be on the receiving end of His illimitable love.

It is because of that love that I am protected and kept, while in the midst of it all. It's also because of that love that I can rejoice and sing songs of victory and deliverance, while still going through. No matter how out of control the world may appear to be nor the lengths that the enemy will employ to attempt to damage, disrupt and destroy; I know that I serve an all-knowing God who is in control of it all.

Suggested Song of Meditation: "In the Midst of it All" by Yolanda Adams

Isaiah 45:8 (Good News Translation/GNT)

⁸ I will send victory from the sky like rain; the earth will open to receive it and will blossom with freedom and justice. I, the Lord, will make this happen."

Being back in New York, when it rains sometimes, it sounds like a melody unlike any other one that I have ever heard; and it just makes me smile.

For a while now, I have learned to look at rain as something positive because of the various messages I have been blessed to hear throughout my spiritual walk.

When the rain pours down, it is not only refreshing, but it is also able to breathe new life into dry areas. Asking God for that rain positions us to receive His power that is capable of touching every dry area of our lives and blessing us with infinite grace, mercy, glory, righteousness, salvation, peace and eternal life that we need. Not just plants need rain to grow, but we do as well.

When we are able to observe and acknowledge the areas of our lives that are in need of renewal and refreshment, that is when God will bring us into a season of rain.

So when we look up and see the clouds forming, we should immediately rejoice in the cloud-forming process. As my pastor back in Maryland once explained it, clouds are formed in this manner: the sun shines, it heats up the water, a lift in force causes the water to evaporate, which forms the clouds and that brings the rain.

What that means for us is, the Son (Christ Jesus) shines, then heats up the water (which are the tribulations, test and trials that challenge us), evaporation is caused by a lift in force and clouds are formed (that's through our praising God), then comes the rain (His Holy Spirit that has the ability to change and strengthen our lives).

We serve a God that will remove that which hinders our walk with Him and send victory from the sky like rain. Just knowing all of that makes me want to do a rain dance of my own.

Suggested Song of Meditation: "Rain On Us" by Earnest Pugh featuring Charles Butler and Trinity

1 John 4:10 (The Message/MSG)

¹⁰ This is the kind of love we are talking about—not that we once upon a time loved God, but that he loved us and sent his Son as a sacrifice to clear away our sins and the damage they've done to our relationship with God.

We should make it our duty to constantly dedicate time to honor and praise the greatest love that there is and that is the love that God has for us.

We learn how to love by recognizing and being grateful for the one who first loved us. The One who knew all we would do and knows all that we have yet to do and still made the commitment to being the source of the most everlasting love we could ever know.

By keeping and applying God's Word to our lives, we show that we love Him. By loving others, we fulfill a fundamental requirement for Christian living. If we just stop and think about all that God has done and continuously does for us, how could we not be in awe and rendered speechless. We do not have enough tongues, nor could there ever be enough time to express how magnificent our God is.

Our love should be expressed to God and others daily. If we don't know anything else, we must know that God is love.

Through our Heavenly Father I have learned that genuine love always results in action, not just sentimental words. It's also through talking to, hearing and learning from God that I have realized that mature love does not produce or incite fear but instead imparts courage.

God is the epitome of all that we could ever possibly need. For that reason and so many more, it is so important that we don't just have information about God, but that we develop intimate knowledge about God. It is when we have that intimate relationship with God that we live within the realm of His love. Through our daily walk with Christ, we are able to both experience and express that love.

I know that God has loved me more than I have loved myself. In learning and understanding God's love for me, I have gained a greater understanding into loving myself and others. I am also reminded that through that same love of His, I have access to everlasting grace and mercy; so even when I may stumble or fall, it doesn't destroy the relationship that I have with God.

Suggested Song of Meditation: "Speechless" by Anita Wilson

2 Corinthians 5:17 (J.B. Phillips New Testament/PHILLIPS)

17 For if a man is in Christ he becomes a new person altogether—the past is finished and gone, everything has become fresh and new.

Being in New York, I recall so many memories from my childhood, from college and since becoming a mother and a wife. With all those memories come a lot of laughter and a lot of tears, but they have all been a huge part of who I am. Well, let me say they were a huge part of what I am. I thank God that I am not who I used to be.

I am thankful for the tests and trials, the heartaches and disappointments and the storms of life that raged so ferociously.

It wasn't until the reality of my life caused me to reevaluate so many things that I realized what was missing. What I needed, who I truly needed was God. I needed my faith to be restored and renewed and for things to be done and received differently. I know I am not insane, so doing the same thing over and over again and expecting a different outcome was not working for me. But seeking that one-on-one relationship with God, learning from Him and who He had called me to be, helped in the transforming of my thoughts, my actions, my way of life... it was the transformation of me as a whole. I realized that when God is in it, there are no limits.

No matter where we have been or currently find ourselves, God has the power to make all things new. Where it may look like the end of one aspect of our lives, God is really setting us up for a new beginning in those areas, if we just believe and seek Him out in all things.

When we are united with Christ, there is a renewal in our heart that takes place in such a way that it is as if we are new beings or creatures. We have new drives for life, new ambitions, new morals and values and new purposes and principles. We no longer carry those things of old. We don't desire to do things the way we used to or to associate and affiliate in the way we did. We secure ourselves in the unbreakable foundation that is Christ Jesus and never lose sight of the fact that our strength is found in God.

Regardless of what we may come up against or how dormant and stagnant areas of our lives may appear, our God does indeed make all things new.

Suggested Song of Meditation: "It's Not Over" by Israel & New Breed featuring James Fortune and Jason Nelson.

Matthew 10:29-31 (Names of God Bible/NOG)

²⁹ "Aren't two sparrows sold for a penny? Not one of them will fall to the ground without your Father's permission. ³⁰ Every hair on your head has been counted. ³¹ Don't be afraid! You are worth more than many sparrows.

As always, I am in awe of just how amazing God is. I was humming a particular song as I was about to head out of the house.

As soon as we opened the door, I heard all this chirping and when I looked up I saw nothing but sparrows flying in the air and perched up on tree branches. There were so many of them and it made me think about the little value that has been placed on sparrows by man and yet God's eyes are still on them and nothing can happen to them without God's permission.

What a sense of assurance and protection I felt in knowing that we are valued so much more than all the sparrows that are inhabitants on this earth. Being reminded that God knows us inside and out, down to the actual number of hairs on our head is worth shouting over.

God did not give us a spirit of fear. We must stand on His Word and remember that nothing nor no one can come up against us without God's permission or direction. Regardless of what you may be currently facing (whatever trials, obstacles, tests or adversities), know that God wouldn't ever give us more than we could handle. As long as we have faith in Christ we can weather any storm. Even when it's the most uncomfortable of situations and it appears to get worse before it begins to get better, we have to know that all of it is working together for our good. We mustn't ever forget how valuable and precious we are in our Heavenly Father's eyes. What we go through aids in helping us get to where God wants us to be and doing what He has called us to do.

I have learned that some of the trials and adversities I have faced in my life were not just about me, but about those who were watching me as I was going through them. If someone was reading you, what would they learn?

As I looked up in the sky this morning, the sparrows clearly outnumbered my daughter and me. But I know that no matter how many there were, we are valued more. We should never lose sight of the value God has placed on us nor should we allow man to be involved in the equation when determining our value or self-worth. Man is not omniscient, omnipresent or omnipotent; God is. Sparrows are found all throughout the United States. The next time you see one flying, remember if God's eyes are on the sparrow, then you know He's watching over you.

Suggested Song of Meditation: "His Eye is on the Sparrow". Lauryn Hill and Tanya Blount

1 Peter 5:10 (New International Reader's Version/NIRV)

¹⁰ God always gives you all the grace you need. So you will only have to suffer for a little while. Then God himself will build you up again. He will make you strong and steady. And he has chosen you to share in his eternal glory because you belong to Christ.

Oh, what a friend we have in Jesus, all our sins and grief to bear. What a privilege to carry, everything to God in prayer.

What another great hymn we used to sing in my church back in New York. As a child and teenager, the words of that song were just that, words to a song that I loved. But as I got older and was introduced to the world and the various aspects of just living life, the meaning of those words really resonated with me. In times of loneliness and when turbulent seasons were upon me, I would search all over not realizing that all I ever needed and wanted, along with the best friend I could ever ask for had been right there all along.

Even when I was lost, God's grace covered me. Grace is defined as the free and unmerited favor of God. We don't deserve it, we definitely haven't earned it and it has nothing to do with where we live, the car we drive, the clothes we wear, etc. How blessed we are that God gives us the grace needed to supply all our needs. It is my hope and prayer that each of you realizes that you are not outside the realm of God's grace. We have been chosen in Christ and are a select people. And although we are not better than anyone else, because we have been redeemed by Christ, we are distinguished.

How we think and what we tell ourselves, significantly impacts the decisions that we make on a day-to-day basis. As Christians, trials are going to come and that will require us to have to suffer temporarily. I think that last part gets lost. When we are going through a rough time in our lives, we can get so caught up and distracted by the trial itself that we lose sight of what God is trying to show and teach us. At times, we also forget that each trial is temporal and comes with its own expiration date.

When I was younger, I used to hear the phrase "No pain, no gain". When I reflect over my life thus far and my spiritual walk, I realize that the situations that have brought me the greatest pain, turned around to bless me in ways I had no idea were even possible.

I have gained the invaluable knowledge of knowing who God says I am and the thoughts that He has for my life. I have been rebuilt, strengthened and know that I have the Lord's unrelenting support and all obstacles shall pass.

Suggested Song of Meditation: "This Too Shall Pass" by Yolanda Adams

Isaiah 11:2 (The Message/MSG)

² The life-giving Spirit of God will hover over him, the Spirit that brings wisdom and understanding, The Spirit that gives direction and builds strength, the Spirit that instills knowledge and Fear-of-God.

It is so important to take note of where our direction and guidance is coming from. Are the decisions that we make navigated by what the world says or does, or are we being led by the Holy Spirit in all aspects of our lives? When we allow the Holy Spirit to speak to our heart, we are blessed to receive wisdom and understanding, the guarantee of instruction in the right direction, strength that is built, knowledge that is imprinted and the privilege of knowing and honoring the Lord.

When we take the time to stop and listen to what the Spirit has to say to us we are reminded of who God said we are and who He knew us to be long before we ever physically came to be here on earth. The words that we can only receive from the Holy Spirit are able to bring new life to any situation that we may be encountering. We are not only given instruction on what we need to do, but are also shown just how much God loves and cares for us.

Living our lives according to God's plan is serious business; as a matter of fact, it's of the utmost importance. Therefore, we shouldn't give the power or authority of speaking over us and/or our situations to anyone else.

I know firsthand what has happened when I have allowed my decision-making process to be guided by the views and actions of others, instead of listening to the Holy Spirit. I further walked down a path that God never intended for me, but when I eventually came to my senses, He received the glory, because like a GPS device, God recalculated my route and got me back on track.

It is imperative for us to be all we were created to be and to carry out all the plans that God has for us. In order to accomplish that, we have to allow the Holy Spirit to guide us and must have God's Word abiding within us.

Suggested Song of Meditation: "Speak Lord" by Tamela Mann

Luke 5:26 (New Living Translation/NLT)

> *²⁶ Everyone was gripped with great wonder and awe, and they praised God, exclaiming, "We have seen amazing things today!"*

I am one that when things are weighing heavily on my heart and mind, it is almost impossible for me to rest. Now I know that's not healthy and so I find myself in a place where I have no choice but to surrender it all to God because I can't allow myself to be consumed by it all.

Watching the sun rise this morning, primarily, reminded me that because our Heavenly Father's beloved Son did rise, I am able to have life and have it more abundantly. Secondly, the sun rising reminded me of how amazing our God is. If He caused the sun and moon to shine, nothing that I am currently experiencing is outside of His realm to bring resolution to.

I celebrate the Lord, praise His name and recognize that throughout my life God has done the most wonderful, incredible and unimaginable things. In order to see those things accomplished in my life, I had to endure some of the hardest tests and trials. And even when I didn't know how or when it was going to come together, I relied on my faith. Who better to trust than the only One who knows it all and who has had every one of our days written and shaped before they have ever existed.

I rejoice knowing that Jesus is the way, the truth and the life. In my midnight hour, I wept and pleaded for the Lord to reveal to me what I have been hesitant to see with my natural eyes. I promised the Lord that whatever was shown to me, I would accept it no matter how much it may hurt. Before the sun even broke through the clouds, the revelations began.

How amazing that God loves me so much that He would personally communicate with me, even in spite of some of the decisions I have made in my life and ones that I have yet to make. He protects me before I even know there could be cause for alarm.

Suggested Song of Meditation: "Amazing" by Ricky Dillard & New G

Zephaniah 3:17 (Good News Translation/GNT)

17 The Lord your God is with you; his power gives you victory. The Lord will take delight in you, and in his love he will give you new life. He will sing and be joyful over you.

I believe that holidays like Mother's Day and Father's Day are nice but being a parent is a role that should be performed and recognized, 24/7, 365 days a year. With all the different Father's Day messages that were being exchanged yesterday, I began to truly reflect on the importance of a father's role within the family. In that same manner, when that paternal presence is absent, the effects of that are felt as well.

No matter what your childhood consisted of or the familial dynamics that currently represent your household, I was reminded of the greatest love that we could ever receive comes from our Heavenly Father. The Lord our God, won't ever leave us nor forsake us and He is unable to fail us. Regardless of the trials that arise, God is right there with us, in the midst of them, ready and able to rescue us. He loves us so unconditionally and infinitely that He allowed His son, Jesus, to die for us. As a parent, I love my children with every ounce of my being and to know that the love God has for me completely surpasses all that, is so profound to me.

I must admit, that some Father's Day holidays are harder for me than others, because for over 25 years, I have had a very disconnected (basically nonexistent) relationship with my biological father. I think that what makes it the most difficult for me is that for those first 12 years of my life, I was the apple of his eye, a serious Daddy's little girl. Because I knew I was my father's one-and-only princess, you couldn't tell me nothing. But as life would have it, things happened beyond my comprehension and all that changed. I allowed my value and self-worth to be determined by my perception of how my father and others felt about me and so any ounce of rejection or non-acceptance pulled me more and more into a shell.

I have to tell you that it has been through Jesus' love for me that I have learned how to love myself and others. I needed the assistance of the One who knows me better than I know myself; the one who loves me in a way that man is unable to. God has shown me so much grace, mercy and favor. His love has covered me through each mistake and twist and turn my life has taken. His ability to love me so eternally and the level of forgiveness He exercises has taught me the power of forgiveness. I may not understand why things happen the way they do, or why people make the decisions in life that they do, but I have learned to forgive and to release that pain. Instead of pain, I desire to be filled with God's love. Although there may be some disconnections in my life, I know that I am fully connected to the Lord.

I am who I am and where I am today because of Jesus' love for me and there's no greater love in the world. Instead of focusing on who may not be in my life at this present time, I choose to focus on my Heavenly Father, who has been here all along. He has provided me with a love so great that it has given me a new life and a new perspective on everything.

Suggested Song of Meditation: "No Greater Love" by Smokie Norful

Hebrews 6:18 (Contemporary English Version/CEV)

¹⁸ God cannot tell lies! And so his promises and vows are two things that can never be changed. We have run to God for safety. Now his promises should greatly encourage us to take hold of the hope that is right in front of us.

This is the day that the Lord has made; we shall rejoice and be glad in it! I feel that if I seek first the kingdom of heaven, first thing each and every morning followed by the physical workouts that I take part in; I am more than prepared for what lies ahead for the rest of the day. When I spend that much needed time with God, I am allowed to work on myself from the inside out. And then having that workout time allows me to work on my exterior; knowing that my body is the temple of the Holy Spirit. I am reminded that my body was created in God's image; therefore, it is my desire to treat it the best I can.

Working out is also a form of meditation for me. It is during that time that I do reflect and address what is currently weighing on my mind. As I press through each set, rep or minute of training, I remind myself of all God has done and continues to do in my life. I am reminded that when others said, "No", Jesus said, "Yes". It is because Jesus said, "Yes" that I am still here today.

God knows every last plan that He has for our lives, which should constantly strengthen us because God's promises are something that we can always count on completely.

I will tell you that one of my biggest pet-peeves is lying. Lies have a way of causing such hurt, pain, disconnection and destruction. And I know that I had made many life decisions based on the lies told to me by others. Once the realization of that smacked me in the face, I knew I needed God to change a few things about me and my perception of reality. I also knew that I needed to do my part and take the responsibility to, apply daily, those changes that needed to occur for a stronger relationship with God and in turn, better life decisions for myself, rooted in truth, to be my outcome.

How reassuring to know that the One person that we can rely on at all times, regardless of the day, hour or number of mistakes we have made, only wants the best for us. Even through our hiccups and missteps, we are forgiven. Before we ever drew one breath here on earth, God knew us and He knew once we entered this earth all the twists and turns our lives would take, and still, He chose each one of us specifically by name.

How blessed are we because no matter what we are currently facing, or how bleak a situation may look, we have that promise of knowing that when Jesus says "Yes," nobody can say, "No".

God's Word is Complete, His Love is Unconditional and His Power is Inexhaustible

God will open doors for us that no one else can close. And in that same light, God will also close doors that no one else can open. If God closed a door, we should be thankful because it wasn't a place we needed to be or visit anymore.

How encouraged we should be because God is in control of it all. When we allow God to guide us and our decisions, we have no reason to worry. It's when we believe that God needs our assistance and we place our hands on a situation, instead of waiting on Him to bring us the resolution, that we make things harder for ourselves. I grab hold tight of the hope that is in front of me because I know we serve a limitless God, who is almighty and all powerful.

Suggested Song of Meditation: "Say Yes" by Michelle Williams featuring Beyonce' and Kelly Rowland

John 4:13-14 (The Message/MSG)

¹³⁻¹⁴ Jesus said, "Everyone who drinks this water will get thirsty again and again. Anyone who drinks the water I give will never thirst—not ever. The water I give will be an artesian spring within, gushing fountains of endless life."

When I was younger, I learned in school that the basic necessities for human survival were water, air, food, clothing and shelter. Over the years I have read unbelievable stories on how people were able to survive days, sometimes weeks with just water. So, this past week, even though as a family we consume water regularly, as I began to feel dehydrated and increased my intake, I started to really think about just how important water is to our survival.

As I reflected on the importance of the water that our physical body needs to continue living, it immediately made me think about the source of the living water that our spirit needs as well; that source being Jesus. I started to acknowledge just how rundown my body feels from dehydration, but more importantly I recognized how jacked up, not just my body, but my whole life would be without the "living water".

My family has had instances when a water main has broken which has caused us to have to hurry to the grocery store to stock up on water because pipes would be shut off for an unspecified, inconvenient, amount of time.

How much favor and grace we are shown in that through Christ we have access to a water source that never dries up or depletes. It is forever overflowing and capable of filling us over and over again for eternity. All we have to do is seek Him out and commune with Him one-on-one. When we are connected to the God of the overflow, we learn firsthand that His presence is water. Every last thing that we could ever need is in God.

Speaking of the importance of the "living water" took me to Jesus' encounter with the Samaritan woman (John 4). What I loved about this particular passage in the Bible was the symbolism. Here was a Samaritan woman with a bucket at the well, because just like for us, even back then, water was very much a necessity and often scarce. But Jesus still used the opportunity in asking the woman for a drink of water, to explain that even once that water had been retrieved and consumed, man would still thirst again and again, but glory be to our Heavenly Father, that through Him, anyone who consumes the water from Him, will never thirst, ever again.

Like so many of us, the Samaritan woman couldn't see past what was right in front of her face and that was a deep well, and a man who was a Jew, speaking of an everlasting water He could provide her and He didn't even have a bucket. I love that in this story we could see the whole transformation process the Samaritan woman went through. She met Jesus, learned more about Him (who knew everything about her), which resulted in her coming to believe in Him and then she took what she learned about Him and went and shared it with others.

The Lord's presence is water. We need it to survive and so that we can be positioned to learn more about Him, believe Him for all things and then share what we learn with others.

Suggested Song of Meditation: "Water", by Anthony Brown and group therAPy

Proverbs 16:24 (Names of God Bible/NOG)

²⁴ Pleasant words are like honey from a honeycomb—sweet to the spirit and healthy for the body.

As I continue to learn more about the Lord, I, in turn, am provided so much clarity into the person that God desires me to be. Growing up, I always felt like I didn't fit in or belong. It seemed as if the way I viewed things and my way of thinking was completely different from that of everyone else.

As I look back, even as a little girl, I used to put so much value on words. Whether in a conversation, in a book I was reading or within a poem or song I was composing, the particular selection and grouping of words was always of importance to me.

Being a words of affirmation person, not only did I seek to receive that affirmation and encouragement from those I was in contact with, but that was also my primary method of communicating when it came to others.

Speaking encouragement over another person hasn't ever been an issue for me. I actually welcome and thank the Lord for any opportunity that I have to be a source of encouragement for someone else.

But I realized that I couldn't offer someone something that I wasn't providing myself. There were so many times when it was hard to encourage myself, when everything around me was so discouraging.

It was in those instances that I learned that my encouragement didn't come from my temporal situations or circumstances or from what people did or didn't say to me. My encouragement comes from the Lord and the truth that I have come to know, by way of reading and gaining a deeper understanding of His Word; not just in my times of need, but each and every day.

Knowing that the Lord is my refuge and strength, a well-proven help in times of trouble (Psalm 46:1) and that greater is He that is in me than he that is in the world (1 John 4:4), keeps me encouraged and provides me with what I need to speak victory when I am in the midst of a storm.

Romans 8:37 reminds me that, "In everything we have complete victory because of Christ who loves us."

I know that the power of life and death lies in each of our tongues (Proverbs 18:21). Therefore, I have made the choice not to speak the lies, deceit, manipulations and defeat that the enemy operates through and then attempts to attach to me. Instead, I remain encouraged by who God says I am. And who is that you may ask?

I am a child of God by faith in Christ Jesus (Galatians 3:26); I am God's incredible work of art (Ephesians 2:10); I am God's witness to the world (Acts 1:8); I am the light of the world (Matthew 5:14); I am fearfully and wonderfully made (Psalm 139:14); I am the salt of the earth (Matthew 5:13); I am one who doesn't ever have to question if God loves me (Romans 5:8) and I am one who knows that all of my help comes from the Lord (Psalm 121:2).

These are just a few of the truths that I have stored up and which assist me in speaking life and encouragement, not just to others, but to myself as well. They are sweet to my soul and health to my bones.

Suggested Song of Meditation: "Encourage Yourself" by Donald Lawrence and The Tri-City Singers

2 Thessalonians 3:3 (Amplified Bible/AMP)

³ Yet the Lord is faithful, and He will strengthen [you] and set you on a firm foundation and guard you from the evil [one].

What a time of reflection it has been for me. Between the numerous conversations that I have had with my husband and children, along with the word that was delivered by my pastor yesterday, I was left reminded of the various ways my life could have ended up thus far, but God blocked it. There isn't one way to group any set of words together to convey how thankful I am that God didn't allow what the enemy had for me to come to fruition.

I know that all that I have encountered has helped to make me the woman, wife and mother that I am today (and I'm STILL a work in progress). Over the past couple of days, my son and I were having some in-depth conversations. It's not uncommon for him and me to do so because we are so much alike and tend to handle situations in the same manner. But I will be the first one to say that some of my attributes that he has acquired, like wanting to fix everything and please everybody, I am working HARD to have him reel in.

Because I had my son at the age of 20, he has basically occupied the passenger seat throughout every twist and turn of my adult life. He has seen what happens when you try to take the wheel and "help God" (who doesn't need our assistance), instead of surrendering complete control over to God and entrusting each destination that you arrive at to be the best one for you, regardless of how it may appear.

Transparency is a must in our household, no matter how uneasy and uncomfortable it may be at times. I have found that by being completely transparent and open with myself and in turn others, the revelations that are uncovered are mind-blowing. When I look back over my life up until this moment and I think about the choices that I made out of pure brokenness and where I could be, I can't help but cry.

God blocked so many terrible things from happening to my family and me. Even when I thought I knew best in a situation or relationship, God stepping in and redirecting my steps prevented me from further heartache and disappointment, even when I thought that wasn't possible. We are so blessed to serve a God who knows our breaking point and who is so faithful to strengthen us and guard us from what the enemy had intended.

Our strength doesn't come from ourselves, but from God's presence in our lives. There is work for each of us to do and I know that is why I am still here today. He didn't let brokenness, depression, car accidents, etc., get in the way of the calling that He had for my life. As a matter of fact, each of the situations in my life that have brought me the greatest pain, God has turned them around in my favor. Because of God's infinite love, grace and mercy, I have been given beauty for ashes.

As God's representative for my children, it is imperative that they understand that God is indeed in control of every aspect of their lives and that yes, living and journeying through life will have its ups and downs. I desire for them to remain encouraged knowing that anything that God allows them to come up against, He has already made the provisions for them to make it through; and that it ALL will work together for their good.

I also want them to know that even when they don't see God working, He's like the construction work that we see anytime we travel along the highways or interstates. We observe the signs that say "Men at Work". Whether we ever see the men working or not, work is getting done. God is the same way. We may not see the work He is doing in our lives right away, but we need to have that metaphorical "Jesus at Work" sign in front of us to be reminded that the Lord is always working on our behalf.

I thank God for all the ways He has and will continue to block what is not His will for my life. If it's not what He has for me, I don't want it. So if I get it, I know it is because He knew I could handle it.

Suggested Song of Meditation: "God Blocked It", by Kurt Carr

Romans 8:37 (Amplified Bible /AMP)

> *37 Yet amid all these things we are more than conquerors and gain a surpassing victory through Him Who loved us.*

Let me tell you that I just love how if we are willing to just stop, listen and wait on God, He will reveal so much to us. I thank Him for the promises that He has made and that I can always stand on.

There was one particular week that I was writing blog posts, that the central theme for that week was the importance of us not holding onto those former things. After publishing each of those posts, it was stirred up in my spirit that there was another part to that which needed to be addressed.

Yes, it is so important to not let past mistakes define who we are. But it is also important that we realize and address the reasons that we make some of the decisions or react in the manner that we do; to take both accountability and responsibility. Whether we realize it or not, generational curses and sins are a spiritual bondage that are passed down from one generation to the next.

The symptoms of generational curses and sins manifest in many ways. They may be in the form of character flaws, financial difficulties, addictions, emotional problems, sexual problems, different forms of abuse, illnesses, etc. They are certain burdens that we get used to having in our lives and in turn, we tend to respond to the problems they cause the same way each time.

In order for the curses to be broken, we have to be transparent with God and ourselves. We know that as children we take on attributes of our parents. I have also witnessed children who have acquired traits of parents and grandparents whom they have not had much contact with throughout their lives. Genetics is indeed very interesting and sometimes the behaviors and thought patterns that we exhibit come from the environment in which we were raised. In no way am I striving to place blame or paint any one's childhood as a negative one. I just know that the enemy is a liar and will use anything that he can to make us feel like we are less than.

Please know that couldn't be the furthest from the truth. We have been chosen by the Most High and are more than conquerors. Regardless of who we are or where we come from, there is not one generational curse that cannot be broken. When we give our lives to Christ, no matter what struggles have been in each of our families, that spiritual bondage is broken through our faith in the blood of Jesus.

I rejoice and praise God because I know that regardless of the generational curses that have been passed down through the bloodline, Jesus' blood, and only His blood, can cancel out each and every generational iniquity that has been carried. The struggle is no longer yours or mine because in all things we are triumphantly victorious because of the One who first loved us.

Suggested Song of Meditation: "The Curse is Broken" by James Fortune & FIYA

Isaiah 58:12 (The Message/MSG)

> *¹² You'll use the old rubble of past lives to build anew, rebuild the foundations from out of your past. You'll be known as those who can fix anything, restore old ruins, rebuild and renovate, make the community livable again.*

While I was participating in Cycle 8 of Dr. Celeste Owens' 40-Day Surrender Fast, which was entitled, "New Beginnings," I just knew that it was referencing the new chapters that my family and I were preparing for in our lives. Boy, was I wrong. It was revealed that what was meant by "New Beginnings" was that, something that God had already started would be revitalized; that He would breathe life, ignite and put fire underneath an area that I believed was dead and/or unproductive.

Let me tell you that when I heard that, all I could do was weep because it all made sense in a way I didn't even expect on just days one through five. If you know me, you know that I was born a Harlem girl and have always been a Harlem girl at heart.

When I was younger, New York City was everything to me; my lifeline. I had my parents, was a dancing child and loved going to the kiddie discos on the weekends; along with attending my preschool with the playground on the roof during the week. I also loved Riverside and Central Park and my NY slices (with extra cheese). As a matter of fact, there was a song by this singer, Taana Gardner, called "Heartbeat" that I would hear all the time. I remember it because when the album was played, a heartbeat sound was heard before the music and vocals kicked in. That was how I felt about NYC; it was my heartbeat. So when we moved from there, I felt like I lost my heartbeat and I wasn't the same girl.

For so many reasons, once I moved from NYC as a child, my whole mindset towards it changed and it became that ultimate source of pain for me. Many of my hopes and dreams were tied to that place. I have spent most of my life trying to steer clear of it because it all hurt too much. But oh, what a mighty God we serve. Because in the same place where there has been a breach, I know God has been molding and shaping me and working on my mindset, so that I could first restore things the right way within myself. One of the definitions of breach that I came across was, "a breaking of relations, an estrangement, a quarrel, a broken state". That is exactly how I have viewed New York City.

I had lost hope in some of my dreams and because of that moving back to the state of New York, let alone within minutes from everything I ever knew, wasn't even an option (or so I thought). If you think that everything you're doing is because of you, think again. There is not one step that we take that God didn't already know we were going to make. Even if we grab onto things He never had for us in the first place, He will still get the glory and every promise that He has made to us will still come to pass.

Before now, I would not have been emotionally or spiritually ready to move back to New York. But I am a new creation in Christ and my mindset has changed. I am becoming all that I am meant to be. I'm not here to hold onto the former things, for they have passed away. I release past hurt, shame and disappointments. I know that if God said He's going to do it, then that is what He's going to do. Giving up hope is not an option when, as my pastor in Maryland once reminded us, "We serve a God who has the capacity, power and might to make our dreams come true and in due season we shall reap, if we faint not!"

We all have areas within our lives that we have deemed dry and unfruitful. Life happens and we become distracted and lose hope in that which we once dreamed. Foundations can be built out of the rubble of our past. Restoration, renovation and revitalization are possible through our Heavenly Father. When our mindsets are transformed we are then able to embrace the new beginnings that God has for us and truly live our lives according to His purpose.

Suggested Song of Meditation: "New Beginnings" by Linda Clark

2 Corinthians 2:14 (New American Standard Bible/NASB)

[14] But thanks be to God, who always leads us in triumph in Christ, and manifests through us the sweet aroma of the knowledge of Him in every place.

What a week I have experienced. When I say that I was tried on every side, I mean, every side. In two separate instances, when my character was tested and who I am as a person was brought into question, I felt victorious. Something inexplicably powerful happens when you let go of your enslaved mentality—one bound by past hurts, disappointments and situations and you boldly surrender it all to God and adopt a new beginnings mindset—one where you know without a doubt that God can do all things and that nothing can stop or restrain the thoughts and plans that He has for you and your life.

The enemy tested me on so many levels and I was reminded of something that I learned last week that has left me so empowered. I have heard it said many ways, but probably the best, from Pastor Donald Chisholm, Sr. of the Latter Rain Cathedral in Lockport, NY, when he stated, "God is the devil's boss." It was reaffirmed that no matter what I am going through, the enemy cannot bring anymore into my life that God does not allow. With God on our side, we are able to proceed triumphantly and with the mentality that we have already won.

Even while standing in the midst of a battlefield, we are victorious because the battle is not ours, but the Lord's. When we know God and carry the knowledge of Him with us, fear is removed because God operates through faith, unlike the enemy who operates through fear.

I know that I have been brought out of bondage and the chains are forever broken. That is why when the attacks come, they don't affect me the way they used to because I know that I have already won!

Where I once felt like the metaphorical piñata, bound by the string and the common target for people to take hits at, it was instantly made apparent to me that I indeed was no longer bound by that string and that those hits weren't even close to landing like they used to because I am FREE!!! The feeling of being healed and the confidence I possess because the chains, strings and strongholds have been broken, is such an indescribably profound moment; one that I desire for each of you to experience.

God has written our destinies and they are before us. I know that He has given us the authority to conquer the enemy because there is no victory over God.

Suggested Song of Meditation: "We are Victorious" by Donnie McClurkin featuring Tye Tribbett

Revelation 1:8 (Amplified Bible/AMP)

⁸ *"I am the Alpha and the Omega [the Beginning and the End]," says the Lord God, "Who is [existing forever] and Who was [continually existing in the past] and Who is to come, the Almighty [the Omnipotent, the Ruler of all]."*

So often we find ourselves needing the Lord to show up in the midst of our circumstances and providing deliverance in ways that we hadn't previously.

Although new tests and trials could serve as opportunities to become utterly perplexed and discouraged, that is the time that we should rejoice boldly, knowing that if our God is for us, who can be against us? Every obstacle that we encounter is an opportunity to get closer to the Lord and develop an even deeper connection and relationship with Him.

Instead of focusing on the details of the temporal situations that we may face, our attention should be turned to the One who is the A and the Z. He is the God who is, the God who was and the God who is about to arrive the Lord is Almighty (Sovereign-Strong).

I understand that when you're going through, nothing about what you're enduring seems insignificant or on a small scale. But regardless of the diagnosis the doctor may have given you, the disconnect that has occurred within marital, familial or other personal relationships, what is reflected in your bank account compared to the financial obligations that you have or any final notice document that may come in the mail; nothing is too hard for the Lord to fix.

He is almighty which means there is no limit to His power. Nothing is beyond the Lord's reach. He created the universe, parted the Red Sea, turned water into wine, fed five thousand with just five small barley loaves and two fish and even the winds and waves obey Him (and we know there is so much more the Lord has done).

Don't you see that He is the One who does impossible things? We know this because each of these events and countless others can be found in the Bible and because of all that He has done in each of our lives.

Through our faith, we are able to stand on His Word. When we take the time to digest and meditate on the Word of God and the truth it provides, our focal point and mindset shifts from our situations to the One who is the first and the last; the beginning and the end of all things.

The Lord observes a need and always provides for us. His name is a strong and mighty tower where we can always run and be raised high above danger. He is our destiny and where we begin. Because He holds all power in His hands, He has the final say in every situation!

Suggested Song of Meditation: "I Am" by Jason Nelson

Isaiah 12:2 (New English Translation/NET Bible)

² Look, God is my deliverer! I will trust in him and not fear. For the Lord gives me strength and protects me; he has become my deliverer."

For so long, I believed that I could do it all on my own, or that if I did allow God in the midst of my situations, that in some way, He would need my assistance. When I look back on that way of thinking, I cringe. What in the world was wrong with me? I'll tell you what was wrong; I was afraid. Afraid of what would happen if I surrendered it all to God. I didn't understand that by always wanting to put my hands back on something that I had made the commitment to release to God, I was not walking in complete faith or trust in the Lord. Acknowledging that was like a sucker punch to the gut, because I know that without God I am nothing and can do nothing.

In learning the importance of surrendering and what needs to be done for it to be accomplished correctly, so much has been revealed to me. I have to recognize all that is available to me if I just trust in the name of the Lord and do not fear. No questions, no negotiations, just pure and radical faith in the Lord and the principles and promises that are located in His Word. I am reminded that God requires so little from us and yet blesses us so exceedingly and abundantly.

We have been told that if we have faith the size of a mustard seed, we can move mountains. I am a visual person, so when I visualize how minuscule the size of a mustard seed is, and in turn think of all the mountains that have been moved in my life, when I have exercised my faith, a song of praise immediately comes to mind. I have seen God do what I thought was impossible in my life; along with provide me with clarity in areas that I didn't even know I was blinded in. When I try to filter situations, circumstances and people through my own understanding, that is when I get hemmed up. I used to be one who internalized everything; no longer is that the case. When things do not make sense to me, I defer to the Lord and wait on Him for understanding. I trust in God and worship Him alone. There is no one like Him in all the earth and I know that my strength and protection comes from Him. No matter what comes our way, we must trust in our Heavenly Father who is omnipotent, omniscient and omnipresent.

He knows all we will face before we ever have the slightest inclination that a storm front is moving in. I have read countless examples of His infinite power and I know that same power is working in the midst of my life and through every situation that I have and will encounter.

Before we place our trust in anyone or anything else, trust in the name of the Lord. He is our deliverer and will always be by our side. He will never leave us nor abandon us.

Suggested Song of Meditation "I Will Trust" by Fred Hammond

Deuteronomy 31:8 (International Standard Version/ISV)

⁸ Indeed, the Lord is the one who will keep on walking in front of you. He'll be with you and won't leave you or abandon you, so never be afraid and never be dismayed."

Recently I had a serious "ah-ha" moment as I came to the realization that sometimes people not being in your life was not meant to punish you, but to do the complete opposite, actually.

You would not believe, throughout the course of my life, all that I have accepted or the concessions that I have made, to have certain people in my life, or to reestablish a connection within a relationship that was no longer what I desired or thought it should be.

Over the years, I have truly learned to appreciate the fact that the Lord goes before me and is with me with on every last step that I take. He is omnipresent (everywhere at the same time) and omniscient (all-knowing). This means that in every season of my life He has known who I needed to be aligned with and at the same time, which individuals either (a) didn't mean me any good or (b) were incapable of being who I needed them to be as I proceeded along the way.

There have been relationships with people that I thought would last for a lifetime, that I discovered were only meant to be for a reason or for a season. When that season ended and I had to move on from them, I thought I had done something wrong. Taking some much needed one-on-one time with God, I realized I wasn't being punished; in fact, it was that God loved me just that much, that moving on was for my betterment. In that same breath, God has surprised me with connections with amazing individuals who have been able to mentor and pour into me, right where I am and in a way that only God could have led them to; and those connections are still thriving to this day.

No matter what the relationship is, whether with a parent, child, sibling, extended family member, someone you have a child or children with or a friendship that has become strained, if you know that you have done all God has instructed you to do, release it and release yourself. We don't know everything about everyone, nor do we know all that someone else is carrying which influences the decisions that they make. When I look back on all that I thought I wanted and all those who I "just knew" I needed in my life, I shiver. I thank the Lord that He has not given me every last thing that I have asked for, because if He had, the level of chaos, toxicity and confusion that would have been welcomed into my life would have been suffocating.

I am grateful that God directs, guides, strengthens, defends, protects and goes before me. I am not afraid nor dismayed because He doesn't ever fail to give us direction and assistance and

He promises to never leave us nor forsake us. Sometimes we place all those expectations on others. Our expectations should never be placed on man, who disappoints, but on God, who can never fail.

I have learned that there is such a thing as a good bye.

Suggested Song of Meditation: "He Will Never Leave You" by Emmett Moffett

Colossians 3:23 (Amplified Bible/AMP)

²³ Whatever may be your task, work at it heartily (from the soul), as [something done] for the Lord and not for men.

Back on December 31, 2014, I typed up what I thought was my Encouragement for Your Journey (EFYJ) end of year message. After I scheduled the post to publish and went on to complete some other tasks, I soon began to feel convicted, because I knew I had been putting off something that, for a while, God had been preparing me for. I had been telling my husband and children that I knew I needed to utilize my EFYJ blog more than just once a week.

For a while, I knew God was calling me to provide, daily not just weekly, motivation and inspiration. Now, I know God did not give us a spirit of fear but of power and love and self-control (2 Timothy 1:7), but my initial response was that I was terrified. There are 365, sometimes 366, days in a year and I knew that once I made the commitment there was no turning back.

The enemy used fear to make me question whether I was even capable of taking on this task. Most people who publish daily blogs or devotionals have parents who are well known pastors, bishops and reverends throughout the world and have taken up the mantle and brought those teachings into the next generation. That, my friend, was not the case for me.

Before I allowed myself to get more distracted and taken off course even longer than I should have been by the enemy, I was reminded that I am not a servant of man, but of the Lord's and that where man may count me out and deem me unqualified, God's grace clothes me in unmerited favor which allows me to accomplish things that can only be done when His super meets my natural. Here is where my source of motivation lies.

It really means the world to me to be able to be a source of encouragement and to provide the truth and good news of the Lord to others. Making the decision to be obedient to the Lord and creating the daily blog provided me with the platform to operate in the grace and the gifts that God has given to me. I know that in everything that I do, whether pertaining to this blog or any other task, I am to complete it from my heart, with good will and a jovial devotion.

Whether what you are accomplishing is within the workforce for a superior, within your own business, in school or within the home as a homemaker, we should always delight in the services we provide, knowing that it's a compliment to God when He sees us returning the gifts He has given to us back to Him. Yes, you may have a boss over you, but what we do is not for man, it should be done as something for the Lord and from our souls.

When we walk and operate in the grace God has given us, we will see doors begin to open for us, positions that we will be elevated to and the connections and relationships that will be cultivated. I learned recently that grace is an acronym for **God's Riches At Christ's Expense**. I won't ever forget that and it just added more fuel to my motivational and inspirational fire!!!

Suggested Song of Meditation: "The Gift" by Donald Lawrence

Proverbs 16:9 (GOD'S WORD Translation/GW)

⁹ A person may plan his own journey, but the Lord directs his steps.

Although I am a Northeast girl, let me tell you, I am one who does not like to get cold; so, the winter season is indeed my least favorite. Although I think that snow is very pretty, I don't need to see it outside my window. My children, of course, feel the complete opposite; especially when getting their first real glimpse of snow (of about one to two inches) meant schools being closed. I definitely took advantage of being able to go back and get some much needed sleep after my early morning devotional call.

As I laid back down, I began speaking to God about all that was on my mind regarding the preparations that my family and I have ahead of us as we get ready for my son to graduate from high school and to relocate back to New York in five months. It was during this time and as I was looking through a couple of my devotional journals that I was reminded of the importance of seeking God's instruction before making any plans.

I know I am quick to come up with what I would call a "master plan" and in the past I would have these "well thought-out" (or so I believed) plans and then would call myself trying to negotiate with God when it didn't appear that He was leading me in the direction that I thought I should go. What was I thinking?

It was at these moments that I truly learned that I could come up with all the plans that my heart desires, but it is God who decides what I shall do and who establishes each step that I take. I was doing things backwards. I would construct my plan and then consult God. Uh negative, I needed to consult God first and then move according to His instruction.

We can have many plans in our hearts but it is the Lord's purpose that will prevail (Proverbs 19:21) A wise person commits his/her plans to the Lord. By making His will for our lives the foundation for our decisions, through the Holy Spirit and His grace, He will order our steps. The only way to know what His will is for our lives is by having a relationship, a deep and connected one, with the Lord.

It is so important that we meditate on His Word, allow the Holy Spirit to teach us how and what to pray for and take the time to wait and hear from Him. When I look back and think about the steps I believed I should have taken and the plans I felt should have come to fruition compared to the direction God has led me in, I am so grateful that God's thoughts are not my thoughts nor are His ways my ways (Isaiah 55:8).

Each step that we take should be established and directed by El Elyon, God Most High. When we trust God with our decisions, it frees us from being preoccupied with our problems.

Suggested Song of Meditation: "*Your Steps Are Ordered*" *by Fred Hammond and Radical for Christ*

Psalm 18:35 (Amplified Bible/AMP)

35 You have also given me the shield of Your salvation, And Your right hand upholds and sustains me; Your gentleness [Your gracious response when I pray] makes me great.

There are mornings when before I am able to do anything else, I need to be ministered to by nothing but songs of praise and worship, back to back. Music is such a staple in my life.

In the songs I was listening to, I was reminded of who God says I am and the provisions He has, does and will continue to make for me. God wrote it in His plan for us that we would be victorious, regardless of what is placed before us. Because of the evidence of all that the Lord has been to and for me up until this very moment, I am confident that in all these things, I am more than a conqueror through Him that loves me (Romans 8:37).

I know that the battle is not mine but the Lord's and that each trial, storm and obstacle is just a test of my faith. They're an opportunity to show God that even when I don't see an end in sight or resolution to what I am experiencing, I will give thanks and praise His name right through it all. I have no doubt that when it's all said and done, I will have won; better yet, that I have already won.

In our destiny, it is written that we shall win. God has given us the authority to conquer the enemy. No matter what we encounter, with God as the source of our strength, we will be victorious through our Lord Jesus Christ. We were born to be the head and not the tail, to be above and not beneath, to be the lender and not the borrower, to be the victor and not the victim.

Because I know who the Lord is, I know who I am. I know my identity. How about you? What's your name? In case you didn't know, my name is Victory!

Suggested Song of Meditation: "My Name is Victory" by Jonathan Nelson

Lamentations 3:22 (New American Bible (Revised Edition/NABRE)

²² The Lord's acts of mercy are not exhausted; His compassion is not spent.

To say that we serve a faithful and on-time God is an understatement. The way that the Lord orchestrates and weaves everything together, both right in front of our eyes and a lot of times behind the scenes, without our knowledge, leaves me astonished.

When I decided to stop shying away from the calling that God has placed on me and began the daily blog on December 30, 2014, I didn't even have a clue as to the battles that awaited me. But let me tell you, that making the commitment to share what the Lord had placed within me, to hopefully reach the hearts and souls of others, has truly blessed me more than any of you could ever possibly know.

It's one thing to take what God is sharing with me, write it down in a journal and keep it for myself as a resource. It's another thing to share with each of you, not only where I am in my journey, but also the truth about God's goodness and faithfulness. Each day I grow stronger in my faith and my walk with Christ.

I am constantly reminded of just how much God cares for us. His love for us is so deep, we are not consumed by the day-to-day woes that we encounter. His mercy and loving-kindness are not exhausted, but are renewed each morning and His compassion is not spent. His faithfulness and stability in our lives is great and abundant. Even if we fall, we are able to brush ourselves off and get back up again.

For me, when the hits and attacks come, they just don't seem to puncture as deeply as they used to. I not only know where my protection lies, but also where my strength comes from; and that is in the Lord. I will continue to trust in the Lord at ALL times, knowing that God won't let me fail. Even when I can't see or don't know the who, what, when, where, why or how's of a situation, I will depend on Him, believe in Him, have faith in Him and wait on Him.

Never stop believing or dreaming. If you keep your faith in the Lord, you will prevail because God won't let you fail.

Suggested Song of Meditation: "God Won't Let Me Fail" by Tamika Patton

Psalm 138:7 (New Century Version/NCV)

⁷ Lord, even when I have trouble all around me, you will keep me alive. When my enemies are angry, you will reach down and save me by your power.

The story of the prodigal son, that is found in Luke 15:11-24, is one that I have truly come to appreciate over the years. It is a constant reminder for me that recovery is part of restoration.

In the "prodigal son" parable, after taking his inheritance, moving to a faraway country and making some bad decisions, when the younger son came to his senses and returned home, his father clothed him in the robe of honor, did not hold his past decisions against his son and offered him only the best.

Our Heavenly Father does that and so much more for us. When we are in trouble and don't make the best decisions for ourselves, God preserves our lives, stretches out His hand against the wrath of others and reaches down and saves us with His power.

Because of the blood of Jesus, like the prodigal son, we are covered. God covers us and all that we have done. He forgives us of our sins and doesn't require us to be clothed in a cloak of shame, with our transgressions numbered and detailed for the whole world to see. What God has for us is so much greater, that if we just confess our sins, the Lord is faithful and just to forgive us and cleanse us from all unrighteousness (1 John 1:9).

We have been redeemed, bought with a price. Our whole life has been changed because of Christ. Through our recovery we become more and more obedient. This aligns and positions us to be on the receiving end of restoration in ways and on levels that are only possible through God. I'm resting on the promise of who our Lord and Savior Jesus Christ is, knowing that I am covered and therefore, not worrying.

Suggested Song of Meditation: "Resting on His Promise" by Youthful Praise featuring JJ Hairston

Isaiah 41:10 (Easy-to-Read Version/ERV)

¹⁰ Don't worry—I am with you. Don't be afraid—I am your God. I will make you strong and help you. I will support you with my right hand that brings victory.

I read a quote by Dr. Martin Luther King, Jr. that stated, "Life's most persistent and urgent question is—What are you doing for others?" That is a question I have begun to ask myself.

I know that in order to be the best servant to the Lord, I must be in tune and aligned with the Lord's will for my life and His Word. Just a touch from God brings that much needed clarity and direction to light my path. No one else can do the things that the Lord is capable of doing.

Each day a new page is revealed in this story of my life. Even though I cannot see how the day will unfold, my faith gives me the reassurance that there is no need to fear or worry because God is with me. He has promised that He will hold and support me with His right hand that holds victory.

All we need is that touch from the Lord. His unchanging hand will turn our losses into wins and will change those wrong things that are in our lives and make them right. When we call on Him, the Lord is faithful and present. We serve a God that sits so high and looks so low. When He reaches down and touches us where we are--healing, transformation, restoration and unspeakable joy and peace are possible.

All we could ever need can be found in Christ Jesus. No matter the mistakes we have made or the season of our lives we are currently in, God will make us stronger and assist us.

Suggested Song of Meditation: "All I Need" by Brian Courtney Wilson

Isaiah 64:8 (The Voice/VOICE)

⁸ Still, Eternal One, You are our Father. We are just clay, and You are the potter. We are the product of Your creative action, shaped and formed into something of worth.

As I have stated previously, when I first started my Encouragement for Your Journey ministry, it began as a weekly Monday motivational that was sent out to family and friends. In one of those morning emails, I spoke about being in the potter's hands and I began to think more and more about that.

Now more than ever I am reminded that no matter what comes my way, because of the molding and shaping, I can indeed make it because my life is in the Lord's hands.

One of the things that I love most about the Lord is that He is an omniscient God, knowing all. I don't have to explain who I am, why I think or do the things I do because He knows me inside and out. Because God knows all about me, including my past, my present and what has yet to come, I can rejoice in knowing that any areas that need to be changed and refined in me, who better to mold and reshape me than the One who knows the path and purpose that He had sanctioned for my life long before I was ever placed in my mother's womb?

Why would we entrust that to anyone else?

I love going to stores like Pier 1 and Kirkland's because they have some really beautiful pottery. Anytime I see a piece of pottery, I think about the intricate and delicate process that occurs from conception to completion, making the item ready for display. When a potter is molding the clay, he/she must be careful when shaping it so that the clay obtains the desired form that the potter had in mind. Once that step is completed, then the clay must go into the fire and it takes a trained eye and gifted potter to know the right amount of time that each piece must endure in that heat. Timing is everything, firing clay too high can cause it to deform, melt or even shatter; too low and it will not be durable.

If the process is so precise for a piece of clay, why would we not expect that and so much more for ourselves?

There is no greater potter than our Heavenly Father and I rejoice knowing that He desires to reshape our lives and change us from whom we were into who He wants us to be.

When you feel yourself going "through the fire", remember two things (a) when you're going through, the Lord knows just how much we can bear and will not allow us to feel the heat any longer than we need to and (b) it's when we're in the fire that, like clay, we are rid of the imperfections and impurities that are blocking, hindering and distracting us from the path and course that God has for our lives.

The end result is a new person, a changed person, with a shine and brilliance for the entire world to see.

Suggested Song of Meditation: "My Life is in Your Hands" by Kirk Franklin

Psalm 55:22 (Easy-to-Read Version/ERV)

²² Give your worries to the Lord, and he will care for you. He will never let those who are good be defeated.

For so long, when obstacles came my way, I automatically believed that the hardships I was encountering were being placed in my path because I was being punished for a sin I had committed; which had caused God to abandon and forget about me. I struggled to carry the weight of everything on my own and thought that it was up to me to find a resolution to the situation.

That did nothing but make matters worse. Eventually I realized that I had a choice to make. I could either give all my burdens to the Lord or try to carry them myself.

Although I was attending church at that time, I was in such a broken place. I was so ashamed and disappointed in the situations I had found myself in and the decisions, I in turn ended up making. The enemy used that time to keep me bound by the shackles of regret and shame, which prevented me from seeking God's presence.

During that time, what I was doing was not working for me and I knew that if the Lord didn't turn things around for me, then it wouldn't happen. Instead of allowing the enemy access to attack my mind any further, I reached for the Word of God, where I found the truth that lifted the blinders from my eyes and helped to illuminate my path and I sought to be in His presence more and more.

As I continued to read and study His Word, I not only learned the definition of what real love is, but also just how mighty, awesome and amazing our God is.

Although so much of what has occurred in my life has caught me off guard, I actually found such a peace in knowing that nothing catches the Lord off guard. He knows everything and has written each of our days long before they ever came to be.

In recognizing the importance of putting all that concerns me on the altar, trusting the Lord, standing on His Word, stepping aside and letting go so that God could be God (with no assistance from me), the entire way that I viewed my God, myself, my life and my circumstances shifted.

I recognize that the obstacles that I encounter, the Lord has allowed; not as a form of punishment but for my betterment and to take me higher in Him. Unlike what the enemy would like to have me believe, I know that the Lord is with me always and would never leave me nor forsake me.

How fortunate I am to serve a God so faithful that I am able to cast on Him whatever He sends my way. He promises to carry my load, to help me out and to never allow the righteous to be shaken or toppled in ruin.

By removing myself and my ways from the equation, my relationship with the Lord has grown stronger and I have come to count it all joy when I meet trials of various kinds.

It is His plan for my life that I choose to follow and trust in. Putting my all on the altar and stepping aside is my way of letting the Lord know that I am fully aware that He is in control of it all.

Suggested Song of Meditation: "Step Aside" by Yolanda Adams

Romans 8:28 (Contemporary English Version/CEV)

²⁸ We know that God is always at work for the good of everyone who loves him. They are the ones God has chosen for his purpose.

Not knowing what lies ahead for me each day, I have certain verses that I retain in my "reserve tank" as my sources of encouragement no matter what I may face. Romans 8:28 is definitely at the top of that list. As I was driving home from running errands this morning, a song that speaks directly to this verse came on and as they say, "That's all she wrote."

What a reassurance there is in knowing that every situation, every circumstance and every encounter, God is working together and fitting in the plan that He has designed and purposed for our lives. The Lord desires the best for us. That is why we have to make sure that the decisions we make, the actions we perform, the words we speak and the person we present ourselves to be are in alignment with God's will for our lives.

May the love and radical faith that we have in the Lord be reflected in all that we do. Weeping may endure for a night, but we can have peace because we know that joy will come in the morning.

Remain encouraged knowing that anything that God authorizes us to endure, He has already made the provisions for us to make it through; and that it all will work together for our good. Regardless of what may be occurring in your life at this present time and no matter how burdensome, what the enemy intends for evil God will turn it around for your benefit (Genesis 50:20).

Never let go. Keep standing on His promises knowing that God is always working on our behalf. So much of what He orchestrates is done without our knowledge. But we can be confident in knowing that we don't have to see the work being done to know that it is being accomplished.

Suggested Song of Meditation: "God's Up to Something Good" by Hart Ramsey & The NCC Family Choir

1 Chronicles 29:11 (New Life Version/NLV)

¹¹ O Lord, You have great power, shining-greatness and strength. Yes, everything in heaven and on earth belongs to You. You are the King, O Lord. And You are honored as head over all.

How grateful I am that we serve a God who is so full of love, mercy and grace. Because of the love that God has for us, each and every morning we are given access to His grace, which grants us more than we could ever deserve and His mercy, which doesn't give us exactly what we do deserve.

At every turn and in each instance of our lives, the Lord has been full of compassion. He has been our resource and the only source of our strength. He is our Redeemer and Creator. It all begins and ends with Him. He created us for His glory and we should eagerly show how thankful we are because He is the Lord God Almighty. He was, is and forever will be all that we ever need.

Everything both here on earth and in heaven belongs to the Lord. No other greatness or power can be found anywhere else. We could search all over, high or low and never find anyone or anything greater than our Heavenly Father. Evidence of His promises being fulfilled can be seen all around us.

Because God is in control of my life and is exalted as head over all, I am able to move forward in the destiny that He has outlined for my life. There are so many reasons that I bow down, surrender it all and worship the Lord. Even though He knew I would make choices that would not be pleasing to Him and hinder my relationship with Him, He still called me out specifically by name. He knows my breaking point and as my refuge and shelter, He covers me with a love so limitless that even when it may appear as if I am losing, I have already won.

Jesus saved me and through His power, I am no longer a slave to sin but am now a slave to righteousness. I would have never made it, if God hadn't been by my side. The Lord God Almighty is the key that unlocked every shackle in my life. For these reasons and countless others, I will forever worship our Almighty God.

Suggested Song of Meditation: "Almighty God" by Brian Courtney Wilson

Psalm 146:5 (GOD'S WORD Translation/GW)

⁵ Blessed are those who receive help from the God of Jacob. Their hope rests on the Lord their God.

Because of the Lord that exists inside of me, I am blessed. I believe in God and God alone. Through the steps that I have already taken in my journey, I have learned the importance of not putting my confidence or trust in man, but in the Lord at ALL times.

Whether we are coming or going, when we keep our eyes focused on the realities of heaven and center our hope on our Eternal Father; it is then that we truly get to know what real blessings are.

We should walk honorably, keeping the Lord's commands close to our heart. Entrusting every concern, worry, anxiety and stronghold to the Lord gives us victory and leaves the enemy defeated. What a joy and assurance we are left with, when we can do these things.

The blessing that we have as children of God means that no matter what our situations look like at this very moment, the power of the God we serve is so mighty that He can turn it all the way around and have our circumstances working in our favor in a matter of seconds.

Any assistance we could ever need can be obtained through Him.

Suggested Song of Meditation: "We're Blessed/Shout Unto God" by Fred Hammond

Jeremiah 31:3 (English Standard Version Anglicised/ESVUK)

³ the Lord appeared to him from far away. I have loved you with an everlasting love; therefore, I have continued my faithfulness to you.

There is absolutely nothing greater than the Lord and the unfailing love that He has for each one of us. It is through the example that has been set by Jesus that we have the opportunity to be on the receiving end of that love and have the ability to reciprocate that love to others and ourselves.

It's a love that doesn't keep tally of our wrong doings and clothes us with His grace and mercy, so that we can have a clean and fresh start. It's a love that gives us the confidence to boldly proclaim that we know that God won't ever leave us, to walk our individual journeys alone.

It's a love that will take what we viewed through our natural eyes as flaws and limitations and through Him, strengths and opportunities will be birthed. It's also a love that will rejuvenate, transform and empower us to a point where everyone will be left wondering, who or what is behind the glow that they see in and around us.

God shows us an everlasting love and a faithfulness that man is unable to display or demonstrate. It's also a love that, when what should have left you broken, has now been the driving force in re-building and re-positioning you. It's a love more than worth fighting for.

On days when we need that added push of reassurance, we have His Word. We don't have to wonder if we can trust Him or if He'll ever abandon us. The Lord loves us so much that He has provided us with countless examples of a love that can always be depended on. Because of God's boundless love and trustworthiness that we are in constant receipt of, we shouldn't ever be ashamed to openly express the love and thankfulness that we have for the Lord in return.

Suggested Song of Meditation: "Love Like Crazy" by Kierra Sheard

Psalm 27:1 (Holman Christian Standard Bible/HCSB)

¹ The Lord is my light and my salvation—whom should I fear? The Lord is the stronghold of my life—of whom should I be afraid?

Since God's grace and mercies are renewed each and every day in our lives, we always have a reason to be grateful. Share that blessing with someone else. You may never see the end result, but think about it, any seed that is planted needs time to grow.

While reflecting on God's love for me, I was so fortunate to take part in an activity, I have no doubts, that what I was able to accomplish was solely because I was being directed by the love of the Lord and not the orchestration of man.

At one of the Homemakers' Ministry meetings that I was in attendance for at my church, we had to create a vision board about the things we intended to accomplish and make reality in the near future.

As I grabbed each magazine, words and images just captured my attention and spoke to the fearlessness and trust that I have in the Lord.

I'm here to tell each of you that because of God's love for me, I could look at an advertisement for scar cream and make that the top center of my vision board. The ad said, "Say Goodnight to Scars." What that ad said to me was those scars of the past, the strongholds, the guilt, the shame, the hurt and the pain, it was time to say "Good night," and better yet "Good bye" to them, because each morning God covers us with all we could ever need to be victorious. I was not going to go one more night into another day carrying those scars with me.

A few more of the slogans that spoke to my life and the vision that God has for it were, "Love", "Family Matters", "Fearless", "Development, it Happens Here," "Bring Your Passion to the Future", "Waste Not, Want Not", "My Moment", "Amazingly Perfectly (because God does everything amazingly and perfectly)", "Empowerment" and "Rejuvenate".

There were many other words and images on my board but I believe that each of you gets the picture without the board being physically present in front of you.

Because of God's love, faithfulness and goodness in my life, fear, rejection and wanting to please everyone doesn't get to rule my thought process and thought life any longer. Right here and now, I am rejoicing because I have arrived to a place where I am fearless and desiring to be authentically me as the Lord created and molded me to be.

Suggested Song of Meditation: "Here Right Now" by Tasha Page-Lockhart

Jeremiah 33:3 (Amplified Bible/AMP)

> *³ Call to Me and I will answer you and show you great and mighty things, fenced in and hidden, which you do not know (do not distinguish and recognize, have knowledge of and understand).*

Over the years I have learned the importance of being productive rather than just busy. Time is so precious and is something we can't get back. I am more mindful of how my time is spent.

I know firsthand how imperative it is that I do not place God in a box by putting limitations on what He is able to do in my life. God continues to reveal to me that, not only will He answer my prayers when I call on Him, but He'll do it in a way that I didn't even know I could ask Him to. Faith kick starts and activates the blessings that are for each one of us.

One of the things that I love about the Lord is that, even when I'm extremely optimistic and expecting greatness, He'll step in, grab hold of my situation and do exceedingly, abundantly, above all I could ever ask or think (Ephesians 3:20).

I have come to realize that what I thought was on the bigger or greater scale hadn't even scratched the surface on all God intended to show me. And the knowledge of that causes me to constantly be excited about all that the Lord has for me.

There are no limits to what the Lord is capable of doing. Therefore, in every area of my life, I am expecting the kind of greatness that can only come from the Lord.

Suggested Song of Meditation: 'Expect the Great" by Jonathan Nelson

Proverbs 3:13 (Amplified Bible/AMP)

¹³ Happy (blessed, fortunate, enviable) is the man who finds skillful and godly Wisdom, and the man who gets understanding [drawing it forth from God's Word and life's experiences],

I have always heard it said that we should strive for joy in our lives because happiness is determined by our external circumstances, whereas joy comes from seeing and knowing the Lord. But in the above verse, the word happy is a synonym for the word blessed.

While journeying the path that God has established for me, I feel so fortunate for the opportunities to obtain godly wisdom. Wisdom is the only path to a full and fruitful life. Oh, how I desire to live life to the furthest extent, until it overflows, constantly gaining wisdom as I travel along the way. It is through wisdom that God formed the earth, numbered the clouds and made the world. Only He can provide us with the wisdom to live righteously and to be able to endure trials optimistically.

At the conclusion of one of the calls associated with the Dr. Celeste Owens' 40-Day Surrender Fast, we listened to a spoken word selection. In those few moments, my sense of identity and purpose in the Lord were electrified. The artist delivered words and phrases of encouragement that resonated so deep within my soul. She proclaimed that this was the season that our dreams would come forth and that our new day had begun. When she declared that what I have been waiting for is here and it is me, I was left with an understanding and clarity that could only come from God's Word and my very own life experiences.

For that reason, when anyone hears or observes me utilizing the word happy, it is in reference to feeling fortunate. We are so blessed to be associated with the Lord because with Him is where we belong. There isn't any possible way that we could ever make it without Him. The Lord makes us whole and takes our pain away. The love that I feel and the eagerness that I have to worship comes from recognizing that Jesus' life saved our lives. My happiness comes from knowing not only who the source is of my wisdom, but who also positions me to gain understanding into His desire for my existence.

Suggested Song of Meditation: "God I Look to You" by Jenn Johnson

Psalm 41:11 (Modern English Version/MEV)

¹¹ By this I know that You favor me, because my enemy does not triumph over me.

There has been a recurring theme lately in my life and that theme has been, "God Favored Me." Throughout my life, so many painful and heartbreaking situations and circumstances have occurred that I know that if it wasn't for the favor of the Lord that has been on my life, the enemy would have been celebrating in triumph over me.

Have you ever been in a situation and was so encapsulated and consumed by it that it wasn't until you were brought out of it by the Lord and took the time to reflect on it, that you observed the countless opportunities there were for it to go all the way to the left and in the most unfortunate way?

I have and upon this realization, all I could do was cry tears of thankfulness and joy for the grace and mercy that kept me in those times when I didn't even know that I needed the Lord's protection.

Depending on the situations that we face, there are some trials, setbacks and attacks that we may anticipate coming our way.

But what about the ones we have no idea are occurring in the background and being waged against us?

I give the Lord all the glory, honor and praise when I think about my life up to this very second that I am typing. I have stated more than once and it still holds true, that affairs of the heart are my Achilles Heel.

During the most murky and dismal periods of my life, when my love was misused, manipulated and abused, God still favored me. For so long, I was bound by the shackle of being stricken with what has been coined the "Polyanna Syndrome". It led to moments where I was overwhelmed with so much pain and found my character and integrity being attacked and lies being told. But through it all, I rejoice knowing that because God has shown me favor in every instance and around every twist and turn; in spite of everything, my enemies have yet to declare victory over me.

These days, Proverbs 4:23, which instructs us to, "Above all else, watch over your heart; diligently guard it because from a sincere and pure heart come the good and noble things of life," has taken on a whole new meaning for me. Seeking the Lord at all times and guarding my heart are necessities for me spiritually, physically and emotionally.

I have encountered some unfavorable circumstances but I thank the Lord that, in spite of it all, what I have endured did not destroy me.

My faith continues to grow stronger as the breadth, length, height and depth of the Lord's unfailing love for me continues to be revealed; therefore, I will not fall, bend or compromise.

Because of the grace and mercy that has shielded and protected me, I am able to speak life, prosperity and health over all of my circumstances.

Suggested Song of Meditation: "God Favored Me" by Hezekiah Walker featuring Marvin Sapp and DJ Rodgers

2 Timothy 1:9 (International Standard Version/ISV)

⁹ He saved us and called us with a holy calling, not according to our own accomplishments, but according to his own purpose and the grace that was given to us in the Messiah Jesus before time began.

Boy oh boy, lately some serious purging, weeding, sifting and sharpening has been occurring. I am so grateful that God loves me so much that He wouldn't allow me to stay where the enemy would like to make me believe I belong.

During this time, I have been really focusing on releasing the hold that regret has had over me. I am one who documents the seasons of my life in journals. In looking back through these journals, something that I never noticed before was that in each season of my life, regret and shame were in the background and the underlying theme in most of the decisions that I had made.

Now, more than ever, I recognize how imperative it is that I surrender anything that is hindering me from being divinely connected to God and walking in the manifestation of who He has called me to be. For so long, I was concerned about being who everyone else wanted me to be. I was short-changing myself on every level when that was the influence behind my decision-making. I can identify that was the manipulative work of the enemy to keep me bound, further separated from the Lord and the plans that He had for my life.

Having those shackles broken, I am a caged bird that has been set free; free to live my life according to God's purpose. Who God has called me to be is not based on any accomplishments or feats of my own, but according to the Lord's purpose and grace that was given to me through Christ Jesus. So much of my energy had been misplaced and misused, but that is no longer the case.

I am saying, "Yes" to the Lord and will not resist His will or His plans. Whatever God tells me to do, I will agree to, knowing that even when I can't see how it's all working, I have confidence that it is all working together for my good.

I desire to be a better representation of God. When people come into contact with me, may they always be able to observe the everlasting love of the Lord emanating from me. I have been saved and I will follow wherever the Lord leads me, so that I may be all that He has called me to be.

I am focused on my destiny, which is that prize worth pressing for.

Suggested Song of Meditation: "Called to Be" by Jonathan Nelson

Psalm 52:8 (Lexham English Bible/LEB)

⁸ But I am like an olive tree flourishing in the house of God. I trust the loyal love of God forever and ever.

Amazing grace, how sweet the sound, that saved a wretch like me. I once was lost, but because of the Lord's unfailing love, I've been found; was blind, but now I see.

Last night at my son's school, they held a Senior Inauguration ceremony. This ceremony was like a mock graduation for all the seniors who had satisfied the requirements for graduation thus far. When I saw my handsome firstborn all dressed in black, entering into the auditorium with the rest of his peers, it was a very emotional moment for me; but I promised myself that all of my tears would be saved for May 27, 2015, when the official commencement ceremony would take place.

Being my oldest, my son has weathered the roughest of storms with me. As a single mom at the time, I would constantly beat myself up because I knew that everything that I said and did, whether directly or indirectly, would affect him and then eventually my oldest daughter. Looking back over the past eighteen years, there has been so much I wish we had never had to experience. But I am so grateful for the love of the Lord that never gave me exactly what I deserved, a love that covered me when I was just striving to live life and figure things out. We are like a sheltered olive tree protected by the Lord himself.

Watching my son last night was such an humbling experience for me. It reminded me of just how clueless I was about everything. I was lost, broken and didn't have a clue as to who Brandi was. What I did know, from the moment that I gave birth to my son, was that I was born to be a mom. Life didn't make sense anywhere else, except for in the role God had assigned and blessed me to uphold as a mother. Regardless of the poor decisions in my relationships, the generational strongholds that had me bound, the stumbling and falling, God's mercy intervened and the blessings and requests that should have been withheld, were still granted. The future that God promised my family and me hasn't ever been canceled out because of the decisions of my past. I rejoice and praise Him constantly when I think of that very thing.

There is so much thankfulness that consumes my soul, when I think about the fact that even when I've done things that the Lord despised, He never took His love away. I promise you, that I have learned how to love myself and others because of the example set forth by Jesus.

Through it all, God reveals to us, in the lessons that we experience, that He keeps on loving us no matter what we encounter or what we do.

I always used to say that I didn't know what unconditional love was until I became a mom. When I would say that, I meant that when I gave birth to my children, I believed that it was the first time I ever truly felt accepted and like my life really meant something. As I have gotten older, I have had to correct that statement because my children weren't the first to expose me to unconditional love. As much as I love them and they love me, there was a love that was protecting, guiding, molding and shaping me through every good and bad step and situation I encountered. God's love guarantees that I will be victorious and that nothing can separate me from the love of our God (Romans 8:38-39).

That steadfast love is not capable of coming from man, but only from our Heavenly Father.

Suggested Song of Meditation: "Good and Bad" by J.Moss. May it minister to you as it does to me.

Psalm 34:18 (The Voice/VOICE)

¹⁸ When someone is hurting or brokenhearted, the Eternal moves in close and revives him in his pain.

I am one who loves to make smoothies, milkshakes and various juice drinks in the blender. When I first started making them back when I was younger, I found it very interesting that the directions would instruct you to add each ingredient in a particular order. I always thought you could just toss the ice, liquid, fruit or yogurt in at the same time and it didn't matter. How incorrect I was. I learned that there was indeed a method to blending the ingredients.

In life, that concept has come full circle for me. Being married now and having a blended family, I have learned firsthand that if one aspect of the equation for any one family member is thrown off, it affects the dynamics and cohesiveness within the entire family. I am also learning that being someone who has a very "black or white" way of thinking, the many facets to blending definitely have posed a challenge to me, at times.

In a perfect world, when two people come together, it should be forever, but we all know that is not necessarily the case. And when children are created from those unions, it is so important to never lose focus on what the child needs, even if you're still striving to figure things out yourself. I was reminded of that last night when two different situations arose in our family.

Even in some of our darkest hours, when the pain feels like it is just too much to bear, we must never lose sight that like all the other days that have come before this one, God won't ever give us more than we can bear. Every aspect of our lives is in His hands. Let us be comforted in knowing that this too shall pass, though honestly, sometimes that is so much easier said than done.

Not knowing what the end result will be in either situation, I still give thanks to the Lord because He is so good and His mercy endures forever (Psalm 107:1). His love is more loyal to us than we could ever be or have ever been to ourselves. In everything I will give thanks. Even when my heart aches or confusion arises, I will praise His name. We serve a God of order. I thank Him that even when I have made some decisions out of order, He has still been there to connect the dots and deliver me from my brokenheartedness.

Realizing that the Lord feels our pain, in times such as these, I retreat into His arms and allow His unfailing love to bring that much needed comfort, peace and direction to my heart, my mind and my soul. I am rejoicing and praising His name because I know that with His strength, we shall overcome.

Suggested Song of Meditation: "This Too Shall Pass" by Yolanda Adams

2 Peter 1:3 (International Children's Bible/ICB)

³ Jesus has the power of God. His power has given us everything we need to live and to serve God. We have these things because we know him. Jesus called us by his glory and goodness.

A couple of nights ago when I went to charge my phone I realized that the power that was being transferred from my USB cable to my phone wasn't strong enough to continuously power up my phone, so I had to go borrow my daughter's cable which was frustrating, seeing as with her being a teenager, her phone being powered up to its fullest capacity is a necessity. Having to share a cord was an inconvenience (even if she never stated it was).

I thought about that same thing this morning when I went to grab her USB cable once again to charge my phone. The power from my cable is so wishy-washy and I didn't have the time to devote to trying to move it around to see if it would begin charging my phone. All of that led me to think about the source of divine power that we have access to because of Jesus.

We don't ever have to worry about not having what we need to live the life that God has called us to. The Lord has given us everything that we could possibly require to live and to serve Him. When we get to know the One who invited us to God, more personally and intimately, we then learn just what it means to be loved and the significance of His grace and mercy in our lives. We not only have a place to retreat and find comfort and peace in, but we also have a place where we can communicate and receive the answers to live our lives according to God's purpose.

We can search for that connection from others. We can make the mistake of thinking that the love we seek can be found in man; but there is nothing like the love of Jesus. Sometimes we don't know that God is all that we need until He is all that we have. I can attest to that for myself.

During seasons of my life when I felt like I was so low and couldn't get any lower, I looked around and some of those who were there, were no longer. It was during those times that I realized that I needed to stop putting expectations on man and begin placing them where they belonged, on God, because He had already made the provisions to bring me through what I was facing. How thankful I am that the Lord knows and sees all and that He still loves me as I am going through the process.

Every day I am mindful that God's divine power has bestowed upon us all things that are requisite and suited to life and godliness, through the full and personal knowledge of Him Who called us by and to His own glory and excellence (virtue).

Knowing the Lord better powers me up for what lies ahead and that is a connection that I am not ever worried about losing its charge.

Suggested Song of Meditation: "Mindful" by Brian Courtney Wilson

2 Corinthians 12:9 (The Voice/VOICE)

⁹ and finally He said to me, "My grace is enough to cover and sustain you. My power is made perfect in weakness." So ask me about my thorn, inquire about my weaknesses, and I will gladly go on and on—I would rather stake my claim in these and have the power of the Anointed One at home within me.

What an indescribable twenty-four hours it had been. As my children and I traveled to Indiana for the home-going celebration of their grandma and the woman who I would always view as my other mom, I began recalling nothing but countless memories that we had with her over the past sixteen years. Through tears, laughter and smiles, I crossed over four states before entering Indiana, where I became a little anxious and nervous, not knowing what to expect. I knew that it would be difficult and I felt so weak. I needed to be strong for my two oldest babies, because I knew this would be one of their toughest days.

I prayed to God for strength, knowing that His grace is sufficient and all I could ever need. I was reminded that God's power is perfected in weakness. Once we arrived in Indiana and I passed by familiar landmarks and locations that I had once frequented with her, feeble couldn't even begin to capture how I was feeling. But oh, I praised the Lord knowing that during my time of weakness, He is made strong and that I am positioned to have His power rest upon me.

In a way that only the Lord could outline, orchestrate and direct, we were blessed to be in attendance for one of the most beautiful home-going celebrations that I have ever attended. Through the tears, I thanked God for the opportunity to know, love and be loved, by such an amazing woman with such an affectionate spirit. During the program, we were challenged to trust the Lord without any doubts. One of the ways to accomplish that was to remember that God's grace is sufficient.

When I heard those words spoken, I felt a sense of peace usher in and I realized that being on the receiving end of God's grace allowed joy to be placed where hurt and pain were once located. Where I thought I would be so overwhelmed with mourning, God's grace provided me with everything I needed to truly celebrate such a special woman.

Although her passing was unexpected and not at all what we had hoped, because as it was stated, "There were still more chapters of her life we had hoped to read," I was able to find contentment in knowing that the Lord's timing is always right and that this beautiful person (both inside and out) was now in the best place and watching over all of us.

No weapon formed against us shall ever be able to prosper when we know who to run to in our times of need. God's amazing grace not only saves, but keeps me as well.

Suggested Song of Meditation: "God's Grace" by Trin-I-Tee 5:7

Romans 5:8 (The Voice/VOICE)

⁸ But think about this: while we were wasting our lives in sin, God revealed His powerful love to us in a tangible display—the Anointed One died for us.

Have you ever taken time to think about just how powerful, amazing and truly unrivaled the love is that God has for us? Without the sacrifice that Christ made for us on this very day, we wouldn't be able to have the relationship with God that we do. We wouldn't have the ability to go directly to our Heavenly Father at any and all times and have our sins forgiven. Jesus bled and died; He paid it all because we were so lost.

Jesus—the Anointed One, unselfishly gave His life so that we may have life and have it more abundantly. I remain in awe when I think about all that Jesus endured for us.

Jesus exchanged His life for ours and now we have been set free. I will honor the Lord and the love that He has for us by keeping the sacrifice that Jesus made up on Calvary at the forefront of my mind. I am here to live and walk according to God's will and purpose for my life.

Because of Christ, our pasts have been canceled and the old things have passed away; behold, all things have become NEW (2 Corinthians 5:17).

Jesus paid it all and I am here to give my all, in return, as a token of my gratitude for the most powerful love that I don't deserve nor could ever do enough to earn; and yet, through Christ, I am a recipient of it.

Suggested Song of Meditation: "You Paid It All" by Wess Morgan

Job 5:9 (New Living Translation/NLT)

⁹ He does great things too marvelous to understand. He performs countless miracles.

On this day, what are you believing God for? What words are you speaking over yourself and your situation? Now, more than ever, it is so imperative that we exercise radical faith and make proclamations and declarations through the faith we have in our Heavenly Father.

This is our time to rest on His promises and to expect Him to accomplish great things that are far beyond our comprehension and miracles that are far too many to even count. The time for walking around with our heads hung low has expired. God is bringing restoration by way of accelerated blessings and with rapid fulfillment.

Since our confidence comes from the Lord, walk with your head held high. By faith, declare that God is about to elevate and take you higher, that your increase is on its way, that you are getting stronger, that your circumstances are getting better and that you are about to move.

Don't begin to settle nor fall into the trap of complacency. The assignments, aspirations and visions that the Lord has placed within you serves as a reminder that what He has for you is bigger than where you currently find yourself.

Get ready for all the great things and countless miracles that are too marvelous and grand for us to begin to comprehend, that only God can perform.

Suggested Song of Meditation: "Something Big" by Jekalyn Carr

Isaiah 60:1 (New Life Version/NLV)

⁶⁰ *"Rise up and shine, for your light has come. The shining-greatness of the Lord has risen upon you.*

I thank God for all the opportunities in which I am fortunate to receive His teachings and instructions via the divine connections that He has orchestrated in my life. One of the greatest divine connections I have been blessed to be linked to took place within the Homemakers Ministry at my church back in Maryland. During one particular meeting, we discussed the topic, *My Heart, My Forgiveness*, which came from Priscilla Shirer's book, *The Resolution for Women*.

At the conclusion of our meeting, I felt enlightened and armed with so much knowledge, as I was provided unbelievable insight into things from my past as they pertained to unforgiveness.

Ten years ago, I had a clothing line called AMJ: A Mother's Journey. I created phrases of encouragement that were screen-printed and embroidered on different types of apparel. One of the phrases that I created, which was very popular among my consumers stated, "Unlike the sun, I cannot continue to shine on something that is not willing to grow."

During that particular season I was in, I wanted to do something to encourage others, especially women, but I was allowing toxic people and situations to rule my life all because I hadn't taken the time to acknowledge the broken state I was truly in. The strongholds of rejection, fear of exclusion and people pleasing at all costs had me so bound.

I am one who loves to smile and who enjoys making others smile, but I was torn between two worlds. I was saved and desired to please the Lord, but also sought that approval and acceptance from man. Of course, like oil and water, that did not mix. So here I was trying to shine the light that Jesus had placed within me in ways that the Lord never instructed me to.

I created a message nine years ago and hadn't even scratched the surface on what God intended to reveal to me. I was so concerned with the "weeds" in my life that I wanted to share my light with, not realizing that upon releasing my situations to the Lord, His Son would shine in my life and thus, facilitate the weeding out process for me.

My issue with forgiveness has not ever been forgiving others. Where I have struggled is in not being able to forgive myself for the situations and circumstances I found myself in, that God didn't necessarily have for me in the first place. Thinking that I knew people better or that the situation would get better if I just held on and waited it out; neither worked well for me and none of that God called me to do. In time that was made abundantly clear. I would beat myself up and was left with so much shame, regret, resentment and guilt. Although I knew if I just repented God would forgive me, I honestly didn't believe I was worthy or deserving of His forgiveness.

But one fine morning, I arose from the prostration that my circumstances had me in, recognizing that because Jesus rose, not only had I been forgiven but I was also able to shine and radiate with the glory of the Lord. I have graduated from my words "Unlike the sun, I cannot continue to shine on something that is not willing to grow," to God's truth that instructs us to "Let our light shine before men in such a way that they see your good works and glorify your Father who is up in heaven (Matthew 5:16)."

I have accepted God's forgiveness in my life and know that God extends an inner peace when we forgive. Do not let one ray of the light that has been placed inside of you be held hostage by unforgiveness. The Lord has brought back the sunshine in my life. His son-shine is my lifeline.

Suggested Song of Meditation: "You Brought the Sunshine" by The Clark Sisters

Titus 3:5 (Easy-to-Read Version/ERV)

> *⁵ He saved us because of his mercy, not because of any good things we did. He saved us through the washing that made us new people. He saved us by making us new through the Holy Spirit.*

Self-worth is defined as the sense of one's own value or worth as a person; self-esteem; self-respect. Let me tell you that when a person knows their self-worth and it is founded and rooted in who God says they are, that person is an unstoppable force. But on the other side of that coin, when a person doesn't know their self-worth and they allow it to be defined by the world and those around them, he/she places themselves in a very paralyzing state.

These past couple of months have been ones of serious retrospect for me. Initially, when I have looked back over the years that the Lord has blessed me with, my honest initial response was met with mixed emotions. I felt abundantly grateful and appreciative, especially when so many that I have loved have left this earth and moved on to be with the Lord; but at the same time frustration and disappointment surfaced. Time is so precious and is something that is not promised to any of us. With that being said, the majority of my life has been spent with me trying to be everything to everyone else. I worked diligently to make sure everyone knew their self-worth and I didn't even know mine.

I allowed myself to be defined by others (in their broken states), by generational strongholds and by events and situations that had occurred in my past. That saddened me, especially when I look around and those who I devoted myself to have since walked away seeing as I no longer served a purpose to them. That sadness and reality check caused me to take some self-inventory. If I was the common denominator in each of those instances and relationships, what was it about me that kept attracting the same situations and causing the same end results? And that answer was, I hadn't addressed or allowed the Lord to dig up the root of the sources of brokenness in my life.

Generational strongholds have a way of being transmitted from one generation to the next so seamlessly that you don't even realize that they're embedded in your DNA. But oh my goodness, no matter what was passed on through my family's bloodlines, none of that could ever be greater, stronger or more powerful than the blood of Jesus!!! Because of His blood and His mercy, I have been saved and the chains have been broken!!!

It may have taken me awhile to get there, but I am here. That is why I am taking the stand to be the Moses for the next generation, my children, and for the rest of my people. The generational blessings begin here and now.

I know my worth because God said that I was worthy of His Son dying on the cross for me. The Lord said I was worth saving and so He has changed my life. He proclaimed that I was worth keeping and so God cleaned me up inside, making me new and giving me a fresh beginning.

When our worth comes from the Lord, we are free, we are whole and filled with the hope, peace and confidence that can only come from the Lord. Aren't you glad that God thought we were worth it?

Suggested Song of Meditation: "Worth" by Anthony Brown and group therAPy

Isaiah 43:1 (The Voice/VOICE)

43 Eternal One: Remember who created you, O Jacob? Who shaped you, O Israel? See, you have nothing to fear. I, who made you, will take you back. I have chosen you, named you as My own.

Now, more than ever, there is peace that fills me knowing that before I was ever placed in my mother's womb, God knew me and before I ever drew my first breath, He had already chosen me to be His prophet and to speak His Word to the nations (Jeremiah 1:5).

I have spent a lot of my life trying to establish a presence and connection with so many, with the hopes of not ever being forgotten. That way of thinking, definitely served as a life lesson for me. I realized that what I was seeking from others could only be found in my Heavenly Father.

I feared not having that validation and acceptance from the masses. What I had to learn (the hard way) was that the acknowledgement and confirmation from the Lord, trumps anything and everything that I could ever hope to receive from a multitude of individuals here on earth. Where others were once present and my name was constantly on the tip of their tongues, those same individuals have since dispersed showing no signs of ever having a connection to me.

That used to bring much sadness to my heart. But during this time, God has shown me that no matter where I am, where I go and what I do, He knows my name and will never leave me nor forsake me. He has been my friend at all times and has given me hope when I felt hopeless.

The Lord has promised to be my light over the darkness, my strength over weakness and my joy and relief over sadness. Continuously, I am reminded that I have been marvelously set apart and am fearfully and wonderfully made. I am no longer consumed by who doesn't know or no longer decides to acknowledge me. The Lord not only chose me, but has called me by name and I am His. I will constantly praise Him!!

Suggested Song of Meditation: "Not Forgotten" by Israel and New Breed

Psalm 86:15 (International Standard Version/ISV)

15 But you, Lord, are a compassionate God, merciful and patient, with unending gracious love and faithfulness.

In thinking about the continuous praise and worship that the Lord is so deserving of, I know that if I had ten thousand tongues I wouldn't be able to fully impart how thankful I am for all that the Lord has done and continues to do for me. Looking back over every day that the Lord has blessed me to see, I have nothing but endless examples of how great the Lord's faithfulness has been in my life.

The Lord is so compassionate, merciful and patient. We have all made decisions that have displeased the Lord and been outside of His will for our lives. Knowing all that we would ever do, God still chose each of us to be on the receiving end of His unending gracious love. Lamentations 3:22-23 reminds us that because of the Lord's steadfast love we are not consumed, since His compassions never end. They are new every morning—great is His faithfulness!

Because of God's grace and mercy, I know that I have been transformed. Although I love working out and desire to be in the best physical shape for myself, I can tell you that the biggest change I have undergone has been internally. I now know what it feels like to be free, because the Lord has torn down the strongholds that were preventing me from being who He has called me to be.

Because of His faithfulness, I am no longer concerned about being weak when I know that my strength comes from the Lord. Because of the Lord's mercy and His compassion that isn't ever limited, when storms surface, I know that I won't ever be completely wiped out. The Lord is my salvation and in Him I find peace. Every morning when I rise, I know that His mercies begin afresh and that means I am covered and prepared to face whatever lies ahead because the God we serve is ever so faithful!!

Suggested Song of Meditation: "You've Been So Faithful" by Eddie James and The Phoenix Mass Choir

Isaiah 61:3 (International Standard Version/ISV)

³ to provide for those who grieve in Zion—to bestow on them a crown of beauty instead of ashes, the oil of gladness instead of mourning, a mantle of praise instead of a spirit of despair." "Then people will call them "Oaks of Righteousness", "The Planting of the Lord", in order to display his splendor.

Sitting here at my dining room table, in so many ways, it's still so hard for me to believe that I am back in New York. Goodness, so much has transpired in the life of this rose who began her journey growing up through the concrete in Harlem.

Even though I was dealt some serious blows growing up and into adulthood, I always held tight to my dreams and would pray; even when I didn't know which way was up. As I reflect from then to now, there is absolutely no denying that the Lord has been by my side every step of the way.

I can tell you, with certainty, that He gives beauty for ashes, strength for fear, gladness for mourning and peace for despair. In desiring to have a deeper understanding of the phrase "beauty for ashes", I learned that the Hebrew word for ashes is epher and that the Hebrew word for beauty is pheer. If you take a look at both "epher" and pheer", to my amazement, you will notice that both words consist of the same exact letters. By moving one of the letter "e", the word and its meaning changes.

Thinking about how moving the letter "e" transforms one word into a totally different word, caused me to think about what beauty for ashes means to me.

It's an exchange between God and me. As easily as epher can be transformed into pheer, God can and will turn our most horrible, embarrassing and painful situations around and from them the most beautiful blessings that were situated just beneath all the shame and regret will break through and spring forth.

Where I once was lost, I have been found. I also have been freed from strongholds and yokes have been broken. Because of the wholeness and healing I have received, a victim mindset no longer has a place here.

I am an overcomer, who has adopted a victor mindset. I operate in the unspeakable joy that I have been given instead of mourning and sadness. I wear my mantle of praise instead of being cloaked in a spirit of heaviness.

No matter how painful the circumstances may be that we encounter, just one touch from our Heavenly Father is all we need. Once we surrender to Him, our ashes are transformed into the most beautiful of things.

We are then made new and planted by God to display His glory and share the good news about His goodness and faithfulness to everyone we come into contact with.

Suggested Song of Meditation: "Beauty for Ashes" by Crystal Lewis

Psalm 5:12 (New King James Version/NKJV)

¹² For You, O Lord, will bless the righteous; with favor You will surround him as with a shield.

There are so many times that I wonder if we ever really stop to think about where we would truly be if it had not been for the Lord who was on our side. I have made the vow to not let one day go by without acknowledging that my reality would be a completely different story if it had not been for God's love, grace, mercy and favor that I have been on the receiving end of.

When we are divinely connected to the Lord and strive to live our lives on purpose and according to His will, we will discover just how blessed we are and will witness God's favor covering and surrounding us like a shield. That is why being in right standing with God is a necessity. In doing so, we are sheltered, protected and encompassed by His love. That same favor will bring us through our toughest trials, tests and obstacles. I rejoice and sing praises unto the Lord because He protects us with His shield of love.

Let us never take for granted that if it hadn't been for Jesus' blood, it would have been us condemned and destroyed by our sinful nature, mindsets and patterns of behavior. But, because of the blood that Jesus shed for us way back on Calvary, we are given the strength that is required day to day to make it through; because that blood never loses its power.

The covering that we receive from the limitless love that can only be acquired from God, faithfully shows us that everything that the enemy meant for evil, God continuously turns it around for our good (Genesis 50:20).

It's astonishing how the Lord has kept us. When we are faithful, obedient and honor God, we are then positioned to receive all that He has already constructed and arranged for us. I charge each of you to never forget how blessed and highly favored you are.

Suggested Song of Meditation: "Blessed and Highly Favored" by The Clark Sisters

John 1:16 (New International Version—UK/NIVUK)

¹⁶ Out of his fullness we have all received grace in place of grace already given.

"Amazing grace, how sweet the sound, that saved a wretch like me. I once was lost, but now I'm found; was blind, but now I see". That song is one that I have heard all throughout my life. It's no wonder that it is one of my favorites. When I would sing it as a child, I enjoyed it so much because of the expressions of praise that it incited in all those around me in church.

As I grew older, the words of that song took on a whole new meaning as I began to observe one spiritual blessing after another occurring in my life. I have never believed in coincidence or happenstance. I learned early on that what we are blessed with has absolutely nothing to do with luck or with our own individual works, but is the direct result of God's favor and the fullness of His grace.

God's grace loves me, adores me, watches over me, saves me and on a daily basis gives me more than I could ever deserve. If it wasn't for God's grace, I would be so lost. I sing songs of praise because the Lord's grace keeps me and is always faithful. I give Him glory for His unmerited favor that I have access to day-to-day.

Because of God's loving-kindness we all receive gifts of grace beyond our imagination. Every day, I can attest to this and I am just so grateful. Being outside of the realm of the Lord's love, grace, mercy and favor is not even an option.

I know what it is like to lose your way, but God's grace and mercy has raised me, freed me and gotten me back on course to living my life the only way I should; and that is on purpose and with the Lord's will being accomplished. Where would we be if it wasn't for His grace?

Suggested Song of Meditation: "Grace" by Tasha Cobbs

Isaiah 42:16 (International Children's Bible/ICB)

¹⁶ Then I will lead the blind along a way they never knew. I will guide them along paths they have not known. I will make the darkness become light for them. And I will make the rough ground smooth. These are the things I will do. I will not leave my people.

The first thing that came to my mind this morning were the following lyrics, "What a friend we have in Jesus, all our sins and griefs to bear. What a privilege to carry everything to God in prayer."

It truly is a privilege to take the weight of all that may be burdening us and being able to release it to the Lord. During a church service in Maryland, I remember being reminded that prayer is not about informing God, because He is omniscient and knows it all anyway. When we pray, we are including and inviting God into our situation.

Knowing that God has not given us a spirit of fear, I have the reassurance in His promises (which never fail), that God will take my hand when I don't know or can't see where I'm going. The Lord will be our personal guide and help navigate us through paths we do not have prior knowledge of. He will cause darkness to transform into light and areas that would normally trip us up, He will cause us not to even stumble.

Through it all and in everything that I face, I know that the Lord will stick by my side and never abandon me for a minute. Being in the particular season of my life that I am currently in, having these reassurances are of paramount importance.

As my family and I prepare to relocate to uncharted territory and maneuver through the process that will assist in getting us there, I do feel blinded in some ways. But I praise Him and rejoice because the Lord is whom I am dependent upon to direct me along this course that I have never traveled.

The Lord understands everything that I am feeling and that is why I won't give up because I know without a doubt that through it all, God has been with me and He has promised to keep me and never leave me.

Suggested Song of Meditation: "Through It All" by Deitrick Haddon

Ephesians 1:11 (The Living Bible/TLB)

[11] Moreover, because of what Christ has done, we have become gifts to God that he delights in, for as part of God's sovereign plan we were chosen from the beginning to be his, and all things happen just as he decided long ago.

Even when it seems as though time just escapes me, I am grateful for days such as today, when I am given the opportunity to gather and fellowship with my Homemakers Ministry sisters. Not having any physical sisters of my own, I truly cherish the sisterhood that has been established with these women.

Today really spoke in volumes to me after we participated in an activity where we were asked to read phrases that were on a piece of paper and discuss if we agreed or disagreed with what the statement said. My piece of paper read, "You are good." When asked if I believed that statement, in all truth I responded, "On some days I believe that, but on other days believing that tends to be a struggle. When asked why I felt that way, I explained that for so long I placed how good, valuable or needed I was based on others. I allowed the current state of my relationships with individuals to determine and define my worth.

That was until I read, Priscilla Shirer's book, *"A Jewel in His Crown"* and I was reminded of who God says I am. After reading that book and sharing the revelations that occurred with my spiritual mentors, I began to change my way of thinking and decided that my perception of myself and what I was striving for in life should first come from who Christ says I am.

These days, among other things, I know that I am good and that I am valuable. I am still a work in progress and so the enemy, at times, tries to get me to question myself and my destiny. But on those days, I confidently proclaim that I know who I am, because I know who God says I am.

Three little words, **"You are good**," brought about a dialogue and a breakthrough that I was in the right place and at the right time to receive. I thank God for choosing me, ordering my steps, setting me apart and appointing me to do work for His kingdom.

Suggested Song of Meditation: "I Know Who I Am" by Sinach

Psalm 147:5 (The Message/MSG)

⁵ Our Lord is great, with limitless strength; we'll never comprehend what he knows and does.

Having a few moments to just sit down and be still, I just started thinking about how great and mighty our God is. One of my favorite words to describe the Lord is omniscient.

To know that we serve a God who is all-knowing and whose understanding is beyond measure gives me endless reasons to rejoice and praise the name of our Heavenly Father.

Because I fully recognize that the Lord is omniscient, the way that I communicate with Him has evolved. Back in the day, I thought I had to break down everything that I was thinking and feeling from A to Z and sometimes AA to ZZ. I believed God needed to understand where I was coming from or why I was in need of what I was asking for. I chuckle when I think back to those days because God didn't need my long, drawn out explanations. He was just waiting for the invitation to be welcomed and included in my situations so that His will would be done thus, causing a shift to occur in ways only He is capable of doing.

I know that the Lord has limitless strength and that my help comes from Him. He is my strength and my shield and my heart trusts in Him because I know that He knows me, knows everything that I need and He has made the provisions for me to receive all that is for me at the exact time I should.

It is inconceivably possible to fully grasp all that the Lord knows and does. I don't have to understand how He does it or when He's going to do it. All I need to know is that when the Lord does bring forth His promises, He does it in a way that is exceedingly, abundantly and far beyond anything I could ever dream to ask or think of. What a mighty God we serve!!

Suggested Song of Meditation: "Great & Mighty" by Byron Cage

Psalm 139:5 (Complete Jewish Bible/CJB)

⁵ You have hemmed me in both behind and in front and laid your hand on me.

There was a time when I thought that I had to search all over to find the Lord. I would pray and anticipate the moment that the Lord would appear and move within my situations.

It wasn't until I truly learned and got to know the Lord for myself that I realized that I don't have to look far for the Lord. He is already here and near me throughout everything I face; good, bad and indifferent.

The Lord doesn't just go before us, He follows us, encircles and hems us in. I love that in some of the translations of the verse above the word "hem" is utilized. According to the dictionary, the word "hem" is defined as forming an edge or border on or around, to enclose or confine and to surround or restrict the space or movement of.

What a source of empowerment I feel when I think of how God will enclose us so that we are surrounded by Him and His love, grace and mercy first. With such a vivid visualization, I view trials so much differently. No matter what comes up against me, God encompasses me and promises to place His hand of blessing upon me; thus protecting me with His power.

There is such power in the "hem". In the Bible, the woman with the issue of blood knew she had to reach Jesus. Upon touching just the hem of Jesus' garment, the woman was healed of a condition that she suffered from and that caused her to be viewed as an outcast for twelve long years.

So when the Lord declares that He hems me in, I rejoice and just say, "Thank you!" He is the salve that covers and protects me. He provides the soothing and healing required for me to be made whole and to walk toward the destiny that lies ahead of me.

There is no debate and I thoroughly recognize that because I am hemmed in both behind and in front; the Lord's presence is already here in every facet of my life.

Suggested Song of Meditation: "Already Here" by Brian Courtney Wilson

Nehemiah 9:6 (Easy-to-Read Version/ERV)

⁶ You are God. Lord, only you are God. You made the sky and the highest heavens and everything in them. You made the earth and everything on it. You made the seas and everything in them. You give life to everything. All the heavenly angels bow down and worship you.

As the days wind down to the time that we have left here in Maryland, I am so excited to see what God has in store. To some, it appears that we have such a small window for all that needs to be accomplished to get done. When I know that I am doing things according to the order and manner in which God instructs me to, I am not concerned.

Anytime the enemy tries to get me to worry or question anything, all I have to do is look in the mirror, outside up at the sky or at my surroundings to be reminded of everything God is capable of accomplishing. The Lord doesn't need our help and will change our circumstances in the matter of seconds, if we just trust and believe in Him. He is Elohim, God "Creator, Mighty and Strong".

The Lord is the only wise and one true God and I don't have to question His greatness, or search far to see His power working in my life and all around me. His everlasting mercy and grace is why I have peace and joy while in the midst of so much that is unknown. Through our Eternal King, the truth is always present and available to us. As long as we have King Jesus, we have everything we could ever possibly need.

Because He is God and God alone, He does wondrous and amazing things (Psalm 86:10). I have seen some of those marvelous works come to fruition. The same God that called everything into existence and gave life to it is orchestrating and working things out on our behalf. Is there anything too hard for God? Absolutely not!!! His knowledge is all encompassing and His wisdom and understanding are beyond measure. My faith, trust, hope and confidence—honestly, my everything, is in the Lord. I fall down and worship the only true God there is.

Suggested Song of Meditation: "You Are God Alone" by Marvin Sapp

John 15:16 (Worldwide English (New Testament)/WE)

¹⁶ You did not choose me, but I chose you. I gave you a big work to do. That work is to go out and do good things and to make the good things that you do remain strong. If you do that, my Father will do anything you ask in my name.

We didn't choose the Lord; He chose us. Before we were ever formed in our mother's womb, the Lord knew us. That means that every day that we are blessed to experience was written long before any of them ever have had the chance to come to fruition.

We should feel empowered, encouraged, motivated and inspired with the knowledge of knowing that we were chosen to be God's children. Because Jesus is the vine and we are the branches, we are divinely connected to a faithfulness and a love that never fails, becomes obsolete or comes to an end; an unfailing love that can only be received from God.

Nothing that occurs in our lives is by way of happenstance or coincidence. When we realize that everything that the Lord does is intentional, we can begin to see things in a different light and can profess that everything is working together for our good; because we love Him and are called according to His purpose (Romans 8:28).

May we accept and always find peace in knowing that anything that we are encountering, although it may come as a shock or surprise to us, is not at all a surprise to God; as a matter of fact, God intended it for specific reasons and it had to receive His approval. If He approved it, that means that good or bad, all of it will be beneficial for us, when it's all said and done.

There is no need to worry because the Lord is intentional and He never fails!!!

Suggested Song of Meditation: "Intentional" by Travis Greene

Isaiah 58:11 (New International Version—UK/NIVUK)

¹¹ The Lord will guide you always; he will satisfy your needs in a sun-scorched land and will strengthen your frame. You will be like a well-watered garden, like a spring whose waters never fail.

It's unbelievable how quickly the weather can switch up. As much as I would have liked to remain inside on such a brutally hot and humid day, I had errands to run that didn't care that the sun's rays needed less than five minutes of contact with my skin before I would be left with an excruciating sunburn.

While out and about, I came upon a place on base that is situated on the Potomac River. It was so picturesque and serene, that I had to take my youngest daughter over there. When she asked me where water came from, we began talking about what God has created and how beautiful it all is. I found a shaded area where we were able to watch the waves from the water and the sun's reflection on it.

As we were leaving, I thought about how scorching hot it was and yet there were areas still thriving and experiencing fullness and abundance in spite of the current weather conditions. It was only a matter of minutes once we got inside, that the sky darkened. Within seconds it was as if the clouds opened up and the rain decided to compose an overture in B flat. The combination of the rain and the ferocious wind made all the windows look like we were driving the building through a neighborhood car wash.

Just moments earlier, everything seemed so parched and now the water had every area saturated and drenched. Observing all of these changes really drilled in the realization that God will give us a full life; even in the emptiest places. Unlike the severe thunderstorms that we just encountered, in life, we won't always get the National Weather Service alert or have the privilege of seeing the clouds change or hear the winds shift to know that our valleys are about to be restored and replenished.

I don't need to see the wind or feel the rain to know that the Lord has already made a way and will fill the dry areas in my life. I recognize the blessing that comes from our seasons of drought. During these times, it's that much more imperative that I move myself out of the way; that I not only take my hands off the wheel but that I keep my hands off of it as well. I am given the opportunity to show the Lord just how much I trust and believe in Him because I know that He will always guide and lead me in the way that I should go.

Through each step that is taken, the Lord will nourish us, satisfy our needs and give us the strength required to persevere. Even if everything around us is dry, we serve a God who will cause us to grow like a garden that has been cared for and well-tended; like a spring that never runs dry.

We don't need to see or feel it to know that Jehovah Jireh is making a way and providing for us.

Suggested Song of Meditation: "You Won't See the Wind or Rain" by Jekalyn Carr

Philippians 4:7 (J.B. Phillips New Testament/PHILLIPS)

⁷ And the peace of God which transcends human understanding, will keep constant guard over your hearts and minds as they rest in Christ Jesus.

Today was one of those days. I can't even tell you how many times I laid down, just to clear my head and instead I found myself just calling out to the Lord to converse with Him. Once I did that, I was able to close my eyes and although I didn't get any sleep, I was able to get some rest.

As each day passes by, I feel like I get that much closer to the door that the Lord has prepared to open for me. But the closer I get, the stronger the attacks from the enemy become and the quantity of road blocks posted up in front of me appear like hurdles in an Olympic trial. Although I feel increasingly weighted down, what keeps me afloat is the peace of God.

It is through that peace that He gives, that my thoughts and heart are kept quiet and at rest because of the trust that I have in Jesus Christ. It is a peace that surpasses and transcends all human understanding. How else could I explain having the desire to rejoice and give thanks, even in the most painful and uncomfortable situations?

I have learned that there is a reason for each painful circumstance and trial that I encounter. If I am completely honest, the home-buying process we have been subjected to has been nothing like I imagined or planned for it to be. Even with a pre-approval and commitment letter from the bank, we have encountered more setbacks than I ever anticipated. I did everything that I could possibly do, because I know that faith without works is dead. I also realized that just because this process has not run its course the way I thought it would doesn't mean I have been dismissed or forgotten.

As Joel Osteen reminded me, the pain and obstacles that I encounter are not here to defeat me, but to elevate me. Through the peace of God, I am comforted and know that my pain is about to be turned into my gain.

I am waiting with expectancy for it to get better, knowing that when I pray and continue to keep my faith in Him and Him alone, I will see the greatness of His power unfold right before my eyes.

Because the Lord's presence is constantly surrounding me, I know that the peace that comes from Him is always within my grasp. At times such as these, my spirit calls on the peace of God to rain upon me.

Suggested Song of Meditation: "Peace of God" by Tarrlyn Ramsey

Jeremiah 10:6 (New Century Version/NCV)

⁶ Lord, there is no one like you. You are great, and your name is great and powerful.

Who is like the Lord? Absolutely nobody. We could search all over, look high and low and still wouldn't be able to find anyone or anything that could hope to be as great as the Lord.

Sometimes we need to be reminded that we serve a great God, who has the capacity and ability to turn things around for us. That means that regardless of the attacks and trials that we may encounter day and night, there is no need to fear because our God is more powerful than any problem or circumstance that we can endure.

Whatever has been taken, stolen and/or withheld from us, God will restore it. After going through, He will bring the rain and will restore above and beyond; with plenty!!!

When I hear the word plenty, it always makes me think of the candy, **Good and Plenty**. Growing up, that candy was a favorite among my friends and family (but not me). I didn't like the taste of it but loved the box it came in because it was purple and white and purple is my favorite color.

I recall my pastor in Maryland sharing with us about how God was about to restore us with more than enough. He further went on to say that when restoration steps into the domain of our lives, we will end up with plenty.

Our God is so awesome. He is omnipotent, omnipresent and omniscient. There isn't any problem, situation or circumstance that is bigger or greater than Him.

Nothing is too difficult for the Lord and with Him all things are possible.

Suggested Song of Meditation: "Great God," by Deitrick Haddon's LXW

Exodus 34:6 (1599 Geneva Bible/GNV)

⁶ So the Lord passed before his face, and cried, The Lord, the Lord, strong, merciful, and gracious, slow to anger, and abundant in goodness and truth.

It has been so brutally hot and humid the past few days that I have truly appreciated and been thankful for the air conditioning that we have at our disposal. Staying inside, at times like these, gives me plenty of opportunity to just sit back and reflect on many things.

I have always been a believer that it's important to never forget where I have come from, but what's even more important is that I make sure that I don't get stuck in the past during these moments of reflection. One of my main reasons for looking back is because I am given endless examples of all the ways that the Lord has kept and covered me.

There have been so many circumstances and situations that were so overwhelming. I had absolutely no idea how I would make it through. At the time that I was in the midst of my troubles, I just knew that what I was experiencing was the absolute worse thing I had ever encountered.

And yet, here I am. I wasn't consumed. I am so much better than I was before. It's more than having a testimony. I am a testimony. I am well aware that by no means have I ever been the reason that my circumstances and situations were overcome. Although the challenges and tests that I face on a day-to-day basis may change, The Eternal One, never changes. We serve a God who is the same yesterday, today and forever; which is why we have not already been utterly destroyed.

There isn't one single thing that our God can't fix. And how do I know that? Because I'm still here and those situations that I thought would break me and cause me to crumble, actually ended up sharpening me and making me so much stronger.

Today, I had to remind myself that instead of being anxious, nervous or worried about what the outcome will be, I must remember that the Lord doesn't change. If He did it before, He most definitely will do it again. The Lord isn't capable of coming up short nor does He go back on His Word.

Quite a bit is brought into perspective when I take the time to think about all the victories I have already won being a child of God. The thought of all of that gets me excited and produces so much hope because I know that there are still many more victories ahead, if I continue to put my trust in Him and stand on His promises.

I won't quit nor will I give up, because I was born to win.

Suggested Song of Meditation: "2nd Win" by Kierra Sheard.

Psalm 56:8 (The Living Bible/TLB)

⁸ You have seen me tossing and turning through the night. You have collected all my tears and preserved them in your bottle! You have recorded every one in your book.

Throughout the years, my perception of crying has changed. I am one who rarely gets angry. Even though I have my convictions and am very black and white, I am not confrontational at all. So, when everything or everyone around me takes an unexpected shift or turn, I am left hurt and consumed with much sadness.

In the past, those tears were tears of disappointment, regret and shame. I would always get so frustrated when things would happen out of my control because, involuntarily, it seemed as if my body's only response to trials and obstacles was to cry. I viewed crying as a sign of weakness and I never wanted to be perceived as weak. But as each tear would fall, I felt that I was cementing my role as the "village crier."

It wasn't until I heard someone speak on just how concerned the Lord is with every aspect of our lives and that because we serve such a compassionate God, He catches every single tear that escapes from our tear ducts, my views on crying shifted. I began to truly understand that every tear, every hurt and every pain matters to the Lord.

In my times of need, I used to look to others as my source of comfort and assurance, until I realized that expectation should only be placed on one person, El Shaddai, the All-Sufficient One. In drawing closer and nearer to the Lord, I know that I am being met where I am by the One who knew where I would be in the first place.

No matter how many words I can formulate into different sentences, sometimes there just aren't any words for what I am experiencing and so I let my tears speak for me. I recognize that no matter how grand or how minuscule my situation may be, the Lord is present when each and every one of my tears is shed. To the Lord, my tears are so precious; they are detailed, collected and recorded.

Crying has transformed from a symbol of weakness to an act of strength; when I know that I am releasing them to our God. With Him, I don't ever have to question if the level of vulnerability I'm expressing is being taken advantage of or mocked. He has promised to wipe every tear from my eyes.

We all need to cry sometimes. Weeping may endure for a night, but joy comes in the morning.

It's not just flowers and plants that need the sun, dirt and water to grow. In my walk with the Lord, I continue to grow as well. We all have dirt and some yucky things that God has brought us through. Those situations that the enemy meant for evil, God not only turned them around for our good, but we have been blessed to grow from them as well.

The tears we shed release those things that should not be kept or pinned up inside of us. Releasing those tears to the Lord also aids in helping us grow. The physical sun can bring about wonderful changes and growth to the things we see on a daily basis. But the level of change that God's only begotten Son is able to bring to our lives is purely miraculous and cannot be compared to anything else.

As I cry, the Lord meets me where I am and I find comfort in knowing that He loves me so much that He has caught every tear.

Today's song of encouragement is, "As We Cry," by Lexi

Isaiah 40:28 (Modern English Version/MEV)

²⁸ Have you not known? Have you not heard, that the everlasting God, the Lord, the Creator of the ends of the earth, does not faint, nor is He weary? His understanding is inscrutable.

Back in the day, anytime I encountered an unfavorable situation or circumstance, I thought that I had to go before the Lord with a PowerPoint presentation and Microsoft Word document, fully detailing the events, individuals involved, my actions, my feelings and the outcome.

I needed the Lord to understand my point of view and where I was coming from. I wanted to plead my case and explain how I ended up where I did and the steps I intended to take, ensuring I didn't end up in a similar situation again.

The same held true, when I was in need of a breakthrough and for God to change my circumstances around. Once again, I felt I needed to present a thesis to Him, with my pages numbered, the appropriate headers and all my sources cited in Modern Language Association (MLA) format.

It wasn't until, awhile back, when I read the verse chosen for today that the first two questions, "Have you not known" and "Have you not heard," made me stop and think about what I was doing. I was offering up explanations when God was waiting on submission from me.

All those words were not required; what I needed to do was acknowledge that it is through the Lord that I am able to have victory IF, I surrender my all to Him, move myself out of the way and allow His will to be done and not my own.

The Lord didn't need all that information because He already knew it!! Before I was formed in my mother's womb, He knew me. He chose me, already knowing the decisions I would make and all the times I would fall. He possesses prior knowledge of everything before it ever comes to pass.

His understanding is inscrutable. It's incomprehensible and impossible to interpret.

He sees where I am and what I am in need of. Not only is He omniscient, He has omnipotent—possessing, unlimited power and has the ability to do anything.

Because I have come to realize that I don't have to explain or remind the Lord of my current circumstances, the quality of my conversations with the Lord has evolved and my relationship with Him has become that much stronger. Nowadays, I take the time needed to meditate on His Word and listen to the instruction that He provides.

Some of the locations I have arrived at may have been a surprise to me, but not ever, are they a surprise to the Lord. That is why I am taking my cue from the One who is not only the author and finisher of my faith, but also the One who has numbered every hair on my head and who has written all my days long before they ever have the chance to be.

Suggested Song of Meditation: "He Already Knows" by Earnest Pugh

Isaiah 26:4 (The Voice/VOICE)

⁴ So trust in the Eternal One forever, for He is like a great Rock—strong, stable, trustworthy, and lasting.

Seven years ago, when I left New York heading back down to Maryland, moving back to New York wasn't even a desire or wish that had entered my mind.

I was a single mom, with the two most amazing children and all I wanted was an opportunity to move forward; to be more and do more for my children. I just knew it would be just my children and me against the world and I was ready for that. Little did I know, the Lord had other plans in mind.

Those plans included me taking the much-needed time (that never seemed available in the past) for me to take some self-inventory and uncover what was holding me back from being all I needed to be for Him, my children and myself. Embarking on that journey was not an easy one at all because in getting to the core of who I am and the decisions I have made, it resulted in some truths coming to light, so many areas of brokenness being revealed and eventually some relationships reaching their expiration date.

Through the revelations and breakthroughs that the Lord provided me with, my heart was mended, which resulted in me meeting my husband and us getting married (a thought that I had given up entertaining years prior) and I was blessed to give birth to another amazing gift from the Lord.

When I think about all that the Lord has done in my life and all the places I could have ended up, He blocked it; with tears I rejoice and am filled with so much gratitude. I will trust in the Lord forever because I can't even imagine where I would be without Him.

He is like a great Rock--strong, stable, trustworthy and lasting.

Years of guilt, shame, disappointment and regret that kept me yoked with such a garment of heaviness, the Lord freed and released me from and **gave me grace to rise above.**

Without the Lord, I would have been inclined to believe that at the bottom was where I belonged, instead of recognizing and owning the spot at the top that He created specifically for me. I am able to walk with my head held high, looking up because I know where my help is located, instead of settling for a place in the back which is not where God ever intended me to be.

Suggested Song of Meditation: "Where Would I Be" by Smokie Norful

Psalm 36:5 (The Message/MSG)

⁵ God's love is meteoric, his loyalty astronomic.

Today as I was driving throughout various places in Long Island, all I could think about was the unfailing love from our Lord and Savior that we are recipients of. When my children and I boarded the subway train heading into the city to see my husband at work, I just sat in awe of the Lord's grace and mercy and how having a direct connection to the Lord has provided me with not just a front row seat to experiencing His marvelous works, but also VIP access to the protection and blessings that come from being a child of God.

The afflictions, trials and obstacles that are presented before me do not get to penetrate or cause the destruction the enemy has intended because God's glory surpasses anything that I could ever endure.

We couldn't ever begin to comprehend the love that the Lord has for us; nor could we ever do enough to deserve it, and yet God still shows us love and on a level that surpasses all knowledge.

Another one of my favorite verses regarding God's love for us is Ephesians 3:19 (which according to the Amplified Bible translation) states, "[That you may really come] to know [practically, through experience for yourselves] the love of Christ, which far surpasses mere knowledge [without experience]; that you may be filled [through all your being] unto all the fullness of God [may have the richest measure of the divine Presence, and become a body wholly filled and flooded with God Himself]!"

His love for us truly surpasses all knowledge and understanding. God's love goes deep and high enough to bring healing from the inside out. His love has gone deep and high enough to look past my faults and still meet my needs even when there was a chance that I could possibly make that mistake again.

God's love has been strong enough to hold me up those times when I was falling down. I used to think because of all that I gave away in the past, I had missed my chance with the Lord. But God has shown me that it is not too late for Him to use me because He hasn't and won't ever give up on me nor will He ever stop loving me.

Throughout the course of the day, I kept basking in God's steadfast love that is meteoric and His faithfulness that is astronomic. With a love like this, my troubles have no choice but to dwindle.

Oh, how He loves us. God's love for us is immeasurable and worth celebrating and rejoicing over constantly.

Suggested Song of Meditation: "He Loves Us" by Immeasurable

Ephesians 4:6 (Expanded Bible/EXB)

⁶ There is one God and Father of everything. ·He rules everything and is everywhere and is in everything [...who is over all and through all and in all].

As my children and I were driving around Long Island today, in search of possible homes, we were having a conversation regarding what we have observed since my husband and I have begun this entire process to acquire a home, back in January.

What I found myself explaining to my babies was that there still is an area that I struggle with, and that area pertains to me unknowingly placing expectations on people, even when I strive not to. I have lived long enough to know that expectations should only be placed on the Lord and no one else.

Through the years, I have learned that I only set myself up for failure and am left with such a sense of disappointment when I place expectations on man. I believe that the reason that I struggle is because in my mind, I'm not placing expectations. I am just requesting to have reciprocated to me, the common courtesy, honesty, respect and attention that I give to others.

During our car ride, my son asked a question that I have been voicing to my husband constantly and that question was, "Why does it seem like our need to buy a home isn't a priority to others, like it should be?" And I had to look at my oldest and tell him that everyone doesn't prioritize like we do, nor do they have the faith and belief in God that we do; therefore, we are not to be dependent on man.

It is God who is everything that we could ever need and who never disappoints. It is the Lord that we serve, who is more than able and has the power and capacity to meet each and every one of our needs. For us, our need is a new home. We continue to believe that the Lord is working behind the scenes on our behalf and is advocating in a way that man couldn't ever do. It will be in His perfect timing that we will have the house He has chosen specifically for us. I continued to explain that we must always do our part, because faith without works is dead!!

There are so many names that the Lord is called by, based on the need we have. Sometimes we may not have those names at the forefront of our minds or on the tip of our tongues, but I know a name we can always call on and that's the sweet, sweet name of Jesus.

Each day, I am reminded that everything I could ever possibly need, I already have because I am a child of God. There is nothing that I require or am waiting to acquire that is greater than or outside of the capabilities of my God. He is greater than it all, above all, through all and is more than we will ever know!!!

Suggested Song of Meditation: "More Than You'll Ever Know" by Byron Cage

Psalm 103:10 (International Standard Version/ISV)

¹⁰ He neither deals with us according to our sins, nor repays us equivalent to our iniquity.

Have you ever taken the time to really begin to breakdown what the Lord's love, mercy and grace has meant in your life? For me, it has meant although my life should have unfolded in a totally different manner, the Lord has never given me what I deserved. I am so far from being perfect and have made decisions and found myself in situations that left me with so much regret, shame and disappointment, and yet, the Lord didn't punish me for my sins and depravity as I deserved. Through His mercy, justice has been tempered with peace.

I am so grateful for the Lord's mercy, which has withheld punishment and results in me not getting what I do deserve and His grace, which is unmerited favor and results in me having more than I deserve.

When I think about the undesirable paths I ventured down or the inappropriate and toxic relationships I encountered and entertained and where I could have been, compared to where I am on this very day, all I can do is fall to my knees and weep with thankfulness for His mercy; rejoicing in the Lord and the greatest love I could ever know.

It's a love that has been patient with me, when instead of just surrendering it all to the Lord, I felt the need to try to figure things out on my own. A love that covers me, cleans me and makes me whole. A love that doesn't deal with me according to my sins nor repays me according to my iniquities.

I exalt His name and am filled with joy knowing that what I have received has occurred because of His grace. So much of what I have acquired, I was told I was crazy to even think I could achieve or obtain. On paper, it may have looked impossible, but because of the unmerited favor that I have received from our Heavenly Father, who is able to do all things, I have been given more than I could ever possibly deserve.

What reason could I ever have to complain, when I know for a fact, that I am so glad God has never given me what I deserved?

Suggested Song of Meditation: "Deserved" by Anthony Brown and group therAPy featuring Gaye Arbuckle

Isaiah 30:18 (The Voice/VOICE)

¹⁸ Meanwhile, the Eternal One yearns to give you grace and boundless compassion; that's why He waits. For the Eternal is a God of justice. Those inclined toward Him, waiting for His help, will find happiness.

I have always been a patient person, but I will tell you that in these past few months, my patience has been thoroughly tested and I have been bombarded with thoughts that under any other circumstance, wouldn't ever have had the opportunity to infiltrate my thought life.

My inquiries have ventured off in two different directions. Either I have questioned whether I'm doing too much and not totally released my situation to the Lord or I have begun to wonder if I'm not doing enough and I am being shown that faith without actions is ineffective and worthless.

Waiting is so difficult at times, especially when so much is dependent on everything coming together. But over the past couple of days, the Lord has reminded me that as I wait for Him to make sense of it all, I am not alone. I am a child of the Most High and He provides me with an unfailing love and promises that I can cling tight to.

Today I read a post from Joel Osteen that stated, "Instead of trying to change your situation, just relax, stay in peace and keep a smile on your face. God is not asking you to control everything. Take the pressure off. He's saying cast your cares, release the control. Do what you can and trust God to do what you can't."

The words, "Do what you can and trust God to do what you can't," have rung in my head all day. When I took the time to reflect on that, I was finally able to relax and stay in peace because I know that I have done all that I can do and now I must just wait on the Lord. Trust, Believe and Wait.

One of the things that is so wonderful and that I worship about the Lord is His graciousness. Today's verse prompted me to recognize that the Lord sincerely waits and longs to be gracious to us. He lifts Himself up so that He may have mercy on us and show loving-kindness to us. Because the Lord is a God of justice, those who incline toward Him and wait for His help, His victory, His favor, His love, His peace, His joy, and His matchless, unbroken companionship; will find happiness. Filled with hope, I anxiously wait for what lies ahead for me.

Suggested Song of Meditation: "The Waiting" by Jamie Grace

Psalm 31:19 (New English Translation/NET Bible)

¹⁹ How great is your favor, which you store up for your loyal followers! In plain sight of everyone you bestow it on those who take shelter in you.

If you don't know by now, I have been soaring on the wings of thankfulness and gratefulness. Prior to watching the Lord move in a mighty way in my situation, praising and trusting in the Lord in all that I do has been my utmost priority.

I know that there have been seasons in my life when I neglected praising the Lord the way that I should have. When I look back on those times, so much regret I felt for allowing myself to be consumed and caught up in people and circumstances that I permitted to take my attention away from what was most important—and that was seeking out the Lord and praising Him through every circumstance.

I will tell you that the same individuals and situations that I pushed God away for; thinking I would eventually have the time to devote to Him, in most instances, I don't even have a relationship or connection with those individuals any longer. Also, those particular temporal situations that I was consumed by could have been diverted a lot sooner, had I just praised the Lord first for His goodness and faithfulness and sought my shelter in Him, instead of others.

Being a people-pleaser never left much time for myself, but then again, wanting to please everyone came from a place of brokenness and the enemy exploited that weakness every chance he got. It wasn't until I called on the Lord and got to know Him and I mean really know Him, that I learned who I was and whose I was. In that time of spiritual growth and maturity, I realized that the Lord had been indescribably too good and too kind for me not to make time to praise Him first.

Before I used to make accomplishing my laundry list of responsibilities my top priority on a day-to-day basis and then if I wasn't worn out at the end of the day, then, I would devote some time to the Lord, thinking He'd understand if I didn't get around to it.

But, I had to be reminded that we serve a jealous God. How dare I put anyone or anything else before praising and giving ALL the glory and honor to His name? It is because of Him that I have the opportunity to be anything.

Without the Lord, we are and have nothing!! It all begins and ends with Him; therefore, each morning that we are fortunate and blessed to see, should begin by us praising Him; and we shouldn't stop there. Praise Him all throughout the day, because when night comes and we look back over the hours that have passed by, we will see evidence of God's unfailing love, grace and mercy surrounding us at every corner.

The Lord stores up His goodness and favor for those of us who are His loyal followers. Make sure to never be too busy to praise Him because words could never truly convey His goodness in our lives.

When we make that time for the Lord and we revere, fear and worship Him, He will bless us in a way that will position us to be witnesses for all the world to see. May we never be too busy to praise Him!!

Suggested Song of Meditation: "Never Too Busy" by Byron Cage

Ephesians 1:4 (Good News Translation/GNT)

> *⁴ Even before the world was made, God had already chosen us to be His through our union with Christ, so that we would be holy and without fault before Him. Because of His love.*

Recently, my family and I went on vacation to our family destination spot, Puerto Rico. One of the biggest drawbacks that I have about traveling anywhere, whether near or far, is that no matter how I try to take every precaution possible, I still end up exposed to the sun, in some way, shape, fashion or form and the skin condition that I have, polymorphous light eruption, always rears its' annoying and painfully visible little head.

Although I am not a superficial person, it's very difficult to look at what appears to be millions of little red bumps all over my sunburnt arms, legs and neck and not feel like some kind of extra-terrestrial.

Anytime I experience this condition, which presented itself for the first time in 2000, my mind immediately begins to recall so many different things from my past that I used to think contributed to this condition.

But during some quiet time in the pool this evening with my daughter, after shedding some tears, I looked up at the stars in the sky; reflecting on all that the Lord had chosen to create and decided to shift my way of thinking.

Being someone who has always loved taking part in every outdoor activity known to man, having this limitation due to an allergy to the sun has weighed on me significantly; especially being a mom who desires nothing more than to create endless memories and be a part of all that I can in my children's lives.

I may not ever understand why this has become part of my journey, but I know that our God makes no mistakes and I am so grateful that with all my imperfections, the Lord has seen and continues to see the good in imperfect me.

I haven't always made the best choices, nor have I always walked down the right paths. How blessed I am to be able to say that, even with all the mistakes that I have made, before the world was made, God had already chosen me to be His through my union with Christ, so that I would be holy and without fault before Him, because of His love.

I was reminded that each situation that I have and will endure has the ability to help someone else. As I think about the price that Jesus paid for my sin debt and the opportunity that I have to do work for my Heavenly Father's kingdom, I will not allow the enemy to make me feel less than.

I have come to believe that even this path that I walk with polymorphous light eruption will be a blessing. Lord willing, I look forward to sharing that testimony with each of you one day in the future.

Tonight, I was feeling kind of low and in no way viewing myself how the Lord sees me. But in a way that only He can, the Lord showed me that He hears me, is always thinking about me and watching everything that concerns me.

Because the Lord's way and His works are perfect, I will forever be thankful that He sees the good in imperfect me.

Suggested Song of Meditation: "Imperfect Me" by Smokie Norful

Jeremiah 32:27 (New American Bible (Revised Edition)/NABRE)

²⁷ I am the Lord, the God of all the living! Is anything too difficult for me?

Oh, how excellent is the Lord's name in all the earth. He sets His glory above the heavens and the earth. Given all that we know about the Lord and the supreme power He possesses, there isn't praise high enough that could express just how amazing and wonderful the Lord truly is.

In just speaking to individuals over the course of the past couple of weeks, I have discovered that many are in a holding pattern waiting for the promises of the Lord to come to pass and others are currently weathering a storm so unexpected that they are just trying make sense of it all and determine which way is the right way.

In both these scenarios, what I hope and pray each person is holding onto is the fact that we serve a God that is so mighty and so much greater than anything we could ever encounter. We serve a mighty God who will turn our situations around within a matter of mere seconds.

Anytime we are waiting, it's our posture during that time of anticipation that dictates and determines it all. It's interesting because as I was thinking about how mighty the Lord is, the very popular film series, "Mission Impossible" came to mind. And the reason that it did, is because when I think about the Lord and the verse from Jeremiah that was chosen for today, I am reminded that there isn't any mission, trial, set, hurdle, obstacle or diagnosis that is impossible for the Lord.

Rejoice and sing praises to the Lord because we know for certain that there isn't any possibility for victory over our Heavenly Father. If the Lord has declared and decreed that it shall come to pass, it will. Regardless of what it may look or feel like, no matter what others may say or think, we serve a God who defies the odds and is able to make the impossible, possible!

The Lord should receive our continuous glory, honor and praise. May we always adore the mighty God we serve.

Suggested Song of Meditation: "Lord You're Mighty" by Youthful Praise

Joshua 1:5 (Names of God Bible/NOG)

⁵ No one will be able to oppose you successfully as long as you live. I will be with you as I was with Moses. I will never neglect you or abandon you.

Today was such a day of reflection for me. As my family and I have finally begun to settle into our new home and our new area here in Long Island, I was reminded of the fact that the Lord has never let me down and that there isn't any way possible that He ever could.

As I look back over where I have been and where I am now, there isn't one instance or moment where God's presence and guidance cannot be observed. God has never failed me and has kept me through every twist and turn and up and down that I have faced. I put all my trust in the Lord and my confidence rests in Him.

There are many things I have yet to learn in life, but what I have learned thus far, is that no matter what I am enduring the Lord is always with me and will make a way. I don't have to know how nor do I have to know when; because the Lord has promised to never abandon me and to be by my side just as He was with Moses.

For so long, New York City and its surrounding areas represented all those whom I had depended upon throughout the course of my life who had let me down. And yet, in only a way that the Lord could do, my spiritual sight was brought into focus and made more keen and I was able to see who has been there for me all along.

I no longer rely or put my trust in man to bring me through or to make a way for me. I know it is the Lord that I am to seek out and wait on. It's so much easier to endure trials and tribulations when I know that the One that I am depending on will always be there for me and won't ever let me down.

Suggested Song of Meditation: "And You Never Will" by Anthony Brown and group therAPy featuring Maurette Brown Clark

Matthew 10:31 (The Voice/VOICE)

³¹ You, beloved, are worth so much more than a whole flock of sparrows. So do not fear.

I believe that one of the absolute best things about New York City is the multitude and diversity of the individuals that reside in and around the metropolitan area. When I was younger, I was fascinated by all the different faces and the various languages that I would hear being spoken. It never got old and it was such a memorable experience.

As I got older, I began to question what set me apart from others and wondered if I was just a face in the crowd. The reason I was burdened with this question was because, growing up, there were so many conflicting familial dynamics that I was just struggling to find myself and make it through; most of the time I felt invisible, irrelevant and very insignificant.

That was until right before I enlisted in the Air Force. I worked at a video store and prior to that, I wasn't much of a TV watcher. I loved music, so it was all about LPs, cassette tapes and then CDs for me. In the video store, we were able to show on the TV monitors, movies that were for rent and for sale as long as the movie rating wasn't higher than PG. As I was cleaning the shelves one day, I came across the movie, "Sister Act 2: Back in the Habit" and decided to cue it up to play. I already was a fan of Lauryn Hill and so when I saw her in the movie, I became more interested in the story line.

I remember it like it was yesterday. I was restocking and reorganizing the candy shelves when I heard Lauryn Hill and Tanya Blount sing the following words," Why should I feel discouraged? Why should the shadows come? Why should my heart be lonely? And long for heaven and home? When Jesus is my portion, A constant friend is He, His eye is on the sparrow, And I know He watches over me. I sing because I'm happy, I sing because I'm free, His eye is on the sparrow, And I know, He watches over me."

It was like I was in a trance, just mesmerized by the melody and the words of the song. It caused me to research what it meant for the Lord's eye to be on the sparrow, in comparison to our value in His eyes. And during that period of time, I grew to understand that, no matter how man may desire to view or treat me, I am cherished and treasured in the Lord's eyes. He sees and knows everything about me.

Our God sees it all. We are His and He calls us by name. We are not just a number or a face in the crowd. To the contrary, the Lord is so concerned with each of us that every hair on our head is numbered. He knew us before we were ever formed in our mother's womb and is in touch with us down to the very smile or frown that crosses our faces.

There were sparrows outside chirping on my porch when I left to go to the grocery store this afternoon. Every time I catch a glimpse of some sparrows, I just smile, hum and rejoice because I know the Lord sees me.

With the enlightenment that came to me via the song, "His Eye Is On The Sparrow" over two decades ago and with the verse and song that was chosen today, I am left with such a sense of protection and assurance knowing that if God takes care of all the sparrows that inhabit this earth and is concerned about their lives; how could I ever question or be concerned about the care and thought that He has for my life and for me?

Suggested Song of Meditation: "I See You" by Forever Jones

Romans 5:5 (Amplified Bible, Classic Edition/AMPC)

⁵ Such hope never disappoints or deludes or shames us, for God's love has been poured out in our hearts through the Holy Spirit Who has been given to us.

Like many, when I was much younger in age and made the decision to surrender and to turn my life over to Christ, one huge misconception I had was that in becoming saved, that meant that things would become so much easier because the trials and obstacles would decrease and the pain and disappointment I was experiencing would disappear because the hard days were all behind me.

Now we know neither of those thoughts were accurate, but it took accepting Jesus as my Lord and Savior for my eyes to be opened and for my ways of thinking and patterns of behavior to be altered. Being saved doesn't mean that there won't still be hard days. As a matter of fact, I have seen my hardest days and tests since making the decision to follow Jesus. But like the song says, "I have decided to follow Jesus, no turning back, no turning back."

Earlier today, I read an inspirational quote from Chrystal Evans Hurst that said, "Some days are just hard, but there is hope in tomorrow." When I read that, I thought about the song that I have chosen for today because it has been one that I have sang numerous times at church.

Yes, each one of us will experience some hard days, but when Jesus is our everything, He becomes our hope for tomorrow. What is so wonderful about the hope that we have is that it doesn't lead to disappointment nor does it delude or shame us because God's love has been poured out in our hearts through the Holy Spirit who has been given to us.

We are reminded to rejoice in hope, be patient in tribulation and constant in prayer (Romans 12:12). With each test, trial, hurdle and obstacle that we face, we can be confident and rest in the hope and peace we have knowing that there are so many roles that Jesus accepts on our behalf. Some of the titles include: Father, Protector, Master, Savior, Ruler, Redeemer, Provider, Shelter, Healer, Way Maker and Deliverer.

Hard days just don't seem as hard when you know that the One who knows all, sees all, created all and is everywhere at the same time, is right with you all along the way. He's everything to me.

Suggested Song of Meditation: "Everything" by Tye Tribbett

Hebrews 10:14 (Amplified Bible/AMP)

¹⁴ For by the one offering He has perfected forever and completely cleansed those who are being sanctified [bringing each believer to spiritual completion and maturity].

There are some self-truths that I had to acknowledge about myself awhile back before I could ever begin to understand who I was and why I processed and responded to situations in the manner that I do. I am a very giving and loyal person who looks for opportunities to help others. Having a humongous heart, I have always been a people-pleaser.

Now, what I also know about myself is that I am very honest. I am brutally and painfully honest to a fault, and that's not just with everyone else, but with myself first and foremost. I know I am a very (and I mean very) black-or-white type of person; I don't operate "in the gray" well at all. I am quick to speak when an action or attitude is wrong.

I have recognized that the firm stance that I have taken on what's right and what's wrong has affected relationships that I have had but my intentions were never to be judgmental. My hope has always been that by addressing situations and acknowledging the truths, it would open up the chance for encounters with God to occur so that He could move in the midst of the situations for all parties involved.

I will be the first to tell you that I am far from perfect. I have had more than my share of wrong-doings and falling short and the Lord still chose to love me in spite of all I have gone through. I know what it's like to be so lost that you can't even see the nose that is attached to the front of your face. I've had some extremely hard and difficult times and if I could prevent some of those days from occurring for someone else, I would gladly do all I could.

Although I know what the struggle is like, I also know that because of the sacrifice that Christ accomplished for us, we have been completely cleansed and set apart for God forever. In Jesus giving His life for me, I recognize that I'm not perfect but that I'm perfect with Him. I am in the potter's hands and each day He continues to mold me into who I am supposed to be.

When I look at my life, I am reminded of how God has and continues to answer prayers that I had completely forgotten I had prayed. The Lord held onto all the aspirations that I had let go of. In those instances, when I missed the mark, it didn't ever stop the Lord from meeting my needs. And where others departed, the Lord has never abandoned me.

With the Lord as my guide, I realize that in keeping it 100% with myself, I am brought that much closer to the spiritual completion and maturity needed to accomplish all that the Lord has placed before me.

With the Lord watching over me, I have come to believe in who He sees when He looks at me.

Suggested Song of Meditation: "Perfect" by Brian Courtney Wilson

Isaiah 59:1 (New American Standard Bible/NASB)

⁵⁹ Behold, the Lord's hand is not so short that it cannot save; nor is His ear so dull that it cannot hear.

I have a question. How many of us have been guilty of putting God in a box by placing limitations on what we believe He can do in our lives? I believe that at some point, we all have done that in some way, shape, fashion or form.

Because of the fear and doubt that we allow to rise up within us, we can't see the limitless power and the endless possibilities that are associated with the one and only sovereign God that we serve.

Until we learn to surrender and give ourselves completely to the Lord, we are the ones who become the barriers and road blocks to witnessing just how far God's reach truly is.

Before making the decision to surrender my life and every aspect of it to the Lord, not having all the answers to what lay ahead for me resulted in me being worried, constantly second-guessing everything and some decisions being made in haste because a victim mentality was what ruled my decision-making process.

But when I began to understand what it meant to surrender to the Lord and the importance that surrendering played in my relationship with Christ and my spiritual walk, my entire mindset changed. My thoughts and actions were no longer attached to a victim mindset, but to one of a victor.

I could no longer be part of the problem; I needed to be part of the solution. Being part of the solution meant recognizing that when I operated from a victim mindset, I wasn't allowing God to move in and throughout my situations the way He desired to; the way I needed Him to.

In order for me to see what God could do in my life, things had to change. Primarily, I had to change. Since changing my mindset and point of view, my life hasn't been the same. I have been set free and my vision is so much clearer than it previously was; because my spiritual senses, as a whole, have been sharpened and enhanced. Trials, obstacles and all that is unknown to me don't get to take me to a place where my initial response is to hit the panic button.

I have seen and I know that the Lord's hand is not so short that it cannot save me; nor is His ear so dull that it cannot hear me. That is a truth that I cling to in my times of need. No matter what it is that I may encounter, I know that nothing is greater than God and that there isn't any limit to the power He possesses.

I am so grateful for His illimitable power that is at work in my life and that is why putting God in a box is no longer an option. Knowing that nothing is impossible with Him, I desire to see all that God can do.

Suggested Song of Meditation: "See What God Can Do" by George Huff

Matthew 11:29 (Revised Standard Version Catholic Edition/RSVCE)

²⁹ Take my yoke upon you, and learn from me; for I am gentle and lowly in heart, and you will find rest for your souls.

I constantly stand amazed at just how God works. When I think I know how things are going to pan out or be resolved, the Lord steps in and makes a way via an outlet you didn't even believe was an option.

Not only am I so glad that trouble doesn't last always, I am even more thankful that we have a friend in Jesus that is unlike any other. He is a friend that is gentle and lowly in heart. That means that pride does not reside in Him and that Jesus is always there concerned about any and everything that concerns us.

We could search all over and would never find anyone else like Him. Jesus knows about every last one of our struggles and has promised to guide us until the very end. When you know that Jesus is with you and walking alongside you, you are given the power and strength to progress on past the tests and trials that you face. Instead of allowing yourself to get stuck where you are, call on the name of Jesus, knowing that there is not one hour of the day, nor a night so dark that He is not near us.

In Jesus we have a friend so high and holy and yet so meek and lowly at the same time. If we just trust and believe in Him, what has kept us bound for so long, we shall obtain freedom from and find the peace that we have been longing for.

Through various seasons of my life, I put expectations on others to be, what I now know, only Jesus could be in my life. And when I look back and think about all those times when I thought I was all by myself, I can recall all the ways that His presence was right there, keeping me and guiding me all along the way.

There's not a friend like the lowly Jesus…No not one…No not one!!

Suggested Song of Meditation: "There's Not a Friend" by Minister Thomas A. Whitfield

2 Timothy 4:22 (New Life Version/NLV)

²² May the Lord Jesus Christ be with your spirit. May you have God's loving-favor.

Over the past couple of days, my children and I have been having conversations about the state of the country that we live in and life in general. We have witnessed so much negativity, ignorance and disheartening events happening all around us. And through it all, what I have been most thankful for, is the grace of God that continues to keep us.

I will never understand why some people do or say the things that they do. And honestly, it's not my job to make sense of it all (although I used to think it was). What I'm supposed to do is trust in the Lord with all my heart and lean not unto my own understanding. It took a while to get that hammered into this cranium of mine, especially when I was the one being affected by the actions and words of others.

But, in the midst of chaos, confusion and strife, I have found that I can still have peace because I have encountered more damaging and unsatisfactory circumstances in my past; and I know that the same loving-favor that shielded and sheltered me then, has no limits and is here to cover me now.

Yesterday, my daughter gave us the fundraiser packet that her school is hosting. One of the items that caught my attention was a votive candle holder that had two glass walls, one in front of the votive and one behind it and the walls had an image in the shape of a footprint, with the famous "Footprints in the Sand" poem inscribed on them.

The "Footprints in the Sand" poem is one of my favorites. It is also one of the first poems I ever remember reading when I was very little and it has stuck with me ever since. That poem illustrates God's grace, mercy and unfailing love for us perfectly.

I know that the reason I am still here today is because of the grace of God. Not only have I never walked alone, but as the "Footprints in the Sand" poem reminded me yesterday, "God loves me and would never leave me. And during those times of trial and suffering, when I saw only one set of footprints, it was then that He loved me enough to carry me."

Because Jesus reigns, there is an expiration date on every obstacle that we will face. And with assurance we can proclaim, that by the grace of the Lord, we will get through it.

Suggested Song of Meditation: "Grace of God" by Sheri Jones-Moffett

Matthew 19:26 (Disciples' Literal New Testament/DLNT)

²⁶ And having looked at them, Jesus said to them, "With humans, this is impossible. But with God, all things are possible".

Each morning when you rise, do you wake up saying, "I can" and welcoming all the possibilities that are ahead of you? Or do you wallow in your current circumstances and allow limitations and short-comings to overwhelm you and distract you from the purpose that the Lord handpicked and selected you for?

"Can't" is a word that I wasn't allowed to utilize growing up and a rule that I have passed down to my children. When I was younger, I wasn't allowed to speak any limitations over myself or my future aspirations. Those sentiments weren't just emphasized at home and at church, but also at school, at dance and track practice.

If I thought to tell my dance instructors what I believed I couldn't do, they would make sure that after doing one pirouette after another, or performing a tap combo repeatedly, that I didn't think to utter those words again.

Track practice was even worse. If my coach was instructing me to push myself harder so that I could shave seconds off my time and I said I couldn't, that meant laps around the track. If you don't know, I was a sprinter, so doing additional laps were not my forte'. Looking back, in each instance, I realize that none of my instructors were asking me to do anything that they didn't believe I couldn't do. I had to learn to trust and believe in myself.

I know the power that words possess and that is why I choose each day to focus on what I can do through the Lord who strengthens me. It is His Spirit that lives within me and that is the source of my encouragement and empowerment. If everything that needed to be accomplished in my life was dependent on me, I would be absolutely nowhere. But because with God all things are possible, there isn't any impediment that I can't overcome, any giant that I can't conquer, nor any mountain that is too high for me to climb.

I may not know all the details or plans but what I do know is that the Lord's ways are perfect and that He knows the thoughts and plans that He has for me. I can do anything, when I elevate my mind and allow my faith in the Lord to navigate my course. Knowing that we serve a limitless God; why would I even dare to welcome limitations, when the possibilities are endless for those who believe?

Suggested Song of Meditation: "I Can Do Anything, by Antwaun Stanley

Revelation 3:16 (J.B. Phillips New Testament/PHILLIPS)

¹⁶ "I know what you have done, and that you are neither cold nor hot. I could wish that you were either cold or hot! but since you are lukewarm and neither hot nor cold, I intend to spit you out of my mouth!"

When the time comes for me to begin working on my daily blog post, the process that I normally go through entails a song ministering to me first; which then results in me searching for a verse that coincides with the lyrics of the song and then whatever thoughts that are stirred up in my spirit, I share.

Sometimes, like today, I won't hear a song first, but will be led to a specific artist and then I wait to see which song speaks to my soul.

The song for today spoke to an internal battle I have had to confront more than once, until I read the verse that was chosen above.

Although I love the verses about God's love, grace, mercy and favor that make me feel all warm and fuzzy inside, I know that in order to grow and mature in my spiritual walk, I also need those verses that speak to what happens if I don't follow and obey our Heavenly Father's commandments.

As a parent, even though I constantly communicate the unconditional love, support and encouragement that I have for my children, it's also very important that they understand and apply the morals and values that we must live by and recognize the consequences of what could happen if those principles are not adhered to.

Because of life experiences, I grew up a very black or white/hot or cold type of person. That was very difficult because I felt like I was just trying to survive in a world illustrated in nothing but gray and flowing in nothing but lukewarm water. I thought something was wrong with me, so I tried to fight what I was made to believe was a huge character flaw.

I encountered some of the hardest seasons of my life stuck in those gray and lukewarm places. That was until I read and researched the above verse and began to apply those words to my everyday life.

In my study Bible, it states that hot water was used for medical purposes and cold water was refreshing. There is a purpose for one or the other. Lukewarm water on the other hand was neither; it's like staying on the fence, trying to have your cake and eat it too. Basically, this meant that the Lord refuses the tepid and half-hearted efforts of self-satisfying Christians.

What I once perceived as a flaw was actually a God-given strength. I embrace and celebrate my black or white and hot or cold characteristics. I realize that growing up, I tried my best to do what was right and follow my parent's rules. Therefore, as I continued to grow, I recognized that my Heavenly Father deserved to know and see that my life would proceed with me serving only one Master and following His commands without any uncertainty.

Neither shades of gray nor lukewarm tendencies are allowed, especially when rejection from the Lord is what we will encounter if they are present.

Suggested Song of Meditation: "No Gray" by Jonathan McReynolds

Malachi 4:2 (Easy-to-Read Version/ERV)

> *² "But, for my followers, goodness will shine on you like the rising sun. And it will bring healing power like the sun's rays. You will be free and happy, like calves freed from their stalls.*

Our greatest triumphs will be birthed from our greatest trials. Because I fear and honor the name of the Lord, His goodness shines upon me like the rising sun; bringing healing power like the sun's rays. Like calves freed from their stalls, I am free and happy, as I step into the joy of the Lord.

This is the freedom that I have been waiting for. I encountered those feelings of healing and freedom this weekend and I wasn't even expecting it.

This past weekend, my son took his first bus ride by himself. We have always traveled together as a family and even when he was chosen for educational opportunities or to participate in another state for his Air Force Junior Reserve Officer Training Corps (AFJROTC) drill team, he was always with other individuals that he knew.

It wasn't until I parked the car so that we could walk my son down into the Port Authority (the New York City (NYC) bus station) that I had such a surreal, yet amazing moment. You see, for those of you who don't know, the Port Authority is the main bus hub in NYC. Bus lines like Greyhound, Peter Pan, Adirondack Trailways, etc., arrive and depart from there.

The Port Authority used to be my only direct connect for transportation in and out of the city when I was younger because my father worked for Greyhound Bus Line. So, seeing the "grey dog", as we called it, meant everything to me.

But then life happened, decisions were made and separations occurred and I no longer desired to travel via Greyhound because it was too painful. Once I began driving and owned my own vehicle, anytime I came across a Greyhound bus, whether in the city or on the highway, it never failed, tears would just come streaming down.

The pain that was tied to my father penetrated so deeply that only my Heavenly Father could meet me at the source of that pain and provide a healing power so profound that decades later when my own firstborn, who is as tall as my father and who carries the same strong, striking and undeniable features of his like I do, was having his moment, all I could do was rejoice and praise the name of the Lord.

A place that was once synonymous with painful memories, I now viewed through a brand new set of eyes and with a whole new perspective.

In that moment, I was free to celebrate and enjoy a milestone that my son was experiencing. As I looked at him standing in line, waiting to be given permission to board the bus, my eyes did water but there wasn't any sadness or regret tied to those tears.

I looked around and saw the same scheduled trips posted on the same walls, with the same newsstands and vending machines that I could recall from over 30 years ago and at that moment I realized that although a lot had remained the same, there had been one major modification and that was within me, because of the Spirit of the Lord that resides inside of me.

And we know, "The Lord is the Spirit. Where the Spirit of the Lord is, there is emancipation from bondage and we become unquestionably free. (2 Corinthians 3:17)."

Even though I have attempted to capture that moment in this post, words truly cannot convey the triumph that has occurred. It's greater than I could have ever imagined.

The freedom that I am now walking (and sometimes running) in produces an indescribable joy that I know I can only associate with the Lord.

This is the freedom that I have been waiting for. Freedom to reconnect, rediscover and fall in love with my birthplace all over again. Freedom to no longer be bound by what has happened, what didn't happen and what I wished had happened; and a freedom to share all of those moments with those who mean the most to me.

Suggested Song of Meditation: "This Is the Freedom" by Tasha Cobbs

Acts 20:24 (New Living Translation/NLT)

²⁴ But my life is worth nothing to me unless I use it for finishing the work assigned me by the Lord Jesus—the work of telling others the Good News about the wonderful grace of God.

One of the greatest Christian hymns that was ever written (over 200 years ago), is "Amazing Grace."

I have heard it sung in many variations, but regardless of the version I have heard or have sung myself, the first couple of lines of that song have always spoken in volumes to me.

"Amazing Grace, how sweet the sound, that saved a wretch like me. I once was lost, but now I'm found; was blind but now I see."

I was raised that I couldn't use or sing a word if I didn't know the meaning of it, therefore, I had to look up the definition of the word "wretch" because when I was younger, I thought the song said, "that saved a **wreck** like me." And that was what I sang, until I came across the official lyrics to the song and realized that although a wreck wasn't far off, a wretch meant an unfortunate, unhappy and sometimes despicable or contemptible person.

Where would we be, if not for the Lord's grace?

I know what it is like to lose your way, but through every season, it has been God's grace that has rescued, freed and gotten me back on course and living my life the only way I should; and that is according to His purpose and testifying to the good news of God's grace.

Through this ministry that I have received from the Lord Jesus, I am able to faithfully attest to His grace.

It's a grace that restores, redeems and releases us to worship and praise His name. God's amazing grace repairs dreams and visions; and releases miracles to happen in our lives.

Where I once felt so unfortunate and unhappy, God's grace reminded me that I was blessed and highly favored. And even though my eyes have always been open, they were more on an "eyes wide shut" status. But I am so grateful for the clarity and insight that I have received because of the Lord.

God's grace has carried me and shown me what the purpose of my life is; and my goal is to complete the task that the Lord has given to me.

Suggested Song of Meditation: "If Not for Your Grace" by Israel and New Breed

Psalm 86:5 (New Revised Standard Version/NRSV)

⁵ For you, O Lord, are good and forgiving, abounding in steadfast love to all who call on you.

The Lord is so good and merciful. When we fall, He forgives us and doesn't keep record of our wrong-doings. I rejoice and am so grateful that He never goes back and makes us wear a garment of shame displaying all that we have gone through and done.

Even when I have made my journey harder by holding onto things from my past, which resulted in me feeling unworthy and not being able to forgive myself for my decisions, God's steadfast love showed me what love, goodness and forgiveness truly is.

God's love, faithfulness, goodness and forgiveness has become the template for how I desire to live my life and walk out the destiny that is before me.

My past sins and situations are no longer allowed to rob me of the joy and peace that I have received from the Lord. When I think about the fact that before I was ever born, each day of my life was already written and the Lord knew each decision I would make, each situation I would face, the date and time I would stumble or fall and He still chose me to love, redeem, protect, forgive, to be on the receiving end of His overflowing grace and mercy and to continue to bless abundantly; words truly cannot begin to convey my gratitude.

But each morning that I rise, I will rejoice and express the love that I have for the Lord, for being the best and loving me the way that He does.

Suggested Song of Meditation: "Reason" by Antwaun Stanley

Proverbs 19:23 (New English Translation/NET Bible)

²³ Fearing the Lord leads to life, and one who does so will live satisfied; he will not be afflicted by calamity.

On this day, I honor and salute all my fellow veterans who answered the call, signed on the dotted line, and enlisted to protect and serve our country.

I still can't believe that was a decision that I made over 20 years ago. I will tell you that my reasons for enlisting came during a period in my life when I needed an escape to find myself and my place in the world.

When I think about how circuitous my journey was while on active duty in the United States Air Force, I remain forever grateful for the steadfast and boundless love, protection, grace and mercy I received from the Lord.

When you take the oath to serve and protect your country, that is a promise that you can't view lightly or go back on. It got REAL really quick. I will tell you that I was afraid and had so many concerns and questions but regardless of the anxiety I felt, what resonated deeper within me was that I had made the right decision and because of all the variables I didn't know, I had to put my trust in the Lord in a way I never had before.

With all the Veterans Day posts I have seen throughout today, I read a phrase pertaining to veterans that stated, "I am a Veteran, and a Veteran is someone, who at one point in their life, wrote a blank check payable to the United States of America for an amount up to, and including, their life." That one sentence spoke a mouthful and every word of it was accurate. I enlisted not knowing what each day would bring.

It was through my enlistment that my relationship with the Lord evolved and became something so secure and powerful, that I knew that as long as Jesus was the fence that was around me every day, all I would need to do is keep still and He would fight my battles.

I was dedicated to protecting and serving my country. But the hardest battles that I ever had to fight came while I was enlisted. They didn't take place on foreign land, but right here, close to home, in the country I was born and raised in. Some of those attacks knocked the wind right out of me, but the Lord continued to be my refuge and guided my footsteps.

I no longer feared man or the potential decisions that could be made to affect my life. I feared the Lord and made Him the focus. He was my light in the midst of so much darkness and the end result became contentment and thankfulness for what I had to endure to make me better and for everything He protected me from, which was intended to destroy me.

Making the decision to serve my country was the best decision I could have ever made. It brought me to a place where it was just the Lord and me. In recognizing the importance of serving the Lord first and then those around me, I was able to accept and navigate through the uncharted path that was ahead of me.

I entered the military with "protecting and serving" representing one thing to me. As I matured and faced what life had for me as an active duty service member, those two words took on a whole new meaning because I had the assurance that the Lord was protecting me along the way.

Suggested Song of Meditation: "Jesus Be a Fence" by Fred Hammond and RFC

John 10:14 (Amplified Bible/AMP)

14 I am the Good Shepherd, and I know [without any doubt those who are] My own and My own know Me [and have a deep, personal relationship with Me]—

One of the great things about bonds that we have with certain individuals is that you are connected in such a way that you don't have to go into great detail with them because they already know where you are coming from and sometimes what you are about to say before you even part your lips to speak.

When I think about the Lord and who He is to me, I couldn't ever transcribe all the reasons that I am grateful for the love that I receive from Him. I know that the Lord knows me in a way no one else does. I don't have to explain my thought process or why I am woven the way that I am to Him. He knows those things that are kept deep within and provides me with a boundless love that provides healing and breaks the chains so I can move forward.

I am a part of His flock and being the Good (more like Best) Shepherd that He is, the Lord cares for me and is concerned about everything that concerns me. Because being who God has called me to be is my top priority, having a deep and personal relationship with Him is imperative.

Just because the Lord knows everything, which includes where I may stumble and fall short, doesn't mean that I desire to do those things. To think that any of my actions could bring pain and hurt to the Lord is very disheartening. And although none of us is perfect, I recognize that by having that divine connection to the Lord, I am able to know the Lord in ways I couldn't in the past, which, in turn, results in a new perspective and way of handling situations.

There was a time when I was that sheep that had gone astray. And even though some of my decisions were not pleasing in the Lord's sight, He cared enough to patiently wait for me to come back and repent. In knowing the Lord and how He views me, I am empowered and encouraged as I follow the path that the Lord leads me along.

How blessed I am to serve a God who knows and is concerned about me and who allows me the opportunity to develop a deep and personal relationship with Him.

Suggested Song of Meditation: "You Know Me" by George Huff

Acts 17:28 (J.B. Phillips New Testament/PHILLIPS)

^{28} Indeed, it is in him that we live and move and have our being. Some of your own poets have endorsed this in the words, 'For we are indeed his children.'

There has been one question that both of my oldest children have asked me, at two totally different times in my life. What they inquired was, "If you could change one thing about your life, what would it be?"

In both instances, it took me less than half a second to begin my reply, but I also knew why I was being asked the question. My two oldest children and I have weathered some pretty tough storms. They never heard me complain because I needed them to know that regardless of what our current situation was reflecting, I was still trusting and believing in the Lord to turn it around. I also knew that no matter how rough it was, it could always be worse and I didn't ever want them carrying the weight of my heavy burdens.

Having once been a child and young adult who carried the weight of those around her, I knew that no matter how hard I tried to keep my children from being impacted by the blows that were coming my way, there was indeed some exposure noted once all the smoke settled.

If I could change one thing about my life, what would it be?

Absolutely nothing. To change one thing about my life would change who I have grown to be, the husband and children I have been blessed to have and the life lessons I have come to acquire.

I thank God for the life that I have. I believe, if anything about my life needed to be changed, then the Lord would have written my days differently to reflect those changes long before I ever entered this world; and my life would have just been that.

Today, I had a much-needed conversation with a very near and dear sister in Christ. In talking to her, I had an epiphany and truly began to realize just how far I have come, recognizing every victory in Jesus Christ that I have seen.

Moments and situations where the enemy wanted me to believe that I had no other option but to fail and remain shackled; Jesus reminded me of His nails and the price that He paid on Calvary so that I could have life and have it more abundantly.

Through all the ups and the downs, the times when I didn't know how I was going to make it and when I felt on the verge of losing my mind; I know, without a doubt, that it was the Lord who kept me.

I am grateful to the Lord for my life and every aspect of it. The tests and trials have and will continue to come to make me stronger.

I count each and every last thing I have and will endure, a joy; because as a child of God, I know that all things will work together for my good. No regrets, just rejoicing and thanking God, who always leads me in victory because of Christ.

Suggested Song of Meditation: "Dear God" by Smokie Norful

1 Corinthians 8:6 (Contemporary English Version/CEV)

⁶ We have only one God, and he is the Father. He created everything, and we live for him. Jesus Christ is our only Lord. Everything was made by him and by him life was given to us.

Each day, I am reminded that I could search all over and never find anyone like the Lord. With all that I am, I praise and magnify the name of our inimitable Savior. The Lord is the One true and wise God who sits on the throne. I don't have to question His greatness, or search far to see His power working in my life and all around me. He deserves all the glory because of the steadfast love and faithfulness He shows us. All things come from Him and we belong to Him.

It's because of Jesus that we are able to be born again; no longer slaves to sin. God alone is mighty and righteous. No one can love, heal or save like the Lord is capable of doing. I give all the praise and honor to Elohim, which means, "God—Creator, Mighty and Strong," because He is worthy of everything that I have.

God's everlasting love, mercy and grace is why I have peace and joy while in the midst of so much that is unknown. Through Our Eternal King, the truth is always present and available to us. I have come to learn that as long as I have King Jesus, I have everything I could ever possibly need.

Because He is God and God alone, He is able to do wondrous and amazing things (Psalm 86:10). I have seen some of those marvelous works come to fruition and I know that the same great God who has performed those wondrous deeds before, shall do it again.

My faith, trust, hope, confidence—my everything, is in the Lord. His knowledge is all encompassing and His wisdom and understanding are beyond measure. I raise my hands and lift my voice to worship our true God, in spirit and in truth.

Suggested Song of Meditation: "You Alone" by Arkansas Gospel Mass Choir

Psalm 34:19 (The Voice/VOICE)

¹⁹ Hard times may well be the plight of the righteous—they may often seem overwhelming—but the Eternal rescues the righteous from what oppresses them.

Lately, I have begun to wonder if it's even possible to turn on the news or access the Internet without being completely overwhelmed and disheartened by the calamity that continues to plague everyone, regardless of where you physically reside or are located.

My thoughts and prayers go out to everyone who has been impacted by the various attacks that have occurred around the world over the past couple of weeks.

Being a mother to three remarkable children who are a part of our future, I have to be honest and tell you that I am truly saddened by everything that is happening in the world today. It leaves me to wonder what the world will be like when each of my babies desire to step out and accomplish the aspirations that they have for themselves.

Immediately, I have to reel myself in, because stressing over "coulda, shoulda, woulda's" and "what ifs" never helped anyone.

In times such as the ones we are facing, I go to the One who has all the answers and who promises to be our refuge in times of trouble. There is so much that doesn't make sense to me; but I've learned that it doesn't have to add up to me, because my days of leaning unto my own understanding are long gone.

I've also learned that when we are striving to live our lives according to God's will, we have to know that afflictions and hard times will come, but I rejoice and thank the Lord for all that He does for us. We are rescued from our adversities and brought safely through.

I may not know what to expect from one day to another, but I know who to depend on and seek out each and every day. I exalt the name of the Lord and thank Him for His love, power and protection in my life.

None of us is a psychic and it doesn't take being a rocket scientist to know that we need the Lord now more than ever. On this and every other day, I am so thankful that through His power, the Lord keeps protecting us.

Suggested Song of Meditation: "Thank you Lord" by Amber Bullock

2 Samuel 22:2 (Easy-to-Read Version/ERV)

² The Lord is my Rock, my fortress, my place of safety.

One of the things that the Lord instructs us to do is to, "forget the former things and do not dwell on the past (Isaiah 43:18)." I thought I had really grasped the concept on how to do that until recently.

There have been only a few areas in my life that have left me baffled; not being able to make sense of how the sequence of events led to the outcome that ended up becoming my reality.

In these particular areas, I was left wondering if there was more that I could have done to help change the reality I was now facing. I was bombarded with so many unanswered questions that I had no choice but to seek out the Lord for insight.

Because our God is omniscient and sees all, I seek out El Roi (God who sees) to be that solid rock, fortress and deliverer that He has been for me over and over again, throughout my life.

I recognize the importance of forgetting the former things, as we do not want to again be bound by circumstances or situations that the Lord has already delivered us from. One of the hardest aspects of forgetting the former things for me is when it comes to certain relationships.

I'm not one to hold a grudge, but honestly, when I had been severely hurt by another, I, in turn, do not desire to place myself in a position where I could be hurt again. At the same time, I don't close the door when it comes to the possibility of reconciliation. But because of the history, it is the Lord that I cling to, because He is the rock that I trust and lean on.

The Lord is always there to comfort me. Having Him to lean on, provides me with the discernment required to prevent hindrances like unforgiveness or a hardened heart from seeping in.

I am in a new season of my life, where unexpected things are beginning to happen. Some are things that I have prayed for, for what has seemed like a lifetime. As I wait to see where the roads will lead, I am grateful for a Heavenly Father who is a mighty rock that I can lean on; One who protects and continuously keeps me safe.

Suggested Song of Meditation: "Solid Rock" by Tasha Cobbs featuring Jamie Grace

Psalm 33:18 (New International Version/NIV)

¹⁸ But the eyes of the Lord are on those who fear him, on those whose hope is in his unfailing love

Who is like the Lord and who is capable of loving us like the Lord? Absolutely nobody!!

I continue to be further educated on the unfailing love that the Lord has for me. When I see where I am today, when so many of the decisions and mistakes that I made in the past should have removed me from this earth, I am fully aware that it is because of God's grace and His eyes being upon me, that I am still here.

I have not, nor will I always do, everything right but I do fear the Lord and place all my hope and trust in His mercy and loving-kindness. I have come to learn that God's eye is on those who worship Him with an awe-inspired reverence and obedience.

Every time I think back on everything I have been through, prayed through and cried through, I recognize that it was only because Jesus' love caught me before I took that potentially devastating and catastrophic fall; that I am able to live my life according to the purpose that He predestined specifically for me.

That is why I worship the Lord with the deepest respect and appreciation because, as undeserving as I am, He doesn't deem it thievery for me to be on the receiving end of His unfailing and unwavering love.

In spite of it, God's love has been that constant in my life, even during those times when I didn't even realize it. It has kept me, covered me, held me, pushed me, healed me and restored me.

We cannot make it without Jesus looking out for us and so presenting ourselves accordingly and making sure that the Lord gets the glory in all that we do takes precedence over everything else.

Suggested Song of Meditation: "Lookin' Out for Me" by Kirk Franklin

2 Peter 3:18 (Amplified Bible, Classic Edition/AMPC)

¹⁸ But grow in grace (undeserved favor, spiritual strength) and recognition and knowledge and understanding of our Lord and Savior Jesus Christ (the Messiah). To Him [be] glory (honor, majesty, and splendor) both now and to the day of eternity. Amen (so be it)!

This is the day that the Lord has made. I will rejoice and be glad in it!!

I had such an "a-ha moment" after typing the sentence above with the beginning lyrics to the very popular praise and worship song, "This is the Day." As many times as I have sung that song in these past 39 years, it took on a whole new meaning for me.

After typing those words, I immediately thought back to something I had just said a few hours earlier to my husband. We were discussing a situation that I am currently facing and I was sharing with my husband that regardless of the tears I have shed and the confusion I am left with; what I am presently enduring was written in my days long before I was ever formed in my mother's womb.

If the Lord made the decision that I must encounter these particular circumstances, that meant that there was much I was expected to learn and no matter how painful or uncomfortable it may be; it was for my betterment and wouldn't ever be more than I could bear.

And that is why on this and every day that I am blessed to see, I will rejoice, give thanks and be glad in ALL things because I am living in the days that the Lord has made.

When issues and trouble arise, I am given more and more insight and knowledge into the God that I serve and love. As the tears fall and I begin to wonder what is what and which way I am to go, the Lord serves as my guide and provides me with the strength and answers to make it through.

It's when the storms are raging and everything is so overwhelming that the Lord steps in and takes all my pain away.

When relationships become distant and disconnected and those whom I thought I could depend on are nowhere in sight, the Lord reminds me that He will never leave me nor forsake me.

When I sin and fall short and am filled with so much shame and disappointment, the Lord covers me with His limitless grace and mercy, which is accompanied by a boundless love that cannot be found anywhere else.

For all that I must endure, I am grateful that I have a name to call on in my time of need. Whether that name is Jehovah Jireh (the Lord, Our Provider), Jehovah Rophe (the Lord, Our

Healer), Jehovah Nissi (the Lord, Our Banner), Jehovah Shalom (the Lord, Our Peace), El Roi (the God Who Sees Me) or numerous others, it is because of the tests and trials that we face that we are given the opportunity to know the Lord on a much deeper and personal level.

Because of the undeserved favor that I have been granted, His grace allows me to grow and to be strengthened spiritually because of the knowledge I possess of our Lord and Savior Jesus Christ.

My perspective on trials and tribulations was modified years back when I realized that if it wasn't for those obstacles that come to make me stronger, I wouldn't know Jesus like I do.

Therefore, all glory, honor and splendor is due to Him both now and to the day of eternity. Amen.

Suggested Song of Meditation: "I Wouldn't Know You" by James Fortune and FIYA featuring Nakitta Clegg-Foxx

Proverbs 15:3 (International Children's Bible/ICB)

³ The Lord's eyes see everything that happens. He watches both evil and good people.

Earlier, I had some questions that kept going back and forth in my head. Those questions included, "What happens when we make plans and they don't pan out the way we hoped they would? What happens when we open our hearts, just to encounter heartbreak? What happens when we start off in one direction and we end up losing our way?

In each instance, nothing that we face is greater than the God that we serve. That is why prayer and meditation is such an important part of my everyday life.

I pray each day; all throughout the day. But there are some moments in my life when "a little more" prayer is needed. Those conversations with the Lord are so sacred and are required for me, so that I don't get held up or distracted by all that seems to be coming my way all at once.

I recognize that the God we serve is omniscient. Because He knows everything, He doesn't need any explanation, in-depth breakdown or analysis of the situations that I encounter. But I am so very grateful that He watches over me and permits me the opportunity to share and release what is burdening my heart, so that instead of being cloaked in a spirit of heaviness; I can still rejoice and give thanks while in the midst of any storm.

Now as much as I love to converse with the Lord through prayer, I have come to truly appreciate the role that meditation plays in my prayer life. It's not always about having something to say to the Lord, but being able to hear from Him as well.

Through meditation, I retreat to that secret place, where I am in the Lord's presence and I wait to receive direction on which path I should take. I refuse to make a move until He instructs me to.

Along with being omniscient, the Lord is omnipotent and omnipresent; therefore, I call on El Roi, God who sees me, and I know that even though I am not able to observe all the various elements or variables that are playing a factor in my situations, our Almighty God knows all and is watching everywhere; and that is why I continue to put my trust and faith in Him.

Faith is the substance of things hoped for and the evidence of things not seen. My faith continues to grow stronger and stronger, because the One I choose to run to in my time of need has promised to watch over and keep me, regardless of what my temporal circumstances may try to get me to believe.

Because I live a surrendered life, there is comfort in knowing that the eyes of the Lord are in every place watching everything. He sees what I can't and is able to accomplish what I cannot. I find strength, peace, joy and protection in that.

Suggested Song of Meditation: "Someone Watching Over You" by Yolanda Adams

2 Timothy 2:1 (Mounce Reverse-Interlinear New Testament/MOUNCE)

² You, then, my child, be strengthened by the grace that is in Christ Jesus

Each day, I recognize that everything I could possibly need, I have in the Lord. It's by God's grace that no weapon that is formed against me has the ability to prosper.

Because of that boundless kindness, I am kept and covered from being overtaken or destroyed by the attacks of the enemy. I am given a name that I can call on at all times and know that my prayers are heard.

It is the grace that is in Christ that has provided protection, insight and clarity, in the moments when I most needed it. Where I was once lost, I have been found, made whole and set free.

The love and grace that Jesus has shown me, I am to reciprocate to others. And no matter the fiery trials and tests that I face, I know that because I have access to God's limitless grace, everything that I endure is working together for my good.

I don't deserve it, nor have I done anything to deserve it, but as I live my life and see what each day holds, I am strengthened and empowered by the grace that has been given to me through Christ Jesus.

Suggested Song of Meditation: "God's Grace" by Trin-i-tee 5:7

Mark 8:36 (The Voice/VOICE)

³⁶ Really, what profit is there for you to gain the whole world and lose yourself in the process?

I just love and constantly stand in awe of how God orchestrates every single detail of my life. I am thankful that He always knows what and who I need long before I ever realize that there is a need to be satisfied.

For the past few weeks, the Lord has been working on me from the inside out; primarily regarding my way of thinking and what I choose to focus on, compared to what I should or need to be focusing on.

There was a song that we used to sing in the choir when I was younger and the lyrics stated:

"Gain the world, Give me Jesus. You could have fortune or fame. You could have worldly acclaim. But I am happy with Jesus alone. You can have this old world, but I'll take Jesus for mine."

In this world we live in, where so much value is placed on who you know, what you have, where you live, what you drive, where you work, what you carry or what you wear; I learned a long time ago that what I value, who I am and how I am defined is connected to my relationship with the Lord and not any worldly connection, friendship, relationship or material item that I currently possess.

Affairs of the heart are one of my greatest challenges and that is why I have taken my focus off the world and have permanently affixed it upon Jesus and the Word of God. There's so much I don't know. So many things appear one way, but have the complete opposite meaning or intention.

I need that discernment so that the choices I make keep me on the path that the Lord has set before me. I do not desire to be distracted by what the world says I must gain in order to be successful or deemed valuable.

There is no monetary amount nor any rare or precious jewel or metal created that is more valuable than Jesus and the place He has in my life.

With God we have the victory, long before the battle ever commences and concludes. Through Him, we have acquired a front row seat to witness His promises come to fruition, that bless us in ways that are exceedingly and infinitely beyond anything that we could ever hope or dare to think of.

So you can take the world, with all the silver, gold, platinum and precious gems in it. With Jesus, we have everything we could ever possibly need and more.

Suggested Song of Meditation: "Silver and Gold" by Kirk Franklin

Amos 3:3 (Modern English Version/MEV)

³ Do two people walk together, if they have not agreed?

While in the midst of tests and trials and when nothing else seems to make sense but the faith that I have in the Lord, I choose to press on.

To say that I have been going through the fire, is an understatement. I felt like I have been channeling my inner Chaka Khan.

I love the Lord for so many reasons, but one reason that is undeniable is the love that He has for me. It's a love that meets me right where I am and communicates in a way that speaks to every character and personality trait and idiosyncrasy that I possess.

The Lord has been nudging me to break free, say goodbye and move on from certain relationships. That is a very difficult task for me, especially because I am a "relational" type of person. I have heard that description numerous times and this evening was the first time I decided to do some research on what it meant to be relational.

According to Louise Phipps Senft of Wagonheim Law, "A relational way of living involves taking an open, positive attitude into our interactions with everyone, assuming that they are acting out of good motives (or, at least, not assuming they're acting out of malice)—and also that their failures might just be attributable to something that we could understand and relate to if we knew them as a well-loved friend. This holds for people we know well and those who are total strangers to us.

Being relational shows in the way we greet others, in the respect and consideration we demonstrate, in the way we don't place our needs and desires above theirs, and in the way we seek to serve instead of be served. Everything we do in relation to others and our world, every day—it all matters. No act or interaction is trivial. We might just reduce this way of being to the Golden Rule—we treat others as we would have them treat us—but being relational goes well beyond that."

Yep, that is me—no ifs, ands or buts about it. Although I believe that being relational is great, it's not-so-great when those principles and attributes find themselves caught up in toxic, broken and unhealthy relationships.

I was born into brokenness. I grew up broken and made many of my life choices out of brokenness before surrendering my life to Christ. Being broken and relational is an oxymoron. It's like oil and water; it doesn't mix.

In each instance, I have always had the best intentions, but because I hadn't taken the time to address my own brokenness and thought that by putting others before myself, eager to serve instead of being served, the enemy was able to take something that was a very great quality and make it my greatest weakness and hindrance as well.

But God. His love has provided a clarity about myself, my actions and those around me in a way that has caused a breakthrough. But with that breakthrough has come some decisions, some goodbyes I have to say in order to press on and move forward toward the abundance He has for me.

Because relationships and affairs of the heart are my biggest Achilles Heel, the Lord knowing I am a visual learner and word person, orchestrated me receiving the right messages, from the right people, at the right time.

While I was viewing a notification that pertained to the blog, I saw the following inspirational quote from Sarah Jakes Roberts that I swore God had her share specifically for me. It read:

"You can't force people to care the way you do. Don't continue to punish yourself by expecting more than they can give. There comes a point when you must release people from the obligation of protecting your heart. You must accept that adjusting your expectations to meet their reality is often the only way to avoid disappointment."

Those words penetrated to my core and I immediately began meditating on them. Later on in the day, when I received another notification regarding the blog, as soon as I opened my Facebook app, the first thing I saw was a Periscope message that Dr. Celeste Owens had shared for #WarriorWednesday.

Let me tell you, I haven't caught on to the whole Periscope movement, but when I saw that the topic of Dr. Owens' message today was, "Goodbye is Just a Hello", my spirit told me to wake up because there was something I needed to hear in the message she had delivered.

My family and I have been completely and abundantly blessed by **Dr. Celeste Owens Ministries**. Her 40-Day Surrender Fasts have been not just game changers, but life changers.

Before Dr. Owens went into today's message, she reminded us about the importance of surrendering; which is "Yielding what we want and putting God at the center." She instructed us not to get caught up or traumatized in the goodbyes because they are preparing us for the hellos associated with the new beginnings that are before us.

While we transition from the goodbye to the hello that is awaiting us, we may often become concerned that God is not present in that "in between" place. But because He is Alpha and Omega, the beginning and the end, that means that He is omnipresent; everywhere at ALL times.

Those words brought such a reassurance to me. But what also resonated so deeply was when she cautioned us on the danger of staying in a place we should have said goodbye to already. In doing so, we risk God's grace leaving and not covering us. That was so real for me and confirmed what I knew I had to do and that was say goodbye to certain relationships because I couldn't risk not having God's grace as a covering.

The Lord had been preparing me to face, accept and embrace the truth that some goodbyes are a necessity for me to press on and move forward towards all that He has for me.

Suggested Song of Meditation: "Press On" by Mandisa

Psalm 107:14 (New English Translation/NET Bible)

¹⁴ He brought them out of the utter darkness, and tore off their shackles.

No matter who you are, each of us has had yokes and strongholds that have kept us bound and shackled. Whether they were sins we have committed, decisions we agreed to, actions we took part in, generational curses we continued to carry on, etc., they all resulted in us feeling some degree of gloom and an isolation into utter darkness.

But as the sunlight, surprisingly, broke through the clouds and lit up my dining room a little while ago, I was reminded of the light and joy I am now walking in because of the shackles that have been torn apart and the darkness that the Lord has delivered me from.

I need someone to know that whatever guilt, shame, regret or disappointment the enemy is trying to keep you bound by, has been covered by the blood of Jesus. As my pastor reminds us each Sunday, unless the enemy is going to go back and retrieve that sin from under the blood, he doesn't get to hold that over your head or use it to hinder your walk and relationship with the Lord.

The Lord loves us so much that we have been redeemed and delivered from our sins and our past. Therefore, we have to do our part and love ourselves enough to adopt a lifestyle of surrendering to the Lord.

There is not one stronghold whose binding power is more powerful than the name of Jesus!!! When we surrender, our mindset shifts from victim to victor as we consult God first in all matters before making a decision or taking part in any situation.

By surrendering and releasing it all to the Lord, the steps that we end up taking in life are ordered by Him instead of being determined by our emotions, other people or previous strongholds that have plagued us.

We serve a God who knows exactly what we need, when we need it and who we will need by our side. Let's sound the trumpets together over the shackles we have heard and will hear fall if we just call on the name of Jesus and allow Him to move in and through every area of our lives.

We must keep our minds stayed on Jesus and the power that is in His name. And because our minds are set on the Lord, we will be positioned to receive the favor, the divine connections and to live in the overflow; where there is no lack.

The chains have been broken and we are no longer bound. Therefore, no matter what may rise up against us, nothing we face will ever be greater or more powerful than God!!

Suggested Song of Meditation: "Break Every Chain" by Tasha Cobbs

Daniel 4:3 (The Message/MSG)

> ³ *"His miracles are staggering, His wonders are surprising. His kingdom lasts and lasts, His sovereign rule goes on forever.*

"Over my circumstance, you've given me another chance, you reign!!" I have been singing that over and over since yesterday evening.

It's amazing that as much as I love music and as many times as I can hear a song, depending on what season I am in or the spiritual warfare and giants that I am facing, a song that I am very familiar with ends up ministering to me in a way it hadn't before. And that was the case last night.

> I rejoice and exalt the name of the Lord who is sovereign; a supreme leader who possesses absolute power. Oh, how excellent is His name. His miracles are staggering and His wonders are surprising.

What a blessing it is to know that no matter how high the Lord is seated on the throne, He isn't ever so high that we can't be seen or heard. He is the King of kings and Lord of lords; a master so loving that He doesn't deem it an inconvenience or intrusion to provide for our needs.

Our God reigns over every circumstance and issue that we may encounter. Whether those situations pertain to our health, finances, marriages, children or any other area; nothing that we face is greater than the Lord and His authority. The Lord knows what we are in need of before we ever part our lips to make our petitions known to Him. There is no one greater than Him. Not only is there no one greater, but there is also no one more faithful than the Lord.

He is our refuge and strength, an ever-present help in times of trouble (Psalm 46:1). He is far above every ruler and authority, power and dominion and every title given (Ephesians 1:21).

It is only through Christ that we have been given another chance. Circumstances and situations that were intended for evil, God intended them for our good. Therefore, no matter what we may face, we will remain encouraged knowing that His kingdom lasts forever and His sovereign rule continues from one generation to the next.

Suggested Song of Meditation: "You Reign" by William Murphy

Psalm 108:4 (Amplified Bible, Classic Edition/AMPC)

4 For Your mercy and loving-kindness are great and high as the heavens! Your truth and faithfulness reach to the skies!

Mercy is defined as compassion or forgiveness shown toward someone whom it is within one's power to punish or harm. When I think about those decisions that I have made in my life that I am not the proudest of, I am forever reminded of just how great the Lord's mercy is for me.

For the longest time, I struggled with understanding how even though the Lord had written each of my days before they ever came to fruition, knowing each decision I would make, every twist and turn my life would take and those times that I would be disobedient and not follow His instruction; He still thought I was worth being on the receiving end of His unfailing love, His great mercy, His amazing grace and limitless tender mercies.

Each day that I rise, I wake up thanking our Lord and Savior, Jesus Christ, because I am well aware that it is because of the blood of Jesus that I am still here. I have access to a loving-kindness which soars overhead far into the heavens and where each cloud is a flag to His faithfulness.

Instead of what I should have received, I have begun to truly comprehend just how phenomenal God's love is for me. Where I could have ended up compared to where I am today (and I recognize that I still have further to go), the endless ways that He has provided for me and the individual and personalized blessings like strength, protection, provision, guidance and spiritual gifts that I am in receipt of, has provided me so much insight into how great the Lord's mercy and grace are toward me.

When I have needed Him, He has always been there. When I have reached out to Him, He has taken hold of me and consoled me. When I have needed direction, He has been the light to guide me out of the darkness. We should be eternally grateful for not receiving exactly what we have deserved in life. It is because of the Lord's love, mercy and grace that we should strive to live according to His will; which means a life surrendered and dedicated to being all that He has created us to be.

Suggested Song of Meditation "Great Is Your Mercy" by Donnie McClurkin

John 1:29 (Disciples' Literal New Testament/DLNT)

²⁹ On the next day he sees Jesus coming toward him. And he says, "Look—the Lamb of God, the One taking-away the sin of the world.

Since heading out the door first thing this morning, until about an hour ago, I have covered so many miles between Queens, Long Island and Manhattan you would have thought I was being compensated for the mileage (but no, I wasn't).

Ever since I attended bible study on Wednesday evening, I have not been able to think about anything but knowing Jesus better and having that relational knowledge of Him and all that is required for me to know and experience that power that raised Christ from the dead.

The Lord loved us so much that He gave His only begotten Son, who was born into sin, so that we may live again. Jesus, the Lamb of God, came to take away the sin of the world.

There have been so many times when I have looked back over some of the decisions that I have made in my life that ended up building barriers between the Lord and me and, in turn, caused His face to be hidden from me; and I was just left wondering, "Lord, in spite of it all, how and why do you love me so?"

Being omniscient, God always has known and always will know every right and left turn we will make, along with everything that is done in the light and that which we would prefer be kept hidden in the dark. Even with possessing all knowledge of every last detail of each of our individual lives, the Lord still thought we were worth loving, choosing and sacrificing for.

When I actually took the time to let all of that sink in, it changed my whole perspective and modified my view on suffering. I used to think suffering was a punishment, but then I had to remind myself that I couldn't say that I wanted to imitate the example that Jesus had provided us with and leave suffering out of the equation.

If the Lamb of God had to suffer, why would I ever think that suffering wouldn't be a part of my journey too? At times when storms are present and I encounter periods of adversity, I have learned to rejoice as I share Christ's sufferings because I know that at the appointed time, His glory will be revealed and He will restore, confirm, strengthen and establish me.

The depth of my gratitude is indescribable because I know that if it wasn't for the precious Lamb of God, I wouldn't have access to God's grace and mercy, which are a necessity for me to finish the race that has been constructed and placed before me.

Why the Lord loves me so, I shall never know; but I will continuously say, "Thank you" for the Lamb of God.

Suggested Song of Meditation: "Now Behold the Lamb" by Tamyra Gray

1 John 4:11 (The Voice/VOICE)

¹¹ So, my loved ones, if God loved us so sacrificially, surely we should love one another.

So much of the state of the world and what I see on the news these days is so disheartening and causes me to grieve. But in those moments, I realize that I am also given an opportunity to pray for the lives of others.

If we just look around in the communities that we live in, we can see numerous examples of the situations that can arise when there is an absence of love. I know that decisions that I made in my life that hurt me the most came from the realization of the love that was missing from my life.

But God... He has loved us so sacrificially. I remember when I was so lost and broken. He rescued me, forgave me, healed me and restored me. And now I desire nothing more than to share that same kind of love with others.

As 1 Corinthians 13:13 reminds us, "So now faith, hope and love abide, these three; but the greatest of these is LOVE." Love comes from God and everyone who loves is born of God and experiences a relationship with Him.

I have learned to love others, not by the love I have or have not received from the world; but by the boundless love the Lord has shown me through every season of my life.

I desire to extend that love to everyone, including my enemies. How do we end up with enemies in the first place? Normally, it's a result of someone wronging, betraying, hurting or causing us pain in some way, shape, fashion or form.

Seeing as none of us is perfect, haven't each of us done something wrong and acted in a way that caused hurt and pain to the Lord and resulted in a disconnection between Him and us?

If it wasn't for God's illimitable love, grace and mercy, where would we be? Since we know firsthand what God's love can do in a person's life, why would we hesitate to take the opportunity to be more like Christ and share that love with those whose paths we end up coming into contact with?

I love the Lord because He first loved me (1 John 4:19). While I kept looking and trying to obtain it from others, there was always one place where it was already being provided and I didn't have to search for it.

We now have the opportunity to reciprocate the same love and forgiveness that the Lord has shown us to others!! Thank you Jesus!!

Suggested Song of Meditation: "Others" by Israel Houghton

1 John 4:16 (J.B. Phillips New Testament/PHILLIPS)

16 So we have come to know and trust the love God has for us. God is love, and the man whose life is lived in love does, in fact, live in God, and God does, in fact, live in him.

You don't have to be married, in a relationship or be a parent to celebrate love and being loved. I wake up every morning thanking and loving the Lord more and more because He first loved me.

The greatest love that we could ever possibly know comes from the Lord. And it's because of the Lord that we are instructed on the attributes that love should possess. Love is patient and is kind; it does not envy, nor parade itself, it's not puffed up, doesn't behave rudely, doesn't seek its own, isn't easily angered, doesn't keep record of wrongs, doesn't rejoice in iniquity, but rejoices in the truth. It's because of God that we have access to a love that bears all things, believes all things, hopes all things, endures all things and it never fails (1 Corinthians 13:4-8).

When I think about God's love and the pureness of it, I weep with such gratefulness and joy in my heart.

God's love for us is everlasting. Through all the tears we shed, the trials we encounter and the mistakes we make, the love of Jesus is always present.

During my times of reflection, I have come to realize that it is through personal observation and experience and the deep and consistent faith that I have in God that I have come to know and trust the love that the Lord has for me.

I have heard and have been one that thought that some of my decisions were so unforgivable that God couldn't possibly love me. I was then reminded and wanted to pass on the same reminder to you today that, "Nothing can ever separate us from God's love. Neither death nor life, neither angels nor demons, neither our fears for today nor our worries about tomorrow—not even the powers of hell can separate us from God's love. No power in the sky above or in the earth below—indeed, nothing in all creation will ever be able to separate us from the love of God that is revealed in Christ Jesus our Lord (Romans 8:38-39)."

God loves us so much that He gave His only begotten Son on our behalf. Because of Jesus, there is not anything in all creation that will ever be able to separate us from the love that God has for each and every one of us.

The Lord instructs us to abide in Him and He'll abide in us (John 15:4). Abide means to dwell, settle in and sink deeper. I desire to settle in the Lord and to be submerged deeper and deeper into His presence and His pure and limitless love that renews me.

God is love!!!

That means that everyday should be viewed as a celebration of the unmatched love that we receive and the life lived in love that we are to show to the Lord, ourselves and one another.

Suggested Song of Meditation: "Love So Pure" by Kim Burrell

Romans 6:17-18 (Modern English Version/MEV)

[17] But thanks be to God, for you were slaves of sin, but you have obeyed from the heart that form of teaching to which you were entrusted, [18] and having been freed from sin, you became the slaves of righteousness.

The other night, I was one of the millions of viewers who watched the Grammy Awards. Music, the artists and the award shows honoring them have changed so much over the years that I had begun to find all of it not worth dedicating three and a half hours of my time to.

As I watched the awards show, there were a few performances that truly stuck out to me; with the main one coming from rapper, Kendrick Lamar. Being a person who is really big on words, I pay attention to what is said in the songs I hear. Kendrick Lamar is an artist who uses his platform to speak to many different issues. Whether you agree with his views are not, he is very talented. But what resonated more with me about his performance was the imagery he portrayed when he first came onto the stage.

Kendrick led a line of men shackled together in chains within a prison setting. Before one word uttered from his mouth, I began to think about what it meant to be a slave and then I drilled a bit deeper and began to reflect on those things that I once was a slave to. My attention left the television screen and I thought about the sin that once had me so bound. If it hadn't been for the abundance of grace and the gift of righteousness that I have received through Christ, I would have given up, lost my mind and everything else a long time ago.

My attention shifted back to the TV when Kendrick Lamar got to the point in his performance where he freed himself from the chains. All of that caused me to think about the power that there is in the name of Jesus Christ to break every chain that we have ever been or could ever be bound by. Those were the thoughts I had as my night began to wind down. Well lo and behold, as I was listening to the radio for a song for the blog I was preparing to create, my youngest daughter (who was four years old) came into my room and questioned if I was about to begin working on the blog. When I replied, "Yes," the next question she had was, "Mom, did our pastor tell us to read Romans 4 or Romans 6?"

I stopped what I was doing and looked at her, because she is always in attendance with us when we go to bible study each Wednesday and I knew that whatever I was going to share in my blog post would come from either Romans 4 or Romans 6..

God is so faithful and to witness the obedience at the young, delicate and impressionable age of four that my daughter had, encouraged and incited me to want to know the Lord even more and to do everything in my power to set the example by living my life on purpose and according to His will so that my family will continue to do the same.

After re-reading Romans 4, 5 and then arriving at Romans 6 and it speaking to the transformation from slaves to sin to slaves to righteousness, it brought back the imagery I had witnessed the night before on the Grammys and what God had spoken to me together and I was reminded, thanks be to God that because I am crucified with Christ, sin no longer has dominion over me and I am no longer a slave to sin.

I entrust, with my whole heart, what I learn from the Lord's teachings on a daily basis. Because I am obeying it, sin no longer controls me and I am being conformed to God's will in thought, purpose and action. I never would have made it without God's amazing grace. I am stronger, wiser and so much better because of the Lord who has always been by my side and on my side.

It is through God's grace that I am connected to Christ and the Holy Spirit to me. Therefore, I have been freed from sin, am able to resist those inclinations to do what is wrong and instead do what is right. Without God and the birth, death and resurrection of His Son, Jesus, I would have never made it to acquire that freedom from sin and the removal of the shackles so that I could be a slave to God's righteousness and a servant to the most faithful and loving Master whose rewards are immeasurable and incomprehensible.

Suggested Song of Meditation: "Never Would Have Made It" by Marvin Sapp

Genesis 50:20 (New International Reader's Version/NIRV)

²⁰ You planned to harm me. But God planned it for good. He planned to do what is now being done. He wanted to save many lives.

After publishing last night's post, for the rest of the evening I thought about various parts from the movie, "War Room" and something that I remembered one of the main characters saying in the movie was that, "There are some landmines that we end up coming into contact with and stepping on, so that others don't have to."

That is so true and I know that I have been through some stuff and given the opportunity, I share those experiences and am completely transparent so that I can tell of God's love, goodness, grace and mercy; how what the enemy meant for harm, God turned it around and planned it for my good.

I believe, wholeheartedly, that there are some things we don't have to experience and God will place individuals in our lives who can see the possibility of us heading down a similar contorted path and those people will help to guide us back to God and His principles, which if we trust and obey, will save us from all the weapons formed against us. We will see that not only will they not prosper but, those devices that had evil intent will be turned into our good and it will put us in a place to do kingdom work and help save the lives of others.

I have always made sure to convey to my children that they could ask me anything and I would always tell them the truth. I know that the truth may not always be pretty, may not always look nice and sometimes may be very hard to swallow and digest. But because of the love, grace and mercy that the Lord has shown me, it's my responsibility to be transparent, open and honest with my children because I want them to make better decisions than I did growing up and to never question God, their worth or whose they are.

I also know that I have a responsibility to share, not just with my husband, children and family, but with others about the goodness of the Lord. I'm not here to be a hypocrite, but I remember all those times when I thought there was no end in sight and I was down for the count. If what I am able to share can prevent someone from taking just some of the steps or keep them from experiencing just some of the heartache that I have endured, then that's all that matters.

The enemy had me bound by so much shame, regret, disappointment and pain but God stepped into my situation and turned it all around. Who better to assist others in understanding the depth, length, height and breadth of God's love, that I have come to know for myself?

The devil thought he had me, but God turned my mourning into dancing and my sorrows into joy. If He did it for me, He will most definitely do it for you.

Suggested Song of Meditation: "He Turned It" by Tye Tribbett

Jeremiah 32:17 (Amplified Bible/AMP)

17 'Ah Lord God! Behold, You have made the heavens and the earth by Your great power and by Your outstretched arm! There is nothing too difficult or too wonderful for You—

Upon waking up a few hours ago, as I was giving thanks to the Lord for another day and just sharing some thoughts with Him, I paused just to listen to the sound of the rain that was falling outside of my windows.

Although I always have been and always will be a city girl, I love nature and am very fascinated by the structure and composition of things and the purposes that they serve.

The minute I walk out the door each day, I am constantly reminded of the enormous power and mighty works of the Lord. With His outstretched arm and great power, it was the Lord (and only Him) who created the heavens and the earth.

Our God is an awesome God who is able to do the impossible if we trust and believe that He can. I don't have to be a psychic to say that there is not one person who will read this post today that cannot attest to what was considered too hard and impossible for them, but that the Lord was able to perform once they released and entrusted their situations to Him.

It doesn't matter how many degrees you can have hanging on your wall or how many books you have accumulated and can boast about reading; I have learned that sometimes the reason that we do not see the Lord doing the impossible in our lives is because we say we believe He will do it, but there is always a "but" or some other form of hesitation behind that statement or we are so limited in our thinking that we are too afraid to seek God for that which we deem impossible.

Matthew 21:22 reminds us, "And whatever you ask in prayer, you will receive, if you have faith!!"

In so many instances, it's our faulty way of thinking that gets in the way of us witnessing God doing exceedingly, abundantly and above anything that we would ever comprehend in our lives. What a disservice we do to ourselves by being the obstacle that gets in the way of all that the Lord desires to do for us.

Whether the impossible you are facing pertains to your health (physical, emotional or mental), your family, your marriage, your finances, your education, your employment, your ministry, etc., nothing is too difficult for the Lord to handle or too wonderful for the Lord to bring to fruition.

We never have to look far to be reminded that we serve a sovereign God who knows all, sees all, is everywhere and capable of any and everything!! The same God who has done the impossible time and time again in your life, is the same God who has the final say and whom all power belongs to, now and forever.

Suggested Song of Meditation: "Yes He Will" by Fred Hammond

2 Thessalonians 3:16 (The Voice/VOICE)

16 And now, dear friends, may the Lord of peace Himself grace you with peace always and in everything. May the Lord be present with all of you.

Over this past week, my family and I have observed God's grace, mercy and favor (and to such an abundant extent) upon our lives.

Now you know that as God continues to move on our behalf, that does nothing but upset the enemy and you can best believe that opposition and adversity, of some form, will be on the horizon. And as the end of the week came upon me, layers to the familial dynamics that are nowhere near where I wish they could be, began to be pulled back by the enemy to see what my reaction would be.

For so long, affairs of the heart, especially where my extended family and those I deemed closest are involved have always been a well-documented source of vulnerability and pain for me. So when the enemy decided it was time for me to revisit a couple of those areas, I knew that none of it could be happening without God's approval and that it was a test of my faith and character; in which the end results would produce a better, wiser and stronger me.

Although what I was encountering left my heart feeling some heaviness; what kept me from shattering into pieces was the peace of God. In recognizing the importance of keeping God at the center of all I do, the enemy doesn't get the access to me that he once had. I cling to the promise that the Lord will continually give me peace in every circumstance (not just one, some or few).

The Bible tells us in Isaiah 26:3 that, "God will keep the mind that is dependent on Him in perfect peace, for it is trusting in Him."

It is through the peace of God that my thoughts and heart are kept quiet and at rest because of the trust that I have in Jesus Christ. It is a peace that surpasses and transcends all human understanding.

How else could I explain having the desire to rejoice and give thanks, even while enduring the most painful and uncomfortable situations?

As I once heard Joel Osteen share, "The pain and obstacles that we encounter are not here to defeat us, but to elevate us." Through the peace of God, I am comforted and know that the pain I may have felt in my yesterdays has been turned into the gains I will have acquired for my today and all the tomorrows that are before me.

Suggested Song of Meditation: "Yesterday" by Dorinda Clark-Cole

Psalm 91:14-15 (The Voice/VOICE)

¹⁴ "Because he clings to Me in love, I will rescue him from harm; I will set him above danger. Because he has known Me by name, ¹⁵ He will call on Me, and I will answer. I'll be with him through hard times; I'll rescue him and grant him honor.

I am relieved to have completed the medication that had been prescribed to me by my doctor, to address the significant increase in my blood pressure due to stress.

There were so many other directions my health could have taken, unbeknownst to me at that time. But because I cling to the Lord in love and have that desire to truly know Him and to have that personal knowledge of His mercy, love, and kindness, trusting and relying on Him, I have been captured by the Lord's grace.

Today, we celebrated the youngest member of our family since the clock struck midnight. My youngest daughter is now five years old.

I don't know where the past five years went, but as I looked back at the first picture that was taken of her after she entered this world on March 8, 2011 at 2:19 a.m., and then looked at her today posing, smiling all hard, just excited to be a year older, I couldn't help but think about all that the Lord has rescued us from and the danger that He set us high above.

Just a few months after her birth, our family was involved in a car accident. With all of us inside the car, everyone was in disbelief, after witnessing the accident and seeing our car, that we walked away without one scratch on any of the five of us. Our car may have been totaled, but in that moment, all we could focus on was the total and awesome power of our God; whose name and hand of protection saved us.

Out of all of us in the family, it has been my youngest daughter who has had to have surgery. At the age of three, she had to be whisked away in an ambulance (my first nerve-wrecking experience in one) and emergency surgery had to be performed because of a strep infection that had attacked one of her lymph nodes, which had become enlarged to the size of a golf ball.

But it was God's amazing grace that kept her, my family and me.

Please understand that I have endless examples of God's faithfulness and goodness. And it's because of who I have come to know the Lord to be and that knowledge and wisdom that I carry with me each day, that I do not fear in times of need or adversity.

Instead of worrying, I have found the power that comes from being able to sing, praise and rejoice my way through each obstacle. And why wouldn't I, when the One I am relying on to rescue and see me through has never lost, can't fail, can't be overcome, has all power in His hands and the final say in my life?

Although it seems that these five years have gone by quickly and we have endured some trials, my family and I have also seen some miracles and blessings bestowed upon us that no one nor nothing in this world can take credit for but the Lord.

Our God will take a mess and convert it into a message, a test and turn it into a testimony, a trial and transform it into a triumph; and where you thought you were a victim, you will discover that victor you were born to be through Christ Jesus.

No matter where I look, and I don't have to gaze far, I am given daily reminders of who God is and all that He is able to do, if we trust and rely on Him.

Suggested Song of Meditation: "Rescue" by Pajam

1 Chronicles 29:12 (Holman Christian Standard Bible/HCSB)

¹² Riches and honor come from You, and You are the ruler of everything. Power and might are in Your hand, and it is in Your hand to make great and to give strength to all.

As I observe all that is happening within my surroundings, I stay in constant wonderment of the Lord and His mighty power.

Regardless of what the enemy may do to try to get me distracted and off course, who the Lord is and what He is capable of performing supersedes all of that.

Our Lord is so mighty!!

He is the One who spoke into nothing and all creation heard; the One who holds all power in His hands and who does what is impossible for man to accomplish.

I recognize that my start and my destiny are found in the Lord and nowhere else. That is why temporal situations do not get to affect me the way they used to; because I am walking in the fearlessness I have acquired from the One who is ruler over everything.

The Lord is Almighty; which means there is no limit to His power. Nothing is beyond His reach.

This is just some of what I remind myself of, on a daily basis because the enemy doesn't let up. As a matter of fact, his attacks have gotten a bit stronger and more personal, but no matter how he may try to change up or intensify his attacks against me, I continue to seek out and surrender to the Sovereign God we serve, so that the enemy doesn't even get the opportunity to penetrate the force field of faith that encompasses me.

I have come to learn and find great peace in knowing that, if I just move out of the way and allow God to be who He has been, who He is and who He will be, He will continue to supply all my needs.

Knowing how mighty the Lord is and that there is no one greater than Him, my focus has shifted from my situations to the One who is the beginning and the end of all things and whom blessings and honor originate from.

Suggested Song of Meditation: "Mighty You Are" by The Walls Group

Ephesians 2:8 (Worldwide English (New Testament)/WE)

⁸ You have been saved by God's love and kindness because you believed. It was not because of anything you did, but it was a gift from God.

As a child of God, I know that I have been saved by grace. My study Bible elaborated on that truth to say that, "The grace of God is the source of salvation; faith is the channel, not the cause."

It is God and God alone who saves. We could never do enough to earn it; pure and simple, it's a gift from God. And I am here to shout and let the world know that there's enough love for everyone. Our salvation originates out of the loving-kindness that the Lord has for us; it does not come by any efforts of our own.

Sometimes we make the mistake of looking to others to save or rescue us. If we trust in ourselves or others, we will be doomed to fail. Make no mistake, there is only one who cannot fail; whose love has won and who reigns supreme over everything!!

God's grace has saved and freed us to live our lives according to His purpose. Because of God's love, there is no need for fear or shame in our lives. Who God has called us to be is not based on any accomplishments or feats of our own, but according to His purpose and grace that was given to us through Christ Jesus.

We are able to find our voices and welcome the new days that are before us through the salvation and the unmerited favor we have received.

I am here to let it be known that my gratefulness for these gifts, that I have not earned, but am able to receive, has caused me to continuously lift up the name of the Lord, higher and higher.

Suggested Song of Meditation: "Let It Be Known" by Casey J.

Nehemiah 1:5 (New Living Translation/NLT)

⁵ Then I said, "O Lord, God of heaven, the great and awesome God who keeps his covenant of unfailing love with those who love him and obey his commands.

While reflecting on the greatness of our Lord, I came across Nehemiah 1:5. Instantly, after reading Nehemiah 1:5, my mind shifted to Psalm 145:3 which states, "Great is our Lord and most worthy of praise; His greatness no one can fathom." I also couldn't read Nehemiah 1:5 without thinking about the message that my pastor recently delivered in church about Nehemiah and us taking the initiative to be like him and rebuilding the walls back up.

Nehemiah had a specific mission and he was able to accomplish it, regardless of the criticism and opposition he constantly faced; because of the relationship that he had with God. Not only did Nehemiah guide his community as they rebuilt the walls in Jerusalem, but he was also the vessel utilized to guide them spiritually by demanding that they obey God's law.

I don't ever want to be outside the covenant of God's unwavering and boundless love. I love the Lord, first and foremost, and strive to obey His commands every day of my life. The Lord is incredible, remarkable, magnificent, awesome, powerful and merciful. He is my everything and that is why I am adamant about taking some pages from the book of Nehemiah.

I have seen the reconciliation, restoration and renewal that is possible; along with the favor and blessings that are provided when we obey the Lord and give Him our most sincere love, respect and praise that He most rightly deserves.

Each of us has walls that need to be rebuilt. Whether those walls are around our homes, our communities or beyond; they need to be built based on the Word of God. We need to set our eyes on those things above and be that source of encouragement by telling others about the truth of all that God has done and is capable of doing. No one nor nothing is greater than our most faithful and loving God. He is the greatest and has provided us with everything we could ever need to accomplish whatever task may lie ahead of us.

Suggested Song of Meditation: "The Greatest" by Dave Hollister

John 6:35 (Lexham English Bible/LEB)

35 Jesus said to them, "I am the bread of life. The one who comes to me will never be hungry, and the one who believes in me will never be thirsty again.

Last night when my family and I were driving in and around Brooklyn, we observed so many Jewish families gathering together to celebrate Pesach (Passover).

As I observed the families coming together, so many thoughts ran through my head. I began to think about just what Pesach symbolized; and that was God's deliverance of the Israelites from slavery in Egypt. Because of the Lord, their lives were transformed from those who were in bondage to now those who had obtained freedom.

While thinking about Pesach, there was no way that I could ignore the parallelism between how the blood of the Passover lamb on the Israelites' doorposts was a sign that God should pass over and prevent the destroyer from entering their homes and striking them; in the same manner that the blood of Jesus protects and covers us and prevents the enemy from destroying us. It's also because of the blood of Jesus that we are no longer held captive or shackled to our old ways. Our lives have also been transformed and we are free and have been granted a new beginning through Christ.

As I studied more about Pesach, I also saw additional similarities between the Passover lamb and Jesus, the precious Lamb of God.

Some of the requirements for the Passover lamb was that it had to be without blemish, young, male, had to be slain in public and none if its bones were to be broken. Jesus, in comparison, was perfect and sinless, young, male, crucified publicly and even though His death was barbaric, none of His bones were broken either.

I am here to testify that there is no question that Jesus is the source of my life.

The sacrifice that He made on Calvary has changed my life's story. In the Bible, we saw how manna fulfilled the physical needs for a certain amount of time; but Jesus fulfills our spiritual needs forever.

We can be lied on, mistreated, discarded or talked about, but like the song says, "Long as we got King Jesus, we don't need nobody else."

Jesus promised that those who come to Him will never be hungry, and those who believe in Him [as Savior] will never be thirsty and will be sustained spiritually.

Jesus' love for us is the reason that I strive to make sure that everyone knows just how good He has been to me and about the life that we can only obtain through Him.

Suggested Song of Meditation: "You Are the Source" by Antwaun Stanley

Psalm 126:5 (Lexham English Bible/LEB)

⁵ Those who sow with tears shall reap with rejoicing.

It's amazing how our sense of direction can be shifted within a matter of seconds. GPS, for me, doesn't stand for Global Positioning System, but God's Purposeful Supervision. Like so many times in the past, I begin my daily blog in one direction and then God ends up rerouting me down another path.

As I was going through and discarding some things here at home, I came across a packet of flower seeds that I had received at a family reunion a few years ago. I held onto the packet promising to plant the forget-me-not seeds one day in the future. As I was looking at the picture of the pretty flowers on the packet, still in my "harvest mindset", I began thinking about all the seeds I have sown over the years and the tears that have watered those seeds.

Although I have strong convictions and principles, I have always shied away from confrontation. I am one that when faced with opposition and conflict, my first reaction wasn't to get mad. My feelings would get hurt and I would cry. That always drove me crazy because I was made to feel so weak when tears would flow.

These days, I am no longer afraid or ashamed to cry. Any painful or uncomfortable situation that I have encountered, I have found crying as a release as I surrender the circumstances of the situation to the Lord. I knew that through my tears, I was growing and even beginning to heal, in the midst of the situation.

Like flowers, I learned some few years back that in order to grow we all need some manure (which are the twists and turns and the messes in our lives that God delivers us from). Also like flowers, for growth we need water, which comes in the form of the tears that fall from our eyes. And most importantly where flowers need the sun to grow and live, we need the Lord's Son to live and grow.

I found it very ironic that the type of flower seeds that I have are the forget-me-nots. Today, God reminded me that He will forget me not and the tears that I have shed won't ever be in vain.

God promises us that if we sow in tears, we shall reap the harvest in joy and with singing. Weeping may endure for a night, but joy comes in the morning (Psalm 30:5).

Suggested Song of Meditation: "Sow in Tears" by Richard Smallwood and Vision

Job 12:10 (The Voice/VOICE)

¹⁰ His hand cradles the life of every creature on the face of the earth; His breath fills the nostrils of humans everywhere.

Although I am fully aware that there are no limits to the dominion that the Lord possesses and that in His Word we have that confirmation that nothing is too hard for the Lord to handle; just as the suggested song of meditation expresses, "I know and believe that God still works miracles, but I am just thankful for what some call the 'simple things' that He does over and over, each day for me."

On a daily basis, life situations arise and I am reminded that the Lord is in control of every aspect. Because the Lord cradles the life of every creature on the face of the earth and His breath fills the nostrils of humans everywhere, worry and fear don't get to live here.

I have been changed and in no way is the Lord through with me yet. I am clay in the potter's hands. He is constantly working on my heart, my mind and my spirit. I continue to see how far He has brought me by the way I react or choose not to react, when the tests, trials and curve balls of life come my way.

I am so grateful for who God is and all that He chooses to do in my life. Please understand that if He decided not to do anything else, He has already done more than enough.

Every day that we are blessed to open our eyes, to be of a sound mind, to have the activity of our limbs and be on the receiving end of His brand new mercies and unmerited grace, I am reminded that our lives are truly in our Lord and Savior's hand.

I continue to witness that there aren't any limits to God's supremacy. All power is in His hands.

I don't need to know what the next step will be because I acknowledge that God is in control and that nothing is impossible for Him.

God continues to make a way for us when there appears not to be one anywhere in sight. He opens doors that no one can close and keeps the ones shut that are not in alignment with what He has purposed for our lives. Therefore, remain encouraged by all He does, both big and small.

For the Lord to keep doing all that He is doing will continue to be one of my daily prayers.

Suggested Song of Meditation: "Keep Doing What You're Doing" by Anita Wilson

Psalm 103:13 (The Voice/VOICE)

13 An earthly father expresses love for his children, it is no different with our heavenly Father; The Eternal shows His love for those who revere Him.

I would like to wish all of you fathers in any form or capacity, a Happy Father's Day. And for those of you who may not be fathers, but took part in honoring and celebrating the father figures that you have or may have had present in your life, I pray that this day was met with an abundance of joy.

Throughout the three years that I have been sharing my walk with the Lord via this blog, I have been very transparent in explaining that the Father's Day holiday has always been a very difficult one for me because for a while now, I have had a disconnected relationship with my earthly father; who, when I was younger, was my everything.

My father was the most loving and compassionate person and I never had to question how much he loved me. I was/am his carbon copy in female form, and felt like I was carrying the Olympic gold every time someone would comment on how I looked just like him; down to his eyes and smile.

Abruptly and for reasons that were way too complicated and intricately entangled for a twelve-year-old's mind to process; our relationship was no more and I was left with my greatest heartbreak.

All of that led to some really dark times for me. So many times, I cried out to Lord, because I felt He was all I had and I knew that when I prayed, He would listen. If it hadn't been for the Lord's compassion for me, I don't know where I would be.

I have spoken numerous times on the effect that "daddy pain" has on a child. But I have also followed up my sentiments by saying I have always believed that God would turn every circumstance I have encountered around for my good.

I am here to tell you that, I know without a doubt, that it has been because of God's eternal compassion, unfailing love and everlasting grace and mercy that on this Father's Day 2016, my daughters and I were blessed with the honor and privilege to spend some time with my father and treat him to a special Father's Day dinner. It still is very surreal to me because it had been 35 years since I last had the opportunity to spend Father's Day with him and 27 years since we've sat done together for a family meal.

Although I am trying to do my best to illustrate the magnitude of what occurred today and my gratitude to the Lord that is bursting from the seams of my heart; I know I can't do it proper justice.

Because of the Lord's compassion for me, I have been forgiven, made new and no longer enslaved by the past. Therefore, given the opportunity, why would I not offer the same compassion that I remember him showing me so early on in life to my father? It's a compassion that the Lord has continuously provided me with because of the awe-filled respect and deep reverence that I have for Him.

Some of the lyrics for today's song speaks to what I was feeling towards the Lord earlier today when it says, *"You've given far beyond my need so I give, my deepest thanks to You for all I've watched You do. And for the things that I am yet to see, still I'm confident and wait patiently. I cry out and you answer."*

Here is another area in my life, probably one of the most meaningful and important areas, where the Lord has given me beauty for ashes (Isaiah 61:3).

In Isaiah 61:3, the Hebrew word for ashes is epher and the Hebrew word for beauty is pheer.

Beauty for ashes is an exchange between God and me. As easily as epher can be transformed into pheer, God can and will turn our most heartbreaking situations around and from them the most beautiful blessings that were situated just beneath all the hurt and pain will break through.

I have been given an oil of joy for mourning and a garment of praise for the spirit of heaviness I have been carrying.

What a day today has been. And when I woke up for church this morning, the first thing I began singing was, "This is the day that the Lord has made. I will rejoice and be glad in it."

When I was younger, I thought the greatest prize I held was the physical attributes of my father; which, in turn, have been passed down to my children. As grateful as I am to have my father's eyes, I am even more grateful for my spiritual sense of sight being more finely tuned and aligned with the Word of God.

Learning to see things (myself, others and situations) the way God sees them, has been the driving force in me living a surrendered and unstuck life for Christ.

Strongholds have been forever broken and I have been set free so that I may receive all that God has for me, in His time which is always the right time!!

Suggested Song of Meditation: "Father" by Jadon Lavik

Jeremiah 1:5 (New Life Version/NLV)

⁵ "Before I started to put you together in your mother, I knew you. Before you were born, I set you apart as holy. I chose you to speak to the nations for Me."

When I tell you that there is never a dull moment in the JeffMot household, with the children I have, please believe me.

I continuously thank the Lord for blessing me with them and remain in awe of how great He is, as I observe my children living the lives that the Lord has handcrafted for each of them.

As a mother, when carrying each of my children in my womb, I did the absolute best I could to follow the doctor's orders; which included taking my prenatal vitamins, eating right, resting and avoiding stress at all costs. But, I always knew that it was completely in God's hands.

To think that before our mothers and fathers ever came together, God knew us and not only did He know us, He chose us and for a specific purpose; and the fact that that same principle applies to our children and our children's children and etc., is so profound to me.

God knew all that we would and wouldn't do and still chose us to do work for Him. We have been selected to be a prophet to the nations; spreading the good news about the Lord.

God knows the holy plans, the blessings and everything else that He has specifically for each of us. Each of those plans and blessings were individually declared and selected for us by name.

What God intended for me, is for me; not for my neighbor, my relative, a previous co-worker or anyone else and vice versa. I have no desire to get caught up in what someone else has because that is for them, nor do I desire to let myself or anyone/anything else get in the way of what God has for my family and me, because no one knows the plans that God has for mine and me, but Him.

And that is why I can wake up with joy in my heart and my mind stayed on Jesus because with Him is where my trust lies.

No matter what each day brings, I have come to recognize that tests and trials are for our betterment and come to make us strong.

Great is God's mercy for us and He is forever faithful towards us.

God has blessings with each of our names specifically etched across them. We will have naysayers and doubters, we will encounter some stumbling and may even fall at times, but count it all joy knowing that before we ever drew our first breath, we had been chosen and God's plans for us are to prosper and not to cause us harm. His plans are to give us hope and a future (Jeremiah 29:11).

Suggested Song of Meditation: "God's Got a Blessing" by Norman Hutchins

1 Thessalonians 5:11 (New International Reader's Version/NIRV)

[11] So encourage one another with the hope you have. Build each other up. In fact, that's what you are doing.

What a special day it was, as we celebrated the 19th birthday of my son today. Just looking at him, I honestly couldn't believe that 19 years have gone by so quickly.

I was actually three weeks from turning 20 years of age when I found out that I was pregnant with my son. I was active duty in the Air Force and hearing from the nurse at the clinic on base that, "I was one of three Airmen whose pregnancy test came back positive," believe me when I say that, those were the last words I ever expected to hear.

I figured I was just dealing with symptoms from the flu shot I had just received days earlier or that my anemia or thyroid were acting up, as they had in the past.

During that time, I was in such a lonely and lost place. I actually had enlisted in the Air Force, as a way of escaping my reality and with the hopes of finding myself. Well, on November 6, 1996, that journey to self-discovery took on a whole new meaning because I was now being tasked with the responsibility of caring for and nurturing another human being.

Nothing else mattered to me but the child that was growing inside of my womb; and without a sonogram, I knew deep down I was having a boy.

In a lot of ways at that time, I was looking for love in all the wrong places. My relationships with those in my family were either strained or non-existent and that was very difficult. That caused me to put my entire focus on the baby and me.

I knew that having sex and not being married was a sin. I was ashamed and felt I didn't deserve God's forgiveness. But, I also knew that I couldn't be the mom I desired to be without God and so I sought out the Lord, confessed my sins and asked for His forgiveness and guidance as I began this new chapter in my life.

It was through my pregnancy and the birth of my son, that I got a glimpse into just how much the Lord loved me. The thought that the Lord chose me to be His representative for this most precious gift was a feeling unlike any other.

For so much of my life I felt non-existent, rejected and unimportant. All that changed when I became a mother.

Being a mom, I desired nothing more than to be as closely aligned with the Lord as possible. Children do not get to choose their parents and it has always been my hope that my children never regretted that I was the one chosen for them.

I couldn't expect my son to show grace, mercy, compassion and forgiveness if I wasn't doing the same. I couldn't challenge him to be his best, if I only opted to accomplish the bare minimum. I couldn't teach him about the Lord and what it meant to have faith, if he always observed me putting my trust in other things or other individuals before taking it to the Lord. Nor could I express the power and importance of prayer, if one minute I'm on my knees praying and then the next, I'm back up worrying and stressing.

Tonight, when we went out to dinner, I felt encouraged and victorious in a way I can't even put into words. Over these past 19 years, it has been my son who has weathered some of the most turbulent storms with me. To look at us, you wouldn't even believe half of it, but God!!

It's because of the faith that we have had in the Lord, that we were able to remain strong and hopeful, even when we couldn't see how it would all work out. Not only has the Lord made it alright, but has He done exceedingly abundantly and gone infinitely beyond anything that we could have ever asked or dreamt of.

That resonated so loudly as my husband, daughters and I had the opportunity to share in my son's birthday celebration with my father. There were three generations of Jeffersons at the restaurant this evening and none of that would have been possible without God.

I am my father's only child and, therefore, my children are the only grandchildren he could ever have. What an amazingly indescribable evening it was; especially given the fact that my father and my relationship had been completely disconnected for the past 27 years.

But in those 27 years, (even when I didn't understand), it was the tests and trials that I endured that helped to make me better and stronger; and provided me with clarity and insight in a way that I wouldn't have been able to receive it otherwise. All of it was preparing me for a time such as this.

I have chosen to forget the former things and am so thankful for this season of restoration and reconciliation that the Lord has not just ushered me into, but my entire family as well.

Looking across the table at the man who is the reason for the features that my children and I have on our face and realizing that we were all together made my eyes tear up.

Gazing back and forth between my father and my son, who not only favor ridiculously but who also share the same initials and mannerisms, reminded me that even though it was my son's birthday, what a gift and privilege the Lord had also granted me.

Given all that I have experienced and all the ways that the Lord continues to provide for my family and me, why would I worry about my life and how could I not be encouraged?

I don't know what each of you may be facing, but I'm here to tell you that if you hang on, don't give up and keep your faith in the Lord, He will make it alright and turn it around for your good.

Watch!! God will step right in and provide right before your eyes, in ways that you can't explain nor will you be able to deny!!

Suggested Song of Meditation: "God Provides" by Tamela Mann

Deuteronomy 32:4 (International Standard Version/ISV)

⁴ Flawless is the work of the Rock, because all his ways are just. A faithful God—never unjust—righteous and upright is he.

How great and greatly to be praised our Heavenly Father is. As I am blessed and fortunate to see the dawning and conclusion of another day, I am reminded of just how perfect, powerful and personal the Lord is.

One thing that I am very guilty of doing is keeping track of those who appear or have shown me that they are not in any way concerned about those things that concern me. Lately, there has been one mountain and giant after another. And although I am a very private person, sometimes you just want to know that people will take time out to think about you in the same way you have for them.

This season of transition has been more difficult and trying than I ever anticipated and yet, I wonder how would I have known what to anticipate when I haven't ever been in the place that I find myself in now?

So many things have changed and a lot of those changes have occurred in me primarily. I have been stripped of my crutches, training wheels and support apparatuses and have been brought to a place where I am depending completely and ultimately on the fact the Lord is my mighty defender and will move the mountains and cause the giants that are in front of me to fall; if I wholly surrender it all to Him and believe in His faithfulness and righteous.

Everything that the Lord does is perfect. He is Almighty, a provider, protector and the possessor of all power in heaven and on earth. There isn't any victory over Him and He is the one person I don't ever question whether He is concerned about me. I know that the Lord is always thinking about me and watching everything that concerns me.

Our God is so awesome. He heals every area where brokenness has resided and provides strength where we once were weakened. Jesus was pierced for our transgressions and by His stripes, we have been forgiven and healed.

The Lord is worthy to receive all glory, honor and praise. Because all His ways are just and His work is flawless, I am stronger, wiser and encouraged to keep pressing ahead in this race that I am running.

Suggested Song of Meditation: "Awesome Remix" by Charles Jenkins ft. Jessica Reedy, Isaac Carree, Da' T.R.U.T.H. & Canton Jones.

PRAISE AND WORSHIP
ARE HOW I EXPRESS
MY GRATITUDE

Psalm 113:3 (Amplified Bible/AMP)

³ From the rising of the sun to its setting the name of the Lord is to be praised [with awe-inspired reverence].

I have always loved watching how the sky transforms both when the sun rises and when it sets. When I think about all that transpires in a day between those two moments, it is with an awe-inspired reverence, that I worship and praise the name of the Lord. Right before noon, my children and I were involved in a car accident. The other driver decided to switch lanes without signaling, and as much as I tried to swerve all the way to the right so that we would not be impacted, the rear section of our vehicle was still struck. I am forever grateful that none of us—my children, the other driver nor myself suffered any injuries.

With everything that has been happening, both here in the U.S. and abroad, the hedge of protection that the Lord provides each and every day is just one of the reasons that at every time and in every place—from the moment the sun rises to the moment it sets—the name of the Eternal remains high in my heart.

Here in New York, the sun normally rises around 5:40 a.m. and sets around 8:20 p.m. When I think about all the circumstances that occur and all those incidents that the Lord blocks from happening within that fifteen-hour time frame, I enter His gates with a song of thanksgiving in my heart. I come into His courtyards with a song of praise, giving thanks to Him and praising His name (Psalm 100:4).

Because it is not an alarm clock that wakes my family and me up each morning, because of the limitless love, grace and mercy that I receive from the Lord, because I am protected from dangers, both seen and unseen, because when I am weak, I am strong; honestly, just because of who the Lord is, I have a worship song to sing.

Suggested Song of Meditation: "Worship Song" by Y'Anna Crawley

1 Corinthians 1:4 (The Living Bible/TLB)

⁴ I can never stop thanking God for all the wonderful gifts He has given you, now that you are Christ's.

I am a person who is very big on reflection. In reflecting and looking back on the past and times of old, my desire is not to go back to those mindsets or situations and remain there, but to rejoice and give thanks to God for where I was and just how far He has brought me.

As I was standing in the line at the grocery store yesterday securing all the items that we needed for the beginning of this week and our Thanksgiving feast, I looked into my cart and began to tear up thanking God for His grace, mercy and favor that had positioned us to be able to pay for all the items that I had. I know what it is like to not know how you're going to get through the day, let alone the week, month or year. And yet, during my times of reflection, I have countless examples of the manna that the Lord blessed my family with during our hardest times and the resources in abundance that have provided us the opportunity to be a blessing to someone else.

Every day that the eyes open and the limbs function for my family and me, I am thankful. Having the opportunity to serve the Lord and others, I am thankful. Because of the reassurance in His Word and the promises that He has made to us, I know that trouble doesn't last always; I am thankful. For all that I thought I should have and where I thought I should be, that the Lord didn't give me and didn't place me, I am thankful. Because of the price that Jesus paid on the cross for our sins, granting us open and free access to God, I am thankful. Trust me, I could go on and on.

We should always give thanks because we serve an eternally faithful God. If we place our focus on man, who is flawed, we will become discouraged and lose hope. But by placing our concentration on the Lord, even during our hardest times and darkest hours we can be filled with praise and thanksgiving.

I don't know and don't need to know each of your personal stories to know that God has and continues to bless each and every one of us. No matter what we may currently be going through, we always have a reason to say "Thank you."

Each morning, before you lay the petitions of your heart before His altar, I challenge you first to just say, "Thank you." Thank Him for all that He has already done before going to Him about what you need. Our Heavenly Father already knows the desires of our hearts and the provisions that are in place for His will to be done. For some people, we may be the only Bible they ever read. If you're going to read my pages, I want you to know that first and foremost, I am thankful!!

Suggested Song of Meditation: "I Want to Say Thank you" by Lisa Page

Hebrews 4:16 (Worldwide English (New Testament)/WE)

¹⁶ So let us trust him when we come to worship God. He is so good. He will be kind to us and help us when we need it.

I am a "words of affirmation" person and so having an encouraging and uplifting word sown into me is truly the gift that keeps on giving. I desire not only to constantly be in a positive place filled with encouragement, but to sow that encouragement into others.

With that being said, I know that sometimes when we are just going through life, it can be hard to always smile or always feel uplifted. Some trials just leave you wondering, "Why, Lord why," or at least for me they do. And it's during these times that I truly realize how much I really do need God. When things just don't appear to make sense, or when the obstacles are so far out of my control, but have a direct and significant impact on my family and me, that is when I feel most fragile and when I look to depending solely on the Lord; who is the same yesterday, today and forever.

I boldly go before His throne, even in a fragile state, knowing that in God, the grace and mercy that I need to make a way for me can always be found. I put all my confidence and faith in the Lord regardless of what may arise. And yes, I will be one of the first ones to say our God may not come when we want Him, but He is always on time; even when I desire resolution or the expiration of that trial to come sooner than later. I reflect on the previous trials that I have endured and the strength, growth and maturity that were by-products of those particular obstacles.

Stretched out before the Lord, making my petitions known and voicing how much I need the Lord makes my relationship with Him that much deeper and my faith that much stronger. Without any doubts, I know who will never leave me nor forsake me.

On this day, I just wanted to remind each of you and myself that victory is ours and that there isn't ever anything wrong with openly expressing to the Lord just how much we need Him. God is indeed the best friend we could ever have. A best friend that not only knows us better than we know ourselves, but who also has all power in His hands.

Suggested Song of Meditation: "I Need You Now" by Smokie Norful

1 Thessalonians 5:16-17 (Expanded Bible/EXB)

¹⁶ Always ·be joyful [rejoice]. ¹⁷ Pray ·continually [without ceasing].

Oh, how I love Jesus, because He first loved me. I pray that each day when you rise, you are filled with such a spirit of thankfulness. We can get so caught up in our day-to-day routines, or waiting on those "big things" that we are believing God for that we forget to thank Him for all the little things that He continues to do for us on a regular basis. And so, before I say anything else, I have to say to the Lord, "Thank you."

I have always been a believer that prayer works and still is the strongest weapon that we have. It's not just praying that is important but how we pray. When we pray, we should still have a rejoicing spirit and be able to pray without losing one ounce of hope or becoming discouraged. Regardless of what our current situation reflects, we need to be thankful in all circumstances. When we believe in our Heavenly Father and know that He hears our prayers and will answer them according to His will, there isn't any room for uncertainty, worry or doubt.

I'll tell you that I am so grateful that my prayers are answered according to God's will and NOT my own. Goodness gracious, when I think about some of the petitions that I have laid before the Lord over the years, that had He granted and given me just what I had asked for, I know confidently that I would have been worse off and nowhere near where I am right now. Some of my prayers were quite limited. In them, I was short-changing myself and putting limitations on the Lord, when He had so much more in store for me.

Praying has been something I have naturally wanted to do, ever since I was very young and my father had me kneel at the bed and taught me the Lord's Prayer. But over the years, through growing closer to God, I have learned that knowing how to pray is imperative. And that my disposition as I wait for the answers to those prayers is equally important as well.

You will see no pity parties here, as I wait on the Lord. I have learned to pray and not faint (Luke 18:1). I submit my petitions before the Lord and then I wait expectantly (Psalm 5:3). I do so with a song of praise and a word of encouragement throughout the entire process. There is only One person in control of our lives. Within Him is where we find our strength and our refuge and through His Word is where we seek our answers, because we know that anything that we ask in HIS name, He will do (John 14:13-14).

As I become more mature in my spiritual walk (because it is an ongoing process), I know that my prayers give me direct access to Him. I do not need to explain all the details; I can just be free to speak to Him and watch Him move throughout my situations. Each test and trial is for my good and so I look at each one as an opportunity to see what God desires to teach and show me.

I have learned and grown to appreciate that things do not get answered on my time, but on His. Let me tell you that there are many life changes that, had they occurred when I thought they should have, I would have missed out on so many other blessings in my life. We serve an on-time God.

The wonderful news is that I know firsthand that prayer changes things. I will rejoice in Christ Jesus' name and give Him all the honor, glory, praise and thanks in the beginning, in the middle and at the end when my deliverance has come. I pray that you will do the same.

Suggested Song of Meditation: "Good News" by Vanessa Bell Armstrong

Colossians 1:11 (Complete Jewish Bible/CJB)

¹¹ We pray that you will be continually strengthened with all the power that comes from his glorious might; so that you will be able to persevere and be patient in any situation, joyfully.

So much happens in my life that constantly reminds me that there is no greater power nor greater God, than our God. He is the God of love, God of power and God of mercy. His hand of grace has touched me and I have been forever transformed. Even on my weakest day, I am convinced that it is through God's strength that I can do anything. I no longer look at tests and trials like I used to.

My initial response to trying times was that, "I did something wrong or I was being punished for this or that decision that I had made." In taking the time to get to know the Lord (having that intimate relationship with Him and being deeply rooted in His Word), I learned how to persevere in the midst of my storms. The power that comes from His glorious might has strengthened me time and time again. When I am going through, I am able to do so joyfully, while praising and glorifying His name.

With God, I am able to hold on. Regardless of what the current situation may be reflecting, I know that with God I am covered. There were times when I felt so alone, not realizing that God was there all along right beside me. Sometimes we get so caught up in our current circumstances and situations that we lose sight of the One who always has been and always will be there for us. It's when we lose sight of who is truly in control of our lives that the enemy is able to take over.

I have made the declaration that the enemy doesn't get an invitation or permission to distract, upset or stress me. If I am living a life surrendered to God, then I believe God for what shall come to pass in my life. Therefore, I cannot waste time being stressed over things that are not within my control or that God never called me to carry in the first place. Time is the one thing we cannot get back once it's gone and I learned yesterday in my Leadership Institute class that how we spend our time reflects the giver of time—God. That one statement was so profound to me because I always say that, "There is not enough time in the day." Therefore, I am learning the importance of prioritizing what I allow my time to be focused on.

In the past, so much of my time was spent on worrying and trying to figure out my life, other people and their situations. I would literally be stressed for no reason. That was until I realized what stressing over situations really meant. It meant that I had forgotten or stopped acknowledging that God was/is in control. That was indeed a hard pill to swallow and yet one I needed to hear because I know that every breath that I breathe is because God says so. I know that every trial that I have come up against and the ones that have yet to surface, my victory in them in no way is because of my strength or me, but because of the strength that comes from above and the all-powerful God I serve.

That power means that I can be going through it, but you would never know it because I am still smiling, praising Him and filled with joy because I know that it is all working together for my good. I am encouraged knowing that nothing can come my way without God's approval. Being equipped with this knowledge provides me with the necessary endurance needed to run this race. My faith does not rest in human wisdom, but in the power of God (1 Corinthians 2:5).

Be encouraged knowing that the same power that resurrected Jesus from the dead lives within us. When we keep our focus on God and walk in His supernatural power, it will overflow into our natural domain.

Suggested Song of Meditation: "With You" by James Fortune and Fiya featuring Kim Burrell

Psalm 103:2 (Expanded Bible/EXB)

² ·My whole being [O my soul], ·praise [bless] the Lord and do not forget all his ·kindnesses [gifts; benefits].

What an amazing day we had celebrating my oldest daughter's birthday and I couldn't help but get emotional.

As I watched her laughing and creating lifelong memories with such a great group of young ladies that she has been blessed to label as friends and extended family, all I could do was thank God for all that He has done and continues to do in our lives.

There are not enough combinations of characters on the keyboard to illustrate and capture just how good God has been to me. When I was just a couple of months into my pregnancy with my oldest daughter, I found myself homeless. Active duty in the military, with an almost four-year-old son and another child on the way, I was in such a broken state because I had placed my expectations on and my trust in certain people before ever thinking about entrusting it all to God first.

It took a broken engagement, having nowhere to live and feeling like the biggest failure to God and my children to get that wake up call. Basically, it took God allowing my world to be flipped upside down where I was so low, I didn't have the energy or the strength to do anything but look up to the hills for the help I was in dire need of.

I needed to be better, to do better and to receive better. There was no way that I could do that by serving two Masters. I was trying to please God and yet, allowing the strongholds of fear and rejection to make me feel like I had to do everything I could to please man as well.

With each bump in the road and each bump on my head I acquired by trying to resolve situations or look for answers my own way, God still was better to me than I ever was to myself.

My pregnancy with my oldest daughter was during the hardest time in my life and I woke up each morning not knowing if I would miscarry her or have half my face paralyzed, due to Bell's Palsy, like it had just been a year prior. I have always called her my miracle baby because it was only because of God that she entered this earth on January 18, 2002, healthy and with a purpose all her own to live and fulfill.

I was not married when I got pregnant with any of my children. That is definitely nothing to brag about, nor was being a single mom ever a plan or aspiration that I had growing up. But even with falling short, and God knowing all my days before they ever came to be, He still called me out by name and chose me.

There is no way that I could ever wake up on any morning and forget to praise, thank and honor God for loving me first. I thank Him for His illimitable love, grace, mercy and kindness. I look at my husband and my children and am constantly reminded of how much God loves me because He blessed me to be attached to and loved by them.

With all that I am, I will praise the Lord. Without God, I am and can do nothing, but with Him all things are possible (Mark 10:27). Please don't ever forget to remember all that God does for you. Nothing that we have is because of anything that we have done. It all comes from the blessings and favor that God has bestowed upon us. Don't ever forget to remember where your blessings come from. I know I won't.

Suggested Song of Meditation: "Don't Forget to Remember" by Donald Lawrence featuring Lalah Hathaway

Ephesians 5:20 (International Standard Version/ISV)

²⁰ You will consistently give thanks to God the Father for everything in the name of our Lord Jesus, the Messiah;

No matter where you may find yourself today, there is always a reason to rejoice. If for no other reason, sing songs of praise and thanksgiving knowing that it wasn't an alarm clock or rooster that woke you up this morning, but the Lord, himself.

Whether we like it or not, trials and obstacles will come into our lives. When we change our perspective and realize that these inconveniences are for a reason and that each test has its time and season, giving thanks comes so much more naturally. I give thanks through each period of my life (and some of them have been pretty rough). I know that there are many more trials ahead of me, and yet I am grateful in the midst of the trials I must confront nonetheless.

My life has seen some amazingly indescribable mountain highs, but also some unanticipated valley lows that resulted in a pain being left so deep within. At times, it appeared that the more I prayed, not only did things stay the same, but they would even get worse. Back then I didn't know the importance of giving thanks just as much (if not more) through the bad times, as I did when everything was flowing my way.

I have learned the significance of putting aside every burden that could so easily impede me from the destiny that God has for me.

Encouraging others is something I love doing and through this journey of my life thus far, I know personally how important it is to be able to encourage myself first. I am able to motivate myself, because in all things, I have discovered how crucial it is to give thanks to the Lord, knowing that it is all working together for my good (Romans 8:28).

Suggested Song of Meditation: "Give Thanks" by Marvin Sapp

Hebrews 13:15 (Complete Jewish Bible/CJB)

¹⁵ Through him, therefore, let us offer God a sacrifice of praise continually. For this is the natural product of lips that acknowledge his name.

Music speaks to the very essence of who I am. Every season and chapter of my life has been marked by songs that spoke to where I was at that particular time.

When I reflect on all that the Lord has done and keeps doing in my life, I don't have a desire to do anything but praise the name of the Lord. Songs of praise are the instruments that I utilize. The songs that I sing come from deep within. When I was younger and had the opportunity to work with a vocal coach, she emphasized the importance of me singing from my diaphragm and not my throat. As a ten-year-old girl, I had no idea what that meant until the vocal coach had me perform a couple of vocal exercises. How surprised I was to hear the fullness of the sound that was coming out of me. She told me to always make sure that when I opened my mouth to sing, it always came "from the gut".

In just living life, I have countless reasons to give thanks to God. And when I do, there is always a song attached to it. Whether here at home, at church, in the grocery store or in my car traveling from point A to point B, there is a praise that wells up from deep within me. I do not restrict it because it is my desire that God never put restrictions on His reach to me.

I have also learned that when you have no problem praising the Lord, others will notice. And yes, they may think you are giddy or maybe even strange, but they also will be curious and want to know what indeed is causing you to act in the manner you are. When opportunities like that happen, we are given a chance to win more souls for the kingdom by being a walking testimony of just how great our God is.

In my life, I have sung and danced for reasons that gave back nothing worthwhile. Please understand that when giving thanks to the Lord, I, joyfully and with the fullness I was instructed to use many years ago, offer up the praise that continues to build on the inside, when I think about the goodness of the Lord. I can't and don't desire to keep it to myself; it is inviting and infectious.

On this day and each day that I am fortunate to see in the future, I will continually part my lips to sing songs of praise, because praise is the way I say thanks. How will you praise Him?

Suggested Song of Meditation: "Praise on the Inside" by J. Moss

Hebrews 12:28 (English Standard Version/ESV)

²⁸ Therefore let us be grateful for receiving a kingdom that cannot be shaken, and thus let us offer to God acceptable worship, with reverence and awe.

How is it even possible to awake in the morning and not be consumed with gratefulness; let alone not take the time to express that thankfulness to the Lord? I have been guilty of rising and becoming immediately consumed with the laundry list of tasks that I am expected to accomplish; thus, hitting the ground running. Those days are over. Just opening my eyes, I say thank you. Knowing that my husband and children have been kept through the night and into the dawning of a new day, I am grateful.

I am so thankful for all that the Lord does on behalf of my family and me; those things seen and unseen, known and unknown. For the protection and covering that He provides us with, before we ever have reason to be alarmed. From every corner of my heart and to the deepest places in my soul, gratefulness flows from me.

In order to be catapulted into anywhere, you have to have some tension.

It's essential that we understand that seasons are inevitable and are a part of life. It's really unrealistic to expect that all we will ever have to endure are the Springs and Summers, without any impact from the Falls and Winters. Each season serves a particular purpose. I am not just grateful for the mountain high seasons in my life, but also for the valley low and despondent seasons of my life as well. It was during those times that I was being sculpted and freed from strongholds.

I am so grateful that the Lord knows what I can bear and that He always knows what I need, when I need it and who I need to be aligned with to receive it. There aren't enough words to convey my gratitude for the divine connections that the Lord has already established and the ones that have yet to be formed. I know that none of this would be possible if I wasn't connected to the Lord and constantly desiring to have a more intimate relationship with Him. With each word I speak, move I make and step I take I want the world to know that I am so grateful for all the marvelous works that the Lord continues to do in my life.

How blessed we are to serve a God, in whom no one nor nothing is greater. We should have a longing desire to worship Him and to show Him the utmost honor and respect because we have been chosen to receive a kingdom that cannot be shaken.

For all the victories we have already won and those we still have yet to win, an indescribable gratefulness resonates within me. Praising the name of the Lord is just one of the ways I know to express my gratefulness.

Let us never hesitate to display that gratitude to the One who consistently gives us more than we could ever deserve.

Suggested Song of Meditation: "Grateful" by Hezekiah Walker

Exodus 15:2 (Common English Bible/CEB)

² The Lord is my strength and my power; He has become my salvation. This is my God, whom I will praise, the God of my ancestors, whom I will acclaim.

When we can confidently proclaim that God is our strong defender, how could we not automatically offer up praise and worship to our Lord? Praising Him should be something that we do without even having to think twice about it. It should be something that just naturally occurs, like blinking. If we look back over any season of our lives, we will recognize the countless places where God was our strength, which resulted in us being protected and delivered from the trials we were facing.

Something that I have come to realize is that there is indescribable power in praising God. Whether there are strongholds or yokes that have had you bound for years, or a sickness or medical condition that has taken residence in your body or just a situation that you can't or don't see a resolution for in sight, praise His name, and have the radical belief in knowing that your worship is shifting the atmosphere. It is causing a shift from what is happening today into what God will have for you in the days, weeks and years to come.

Sometimes when we are going through, we have to be able to get ourselves out of the way enough to be able to just utter the words, "Lord I need your help." I have experienced instances in my life when I was knocked down so low; I believed that going any lower wasn't even a possibility. But, I also knew I didn't want to stay where I was. I honestly didn't have the inclination or energy to do anything but, raise my hands, open my mouth with words and songs of worship to the Lord because I knew that He was the only way I would see a breakthrough in my circumstances. God not only shifted my circumstances, He changed my entire way of thinking and where I thought I was being punished, I learned to be grateful for the very trial that I thought would leave me broken forever.

When we praise and worship the Lord and get to the place where we bless His name at all times, situations and outcomes begin to move in our favor. Don't ever downplay or underestimate the power that comes from praising and worshipping the Lord. If you want chains broken, healing and for God to usher you into that new season in your life, worship our Heavenly Father and prepare to witness a shifting in your life.

Suggested Song of Meditation: "Shifting the Atmosphere" by Jason Nelson

Psalm 139:14 (Authorized (King James) Version/AKJV)

¹⁴ I will praise thee; for I am fearfully and wonderfully made: marvelous are thy works; and that my soul knoweth right well.

I have been able to take some much needed time to really reflect on all that had been revealed to me lately. Chains that I didn't even know I was confined by were broken.

During this time, I have said "goodbye" and "so long" to regret, shame and all those former things that were deeply rooted and had to be uncovered so that I could be released from them. For so much of my life, I felt like an outcast. Now, anyone who knows me probably would find that very hard to believe. I learned early on that if I took more time to focus on and tend to everyone else, then that didn't leave much time for people to focus on me and what it was that I truly needed and the areas where I felt lack.

I remember during my teenage years, most of my friends would be primping in the mirrors at school or at their homes when we would get ready for dances and other social events. They would have all their foundation, eyeliner, lip liner, lipstick and mascara out and I would be lucky to have some flavored AVON chap stick. My parents did not play me wearing anything on my face. Honestly, that didn't even bother me because I didn't like looking in the mirror anyway. When I glanced in the mirror, I saw one thing and one thing only, all of my father's features. I was his carbon copy.

From birth until the age of 12 years old, I wore that badge of being my father's twin proudly, like a new sheriff at the O.K. Corral. You couldn't tell me nothing!! But at the age of 12, because of reasons I still have yet to fully comprehend, my father's presence was removed from my life and my definition of myself was tied to that catastrophic event. I, therefore, had no desire to be in the mirror any longer than I had to. If I did, I saw his eyes, his eyelashes and eyebrows, his nose, his lips; just his face. I carried those sentiments for all of my adolescence and into adulthood.

It wasn't until I became a mom for the first time at the age of 20 years old and I looked into my baby boy's beautiful and perfect face; that possessed those same eyes, eyelashes, eyebrows, nose, lips, etc., that I realized that my focus had been on the wrong father. I will always love my biological father, but it is my Heavenly Father who knew me before I was formed in my mother's womb and created me in His own image. How could I ever be ashamed again knowing that I am fearfully and wonderfully made? How could I shy away from one aspect of my bone structure when all of the works of God are wonderful?

In trusting in the Lord, I am free and ascending to new heights. I have let go of the hurt and disappointment that others have brought to my life. Those thoughts that have tried to control me are no longer granted access to me. God has ushered me into a new season and place where it is time to dust off my dreams. Those aspirations that were planted so long ago have sprouted and it is harvest time.

I know that there is a book on the horizon. There are quite a few more pages that need to be written before it's brought to fruition. But there are also some pages, in the story of my life, which I no longer desire to read anymore. God has instructed us to, "Forget the former things and do not dwell on the past." (Isaiah 43:18) That was then and this is now.

I am walking confidently in my uniqueness; being strong and courageous, as the person God created me to be. I have been kept and held by His love, grace and mercy. I sing praises to the Lord because I am His accomplishment, created in Christ Jesus to do good things. God planned for these good things to be the way that we live our lives (Ephesians 2:10). Can you imagine me?

Suggested Song of Meditation: "Imagine Me" by Alexis Spight

Psalm 146:2 (International Children's Bible/ICB)

² I will praise the Lord all my life. I will sing praises to my God as long as I live.

I will always rejoice in the Lord. The love that He provides us with alone is more than enough reason to rejoice.

I am so grateful to Jesus for taking my place on the cross and that is why I will praise the Lord all my life. I will sing songs of praise to our God for as long as I live. I will not just praise Him when everything fits together and appears to be flowing smoothly. I will praise Him through all things and that praise will be in advance. I will praise Him because I know that His spirit lives within me and I am certain that whatever He has spoken over my life, shall come to pass regardless of what may appear in front of and all around me.

The enemy will try to distract me, but I know I have favor with God. I will praise Him and through my praise I will speak those things that are not as if they already were. Based on our circumstances, it can be so easy to fall into the mindset that, "Things won't ever change or get better." But when we can praise God before His promises ever begin to manifest in our lives, we are allowing our thoughts to align with the thoughts and plans that the Lord has for us.

We can praise Him in advance because we have the Word of God nestled inside of us. Go ahead and confuse the enemy by praising the name of the Lord while in the midst of our storms and trials. In spite of what you may be enduring or what you may be waiting and believing God for, start singing, dancing and offering up applause to the Lord.

With my praise, I will give God the glory that only He deserves. In my praise, I will open my mouth, tell my story and offer up thanksgiving because He is so worthy. My whole life I will praise Him and praise Him in advance.

Suggested Song of Meditation: "Praise Him in Advance" by Marvin Sapp

1 Thessalonians 3:9 (New Living Translation/NLT)

⁹ How we thank God for you! Because of you we have great joy as we enter God's presence.

As the sun's rays began to peek through my blinds this morning, I woke up singing, "Joy cometh in the morning, it comes in with morning light. Weeping may endure for a night, but joy cometh in the morning."

It is so encouraging to know that regardless of what we are up against, as we enter into God's presence, we have a joy within us that cannot be taken away. Because of the sacrifice that Jesus made on our behalf, we are filled with joy because we have that expectation of sharing in God's glory.

We may feel pressed on every side by troubles, but will not be crushed. We may end up feeling perplexed, but will not be driven to despair. We may at times be hunted down, but never abandoned by God. We may get knocked down, but we will not be destroyed (2 Corinthians 4:8-9). There is something that the world can try as hard as it can to take from us, but it will be unsuccessful in obtaining; and that one thing is our joy.

I desire to show my gratefulness and appreciation by the life I live. It's easy to say we've got joy, joy, joy, joy down in our hearts to stay when everything is falling into place. What about when we're up against sickness, trials and persecution? Are we still proclaiming that same joy, joy, joy, joy is here to stay?

When we realize that our joy is not influenced or dictated by our external circumstances and situations, we can make that declaration that the joy that we have within us is not going anywhere. We also won't hesitate to proclaim that we are survivors and that we will overcome.

Remember that the Lord knows the plans that He has for us and those plans include giving us hope for tomorrow and joy for our sorrows. The joy that we have, the world didn't give to us; therefore, the world can't take it away!!

Suggested Song of Meditation: "Can't Take My Joy Away" by Vashawn Mitchell

Deuteronomy 10:21 (New International Version/NIV)

²¹ He is the one you praise; he is your God, who performed for you those great and awesome wonders you saw with your own eyes.

If I don't know anything else, I recognize the importance of being able to praise the Lord at all times. I will constantly have a song in my heart that my lips will always be ready to part and sing. It doesn't matter whether good or bad, I vow to praise the Lord.

I know that when we are dealing with so much, being able to raise our hands and offer praise to the Lord may be the last thing we are inclined to do. It is so important for us to do an about face in regards to that way of thinking. Praising the Lord has to become a lifestyle that we eagerly invite and adopt into our lives. Whether happy or sad, we need to worship and honor the Lord through our worship.

In just living life and with our very own eyes, we have witnessed the great, wondrous and mighty miracles that only God is capable of performing.

Praise Him because He is a God that knows the thoughts that He has for each of us and everything that He has begun in us, He will continue until its completion.

Even when I'm going through and with everything that may come my way, I have learned that there isn't any circumstance that even stands a chance because my faith outweighs all that appears to be unfortunate or uncomfortable in my life.

Praising God brings me closer to the Lord; and near Him is exactly where I need to be. I owe it all to God and my praise is one of the ways that I show my appreciation and gratitude.

Suggested Song of Meditation: "Praise Is What I Do" by William Murphy

Psalm 63:3 (The Message/MSG)

³ In your generous love I am really living at last! My lips brim praises like fountains.

During a conversation with someone who is like a big brother to me, we were discussing how not knowing one's self-worth can be such a detriment.

When I reflect on the situations that have caused me the greatest amount of heartache, shame, guilt and regret, it was because my self-worth and my definition of love was not based on who God said I was, or what God's love had shown me; it was determined by how others chose to define me and by the love they did or didn't decide to show me.

It took a lot of twists and turns and bumps in the road to really see and comprehend just how amazing and unfailing God's love is. Even when I was all the way to the left and navigating towards the right didn't appear to be in sight, His love still covered me. That which could have destroyed me, didn't. God has never abandoned me, even when I abandoned myself.

My family knows that anytime I see a homeless person, my heart truly goes out to them. I strive to take nothing for granted because I remember a season in my life when because of the choices I had made and ones that I had allowed others to make for me, I found myself active duty in the military, with a four-year-old, pregnant with my second child, now homeless and over $15,000 in the hole over a wedding that ended up never happening. There are no words to convey how deeply swallowed up in a dark abyss I felt. Where the enemy attempted to take me mentally and emotionally during that time in my life; with the enormous amount of shame, disappointment and regret I carried, was unimaginable. That was a pivotal moment in my life. I know that the only reason that I made it through was because of God's grace and mercy that kept me.

What could have been my breaking point, broke me down just far enough for me to realize that I was attempting to serve man and the Lord at the same time.

I could not live my life that way anymore, if I desired to be whole and acquire the destiny and inheritance that God had already chosen and appointed beforehand for me. That's why you won't hear me complaining. When I see others going through, I immediately pray for them, because I understand how missing one piece of the puzzle can bring a halt to everything.

Who I am, who I shall be and how I love myself and others is rooted in who God says I am and the love He has for me. With my lips, my praises to the Lord will forever overflow like fountains and I will constantly thank Him for all the other "could haves" that He prevented me from experiencing; because He didn't have to.

Without Jesus' love for me, I do not even want to think about where I would be. His love has covered, guided and protected me. I am eternally grateful for the relationship that I have with the Lord. When I think about all that He has and continues to do for me, my heart leaps with joy.

Suggested Song of Meditation: "Could've Been Me" by Kirk Franklin featuring J. Moss and Tye Tribbett

Isaiah 12:5 (Contemporary English Version/CEV)

⁵ Because of your wonderful deeds we will sing your praises everywhere on earth."

There are some days when just hearing a song that reminds me of how awesome our God is, is exactly what the doctor ordered. With my son about to graduate from high school in less than a week, I have been on such an emotional roller coaster and it has been such a time of reflection for me.

When I think about my life, I am left in awe of the 180 degree turn that the Lord has performed in my life. I remember when I wanted to know everything and in so many ways didn't know anything. I gave everyone else the access to define me and determine the paths I would take. For someone with pretty good vision, book knowledge and common sense, I was walking around this earth so blind and misguided. But God....

Every area where I was broken and experienced lack, God took everything that I was and not only turned it around for my good, but used it to make me who I am today. Those places where I felt emptiness, the Lord not only filled them but caused an overflow to occur. Where I felt inadequacies, the Lord reminded me of who He said I was and that knowledge brought a wholeness and completion to my life that I didn't even know was possible. What I viewed as the absolute worst in me, God turned it around and made it the best in me. He gave His absolute best to me.

I rejoice and sing praises because although I may not be where I am supposed to be yet, I know hands down that I am not at all where I used to be. I will continuously worship the Lord for deeming me worthy enough to be on the receiving end of His amazing and infinite love. For all my days and with all I am, my worship will be in spirit and in truth. Through songs, my words and my actions praising the Lord will be at the forefront of all that I do.

Suggested Song of Meditation: "I Worship You" by Mary Mary

Hebrews 13:16 (The Message/MSG)

16 Make sure you don't take things for granted and go slack in working for the common good; share what you have with others. God takes particular pleasure in acts of worship—a different kind of "sacrifice"—that take place in kitchen and workplace and on the streets.

As I sat at my dining room table this morning, I began to think about a conversation I was having with a few of my son's fellow classmates, regarding taking on roles and responsibilities and when we volunteer ourselves, what should be the foundation for all those things.

I was explaining to them that even though I am very much a people person and will be the first one to volunteer and help out, I never do it with the hopes of recognition and accolades being attached to it. I love being that go-to person for others, but definitely do not do it for the attention because that is not what it is about for me, plus I do not like the attention to be on me.

I learned early on that God had placed within me a heart of service and one that adores giving. It isn't always about the material things that we give others. The best acts of service that we can do, are the ones that come from our heart. We all have gifts and talents. They were given to us for a reason. In all things, I strive to be good to others and to share what I have in ways that are most pleasing to God.

When what I'm doing is what God has called me to do, I never view that as a sacrifice. To me, that's an opportunity to let the God in me shine for the whole world to see.

Taking the time to do for others doesn't have to be elaborate or extravagant. Calling and checking up on one another or just listening and praying for someone else means more than most ever realize. When we take the time to do things like: making a meal, providing transportation, offering to assist in cleaning someone's home, babysitting so some downtime can be enjoyed, or helping someone to study for an upcoming exam; all of these are examples of things that may seem insignificant to one person, but would warm the heart and show God's love to someone else.

Each day, I seek God not to just be a strong leader in my home and community, but to be a strong and caring servant leader within my home, community and the areas I am fortunate to travel to.

Remember when we are happy and smiling, someone else is hurting and crying. On those days when our skies are filled with the sun, others are feeling the downpour from the storm clouds of life that are raging. We are given countless opportunities to help others.

Seek out the Lord so that you don't ever miss your opportunity to be a blessing to others as God continues to bless you.

Suggested Song of Meditation: "Help Somebody" by Deitrick Haddon

Psalm 35:28 (Amplified Bible/AMP)

²⁸ And my tongue shall talk of Your righteousness, rightness, and justice, and of [my reasons for] Your praise all the day long.

Throughout my life, every last one of the unimaginable blessings that I have received from the Lord came after a season of trials and opposition. I have a reason to praise the Lord each and every day because I am a breathing and walking example of His continuous goodness.

Where others discounted and wrote me off, the Lord had already written victory in the pages of my life. Praising the Lord causes everything around me to look and feel better. When we praise and give thanks to the Lord, strongholds and yokes are also broken and destroyed. Our praise has the power to eliminate the temporal woes that we endure throughout our journey.

With my whole being, I will praise the Lord all day long because I can see everything so much clearer now. I recognize that before the Lord can bring the level of restoration that He has for my life, there are some things I must undergo and encounter first. And I will shout Hallelujah, all day every day proclaiming how great our God is knowing that everything is working together for my good.

In all that I go through, praising the Lord brings me closer to Him. My praise will always outweigh the bad and therefore, my circumstances don't even have a chance.

Believe me when I say that praising Him causes things to look so much better.

Suggested Song of Meditation: "Bettah" by Jonathan Nelson

1 Thessalonians 5:18 (The Voice/VOICE)

¹⁸ give thanks to God no matter what circumstances you find yourself in. (This is God's will for all of you in Jesus the Anointed.)

No matter where I am nor the circumstances that I face, I am always in the Lord's hands. And there is absolutely no better or more appropriate place to be.

There is such freedom that comes from expressing appreciation regardless of what currently could have us anchored or weighed down. I have included as a part of my daily routine, taking the stance and being committed to rejoicing in the Lord no matter what comes my way. I know that this is His will for me and I do not want to do anything or respond in any way that does not fall in line with me walking in the will of the Lord.

I desire to achieve the destiny that He has for me. I know that lately I have been so caught up in moving forward, that I needed to step back and acknowledge that I have more than I ever expected to, more than I could ever deserve. I realize that the best way to move forward is by continuously thanking, praising, trusting and believing in the Lord.

Through the highs and the lows, I will remain vocal, expressing my gratitude every chance that I get. I've got my mind made up and I won't go back to allowing my temporal situations (which all have an expiration date) to rob me of the joy, peace and hope that is rooted in the connection and love that I have for the Lord. In everything, I will praise Him and give thanks. I recognize that in order for that to happen, my mindset and decision-making process must be focused on only those things that are of God.

I don't want to miss out on anything and that is why nothing but gratefulness flows from my heart and my lips.

Suggested Song of Meditation: "Grateful" by Morgan Harper Nichols

Psalm 71:14 (Wycliffe Bible/WYC)

¹⁴ But I shall hope ever [more]; and I shall add to ever over all thy praising. (But I shall have hope in thee forevermore; and I shall praise thee more and more.)

When it is time for me to complete my blog post, nothing is more frustrating than not having access to any Internet connection of any kind for over two hours. But it was during that time of powering down, restarting and making phone calls to see if there was a quick fix, that a "be still" moment was ushered in and I took some time to just reflect on how good the Lord is to me.

When I think about the Lord's greatness, I am given the hope needed to carry on and face whatever comes my way. I wake up to worship and praise the Lord because He is deserving of the highest praise; one that has the capabilities of reaching His heart. I lift up my hands and sing songs of praise because the Lord is so worthy and deserving of it all.

The Lord is the most faithful and steps in right when we need Him. He provides us with an unfailing love, encourages us and supplies us with the strength that is required to persevere.

My life has been given a new direction and I have been on the receiving end of such extraordinary and astounding blessings. I have come to learn that no matter what arises, I must continuously praise His name. Because of who God is, I have hope now and forevermore. And because my hope is rooted in Him, I will praise Him more and more.

Everything that the Lord does in my life is on a level greater and more profound than any other and for that reason, what I reciprocate back to Him has to be the absolute best that I have to give; anything other than that would be a pure disservice. I am thankful and grateful for the opportunity to know Him like I do and will spend my days praising Him for loving me the way that only He can.

Suggested Song of Meditation: "You Bring Out My Praise" by Patrick Dopson

Psalm 150:2 (The Living Bible/TLB)

> ² *Praise him for his mighty works. Praise his unequaled greatness.*

As I was preparing to type a particular blog post one morning, my mind was focused on something completely different, until the Lord stepped in and I was shown another reason why praising God and lifting His name on high must remain a constant in my life.

The life we live is significantly impacted by the choices that we make. I remember being instructed to always think hard about the decisions that I make, because I would be the one who would have to live with the consequences of them. Getting in trouble wasn't ever something I wanted to experience as a child, but once becoming an adolescent and into my early adult years, it seemed as if trouble had a tracking device on me and found me ever so easily.

There were seasons in my life in which I was so lost. Through the twists and turns and ups and downs it became evident and I had to admit to myself and the Lord that I couldn't live my life according to His will or be who He had called me to be on my own or by allowing myself to be controlled by the world.

The day that I rededicated my life back to the Lord, I did so, praising and thanking Him for redeeming me. With the Lord, I am given a clean slate and am a new creation. I am set free and no longer bound by my past and all it entailed. I have been found and blessed with spiritual senses that are more finely tuned and a spirit of discernment that I rely on to help filter what is of God and what is not.

I feel very fortunate to be on the receiving end of the Lord's mighty acts and His unequaled greatness. I know that because of the never-ending love, mercy and grace that He provides me with, I have all I could possibly need to make it through each day.

When I think about all that He does in my life, I am left in awe and completely humbled. As I sit here and think about where I was compared to where I am; or how I used to think compared to the mindset that I possess now; or the level of faith I used to have compared to the radical and ever-growing faith that I have in the Lord at this very moment, my whole being praises the Lord because there is no possible way that I could ever forget all that He has done and continues to do for me.

No matter who you are, you have a story. On every page and through every chapter that has been lived and read thus far, the Lord's mighty works and surpassing greatness has been covering you each and every day and through every step along your way.

Therefore…. Praise Him!!! Praise Him!!! Praise Him!!! Extol the Lord at all times and let His praises always be on your lips.

Suggested Song of Meditation: "Praise Him" by Jeremiah Hicks

Psalm 103:1 (Amplified Bible, Classic Edition/AMPC)

¹ Bless (affectionately, gratefully praise) the Lord, O my soul; and all that is [deepest] within me, bless His holy name!

Growing up, one of my favorite hymns to sing in church was, "Bless the Lord, O My Soul and all that is within me, Bless His Holy name. He has done great things, He has done great things, He has done great things; bless His holy name!" As a child, that song always seemed to come from a place deep within, a place I couldn't fully explain, but a place that I just knew was sacred and right.

As I travel the path that is set before me and have had the opportunity to get to know the Lord more intimately and thus, establishing a relationship, rooted in love and my desire to be where He is and where He desires for me to be; I have realized that sacred place that I couldn't really explain when I was younger, was the heart of worship that was nestled deep down inside of me.

I'm not here to chase the insubstantial and unproductive wiles of the world. My desire is to pursue the Lord in every way and be in the presence of all that is Him. My heart yearns to be as close as possible to the Lord and to not venture too far away from Him. I praise the name of the Lord because we serve a great God; an awesome God, that will do great things in our lives, if we can learn to just obey, worship and praise Him.

We must recognize that our worship has the power to reach the Lord no matter where we are and no matter where He is. When we have a heart of worship and submit it to the Lord, we position ourselves to enter into a place of complete submission upon Him and His will for our lives. This heart that I have has been praising the Lord from a very young age. Even when I didn't understand everything that was happening around me or to me, I knew it had to be right because it was connected to the Lord. Here is my heart of worship and with my whole heart I will affectionately and gratefully bless the Lord!!

Suggested Song of Meditation: "Heart of Worship" by Tasha Cobbs

Isaiah 43:21 (The Voice/VOICE)

²¹ My people, the ones whom I chose and created for My own, will sing My praise.

Something that I discovered a long time ago was that each of us has his or her own individual gifts and talents that were provided to us by the Lord.

He handcrafted and specifically formed each of us and with a definitive and distinct purpose in mind. As we serve the Lord and seek to live our lives according to His purpose, we are given endless opportunities to utilize the gifts that we have to show Him the praise, honor and glory that He is so deserving of.

If you have been gifted to have a natural ear for music and possess the ability to master the use of instruments, you could compose a melody of praise to offer up to the Lord. Or if you have been given a beautiful voice that is able to provide harmonious praise unto the Lord, then that is what you should do.

Some people have been given the gift of public speaking and are able to formulate and articulate the gratefulness and gratitude that they have for the merciful and wonderful God that we serve. Then there are others who have been blessed to have a passion for research. They take what they have uncovered and present their findings in such a well-formulated and detailed manner for others to appreciate.

No matter who or what you are, you have been blessed with a gift. Those gifts should be used to honor the Lord, not for what He has done in our lives, but for who He is to us.

May we never lose sight of the fact that our lives are not our own. We were chosen and created for the Lord. All that we do should be done for God's glory and the advancement of His Kingdom. With our gifts, we should exalt the name of the Lord, in love, in spirit and in truth.

Because I am a believer and follower of the Lord, I use everything that I have to bless His name. He has been so good to me and I desire for everyone who I come into contact with to know that.

The Lord is so worthy of all our praise.

Suggested Song of Meditation: "We Must Praise" by Amber Bullock

Psalm 118:21 (International Standard Version/ISV)

²¹ I will praise you because you have answered me and have become my deliverer.

If I had ten thousand tongues I still wouldn't be able to thank the Lord enough. He has been my redeemer, my protection, my deliverer, my way maker and so much more.

Today, as I was driving to my son's college and I was just observing everything around me, I couldn't help but reflect on how my life has been transformed over the past 21 years, since I first stepped on the same campus as an incoming freshman. To say everything has come back full circle is truly an understatement. If each of you only knew all that I have encountered as I began my journey into not just adulthood, but womanhood, you would see just why I don't hesitate to praise the Lord and give thanks for who He is.

I can't believe I am back here in NY. Just as Harlem, the place where I was born and spent my first years, has gone through some significant changes, so have I. Although my exterior may still look the same, the shaping, molding, sharpening and sifting that has occurred on the inside is the real reason that in spite of everything that I have been through, my immediate and natural response to everything that happens in my life is to just say, "Thank you, Lord."

There were so many times when I couldn't understand why my life had to be flipped upside down or why relationships seemed to meet their expiration date without any forewarning.

Through each test and obstacle, with a smile and jovial disposition, I say, "Thank you." I am so thankful that even though our Heavenly Father sits so high, He kindly looks low. In each situation that I have faced, I know that the Lord has been right there by my side.

I have had some circumstances and found myself in the middle of some messes that when I think about them now, all I can do is shake my head. But God never gave up on me, even during those times when I began to give up on myself. And it has been because of Him that I have been victorious and not consumed by my situations.

Every step of the way, the Lord continued to bless me and show me the true definition of what love, forgiveness and salvation really is!! Before I fix my lips to begin any other thought or statement, I say, "Thank you." And for the rest of my life, no matter what comes my way, I will continue to bless and honor the Lord at all times, because my praise is the way that I demonstrate my gratitude to the Lord.

Suggested Song of Meditation: "Still Say Thank you" by Smokie Norful

Psalm 136:26 (The Voice/VOICE)

²⁶ Let your heart overflow with praise to the True God of heaven, for His faithful love lasts forever.

Thanksgiving has always been my favorite holiday because I have endless reasons to be thankful and I just love being in the kitchen, which results in the house being filled with the delicious aroma of all the menu items my family has come to expect. I haven't ever been one to wait until the fourth Thursday in November to express my gratitude for a supernatural love that endures forever. My heart continuously overflows with praise because the Lord is always loving me.

For so much of my life, I hid behind walls, created masks and kept a smile that everyone came to expect, so that no one had the opportunity to catch a glimpse of the brokenness I was plagued by as I was growing up.

Looking back, I realize that I fought and did all I could to receive love from others. Back then, I allowed my ability to love myself to be influenced by those whom I deemed most important and the extent to which they did or didn't show love to me. All of that caused me to view myself as less of a person and I became envious of the affection that I saw others receive; especially when it appeared they didn't have to do anything to be on the receiving end of such devotion.

It took being at my lowest point to discover a love that I always had within my grasp. It was a love that waited patiently and covered me as I navigated through the twists and turns of life. It was also a love that taught me about me, along with how to love myself.

Through it all, I thank the Lord for always loving me. God's graciousness, mercy and compassion has kept me, in spite of the mistakes that I have made. And during those times when family and friends chose to walk away, He kept on loving me still.

The inexhaustible love that I receive from the Lord incites such a level of praise and worship inside of me, because I recognize that without His steadfast love, I would be eternally lost. I am grateful that during those seasons of my life when I felt like giving up, God's love never faded.

Suggested Song of Meditation: "Lovin' Me" by Jonathan McReynolds

Isaiah 42:12 (Amplified Bible, Classic Edition/AMPC)

¹² Let them give glory to the Lord and declare His praise in the islands and coastal regions.

Over the past twelve months, my family and I have been through so many transitions. From one geographical region to another, we boldly praise the name of the Lord and lift up our voices to rejoice in Him.

We give God all the glory because of who He is and the privileges that we have been granted, as children of the Most High.

The Lord continuously gives us victory out of the hands of the enemy. We thank the Lord for the doors that were closed; ones we weren't ever supposed to pass through in the first place. We also thank the Lord for the doors that only He could open, which no one else has the ability to close.

For the illimitable love, grace and mercy that we have access to, we give thanks to the Lord. For the peace, joy and protection that comes from Him, we rejoice.

For the life, health and strength that our merciful Lord and Savior provides us with, we offer up total praise to Him.

For every situation and circumstance that the enemy intended for evil, that God turned around for our good; in which we were given victory out of the hands of the enemy, gratefulness overflows from our hearts.

Each day that I rise, knowing that I have been redeemed, I am given endless reasons to sing the Lord's praises and to exalt His name from one place to another.

I desire for the whole world to know about the merciful and loving Savior who chose us and calls us His own. It is because of Him, that we are able to be and do anything. And for that, I will continue to praise Him.

Suggested Song of Meditation: "I've Got a Reason" by Byron Cage

2 Corinthians 4:15 (GOD'S WORD Translation/GW)

¹⁵ All this is for your sake so that, as God's kindness overflows in the lives of many people, it will produce even more thanksgiving to the glory of God.

Our first Thanksgiving holiday back in New York was a very special one for my family and me. As I spoke to each of my family members throughout the day and we recalled the many ways that God's divine favor and spiritual blessings not only covered us, but had brought us into new seasons and chapters of our lives, we couldn't do anything but rejoice in the name of the Lord.

The Lord has done far too much and has carried me through more than I could ever put into words, for me not to continuously give thanks. I know that because of His boundless grace, every detail of what I encounter in my life is working out for my benefit and for His glory.

As we were recalling all that the Lord has done in our lives, individually and collectively as a family, we realized that as God's grace continued to extend from one of us to another, a growing sound of thanksgiving began to be expressed as we relished in the glory of the Lord.

For all that the Lord has done, is doing and will do, may we never hesitate to say, "Thank you." For the promises and provisions that He has made on our behalf, may it never slip our minds to say, "Thank you." For the limitless love that He provides and the power that He possesses to break chains and destroy strongholds, may we always be quick to say, "Thank you."

In everything, I will give thanks to the Lord. I have to tell you that growing up, so much from my past didn't make sense. But as I got out of the driver's seat and deferred to the Lord's instruction instead of my own understanding, I gathered greater insight and began to see how everything was working together to benefit me in the long run. I will forever be eternally thankful to the Lord for who He is. Even with the gratefulness that flows from my heart, I know that the holiday season can be a difficult one for various reasons. Please know that our God is greater than anything we could ever face and that no matter what season we may find ourselves currently in, we must not ever hesitate to give Him thanks.

Suggested Song of Meditation: "Thank you, Lord" by Hillsong

1 Chronicles 16:8 (New Living Translation/NLT)

⁸ Give thanks to the Lord and proclaim his greatness. Let the whole world know what he has done.

With 2015 being my last year in my thirties, I truly began thinking about the Lord's goodness and all the marvelous works He has performed in my life throughout the years.

The more that I think about my life and all that I have experienced thus far, I eagerly seek opportunities to share with the world what the Lord has done for me.

What has been reaffirmed in my life is the truth that, "NOTHING is impossible with God."

I am here to tell someone that whatever you are believing the Lord for, don't stop. No matter how long you have been hoping and praying for that situation to turn around, keep the faith and continue to trust in the Lord.

We can begin to lose hope when things don't happen in the time frame that we desire it to. But once the Lord begins to bring those promises to fruition in your life, they end up being delivered in such an abundant manner; it is not until then that we truly get a glimpse of all that the Lord was working on behind the scenes to bring everything together on our behalf.

As I celebrated my birthday, I couldn't stop thanking the Lord for making me stronger, keeping me whole, intervening on my behalf, holding me close and never leaving me alone when the storms of life raged and I encountered the tests and trials that were before me.

With the wisdom that I have acquired in these first 39 years, I can attest to the love, grace and mercy that has covered me every step of the way. I know that God will do just what He said He would do.

The more that I reflect, the more thankful I am, because I know and the Lord has shown me that He's more than able!!

And the more that I think about it, I continue to have no doubts about the steadfast and incomparable love that the Lord has for me.

Suggested Song of Meditation: "The More I Think" by J. Moss

John 4:24 (The Voice/VOICE)

²⁴ The Father is spirit, and He is seeking followers whose worship is sourced in truth and deeply spiritual as well.

Some time ago, I read a quote from Dianna Hobbs, the popular Christian blogger, where she stated, "Worship is not a style. It is a lifestyle."

I actually had to chuckle because I knew I had been guilty, at one time in my life, of compartmentalizing my worship according to the feelings and circumstances I was dealing with at that time.

But like surrendering, I came to realize that worshiping the Lord was not just something that I did for a specific period of time or because I was looking for something in return.

Worshiping was to be recognized and adopted as a lifestyle and as a means of praising the Lord for who He is, has been and will be each and every day of my life.

Because of the divine connection that I have with the Lord and all that I have learned from His teachings and the life lessons that I have experienced, I call on the name of Jesus and commit to displaying worship that is rooted in truth and that is also deeply spiritual.

I worship and bow down before the Lord in appreciation and admiration. I praise His name because of the illimitable love, grace, mercy and protection I have been granted access to.

When I worship the Lord, it brings a peace to my soul that surpasses all understanding. Worshiping the Lord keeps me encouraged; especially during those times when my external circumstances are anything but uplifting and inspiring.

I rejoice and give thanks because when everyone else walked away, not only did the Lord remain but He carried me when I was too weak and broken to continue along the way. The Lord has always been there for me and I haven't ever known another to love me the way that He does; and that is why, for the rest of my days, I will worship the Lord with all my heart and all my soul.

No matter how high, low, near or far I could search, there is no one else like the King of kings, Lord of lords; our Everlasting Father. I worship the Lord in spirit and in truth because He is my everything and without Him, I wouldn't be.

There isn't anyone anywhere who neither compares to nor could ever come close to the Lord.

Suggested Song of Worship: "Just to Worship" by James Fortune & FIYA

Psalm 34:1 (Common English Bible/CEB)

³⁴ I will bless the Lord at all times; his praise will always be in my mouth.

When I was in the children's choir in my church here in New York, "Bless the Lord" was another one of my favorite hymns to sing on Sunday mornings.

With everything that is happening locally, nationally and internationally, the fact that I am here to see another day, I have more than enough reason to bless the Lord at all times and with all that is within me.

I will bless and worship the name of the God of mercy and Lord of grace who brought me out, to take me in. Throughout those seasons of my life when I was lost and felt so alone, worshiping and blessing the Lord was what I chose to do. The Lord was always there; He never left my side and promised to be the same yesterday, today and forever; never changing.

When we have a heart of worship and submit it to the Lord, we position ourselves to enter into a place of complete submission and dependency upon Him and His will for our lives. This heart that I have has been praising the Lord from a very young age. Even when I didn't understand everything that was happening around me or to me, I knew that the Lord was the answer.

His praise will always be in my mouth for countless reasons that are tied to the love that the Lord has and continues to show me. I have seen, firsthand, that "Can't nobody do me like Jesus, can't nobody love me like the Lord can." Not only did He love me when I didn't even love myself, but His love prevented me from being consumed by the enemy (more than once). And in those instances, when I felt like I didn't have the endurance to press forward, He made a way for me somehow.

I am here to share the great things that the Lord has done and continues to do in my life; hopefully to serve as a source of encouragement and to have you accompany me in blessing the Lord for what He has done for you as well!!

Suggested Song of Meditation: "I Will Bless the Lord" by Byron Cage

Psalm 100:2 (Modern English Version/MEV)

² Serve the Lord with gladness; come before His presence with singing.

Being one who loves to communicate through music, song and poetry, it's with pure gladness, that I come into the presence of the Lord singing countless songs of praise and thanksgiving. Honoring the Lord through song is an integral part of my lifestyle and the way I choose to live my life as a child of God.

As I glanced over at the most amazing Christmas tree that my family and I have ever had (thanks to our wonderful children), I can't help but to think that the reason that this holiday season feels that much more special, has to do with more than just the fact that I am back home in New York.

From last holiday season until this very moment, the Lord has revealed and disclosed so much to me; which has resulted in me gaining the most unexpected and profound insight into what Jesus' birth and death meant for me and my everyday Christian walk and what God's inexhaustible loving-kindness, grace and mercy has granted me the permission and authority to be on the receiving end of.

The Lord is orchestrating some life-changing events in my life and very soon, I will divulge the details with all of you.

But just know that the Lord's love, goodness, grace, mercy, protection, favor and so much more are the reasons that I will always have a song of praise to sing to the Lord.

Suggested Song of Meditation: "Song of Praise" by Andrea McClurkin Mellini

Jeremiah 17:14 (Expanded Bible/EXB)

14 Lord, heal me, and I will truly be healed. Save [Rescue] me, and I will truly be saved [rescued]. You are the one I praise [my praise].

The Lord is the One that I praise. I rejoice in knowing that whenever I am experiencing hurt or pain, the Lord desires to heal me. Whether that healing is for my mind, my spirit, my heart or a particular area of my physical being, I know that God will see me through and take the pain away.

I'm not a New Year's Resolution type of person. My motivation and aspirations in life are geared more towards the lifestyle I desire to lead, which is a surrendered life for Christ. With that being said, all throughout the year, I do an enormous amount of reflecting, especially when some years seem to come with a little more "heat" than others.

I look back on the tests and trials to see what caused them, the role I played in them and most importantly what I learned from them. If areas where pain or strongholds were so deeply covered and hidden are revealed, then I immediately seek the Lord for a breakthrough and healing in those areas because I do not desire for anything to get in the way of my relationship with the Lord and the destiny that He has for my family and for me.

The Lord knows everything that I am in need of and provides for me each and every day. He is Jehovah Jireh (my provider) and Jehovah Rophe (my healer); the One that I run to and entrust with alleviating those areas of my life where there is pain.

God is a healer, a provider, a protector, a comforter, a way-maker and so much more. I worship and praise the name of the Lord for the healing He has already brought to my life. If we just trust in the Lord and submit ourselves and our situations to Him, the Lord will heal us, remove the hurt and pain and bring restoration in a way that only He can.

Suggested Song of Meditation: "God Wants to Heal You" by Earnest Pugh

Psalm 30:12 (The Voice/VOICE)

¹² You have restored my honor. My heart is ready to explode, erupt in new songs! It's impossible to keep quiet! Eternal One, my God, my Life-Giver, I will thank You forever.

Do you know why there is a praise on the inside that I can't keep and do not desire to keep to myself?

Because if you knew all that the Lord has done and continues to do for me; where I was, compared to where I am (and remember, He's still not finished with me yet), you would desire to do nothing but sing praises to Him as well.

Every opportunity that I have to openly share the faith that I have in the Lord, you can best believe that I do. As Hebrews 13:15 instructs us, "Through Jesus, therefore, let us offer God a sacrifice of praise continually. For this is the natural product of lips that acknowledge His name."

When I look back over my life, thus far, and recall all the areas that once brought indescribable sadness to me, I praise the name of the Lord because it is only because of Him that where I once mourned, I have been set free and now dance and make a joyful noise unto Him continuously. Where I was once cloaked in heaviness, I am now clothed in joyfulness.

It's a joy that neither the enemy nor his tactics can take away from me, because he didn't give it to me. Thank you Jesus!!!

As much as I love to sing, I'm here to tell you that when I open my mouth it's for God to get the glory. It's not a game to me and that is what I want my praise to convey. My gratitude for all that the Lord has done for me runs so deep that there is no possible way that I could keep it to myself. It is inviting and infectious.

Praise is the way that I say, "Thank you Lord!!"

I have learned that when you have no problem praising the Lord, others will notice. And yes, they may think you are giddy or maybe even strange; but it also incites a curiosity in them to want to know what indeed is causing you to act in the manner you are. When opportunities like that happen, we are given a chance to do kingdom work; by being a walking testament of just how mighty, faithful and good our God is.

Our God has promised to never leave us nor forsake us; to be our fortress and cover us with His illimitable and steadfast love. Do you know what that means?

It means that because the Lord (my Life-Giver) is always by my side, to illuminate my path and guide me, I won't ever run out of reasons to share with others the praise that I have overflowing for Him.

Suggested Song of Praise: "I Can't Hold It" by Byron Cage

Psalm 71:8 (Wycliffe Bible/WYC)

⁸ My mouth be filled with praising; that I sing thy glory, all day thy greatness. (My mouth shall be filled with praise; and I shall sing of thy glory, and of thy greatness, all day long.)

As I have gone throughout the day, today, I have had so many different thoughts and found myself thanking the Lord for so much (just as I do each day).

Now that the day is winding down, the following lyrics have played over and over in my head; "You deserve the glory and the honor, I lift my hands in worship and I bless your Holy name. You are great, you do miracles. So great, there is no one else like you. There is no one else like you."

When I think about where my life would be if it wasn't for the goodness of Jesus and all that He has done for me, my mouth fills with praise, declaring the splendor and glory of the Lord all day long.

We could search all over, look high and low, and still would never find anyone else like the Lord. No one is capable of doing all that He has done or being all that only He can be in our lives. The Lord continues to show me that His abilities are much stronger and greater than any one of my worries.

If I had 10,000 tongues, I wouldn't be able to thank the Lord enough for my life and for the perfect way that He loves the authentically imperfect me, that I am. That doesn't hinder me from expressing the worship, praise, adoration and glory that I feel and that belongs only to the Lord. Praise is the way that I say, "Thank you Lord," so that I convey the gratitude that He is most deserving of.

I won't ever stop offering up my praise to the Lord. I intend to talk openly, each day, about my faith in Him so that my words will be like an offering to God (Hebrews 13:15).

Suggested Song of Meditation: "You Deserve" by Chrystal Rucker

Psalm 63:4 (The Message/MSG)

⁴ I bless you every time I take a breath; My arms wave like banners of praise to you.

As I was watching the sunrise in San Juan, before we boarded the plane to head home (regretting that our eight-day stay had already come to an end), I couldn't help but think about how amazing the Lord is.

It is because Jesus died for our sins and rose again, that we are able to have life and have it more abundantly. Secondly, the sun rising and setting is a reminder of the awesome power the Lord possesses.

If God created the two great lights that would rule the day (the sun) and the night (the moon), nothing that I am currently experiencing is outside of His realm to bring resolution to.

I celebrate the Lord blessing Him with every breath of my life and waving my arms like banners of praise to Him.

Great is His faithfulness. I rejoice because His steadfast love for us never ceases and His mercies never come to an end.

Our situations may change but the Lord remains the same. Even when I haven't known how or when it will all come together, I have relied on my faith knowing that the same God that I am trusting and believing today, is the same God who has brought me through countless times in the past.

When I look back over my life thus far, I am rendered speechless when I think about all the ways that the Lord has provided for and made a way for me.

So many things have changed and a lot of those changes have occurred in me primarily.

I have been stripped of my crutches, training wheels and support apparatuses and have been brought to a place where I am depending completely and ultimately on the fact that the Lord is my mighty defender and that He will move the mountains and cause the giants that are in front of me to fall, if I wholly surrender it all to Him and believe in His faithfulness and righteousness.

Flawless is the work of the Rock, because all His ways are just. Everything that the Lord does is perfect. There isn't any victory over Him and He is the One I don't ever question whether He is concerned about me. I have the assurance, in His Word, that the Lord is always thinking about me and watching everything that concerns me.

The Lord is worthy and most deserving of all glory, worship, honor and praise.

Because He has been so amazing to me, my praise and worship will forever originate from a place of pure and complete adoration.

Suggested Song of Meditation: "Adoration (So Amazing) by Forever Jones

LIFE IS FRAGILE, HANDLE IT WITH PRAYER

Psalm 5:3 (Common English Bible/CEB)

³ Lord, in the morning you hear my voice. In the morning, I lay it all out before you. Then I wait expectantly.

The wee hours of the morning are probably my favorite time of day because that is when I have my one-on-one time with the Lord. I love it being so quiet and the sun still hidden.

I am still reminded of and am able to observe some of God's most marvelous works. Now I pray and talk with the Lord all throughout the day, but before my day gets started, I have to take that special time to converse with our Heavenly Father. It's very important to me to first thank Him for grace and mercies that are made afresh each morning.

Since we are not the One who is omniscient, it is imperative that we look up to the hills from where our help comes (Psalm 121:1). God is the only one who knows what each day will bring for each of us, so why not seek Him out during the earliest part of our day before we get caught up in just living life?

Going to God, connecting and establishing that ultimate and intimate relationship with Him, provides us with the peace and reassurance of knowing that no matter what the day may bring, through consulting Him and waiting on His Word and instruction, the provisions will already be in place to cover us.

We should not only speak to the Lord, but quiet ourselves to hear from Him as well. If we just trust and wait with expectancy on Him, we will see that God always keeps His Word and that no matter what we may endure, He has not brought us this far to leave us.

The days tend to go by so fast; therefore, setting aside that time first thing in the morning to go to God has the ability to change your whole perspective on what lies ahead of you for the hours to come.

Suggested Song of Meditation: "Ultimate Relationship" by Donald Lawrence featuring Lalah Hathaway

1 Peter 5:7 (The Living Bible/TLB)

⁷ Let him have all your worries and cares, for he is always thinking about you and watching everything that concerns you.

I have to tell you that the end of last week leading into this past weekend was a very trying one for me. My husband, children and I have had several conversations lately about familial dynamics that have brought us pain and that are nowhere close to where we desire them to be. Regardless of the reason for the disconnect, it doesn't mean that it hurts any less, especially when you are the person trying to figure out what you have done wrong. I have learned that a lot of times it's not that we have necessarily done anything wrong, but some people are just not going to be who we need them to be or do what we need them to do for us.

And no matter how many times I have been told and have said myself that expectations should be placed on God and not individuals, I myself am guilty, even when I try not to be, of unconsciously still placing expectations on others and ending up disappointed. And that was the conversation that I first was having with my two oldest children, who were expressing their feelings regarding situations they were encountering. My husband and children are everything to me and so when anything bothers them, this prayer warrior right here goes into some serious overtime.

I know that each us has had situations where we know, hands down, that the only reason that we made it through was because of God. There have also been times when we didn't have a clue as to why we have found ourselves in the situations that we are currently in. What we did know was that if God allowed it to happen, we would be better for it on the other side.

No matter how many times we have cried over a situation, God already knows each tear that will fall from our eyes even before they pass through our tear ducts.

I have no desire to carry unnecessary weight and so for that reason, anything that I have been worried about or burdened by, I put it on the altar. I know that God already has every situation worked out for my good and making that declaration, I can find peace even in the midst of a storm. Whatever may be weighing on you, release it to God because He is the best problem solver and the only one who truly knows us, what we need and what His plans are for our lives.

Anything that you may be anxious about or worrying over, give it all to God, leave it with Him and do not make the mistake of trying to go back and pick it up yourself. May peace reside within you knowing that everything is in His hands and that He is undoubtedly concerned about you.

Suggested Song of Meditation: "Put it On the Altar" by Jessica Reedy

Luke 18:1 (The Living Bible/TLB)

¹⁸ One day Jesus told his disciples a story to illustrate their need for constant prayer and to show them that they must keep praying until the answer comes.

Prayer is such an essential component that cannot be neglected. I know that through prayer we are given the opportunity to experience a relationship with God. I remember being taught that prayer is talking to God, listening to God and enjoying the presence of God. The quality of our relationship with the Lord is determined, significantly, by the condition of our prayer life.

Sometimes when we pray, we expect God's response to our situation to be immediate. We tend to quit and give up way too easily in prayer. Let me tell you that I am so grateful for the life lesson that God has revealed to me and that lesson is that a delay is not a denial. When we surrender our circumstances to the Lord, we do so with faith in the Most High.

During those times that we are awaiting God's response, we cannot allow ourselves to become discouraged. Many times, God is striving to work on us as we press forward and wait on Him with expectancy. The Lord delights in answering our prayers. In so many instances, God's timing doesn't ever correspond with the time frame that we are expecting or believing for a resolution to be provided in. We can't ever forget that God's time is the perfect time. What appears to be a delay for us is actually God working on and bringing together every single detail on our behalf. Prayer is a necessity because we cannot direct the circumstances of our lives in our own capabilities or strength.

In no way could we ever be greater than Jesus and each day that He was here in this world, He prayed. As a parent, I do not give my children everything they ask for right when they ask for it. To do so would invite and possibly encourage a behavior or way of thinking that I believe would not be favorable for them now or as they grow older. Our Heavenly Father responds to our prayers according to His will and the plans He has for our lives. When we put our faith and trust in the Lord, no matter how long it takes to receive the answers to our petitions, we can't allow ourselves to lose heart.

It is so important to have that personal time with the Lord. Having a relationship with the Lord will grant you the peace needed in all situations and will give you a better comprehension between when God says, "No" and when He says, "Not yet."

Suggested Song of Meditation: "Prayer Changes Things" by Ametria Doss

1 Kings 8:28 (Easy-to-Read Version/ERV)

²⁸ But please listen to my prayer and my request. I am your servant, and you are the Lord my God. Hear this prayer that I am praying to you today.

When we go before the Lord and make our petitions known to Him, He hears each and every one of them. I know that prayer is such a powerful tool and has the way of changing things in our lives. It is through prayer that we are given the opportunity to strengthen and deepen our relationship with God.

Our prayers should be pure and sincere and should not be used to try and impress others or as a means to negotiate with God. We serve a God who doesn't read our lips, but instead reads our hearts. I am constantly reminded and have shared in the past that prayer is not about informing God (because He already knows it all); it's about incorporating and inviting Him into our situations.

As we take our will out of the equation and focus solely on God's will for our lives, we experience peace as a result of our prayers. Anytime we feel anxious, scared or worried, those are triggers that we need to pray. When we cast all our cares and worries upon the Lord and are able to magnify His name at the same time, we see that Jehovah Jireh, Our Provider, is bigger and mightier than anything we could ever face.

As we pray and praise the Lord, we must take time to recall all that the Lord has already done for us and never lose sight that even when what we face changes, the God we serve doesn't. Every day that God blesses us to see and to be in receipt of His grace and mercies that begin afresh each morning, we should never hesitate to go before Him with the assurance that He hears our humble cry.

Suggested Song of Meditation: "The Prayer" by Donnie McClurkin & Yolanda Adams

Matthew 6:6 (The Message/MSG)

⁶ "Here's what I want you to do: Find a quiet, secluded place so you won't be tempted to role-play before God. Just be there as simply and honestly as you can manage. The focus will shift from you to God, and you will begin to sense his grace.

Something that I have noticed over the past year is that the amount of time that I devote to spending with the Lord, both in conversation with Him and in silence waiting to hear a word from Him has increased significantly. Whether I'm going to pray or not is not even up for discussion. It's a mandate that I take any and every opportunity that I have to converse with the Lord. Believe me when I say that my prayer life is essential for my survival.

I walk around with the Lord in my soul. I have discovered that it is through the time that I have with the Lord that I am renewed, rejuvenated and revitalized.

I used to think that all my interaction with the Lord had to take place at home or at church. Oh, how I was limiting myself. I felt that if I wasn't located in a secluded place or prayer closet, then that rendered my prayers less effective. Being someone who has always had responsibilities both inside and outside the home, I knew that I needed to make that time with God before I thought to do anything else.

As Pastor William Murphy, III explains in the suggested song of meditation that I have chosen for the above verse, I came to learn that my prayer closet wasn't necessarily a place where I resided, but a place in my heart. When I discovered that, I began to bring the Lord with me in the car, to my office, to the grocery store and everywhere in between. I realized that I could talk to the Lord anywhere and at any time.

It seems as if there is always something on my heart that I need to discuss with the Lord and knowing that He is with me wherever I go means that I have every opportunity to get to know the Lord and thus, be on the receiving end of His continuous instruction and guidance. The answers I seek can only be found in Him. And I know that God already knows what I need before I ever even ask. When my focus shifts from me to the Lord, I begin to sense His grace and start to observe that the petitions which are submitted secretly, the Lord rewards openly.

Suggested Song of Meditation: "All Day" by Tasha Cobbs featuring Pastor William Murphy, III

Psalm 145:18 (Expanded Bible/EXB)

18 The Lord is close [near] to everyone who ·prays to [calls on] him, to all who ·truly pray to him [call on him in truth/faithfulness].

There is not a day that passes by that I do not recognize just how powerful prayer is. I think about the fact that it is because of God's unconditional love for us that His only begotten Son made the ultimate sacrifice on our behalf. And because of that sacrifice, we are granted unlimited access to the Lord. We do not need anyone to go before the Lord on our behalf.

I realize that God is just a prayer away and I am able to put all of my faith and trust in His care, knowing that He will always be there. No matter what it is; any concerns, doubt, fear or worry that I am plagued by, God will cast them away.

It was so important that I realized that because there were seasons when I looked to others for the answers that I needed. I have always been one to tell individuals that "I was only a phone call away," if they ever needed anything. And it seemed as if my phone always rang off the hook when I was needed for something. But ironically, my phone never seemed to ring because of the concern others had regarding the well-being of my family and me. That observation was a very painful one and an extremely difficult pill to swallow.

That was until I noticed that the One who loves my family and me the most, the One who is always concerned about any and everything that pertains to us, has always been there, will always be there and is just a prayer away. I don't have to go looking for Him and when I seek Him, He hears every single word that I communicate to Him during my time of prayer.

I am no longer concerned about the phone calls that I do or don't receive when the One who first loved me and who protects and keeps me is just a prayer away.

Suggested Song of Meditation: "Just A Prayer Away" by Yolanda Adams

Colossians 4:2 (Amplified Bible/AMP)

² Be earnest and unwearied and steadfast in your prayer [life], being [both] alert and intent in [your praying] with thanksgiving.

Reading has always been one of my favorite pasttimes. Growing up, every librarian knew me and I just believed I was doing something from the moment I was issued my first library card. The world was mine to discover and there were endless options for me to choose from.

My love for reading gave birth to my love for writing. If you don't know by now, I'm a "words" person. Uncovering the various ways that words are grouped together and the vivid illustrations that one's mind conjures up, has always been very intriguing to me. As I've grown and transitioned from one stage in my life to another, books have played an enormous role in that transformation.

The Bible is my number one reference and "go to" book for it all. I also appreciate spiritual and self-improvement books, where authors utilize God's Word as their foundation for that specific literary work. One of my favorite authors is Priscilla Shirer. It was during the hardest and most pressing seasons of my life that one of her books, "A Jewel in His Crown," God used to provide me with the template, viewpoint and instructions to press through and move forward.

A few weeks ago, my husband had mentioned that he had seen a poster for the upcoming movie, "War Room", that Priscilla Shirer was starring in. He stated that it looked like a great movie that we needed to see. Last night, I saw the trailer for "War Room" on television and it was so reminiscent of what I had experienced and the power that is available when you have that place where you are able to go through some serious spiritual warfare and find yourself praying and laying it all before the Lord in ways you never knew you could or had to before.

Every time I open my mouth to pray, I am thankful. Just to be able to talk to the Lord for myself and not have to wait on someone else to speak on my behalf, is a blessing that no words can be grouped together to truly convey. No matter where I have been; whether in my own residence or staying in the home of someone else, hey, even when lodging in a hotel, I had that war room identified.

My war room is the place where I surrender and leave my flesh and the ways of the world and seek out the Lord for guidance and wisdom. It is the place where I devote myself to prayer and am unwearied. I strive to keep an alert mind by taking hold of His commandments and letting His name be my petition.

We are fooling ourselves if we don't acknowledge that there's a war out there. It's a constant battle. Having that place where we are able to communicate with the Lord and know that He hears our cries; where the Holy Spirit is able to take us higher, is crucial.

Prayer is a prerequisite if we desire to be divinely connected to the Lord and victorious in our spiritual walk. I believe sometimes we get so caught up in responsibilities and roles that we take on day-to-day, we forget just how powerful it really is.

When we pray and lean not unto our own understanding, the Lord will show us the way. Prayer is not something that we do for a season; it is what we do every day for survival.

Suggested Song of Meditation: "When We Pray" by Jonathan Butler

Exodus 33:14 (Complete Jewish Bible/CJB)

¹⁴ He answered, "Set your mind at rest—my presence will go with you, after all."

When unexpected circumstances or situations arise in my life, I have learned to be appreciative, to count it all joy and to praise the Lord while in the midst; even if I feel blindsided or the timing doesn't appear to be the most opportune for me. Nothing about my life is a surprise to the Lord. Therefore, if I must go through, I have the assurance that all I need to be victorious has already been placed within me.

As I look back over my life, I think about the times when I felt the most outside my comfort zone and pressed on all sides in a claustrophobic kind of way, and I realized that it was also during those times that I encountered the greatest breakthroughs. Having that one-on-one time with the Lord is imperative for me to find that peace that surpasses all comprehension, during times of such uncertainty and perplexity.

When I am able to just sit or lie down and close my eyes, I am transported to a place where it is just Jesus and me. There's a peace in this secret place that ushers in and soothes my mind, before the enemy has the opportunity to infiltrate my thought life by having fear or worry take center stage. When my mouth can't formulate the words to say, my heart composes a melody and croons, "Jesus, Jesus, Jesus." There is just something powerful that occurs when I call on the name, "Jesus." It is indeed the sweetest name I know.

I am able to set my mind at rest and am left feeling secure, because I know that the Lord is present in my life at all times. When I close my eyes, I am able to just be still. All the distractions of the world are eliminated and I'm given the opportunity to communicate with God and receive the guidance to help me press forward through the tests, trials, twists and turns that are associated with this marathon of a race that I am running.

Suggested Song of Meditation: "When I Close My Eyes" by Jessica Reedy

Psalm 141:2 (Names of God Bible/NOG)

² Let my prayer be accepted as sweet-smelling incense in your presence. Let the lifting up of my hands in prayer be accepted as an evening sacrifice.

Recently, after posting one of my blog posts, I was up for quite a bit afterwards because my youngest daughter was very congested and couldn't get to sleep. As I was watching over her and was replying to a few notifications, I saw the following quotation from Martin Luther that stated,

"To be a Christian without prayer is no more possible than to be alive without breathing."

As the congestion that my youngest was frustrated with began to subside, I got ready for bed thinking about the above quote and just how vital my prayer life has been and continues to be to my relationship with the Lord and honestly, my everyday survival.

To be able to communicate with the Lord is unlike anything else in the world. During my time of prayer, whether the conversation is relayed via spoken word, through a song or by the tears or groans of a difficult situation where words can't even be formulated; I know that a dialogue is taking place and flowing between heaven and earth.

To be in the presence of the Lord is such a sacred and holy place. It's a place where the Lord feels so near and I remain captivated by all that He is.

Whether I am experiencing the highest of the highs or the lowest of the lows, when I pray, I find that peace and joy that surpasses all understanding and it leaves me wishing time could just stand still, so that I could stay right where I am.

In those moments, I feel so protected and am able to rest because I know that the Lord is there and that He hears all that has been laid upon my heart to share with Him.

Because of the powerful blood of Jesus, we have direct access to the Lord. I am able to confidently go before God's throne of grace, so that I may receive the mercy and find the kindness to help me in my time of need.

I couldn't live my life on purpose and according to God's will if prayer was not an integral part of my daily routine.

Every day, I burn four different candles, at different times in my house and they represent my husband and my three children. When I burn the candles, the aromas fill up my home and remind me of the love I have for them and they for me.

It is my prayer that, like those candles, when I pray to the Lord each day, that my prayers are accepted as an offering of sweet-smelling incense that rises in the presence of the Lord.

Suggested Song of Meditation: "Stay Right Here" by Todd Vaters

Psalm 138:3 (The Voice/VOICE)

³ On the day I needed You, I called, and You responded and infused my soul with strength.

What a day it has been. Honestly, what an emotionally draining few months it has been for me. The first few words from the suggested song of meditation, sums up how I have been feeling when it says, "If it ain't one thing, then it's another."

That has been my life lately; it's either been one thing or another. Instead of questioning why I have had to encounter numerous situations that have left my heart filled with so much heaviness and sadness, I have instead stepped back and begun to take the time to see what it is the Lord is desiring to teach me with each circumstance.

Although I have a huge heart, oftentimes I have gotten ahead of myself, trying to be the "fixer" and "problem solver" in the lives of those who weren't in a place to receive all I was trying to be for them.

Earlier this week, I read a quote online where someone said, "Be careful when trying to fix a broken person. For you may cut yourself on their shattered pieces." I'm not one to follow celebrities on social media, but when I saw this particular sentiment, it did resonate with me because I have the scars from some of those cuts.

I know that I have sinned, fallen short and am far from perfect. I have never thought I was better than anyone nor have I ever wanted to come across as being judgmental. But being someone who is very black and white and who likes to get straight to the point, that is not always received well.

It's because I too, know what it's like to be broken and what happens when life decisions are made while in a state of brokenness, that I strive to prevent others from having to endure some of the hardships and adversities I have faced.

I also know what it means to be saved, changed, freed and delivered from those strongholds and yokes and that is what I desire for those that I love and anyone that I am fortunate to come into contact with, to have the opportunity to experience.

Having that divine connection and intimate relationship with the Lord has changed my life and blessed my family and me in ways I couldn't ever put into words.

I am so grateful that all I have to do is call on the Lord and He will encourage me and infuse my soul with the strength it needs to make it through.

Even though the past few months have been anything but easy, I know that I am stronger than I have ever been. Because my strength comes from the Lord, my whole outlook has changed. In the past, I would become so overwhelmed by the situation itself, I couldn't focus on anything else.

But these days, I have chosen to keep my focus on the Lord, who when I cry out to Him in prayer, answers me and makes me bold with strength. There have been many tears that have fallen, several sleepless nights and some doors that have closed unexpectedly. But I rejoice because these situations have assisted in my growth.

And that is why when you see me, I'll still be smiling; because I know, without a doubt, that it's because of the Lord, who has never left my side, that I'm stronger, better and wiser than I have ever been.

Suggested Song of Meditation: "Stronger" by Myron Butler & Levi

Jeremiah 29:12 (Amplified Bible/AMP)

¹² Then you will call on Me and you will come and pray to Me, and I will hear [your voice] and I will listen to you.

"I love the Lord, He heard my cry and He pitied every groan. Long as I live and troubles rise, I will hasten to His throne. Trust in the Lord with all thine heart. Lean not to thy own understanding. Trust in Him and in Him only. You can depend on Him."

Those are lyrics to a song we used to sing in church when I was younger. I may not have known the full extent of what they meant when I was singing them then. But, please know, that I do now.

Spiritual warfare is no joke. When the enemy uses those closest (or ones who should be closest) to you to deliver blows and attacks, that has the capability of knocking the wind right out of you; especially when you don't expect it.

As hurt as I have been, there is more to the story and it's because of how far the Lord has brought me and the recollection of all the answered prayers that He has provided me with in the past, that I am able to remain encouraged throughout every twist and turn; instead of being burdened by anxiousness and uncertainty.

My prayer life has been and will continue to be the lifeline that has assisted me in moving forward when the storms of life, the sleepless nights and the desperate pleas to the Lord for guidance have all come upon me at once.

Anything that concerns me, I take it to the Lord, leave it on the altar and am confident that His Word will be manifested. Because I know that when I call on the Lord, come to Him and pray to Him, He'll hear my voice and listen to me; I can't allow worry to set in. Worrying works against all of that. When we worry, doubt is ushered in. We can't be strong, confident and doubtful in the Lord.

That is why being divinely connected to Him is vital. When we have that relationship with the Lord, we discover what His plan and purpose is for our lives. We are then filled with an assurance and boldness in Him, knowing that if we make any request or petition that is according to His will, God listens to and hears us (1 John 5:14).

I don't despise one tear that has been cried because I know that the Lord has captured each one. Nor do I believe that any prayer that I have uttered has gone unnoticed. God has heard every word and the answers that I seek are on their way.

Suggested Song of Praise "Every Prayer" by Israel Houghton featuring Mary Mary

Mark 11:24 (Amplified Bible/AMP)

²⁴ For this reason I am telling you, whatever things you ask for in prayer [in accordance with God's will], believe [with confident trust] that you have received them, and they will be given to you.

Mark 11:24 has always been on my list of favorite verses. But no matter how many times I have read Mark 11:24, I always have to follow it up with 1 John 5:14, which reminds us that, "This is the confidence (the assurance, the privilege of boldness) which we have in God: [we are sure] that if we ask anything (make any request) according to His will (in agreement with His own plan), He listens to and hears us."

What I have discovered, is that in those seasons when I was praying to the Lord and worrying at the same time, the anxiousness and fear that I harbored was because what I was praying for was not in agreement with God's will for my life. So, for that I say, "Thank you Jesus for not giving me all that I asked for!!!"

But now, because of the closeness, strength and depth of the relationship that I have with the Lord; it is with wisdom and discernment that I make my prayer requests known to Him.

When we have that relationship with the Lord, we discover what His plan and purpose is for our lives. We are then filled with an assurance and boldness in Him, knowing that if we make any request or petition that is according to His will, God listens to and hears us.

When we pray and believe, we position ourselves to receive those things that we have asked for. So tonight, we are going to be bold and declare that we shall have what we decree.

We are making the affirmation that whatever we are believing God for, belongs to us. We have to have that radical faith and courage to speak it into the atmosphere; believing, that no matter what it is, all things are possible through Christ, if we just believe.

We are told that the heartfelt and persistent prayer of the righteous makes tremendous power available and great things happen (James 5:16).

The Lord will never fail or neglect us. He knows where we are and all that is before us. It is God who holds the future and He knows each and every thought and plan that He has for us.

And that is why I can no longer give worrying permission to contaminate my faith or my prayer life. I have a confident trust in the things that I ask for in prayer.

I believe it and then leave it on the altar. If we're going to pray why worry and if we're going to worry, why pray?

Suggested Song of Meditation: "Don't Pray and Worry" by J. Moss

SURRENDERING MUST BE ADOPTED AS A LIFESTYLE

Matthew 6:33 (The Message/MSG)

³³ Steep your life in God-reality, God-initiative, God-provisions. Don't worry about missing out. You'll find all your everyday human concerns will be met.

Praise God from whom all blessings flow!!

In each situation and with every decision that I must make, nothing else matters to me than seeking the Master. Even when I feel overwhelmed and it appears as if the odds are stacked against me, I seek and wait for the consolation from the Lord that I am in need of.

Clearly hearing from the Lord sets my soul at ease and keeps my mind and me God-focused. I have come to learn that when I saturate my life under God-reality, God-initiative and God-influence, I am made complete because my mind and thoughts are set on those things above.

It doesn't matter what my circumstances may look like or how intense the pressures surrounding me may be; when I am concerned, above everything else, with the Kingdom of God and what He requires of me. When I pursue what has His approval, the One who reigns over my life, promises to provide and meet all my other needs and everyday human concerns.

When I find myself encountering hurdles, road blocks and setbacks; being in the presence of the Lord is the ONLY place that I desire to be. I require the Lord's presence daily; but in those most trying times, the importance of spending time with the Lord is realized on a completely different level. Just sitting at His feet and receiving the compassion and comfort that could only come from the Lord, has brought indescribable healing and restoration into my life.

When I seek first the Kingdom of God, I have no desire to worry because I know that the Lord is all that I could ever want or need.

Suggested Song of Meditation: "Nothing Else Matters" by Marvin Sapp

Romans 12:2 (The Voice/VOICE)

> ² *Do not allow this world to mold you in its own image. Instead, be transformed from the inside out by renewing your mind. As a result, you will be able to discern what God wills and whatever God finds good, pleasing, and complete.*

What an amazing week last week was for me. I pray that each of you had an awesome Holy Week, leading to an even more memorable Resurrection Sunday. I am filled with so much thankfulness and gratitude for God's infinite and unconditional love that surpasses any other love we could ever hope to be on the receiving end of.

In last Monday's blog, I spoke to how *The 40-Day Surrender Fast* that I have participated in was concluding on this past Friday, Good Friday. Well, I definitely misspoke when I said that. In beginning this journey under the guide of Dr. Celeste Owens' Surrender Fast, I have to tell you that each day brought so much promise and revelation that I wasn't even paying attention to the fact that each day was bringing me closer to the conclusion of this cycle of the fast. So as last Friday approached, I began to have mixed emotions because yes, I was thrilled to have finished the fast strong, with a stronger faith, stronger relationship with God and stronger desire to fulfill the plans and live out the life that He has created specifically for me; but I also wasn't ready for the fast to end. It had become a staple in each of my mornings. It was then that I realized that surrendering was not intended to be cyclic for me. I was meant to Surrender 365.

Jesus was not only wounded for our transgressions and bruised for our iniquities but Jesus being born, living, being crucified, buried and rising on that third day means we have direct access to God. We no longer have to enlist the services of a high priest to go to God for us because Christ that lives in us is our High Priest, Mediator and Intercessor who stands before the throne of God on our behalf.

Last week, I said Jesus did it "just for me". Being armed with that information, it is imperative that I walk as this new creation that I have become. I cannot be concerned with who the world wants me to be or what the world would desire I do, because I have God working, molding, sifting, shaking free and loosing me of anything (or anyone) who is not part of the purpose that He has for my life. And that is not something that just ends at the 40-day mark; it is a continuous process.

I have learned the importance of being able to surrender to God and that should be a lifestyle. Lifestyle is defined as a way of life or style of living that reflects the attitudes and values of a person or group. I have changed and been transformed from the inside out, due to The 40-Day Surrender Fast. God has revealed Himself in ways that only He can and continues to bless not just me, but my family and others as well. Thus, I want my lifestyle to reflect that my values and attitudes are rooted in what the Lord says.

Joel Osteen said, "Put your shoulders back knowing that the same power that raised Christ from the dead lives on the inside of you. If death couldn't keep Christ in the grave, nothing can hold you back. Jesus said in Luke 10:19, "I give you power over all the power of the enemy." The same power God had, He gave to us. Now you and I have resurrection power."

How empowering is that? But we won't ever know all that God has placed within us if we allow ourselves to be molded by this world and don't seek to surrender what is not of God. I cannot be the reason that my household and I are not being blessed by the Lord so that we can, in turn, be a blessing to others. The changes that have begun in me are just the beginning; I know that there is more that God desires from me and so that is the goal that I am working towards; to be more, to depend on Him MORE and live according to His commandments and principles more!!!

Yesterday, as my husband was driving us to church for Resurrection Sunday service, I began pondering what song I would use for today's devotional. And once again, God showed up and showed out (smile). During praise and worship, the choir began to sing a song that not only spoke to where I am but it was also a song that I haven't heard in years and I was filled with so much emotion.

Suggested Song of Meditation: "Changed" by Tramaine Hawkins

John 15:5 (J.B. Phillips New Testament/PHILLIPS)

¹⁵⁵ I am the vine itself, you are the branches. It is the man who shares my life and whose life I share who proves fruitful. For the plain fact is that apart from me you can do nothing at all.

As I have gone throughout the week, the importance of being rooted, connected and abiding in Jesus has been illustrated and presented to me in various ways.

BJ's Wholesale Club has always been one of my favorite places to purchase fresh produce. As I was preparing to create another blog post, I opened up my refrigerator to grab my smoothie and gazed upon the three-pound container of green grapes I had purchased there a couple of days ago.

As I looked at the grapes and recalled what I had learned at bible study the night before, all of those elements brought me to John 15:5.

Last night in bible study, I gained such a profound and insightful understanding of Jesus Christ, my Lord. Receiving and accepting Jesus Christ as my Savior was that essential part for my spiritual rebirth; but that was just the beginning.

Because Jesus is the vine and I am the branch, not having that divine connection and relationship with Him is not an option; when it's clearly evident that apart from Him we can do nothing at all.

It's not until we completely yield to the will and control of Jesus Christ in every area of our lives, that we are able to bear abundant fruit.

In order for a branch to produce fruit, it must abide (meaning to dwell, settle in and sink deeper). I desire to settle in the Lord and to be submerged deeper and deeper into His presence. By obeying, we abide in the Lord. To abide in the Lord means living in Him as He lives in us.

As I seek refuge by hiding in Him, the Word of God reminds me that the Lord will protect me because there is safety in His arms. When we are able to keep the messages in our hearts that we have heard from the beginning, we will remain in the Son and the Father (1 John 2:24). God has promised to safeguard the aspirations that were sown many years ago. Respectfully obeying God's Word produces much fruit.

It is through Christ that we live, move and have our being. Yielding and having that vital union with Christ as our Lord is not a one-time event. As my pastor reminded us last night, it's a "life-long process"; a lifestyle we must adopt.

Suggested Song of Meditation: "Nothing Without You" by Jason Nelson

1 Peter 2:9 (The Living Bible/TLB)

⁹ But you are not like that, for you have been chosen by God himself—you are priests of the King, you are holy and pure, you are God's very own—all this so that you may show to others how God called you out of the darkness into his wonderful light.

What a journey and process it has been to sever the unfruitful source of darkness that resulted from me being so consumed by what others thought and said about me.

One of the greatest realizations that I have had is in recognizing that no matter what you say or do, there will always be someone ready to naysay, discourage, ridicule or even lie on you.

You can have the biggest heart and the best intentions but that doesn't mean that everyone is as excited about who God is to you, all that He's done for you or all that He's still preparing to do for you, like you are.

And you know what? That is absolutely alright because we do not serve two masters.

When we allow ourselves to become so consumed with what the world says about us, we begin to lose our way and in turn, end up blinded and deaf to the truth that the Lord has declared about us and that we have available to us in His Word.

My whole life I dealt with rejection, unjust treatment and exclusion on so many different levels that I believed I had to be a people pleaser to get that acceptance, approval and inclusion that I was yearning for. That way of thinking was attached to a victim mindset. And the more that I operated from that mentality, the more my life spiraled out of control.

I'm a "words of affirmation" person, but made the unfortunate mistake of entrusting my validation and self-worth to man instead of feasting on the Word of God and walking in the truth of who He says I am.

I thank God for the spiritual mentors He placed in my life who knew me well enough to know what I needed to break that victim mindset. I was introduced to various written resources that were rooted in God's Word so that I could ingest and then digest His words which became the blueprint for my life.

Before I used to focus on who made the decision to leave or no longer be connected to me. Now I focus on the fact that I am a chosen generation. I am God's very own, that He chose himself.

Where so many counted me out and placed limitations on me, I find encouragement, boldness and confidence in knowing that I was fearfully and wonderfully made and that God has already declared in His Word that He would make me the head and not the tail, above and not beneath and more than a conqueror.

Because I hunger for and desire a deeper and stronger relationship with the Lord, I take my cue from what He says and not what they say.

I can't go back and redo all those years that I allowed all that came from the mouths of man, to make me feel or the place of darkness it took me to. But I rejoice in the renewed mind that I now possess and the new creation I have become because God has called me out of darkness and into His marvelous light.

Suggested Song of Meditation: "They Said, But God Said" by Jekayln Carr

Isaiah 9:4 (Names of God Bible/NOG)

⁴ You will break the yoke that burdens them, the bar that is across their shoulders, and the stick used by their oppressor, as you did in the battle against Midian.

When I lived in Maryland, I took full advantage of participating in three different cycles of Dr. Celeste Owens' 40-Day Surrender Fast.

With each cycle, my deepest desire was to release plans, mindsets, strongholds and patterns of behavior that were creating a barrier within my relationship with the Lord.

It is said that the definition of insanity is doing the same thing over and over again and expecting a different outcome. Now I can be very silly, but do not believe I am insane. Although when I took a step back, I realized that in some areas of my life, I was still dealing with the same people and the same situations and kept expecting a different outcome in the end.

It's really easy to stay in your comfort zone, where you don't have to take risks or face disappointments, judgments or rejection. In taking some self-inventory lately, it became apparent to me that a lot of who I have been and the decisions I have made have been driven and guided by the strongholds that have kept me bound.

Not wanting to be rejected, disapproved or viewed as the "bad guy", I found myself in situations that never meant me any good, dealing with individuals whose least concern was my well-being or having my best intentions at heart. I used to always do the law of averages, meaning the more people I surrounded myself with and went out of my way for, the higher the percentage of connections and relationships I would have in the end. With getting older, maturing in my spiritual walk and my faith continuing to grow, I have learned that strongholds are just tools of the enemy to try and keep us away from the life that God has decreed for us. Those strongholds or chains can only keep us bound if we allow them to. The hardest part is recognizing and admitting they exist. Once we do that and surrender our all to God, He is able and will break those chains. The areas where we once were overwhelmed and oppressed, we will be left feeling triumphant and victorious.

There is not one yoke with binding power more powerful than the name and blood of Jesus!!! For me, surrendering it all means consulting God first in all matters; before making a decision or taking part in any situation. In the past, I would enter into a situation and then once in the thick of it, I would immediately call on God's name for deliverance. I have learned that had I first consulted God, I would have saved myself a whole lot of pain, heartache and unnecessary drama. By surrendering and truly putting all power in His hands, I take my cue from God and not from my emotions, other people or the strongholds that once kept me bound.

I am desiring to be all that God has called me to be and that means living a surrendered life 24/7. Only God knows what is and isn't for me. And if it's not for me, TRUST, I do not want it.

Suggested Song of Meditation: "Break Every Chain" by Tasha Cobbs

Galatians 2:20 (New Living Translation/NLT)

²⁰ My old self has been crucified with Christ. It is no longer I who live, but Christ lives in me. So I live in this earthly body by trusting in the Son of God, who loved me and gave himself for me.

A lot of us have ancestors, whom in centuries past, were enslaved and bound by physical chains. But in present day, there are still so many of us who are emotionally, mentally and spiritually bound by our sins and circumstances that we have encountered. Jesus dying on the cross means that we are free and that no matter what permission the enemy is given, with Christ that lives within us, we have power over that permission. We have direct access to the Heavenly Father, who loved us so much that He gave His only begotten Son so that we could be saved and have everlasting life.

When I think about Jesus being crucified for my sins, I don't desire for the way I carry myself as a Christian wife, mother and woman to be perceived that what Jesus did is being taken in vain. Yes, we are human and we will fall. But what I know is that there are things that we carry that God desires for us to surrender to Him. He desires for us to have such a deep connection with Him that when situations arise, our decisions are not based on our will for our lives, but His.

God wants to see the plans and the promises that He has for us come to fruition, but a lot of times we get in the way of living life abundantly. There isn't any room in my life for the "old" me who made decisions by trying to figure things out on my own and then turning to God when I was about one step away from losing my mind. I walk in the flesh, but the real me is a spirit who puts all her trust in the Son of God.

By partaking in Dr. Celeste Owens' 40-Day Surrender Fast, God spoke to every area that I was surrendering to Him and blessed my family and me in ways that only He can. Not only did God bring restoration and renewal to the areas I brought before Him, He also revealed areas that I subconsciously was not trying to face. I love God so much because He knows me better than I could ever know myself.

Through this entire process, I have been in awe of God and I am a new person. I am stronger, wiser, and have more clarity and peace. Additionally, the fear of rejection or not being accepted no longer gets to guide my relationships. Because of what Jesus came and did for us, I have become a new being and there's no going back.

Suggested Song of Meditation: "Just for Me" by Donnie McClurkin

2 Timothy 1:7 (New International Reader's Version/NIRV)

⁷ God didn't give us a spirit that makes us weak and fearful. He gave us a spirit that gives us power and love. It helps us control ourselves.

No matter how many reasons we may have for doing something, all it takes is one drop of fear to deter us from what we were called to do. As I shared with all of you when I was taking part in Dr. Celeste Owens' 40-Day Surrender Fast, one of the main areas of my life that it was imperative that I surrender to God was fear. Fear had been the driving force in 95% of the relationships that I have had throughout my life. From childhood into adolescence and all throughout adulthood, the fear of rejection, disapproval, non-acceptance and exclusion had me in situations I should have never been in, tied to individuals who didn't mean me any good or seeking approval from individuals who were broken themselves; which resulted in me being on the receiving end of things that God never had for me in the first place. Being a mother and God's representative for my children, there wasn't any other choice, only one option existed and that was to usher fear out and walk within that spirit of power and love that God has placed within me. The spirit of fear would not be passed on to my children.

Fear no longer has the right nor the opportunity to live here because it's been served its eviction notice. We cannot be all that God has called us to be, while harboring a spirit of fear. How can I have radical faith and be fearful? I'm not here to be a walking contradiction, nor am I trying to be the one getting in the way of what God has for mine and me. That same energy that was once given to fear, has been redirected to encourage myself, by speaking God's promises over my life.

If you let it, fear will render you powerless. All your hopes, dreams and aspirations will go out the window. In the midst of whatever decisions we must make or situations we find ourselves in, we are to be encouraged and defer to the spirit within us that provides us with power, love and a sound mind.

The role fear plays in each of our lives is truly up to us. During one of Oprah's Lifeclass programs, I read a quote that Bishop T.D. Jakes shared and he said, "You can't be who you're going to be and who you used to be at the same time." The old me was at the door and I said, "Goodbye" and welcomed the new me I have become. The old me was fearful, but the new me is fearless, fierce and radically faithful!! It's time for you to love yourself enough and want what God has for you; you should be able to say, "Hello fear, goodbye, farewell, so long."

Suggested Song of Meditation: "Hello Fear" by Kirk Franklin

Revelation 21:5 (Disciples' Literal New Testament/DLNT)

⁵ And the One sitting on the throne said, "Behold—I am making all things new". And he says, "Write, because these words are trustworthy and true".

There is just something about knowing that when you call on the name of "Jesus", you are calling on the One who makes all things new. It doesn't matter what has happened in our past, or how many times we have fallen and done it over and over again. Because of God's infinite love for us and the price that His Son paid on Calvary for our sins, we have been given a second chance and are able to move forward as new creations.

We have the opportunity and access to new beginnings. God makes all things new, not just one thing or some things, but all things. And that is a promise that Jesus instructed, "Write it all down because these are words that are dependable, accurate, trustworthy and true."

I don't know about you, but there have been some areas of my life where I needed God to do something new. I needed Him to breathe life in a way that only He can. There is a freedom when we surrender our lives to Christ; relinquishing it all to the One who is truly in control.

Since we cannot move backwards and forwards at the same time, we must decide which direction we desire to travel in. It is my deepest desire to move forward in every aspect of my life. I parallel the decision of moving forward to driving.

When any of us are in our cars driving, the windshield that is in the front of the car is very large, whereas the rear-view mirror is considerably smaller. We cannot expect to get to our destination if we only use the rear-view mirror. In doing that, we aren't ever looking in front or for what's ahead, but instead we stay constantly looking behind us and at places we have already passed.

Yes, the rear-view mirror is needed as a reference for road safety, but the windshield gives us a bigger picture and allows us to see what is ahead of us as we move forward. In life, like the use of a rear-view mirror, I may glance back momentarily at times, as a reference to all the marvelous works God has already done in my life and just how far He has brought me from. But I can't stay in rear-view mirror mode because that's not safe and it will only hinder my journey.

I know that I belong to Christ and therefore, I am a new creature. I don't have the time nor the energy to focus on my old way of living because it is no more and my new way of living has come into existence (2 Corinthians 5:17). New beginnings through Christ means limitless possibilities because with God all things are possible (Matthew 19:26). We also have the reassurance that we can do all things through Christ who strengthens us (Philippians 4:13).

It is imperative that I have God's instruction and His guidance in my life. We serve an All-knowing God who is not surprised by anything and so I choose to follow Him forward.

Suggested Song of Meditation: "Moving Forward" by Israel Houghton

Psalm 139:16 (The Message/MSG)

¹⁶ Like an open book, you watched me grow from conception to birth; all the stages of my life were spread out before you, the days of my life all prepared before I'd even lived one day.

I know that if I had 10,000 tongues I still wouldn't be able to express how thankful I am for who God is and all that He has done and continues to do in my life.

I began Dr. Celeste Owens' 40-Day Surrender Fast going throughout this world, as a caterpillar, in need of a transformation. Taking part in this fast brought me into my cocoon experience, in every aspect of the words. I have always been infatuated with butterflies, not realizing that I was going through the transformation process myself to reach that stage in life.

I am no longer bound or restricted within my chrysalis, a place where I was surrounded by both thoughts of hope and elements of fear. In order to really let go and break free of our cocoons we have to be willing to let go of our old ways of living, thinking and behaving, because we cannot live in abundance and in fear at the same time. *The 40-Day Surrender Fast* provided me with the spiritual resources that were imperative so that I could work on myself from the inside out; within my metaphoric chrysalis. My mindset had to change in order for me to embrace the radical change that was about to occur within, in and around me.

Now that I have broken out of my chrysalis and transformed into my butterfly stage, the world looks completely different and brighter. My natural and spiritual sight have become aligned, providing me with the clarity needed to soar and be catapulted into my destiny; doing the work for the Lord that He called out specifically for me, long before the foundation of the earth was ever set.

I have so much more freedom. I no longer desire to walk around in circles, waiting for everything around me to change. I had to take the necessary steps to begin that change within myself. It wasn't easy, but it wasn't done in my own strength either; it was done in the Lord's. I feel a sense of protection, covering and hopefulness that I hadn't known before because I was bound and my mindset was one of poverty (rooted in fear and lack) instead of prosperity (rooted in abundance, faith and love). It's just poetic and symbolic that I had to go back to move forward, because now that my chrysalis stage has transformed me into a butterfly there is indeed NO going back. I am free to fly high, for the sky is not the limit for me.

In researching butterflies, I learned that they carry pollen from one flower to another, helping them with the pollination process. Thanks to butterflies, some flowers are able to bear fruit. It is my desire to emulate the ways of the butterfly, by pouring into others and imparting godly wisdom so that we are able to blossom as children of the Most High.

I am so grateful that the days of my life were all prepared by God before I'd even lived one day. And that is the source of my empowerment, because I know that anything that comes my way had to have God's approval and that every promise that He has spoken; He is faithful to bring to pass, if I just wait on Him. This is not the time to get distracted, to go off course or to lose focus.

The destiny that God has for us is too important to give up for anything!! It's so important to take self-inventory and surrender anything that is getting in the way of you being free to be who God has called you to be. Let's fly high together!!!

Suggested Song of Meditation: "Your Destiny" by Kevin Levar

2 Corinthians 4:7 (The Voice/VOICE)

> *⁷ But this beautiful treasure is contained in us—cracked pots made of earth and clay—so that the transcendent character of this power will be clearly seen as coming from God and not from us.*

It's another day's journey and I'm so glad about it. I thank God for another opportunity to share with each of you just how awesome the God is that we serve.

Every day, I am reminded of just how fortunate we are that we serve the God of the "underdogs". I am so grateful that where man overlooks, discounts or rejects us, the Lord will use us in our imperfect state for His will to be done. There are countless examples in the Bible of how ordinary people were able to accomplish extraordinary tasks because of the supernatural power that was housed within them. We were indeed created for His glory (Isaiah 43:7).

Whenever I look at a clay jar, I am reminded of just how weak jars of clay are. They shatter easily and if filled with cracks, they are not able to hold the contents effectively. Within our physical bodies, we have a treasure that is more valuable than any combination of jewels or any monetary amount; it's an immeasurable treasure. God has placed the light of His message and grace within us and it was obtained by Jesus' blood. It is constant, eternal and is manifested in all His attributes together.

I searched for a specific definition of glory and after reading a few of them I learned that, "God's glory is the infinite beauty of His spirit and the greatness of His multifarious perfections." We are able to glorify God because of the things belonging to Him that we carry within our clay pots. When we love, serve one another and use our gifts so that His will is done, God gets the glory. It's important that we realize that our physical bodies really hold nothing of value, whereas the value of Christ that is inside of us is unsurpassed.

We are earthen vessels, made from dirt and clay, two things that are quite insignificant. And yet, we have within us a power that is above ourselves and beyond ordinary. A power that is able to bring things together and also cause barriers and strongholds to collapse and fail. When we allow God to manifest through us and in our situations, it becomes clearly evident that the power does not originate in us ourselves, but in God. As we live our lives each day, it is so imperative that we do anything and everything to glorify our Heavenly Father. To find favor in His sight is what I strive for in my own life.

As I walk this journey of mine, letting the God that is in me shine is more important than anything else. I want to be where the Lord is and do what He has called me to do. All that I am able to do and able to be, my power-source is the Lord. Glory is the "essence of who God is" and I need to be in the presence of that each and every day.

Suggested Song of Meditation: "For Your Glory" by Tasha Cobbs

Psalm 90:12 (New Living Translation/NLT)

¹² Teach us to realize the brevity of life, so that we may grow in wisdom.

I remember the morning that I woke up and saw that longtime ESPN anchor, Stuart Scott, had passed away. It got me to thinking about family members and friends who are no longer here. The loss of a loved one is never easy, but there is so much we can learn.

As I watched the tribute to Stuart Scott that was on the television, I began to recall everyone talking about the unforgettable speech that Stuart Scott gave at the ESPY Awards and the raw and honest words that were so inspiring to me. He said, "When you die, it does not mean that you lose to cancer. You beat cancer by how you live, why you live, and in the manner in which you live."

It is imperative that we realize the brevity of life and make every last moment count. Those who gain wisdom and understanding from God's Word and life's experiences are so fortunate (Proverbs 3:13). It is my hope that with each day that the Lord blesses us to see, the following questions stay at the forefront of our minds.

How are we living? What is our purpose for living? Are we being busy or productive (because there is a distinct difference)?

I pray that you will take the time to reflect on these questions and allow God to move in the areas that need guidance and improvement. It should be our desire that God is reflected in everything that we do.

Our days are indeed numbered. My question to you is, how will yours be numbered?

Suggested Song of Meditation: "I Want to Live My Life for You" by The Clark Family

Galatians 5:1 (World English Bible/WEB)

⁵ Stand firm therefore in the liberty by which Christ has made us free, and don't be entangled again with a yoke of bondage.

It is my sincerest belief that if you questioned ten different people and asked them, "What does it mean to you to be free?", you would probably get ten different answers. The reason for that being although we all face challenges and adversities, each of our spiritual journeys is different.

Last night, my husband and I were having a conversation about some of the revelations that the Lord has provided me over the past few years and especially within the last twelve months.

I have always been a very fact- and knowledge-seeking individual. I love doing research and having a better understanding of things; especially when they have the potential to affect me. Regardless of what the truth may uncover or reveal, that is the realm from which I need to operate.

For so long, I was made to feel like the way I was woven was a deformity or abnormality. Although I am a very personable and relational person, I never really fit in anywhere and became enslaved by the chains associated with being concerned about the world's opinion and perspective about me. I worked so hard to put the focus on everyone else, so that no one had the opportunity to even catch a glimpse of all the weight I was carrying on the inside.

These chains affected my mindset, my faith and my view of myself.

That was until the Lord caused a shift to occur and I found myself in a place where I had no one but Him to lean on and to seek answers and direction from. To the rest of the world, I appeared to be withdrawn and anti-social but in reality, God was doing some much needed work and repair on me.

He was providing me with the truth that I needed to survive. I was being reacquainted with Him and what He declared over me long before the foundations of the earth ever came into existence. I was chosen and am a part of the family of God; therefore, there is no condemnation, because of the blood that Christ shed on Calvary for us. As one of my favorite verses reminds me, "Whom the Son sets free, is unquestionably free (John 8:36)."

I have been set free and am living in that freedom that Christ has given me. That means I'm not going backwards and snatching those chains back up to be enslaved again. The Lord has brought me way too far. Those decisions out of brokenness that I used to make and the way I used to place the world's perspective above God and His Word (yikes) are no more!

I'm walking (and often skipping, dancing and running) in the liberty I have been given.

Suggested Song of Meditation: "Free" by Anthony Brown and group therAPy featuring Crystal Rucker

Isaiah 26:3 (Amplified Bible/AMP)

> ³ *You will guard him and keep him in perfect and constant peace whose mind [both its inclination and its character] is stayed on You, because he commits himself to You, leans on You, and hopes confidently in You.*

With each day that I am so fortunate to see, God blesses me to gain so much perspective into the life He desires me to live. It's amazing how you can have a definition of a word and believe it's a pretty solid one until someone else's perspective redefines that same word and causes a moment of enlightenment to occur. That was what transpired for me yesterday.

While participating in cycle 8 of Dr. Celeste Owens' 40-Day Surrender Fast, I had dialed into the Wednesday morning call, and First Lady Malinda Chisholm of The Latter Rain Cathedral in Lockport, NY began to relay to us what it means to surrender. The manner in which she defined it was so profound that I had to share and comment on it with others. She conveyed it in a way that I will retain and carry for the rest of my life.

If I ever begin to lose sight or am ever questioned about what surrendering really is, I will recall what was disclosed yesterday. Surrendering means to agree to stop fighting, hiding and resisting and instead, living in obedience and letting God do in me whatever is necessary for Him to get the glory and for me to become the person He is after. Surrendering also means following God's lead without knowing the direction in which we are headed. When we surrender our lives to Christ, it means waiting in God's time without knowing when it will come to pass and trusting God's purpose even when we don't understand the circumstances.

In surrendering to the Lord, I am committing to having my mind stayed on Him. I am making the choice to seek those things that are of God before the things that are connected to the world. I know that God will guard and keep me in perfect and constant peace. I believe in the promises that the Lord has spoken and that the deliverance that I am seeking will be received.

During cycle 8 of *The 40-Day Surrender Fast* (in which the theme was "New Beginnings"), I surrendered generational strongholds and curses that had been passed down and that I eventually found myself shackled by. The Lord delivered me from those strongholds and broke chains that kept me bound for years.

Because of strongholds that have been defeated, I have peace and am now free to be launched into my new season. The only thing that can impede me from being propelled into the advancement that God has for me, is me. I will not be the obstruction that prevents me from obtaining all that God has for me. By faith, I believe and trust in the Lord with all my heart; therefore, my mind cannot be changed. I commit myself, lean on and hope confidently in the Lord.

Suggested Song of Meditation: "That's What I Believe" by Donnie McClurkin

John 15:4 (The Message/MSG)

⁴ "Live in me. Make your home in me just as I do in you. In the same way that a branch can't bear grapes by itself but only by being joined to the vine, you can't bear fruit unless you are joined with me.

Yesterday, as I was preparing lunch for my children and I was placing grapes in their individual Ziploc bags, I remembered John 15 and I went first to verse 16, where Jesus spoke the words, "You did not choose me, but I chose you and appointed you that you should go and bear fruit, and that your fruit should remain, that whatsoever you ask the Father in My name He may give you."

That particular verse has always been a special one to me because where, in the past, I had worked so hard to avoid exclusion and rejection, with the hopes of just being the chosen one, Jesus reminded me that from day one I was chosen and have been tasked to produce fruit that will last. In doing so, whatever I may ask of the Lord, in Jesus' name, He will give. That doesn't mean that God will answer instantaneously; waiting is part of the equation. It is so important that we are brave and courageous as we wait on the Lord.

The only way to receive what we are waiting on and believing the Lord for is by abiding in Him and being connected to Him similar to the way grapes are attached to a branch. Focusing on the importance of abiding in the Lord led me to John 15:4.

In order for a branch to produce fruit, it must abide (meaning to dwell, settle in and sink deeper). I desire to settle in the Lord and be submerged deeper and deeper into His presence. By obeying, we abide in the Lord. To abide in the Lord means living in Him as He lives in us. As I seek refuge, by hiding in Him, God's Word reminds me that the Lord will protect me because there is safety in His arms. When we are able to keep the messages in our hearts that we have heard from the beginning, we will remain in the Son and the Father (1 John 2:24). God has promised to safeguard the aspirations that were sown many years ago. Respectfully obeying God's Word produces much fruit.

Suggested Song of Meditation: "Abide" by Lexi

Ephesians 4:31-32 (New Life Version/NLV)

³¹ Put out of your life all these things: bad feelings about other people, anger, temper, loud talk, bad talk which hurts other people, and bad feelings which hurt other people. ³² You must be kind to each other. Think of the other person. Forgive other people just as God forgave you because of Christ's death on the cross.

I remember that in the beginning of December 2015, there was a theme to my daily blogs. Because of the heartfelt response and transparency I had received from my readers regarding forgiveness and the feelings of unforgiveness we may knowingly or unknowingly harbor, I created the theme, "The Pathway to Forgiveness."

As I was reminded in church, "Forgiveness is not a moment, but a process." Those eight words fell right in line with the theme that the Lord had led me to share with everyone. And although everyone's process and path to forgiveness is different, it is crucial that we have a heart that forgives; because that heart knows so much freedom.

Those sentiments took on even greater meaning for me when I read the following inspirational quote on my friend's page, "Life becomes easier when you learn to accept the apology that you never got."

That one phrase paralyzed me momentarily because I knew that although I had surrendered my situations to the Lord and believed I had forgiven those who had wronged, harmed or misused me, the fact that deep down I was still waiting for the apology that I hadn't ever received instantly opened my eyes to the unforgiveness and resentment that I was unknowingly harboring.

Couple that phrase with the song, "A Heart That Forgives" by Kevin LeVar and I was a wrap and needed to express those feelings.

Why Should We Forgive?

Because none of us is perfect. We all stumble and fall short. As much as I love the Lord, I know that some of the decisions that I have made have hurt and displeased the Lord and yet He continues to forgive me and cover me with a love that is limitless. Being armed with that information and having the knowledge that resentment, malicious remarks, bitterness and anger hinder our relationship with the Lord, how dare we not forgive others as God has forgiven us? If only it was that easy. It should be, right?

If the truth be told, some things that we carry have penetrated and resided so deeply within the marrow of our physical being, that the only way that we can let it go and be freed from the shackles of unforgiveness is by seeking and relying on the never-ending power that comes from the blood of Jesus. It is greater than any stronghold or yoke that we may come up against.

When we learn to take our instruction from the Lord, He guides us through the process of letting whomever/whatever it is go; along with being right there by our side as we acquire the freedom that comes from forgiveness; which gives us a heart that learns to love over and over again, as if the offense never occurred in the first place—similar to the manner in which the Lord loves us.

So much of what we carry has been passed down through generations and decades. No one has a time machine nor can we can go back and change the past. We must forgive others as God has and continues to forgive us. We cannot allow the former things to prevent us from receiving the healing, restoration and freedom that God has for our lives.

We may not have always had a say in some of the details pertaining to our lives, but we do have a say in our response to our circumstances and how we choose to move forward.

As I take these steps along the Path of Forgiveness, I never lose sight of the One who has gone before me, the One who walks alongside me and the One who carries me (when needed).

Jesus set the example that we are to follow, with the love and forgiveness that He showed others (especially within His inner circle), up until He paid the ultimate price and died on the cross for my sins.

Suggested Song of Meditation: "Whatever It Is (Let It Go)" by Gail Holmes

Colossians 3:10 (International Children's Bible/ICB)

¹⁰ You have begun to live the new life. In your new life, you are being made new. You are becoming like the One who made you. This new life brings you the true knowledge of God.

According to the Merriam-Webster Dictionary, the word "different" is defined as partly or totally unlike in nature, form or quality; not ordinary or common; not the same.

Growing up, I was very different. I had different dreams and aspirations and my beliefs and thought processes were woven totally differently than everyone else's. I wasn't ever truly convinced that being different was a great thing. From where I stood, being different left you exposed and susceptible to being ridiculed, mocked or excluded. And as much as I knew I was born to lead, I felt I had to follow just close enough so that I wouldn't be on the receiving end of the brutal judgments and opinions of my peers and, at times, some family members.

That mindset led me down a spiraling path of chaos and destruction, which resulted in one pitfall after another. When I think about my teenage years and early twenties, it's only by the grace of God that I am still here. I tried everything in my power to run away from what made me different, when in all actuality, what made me different ended up saving my life. I couldn't run from who God called me to be. God's presence in my life has been one of very few things that I can remember being a part of my entire existence. Coming from someone who remembers her first birthday and my father always making sure we said the Lord's prayer, God has always been there for me.

Those times when I went astray and fell short, He loved me. No matter how deep the trench was that I found myself in, He reached down and saved me. What I once tried to flee, I desired to sprint to embrace. The characteristics and convictions that I possess that were once ridiculed, I own and embrace knowing that they are being used for God's glory.

Being different is a beautiful thing, especially when our main connection is with the Lord; we have the gift of the Holy Spirit residing within us and we have discernment; which allows us to operate in God's wisdom.

At the conclusion of our Thursday Morning Surrender Fast Call yesterday, Dr. Celeste Owens played another spoken word piece by Sundra Ryce entitled, "Expression." When I listened to this empowering and uplifting example of poetic articulation, it reminded me of how I have changed, am different and not the same. Everything that Sundra Ryce expressed I could relate to, but the lines that hit the closest to home were when she said, "The favor of God surrounds me. Love is a gift. I give that gift to myself first. My incredible life starts with me. My ideas are God's ideas; it is God within me, hearing His own voice."

The favor of God does indeed surround me. It invites and encourages me to walk in what makes me different, because I know that I've been chosen. If I don't give the gift of love to myself first, how can I honestly be in the position to give it to anyone else, especially when God instructs us to love our neighbors as we love ourselves?

The thought that when I speak, write, sing, etc., God should be hearing His own voice within me and that my ideas should reflect His ideas; it doesn't get any realer than that.

I don't know what your definition or perception of different is, but I celebrate being different. I am free and like a butterfly to its chrysalis, I am boldly saying, "Goodbye to the old and hello to the new."

Suggested Song of Meditation: "Different" by Tasha Page-Lockhart

Jeremiah 31:19 (Common English Bible/CEB)

¹⁹ After I turned away from you, I regretted it; I realized what I had done, and I have hit myself—I was humiliated and disgraced, and I have carried this disgrace since I was young."

It's amazing to me and I constantly stay in awe of how God works in our lives. While preparing for cycle 9 of Dr. Celeste Owens' 40-Day Surrender Fast, I expressed that there were some "rotten fruit" that God still had to pluck from within me. I believed I knew all the areas that required refinement in my life, until God revealed to me that wasn't necessarily the case.

The morning calls that we take part in speak so much truth about God and what He desires from us and for our lives. For a couple of days, we addressed the impact that regret has; along with the disappointment we felt over things that had been done and opportunities that had been lost or missed. The weight of those situations can weigh down on us more than we ever realized. It's not until we are able to uncover those concealed areas of regret that we are able to be free and move forward on the path that God has for us.

Yesterday morning's call was so dynamic and what I loved most was how, through Dr. Celeste Owens, God was able to speak directly to me, the queen of harboring regret and shame for the decisions I have made in my past. But for me, it drills down so much deeper. Forgiving others for what they have done to me in the past hasn't ever been my issue; forgiving myself for my past decisions has been my greatest nemesis. The amount of shame that has laid dormant inside of me for not only the poor choices that I have made, but more so for the access I unknowingly, at the time, granted individuals to hurt, harm and take advantage of me has led me to be as triumphant as a person attempting to walk through a windstorm with cement blocks shackled to their feet.

Yesterday, God had to sound the alarm for me. In order to truly be free and move forward, I must let go of the regret and shame. I beat myself up constantly for not handling decisions and situations in my youth, adolescence and early adulthood in the manner in which I would today. That wasn't even possible and yet the enemy has used those regrets to make me feel unworthy and enslaved within myself. Let me correct that statement. The enemy used to make me feel unworthy and enslaved to my past. No longer will that be the case.

I'm letting go and making the conscious decision to live my life with no regrets!! God has led me to this finished place and there isn't any room for shame. I learned yesterday that not only do I need all my energy; I also need all of God's supernatural energy to move forward. We can't be filled to capacity with all that is of God, if regret is also taking residency. When we live with regrets, we are left with that victim mentality, but God has already told us that we are victorious. Once again, we can't be both and I'm choosing victory over a victim mindset.

When we get to a place where we can trust God with those choices and areas of regret, God will get the glory. I'm letting go because I can't and wasn't ever tasked with carrying this load. I am one of the first ones to say that God knew me before I was ever placed in my mother's womb and that all my days were written before they ever came to be. What I wasn't grasping in proclaiming that was that in those very days that God had written out for me, my mistakes were included in His plans for my life.

No more shame and no more guilt. I'm letting go, knowing God will handle it and handle it well.

Suggested Song of Meditation: "Let It Go" by Le'Andria Johnson

Luke 11:28 (The Living Bible/TLB)

²⁸ He replied, "Yes, but even more blessed are all who hear the Word of God and put it into practice."

A couple of weeks ago, when I was at bible study, I was sharing with my pastor and church family about how eager my youngest daughter is to learn about God. Her fascination and desire to know more about the Lord led me to download the Bible app for children onto her tablet.

With the app now on her tablet, my daughter is always watching videos from the Bible and requires that I read five bible stories each night to her before she goes to sleep.

It's so amazing to me how times have evolved. What I used to do for my two older children via a thick Children's Bible storybook; I am able to do by way of an app.

My children have always been my greatest motivation in life and the realest accountability tools for me. I'm not a "do as I say and not as I do" kind of person and I know that the only way that I could be the parent and representative of God that I was created and chosen to be, meant that I had to faithfully seek the Lord so that I could hear a word from Him and, in turn, make the Word of God my way of life.

Reading the bible stories to my daughter each night, not only imparts the Word of God into her, but it also blesses me exceedingly as well. Through those stories, I have been reminded of how God favored those individuals, who when they heard from the Lord, obeyed, practiced, kept and guarded that word (teaching) with their lives.

The bible stories also prompted me to remember the consequences that we will encounter if we disobey and do not continually observe the Word of God.

I love to research and have resources at my disposal where I can find the answers to the questions that I have. I am so glad that we have the Bible to reference, no matter where we are in our spiritual walk. I can tell you that I know that there isn't any situation or circumstance that we could face that the Lord has not already addressed in the Bible.

Being armed with that knowledge puts me in the position to be better aligned with the Word of God and to receive the teachings from the Lord that will serve as my blueprint and road map for the footpath that is ahead of me.

These days I am very discerning and attentive about where my instruction and direction comes from. The word I hear HAS to come from the Lord. If it's not coming from Him, it has no place in my life.

Suggested Song of Meditation: "Heard A Word" by Michelle Williams

Philippians 3:13 (Expanded Bible/EXB)

¹³ Brothers and sisters, I know that I have not yet reached that goal [taken hold of it], but there is one thing I always do. Forgetting the past [things that are behind] and straining toward [stretching/reaching forward to] what is ahead.

I woke up this morning thinking about a song I used to hear in my grandmother's church and the refrain stated, "I know I've been changed, I know I've been changed, I know I've been changed, the angels up in heaven done signed my name." In those brief moments, I began to meditate on just how much change has occurred in my life and within me.

I know that I have been healed, freed and delivered. I have been healed from the pain, hurt and disappointments that have been nestled so deep in the core of who I was. I have been freed from the chains and strongholds that had me so bound; it was like trying to swim in the ocean with anchors placed on my feet that were lodged deep within its abyss. I have been delivered from ways of thinking and patterns of behavior that were connected to the brokenness, rejection and exclusion that shaped my thought process throughout my entire life.

I thank God for the undeniable contrast from who I was to who I am now. I appreciate and truly value the life lessons and the tests and trials that have shaped and molded my character. There isn't any possible way that I would ever want to go back to the way things used to be. The Lord's presence in my life has refined the essence of who I am. I know that, in no way, am I where I am supposed to be yet, but I rejoice that I am not where I used to be. I am trusting and believing God for far too much in my present and future to get held up in the past.

In surrendering my life to the Lord and giving it all away to Him, my sins, guilt and shame have been forgiven. All those things have been replaced by joy, peace, grace and favor. I can be going through it but will still have a song of praise and desire to worship the Lord because my joy comes from within. Man didn't give it to me and, therefore, man can't take it away. I have a peace that surpasses all understanding. It's a peace that comes from the confidence and the trust that I have in the Lord. I know that each trial that I face has an expiration date and that ALL things that occur in my life are working together for my good; that brings peace to my soul. I am blessed to be on the receiving end of God's grace, which is defined as unmerited favor and the power to do what we could not do in our own strength.

When I look back over my life, I know that what I have been able to accomplish and the situations that I have been delivered from were not due to my own works or the strength I possess, but that of our Heavenly Father's.

From who I was then, to who I am now, I have not only gained knowledge but also the wisdom that serves as a point of reference as I am strained toward and look forward to what lies ahead. Going back is not an option as I continue to chase after the Lord and press toward that goal that is before me.

Suggested Song of Meditation: "I Won't Go Back" by William McDowell

Matthew 5:16 (New Century Version/NCV)

¹⁶ In the same way, you should be a light for other people. Live so that they will see the good things you do and will praise your Father in heaven.

After the week that my family and I just had, waking up this morning while it is still dark and being able to witness the sun rise over the horizon holds more meaning than it ever did before. To say I am grateful doesn't even scratch the surface on how I feel.

On this morning, I was ignited with the realization that life is way too short to pursue anything but what pleases God. It's not about me, but indisputably about the Lord. I will follow through and do what the Lord tells me to because I want Him to have His way in my life each and every day. I can't and don't want to do any part of this on my own. I have the assurance that through His love I can face any obstacle that may come my way.

Absolutely no weapon that is formed will have the opportunity to prosper. It really doesn't matter what the enemy attempts, because I can do all things through Christ who strengthens me. I know that when I surrender my will to the Lord's, God will mold and shape me into who HE calls me to be and not into who I think I am supposed to be.

I know how my mind works. I know that the personality type that I possess causes me to be very introspective and constantly in deep thought. None of that matters if I'm not doing what God calls me to do, when He calls me to do it. It's not about me, but it's about Jesus. It was so silly of me to think that I could navigate through this enigma called life to what I thought my destiny should be. There is no need for me to try to rationalize or negotiate anything that the Lord commands me to do because I know that if God calls me to do it, that's the end of the statement. There isn't a need for a comma, semi-colon, colon, dash or anything else. I will do what He tells me to, because it's all about Him (period).

I desire to live a life of such obedience that, yes, when others see the things that I am doing, they will praise and give God all the glory because as I have learned, "Every good thing is not a God thing."

I only want what is attached and connected to the Lord and His plan for my life. I desire for the light that He has placed in me to shine for all to see. All who knew me before and see me now, will have no choice but to conclude that God has been at work and is still working in my life. I'm rejoicing that He who has begun a good work in me, shall complete it.

Because pleasing the Lord is the focus of all I do, as one of my favorite children songs boldly states, "This little light of mine, I'm gonna let it shine; let it shine, let it shine, let it shine."

Suggested Song of Meditation: "It's All About You" By Anita Wilson

Jeremiah 29:13 (Amplified Bible/AMP)

¹³ Then you will seek Me, inquire for, and require Me [as a vital necessity] and find Me when you search for Me with all your heart.

Anytime the weather is beautiful, we always observe so many people who take advantage of the awesome temperatures and get some running in. I love to run; I always have. Every time I would go running, I would place a certain goal in front of me that I would be chasing after. Whether that goal was to run farther than I had the day before or to knock some time off the clock, there was always something I was seeking to achieve.

As I thought about that, I began to ponder on that vital necessity that is required for me to be victorious and achieve the goals and plans that the Lord has set before me; that essential component is me constantly chasing after Him. Each day, it is so evident that we need God more and more. How can we ever expect to make it through without continuously seeking Him?

Some people chase after fame, fortune, other material things and people. I have learned that if we chase after the Lord, we will find Him and He will provide us with all we could ever need and more. When we search for Him with our whole heart and soul, we are brought that much closer to God.

Without constantly running after the Lord, we will not have the fuel, patience and endurance needed to run the race that is set ahead for each of us. As I run hard after His glory, I am praising my way through. I rejoice in knowing that the Lord won't ever leave me nor forsake me.

The God we serve is a mighty God. In James 4:8, the Lord tells us that if we come near to Him, then He shall come near to us. That's what I desire, for my relationship with the Lord to be strengthened and deepened on every level.

I spent so much of my time chasing after the wrong things and individuals, that now that I am no longer blind and have been freed, it is the Lord that I vow to chase after, no matter what I have to do.

Suggested Song of Meditation: "Chasing After You" *by Vashawn Mitchell*

Matthew 5:14-15 (J.B. Phillips New Testament/PHILLIPS)

¹⁴⁻¹⁵ "You are the world's light—it is impossible to hide a town built on the top of a hill. Men do not light a lamp and put it under a bucket. They put it on a lamp-stand and it gives light for everybody in the house.

Sometimes we can get so caught up in what others see in us that we lose sight of all that God has declared that we are. Other times, we allow our current situations or even past circumstances to dictate how we view ourselves.

I'm at a place in my life where it's so crucial that I do not allow the light that has been placed within me to dim. I know that the best way for us to keep that light shining brightly is by constantly reminding ourselves of what El Roi, God who sees us, observes when He looks at us.

Where we see pain, disappointments and failures, the Lord sees victory and tells us that in all things we are more than conquerors through Him who loved us (Romans 8:37). When we can't see past what is right in front of us or where we currently are, the Lord sees where we shall be. God reminds us that we did not choose Him, but He chose us and appointed us so that we might go and bear fruit—fruit that will last—and so that whatever we ask in His name, the Father will give us (John 15:16).

In those instances, when what makes us unique and different we try to hide, suppress or change, we need to embrace the individuality that has been placed within us. The enemy will attempt to prevent us from utilizing our gifts for God's glory, but the Lord has declared that we are His handiwork, created in Christ Jesus, to do good works, which God prepared us in advance to do (Ephesians 2:10).

We have been called to be the light and when the source of our illumination comes from the Lord, we don't ever have to worry about our light being subdued because His power is everlasting. Because I believe that I am what God sees in me, my light can be used to help others see what God sees in them.

Suggested Song of Meditation: "I Am What You See" by Bishop Paul S. Morton

Philippians 2:13 (International Standard Version/ISV)

¹³ For it is God who is producing in you both the desire and the ability to do what pleases him.

It is my prayer each day that more of God and less of me is what is observed through my words, actions and walk with Christ. What I desire out of life is derived from what God seeks from and for me and not from or for my own selfish gains.

I desire to be obtainable for the Lord to consistently use me for His service. In order to accomplish that, I know that surrendering and submitting all things that may get in the way of me being completely available to the Lord is extremely imperative. I no longer wish to be consumed by nor have space taken up by mindsets or patterns of behavior that are not pleasing to God.

Because I have accepted and implemented surrendering to the Lord as a permanent lifestyle, my storage is now empty and God has full accessibility to fill me up; to move in and through me as He pleases. I am God's representative and I am energized by the power and desire that the Lord has created in me to work for His good pleasure, satisfaction and delight.

I am able to communicate via my daily blogs and reach out to man to share God's love and His perfect plan. With my ears, I am able to hear the Lord and others so clearly, which allows me to discern God's will and how I may intercede on behalf of someone else. With my voice, I am able to speak the Lord's Word confidently and joyfully sing His praises to those who've never heard. With my eyes, I detect such a need for more availability.

If every test I have endured, mess I have stepped into, trial I have encountered and stronghold that has been conquered can be used to show someone else the way, God's way, then I say, "Use me Lord." My utmost desire is to obey the Lord; which, in turn, results in me being used by Him to do what is pleasing in His sight.

Suggested Song of Meditation: "Available to You" by Melinda Watts (featuring J. Moss)

Isaiah 43:19 (The Living Bible (TLB)

¹⁹ For I'm going to do a brand-new thing. See, I have already begun! Don't you see it? I will make a road through the wilderness of the world for my people to go home, and create rivers for them in the desert!

Something that I have learned as I continue to grow in my spiritual walk with the Lord is that things will happen in our lives sometimes that we truly will not understand. Circumstances will arise that will completely blindside us and leave us feeling so low that we have no other choice but to look and reach up to the One who desires so much more for us. The Lord desires to do a new thing in our lives but, at times, we get in the way of that happening.

When I reflect on certain seasons in my past (and believe me, I don't stay there long, because I don't want my reflecting to lead to me retaining those past mindsets or behaviors once again), I realized how situations in my life had a way of changing me into an individual I never intended to be; one, at times, I didn't even recognize.

In order to be in the place to receive all that God desires to do in our lives, we have to submit it all to Him. We can't compartmentalize or ration out certain areas of ourselves to the Lord and fight to hold onto the rest. We have to release all of ourselves and our circumstances to Him who is able to do exceedingly, abundantly and infinitely beyond anything we could ever dream to ask for, if we allow His power to work within us (Ephesians 3:20).

Through His power, we are molded and shaped from within. It may not always feel good, but I can tell you that when I'm in the potter's hands and I'm going through the fire, no matter how uncomfortable it may be or how long the firing and sharpening process may last, I know that once it's completed, the end result will be for my betterment, so that I am established as that new creation with my mind focused on God getting the glory in all I do.

In order for new things to sprout up in our lives, God has to uproot some things that have been so deeply entangled beneath the surface. That way, what was restricting us, meaning us no good and taking residence to keep us disconnected, can be removed and thus, fresh fertile ground becomes available for all that the Lord desires to spring forth in our lives.

When we are able to get out of our own way and the Lord's, He will do a brand new thing and we indeed, will never be the same.

Suggested Song of Meditation: "Never Be the Same" by Shana Wilson featuring Tasha Cobbs

Psalm 119:105 (Easy-to-Read Version/ERV)

105 Your word is like a lamp that guides my steps, a light that shows the path I should take.

One piece of technology that I appreciate but that can be a real inconvenience sometimes is the GPS Navigation. Whether I utilize the one in my car or on my phone, neither is without its occasional hiccup or setback. And normally this mishap will occur when I am traveling to a location that I am completely unfamiliar with. It is during these times that I become frustrated because of the dependence and reliability I place on my navigation system. Eventually, it reroutes and gets me back on course, but it still can be quite bothersome.

I know that in life, what lies ahead for me is still yet to be revealed, but I thank God that in His Word, I have been provided with what I need to navigate through the course set ahead of me. His Word is that lamp that guides my steps and that light that shows the path I should take. In reading, familiarizing myself and meditating on His Word, where I could feel blinded, I am given keen insight and am able to discern the move that I must make next.

In His Word, I am reminded that the Lord will always be right by my side and near me until the very end. Even when I may get off course, the Word of God recalibrates me, providing me with the instructions to help get me back where I'm supposed to be. I don't ever have to be concerned about being completely lost or in darkness because I have His Word to illuminate my path.

There is not one circumstance that I have encountered that I have not been able to find referenced in the Bible. In His Word, I not only find direction and purpose, but I also find healing and encouragement and more importantly, the truth. I will follow the commandments, principles and instructions set forth by the Lord because it is my desire to serve Him with all my heart. We have nothing to fear with Jesus by our side and His Word brightening and revealing the route we must take in our own individual journeys.

Suggested Song of Meditation: "Thy Word" by Amy Grant

John 8:36 (Amplified Bible/AMP)

³⁶ So if the Son liberates you [makes you free men], then you are really and unquestionably free.

Not one day goes by that I don't think about all that He has done for me and all the ways that I have been set free.

I know that if it wasn't for the Lord who was on my side, I would still be bound by both those chains I was aware of and the ones that I hadn't even dug deep enough to acknowledge were present. There is so much power in the name of Jesus. His name is a strong tower and is the key that will unlock and break every last one of the strongholds that binds us.

It's when we seek the Lord and are in His presence that He is able to lift us up, break the chains and give us a new life. The Lord is the Spirit. Where the Spirit of the Lord is, there is emancipation from bondage and there is freedom (2 Corinthians 3:17).

Through Christ Jesus we have victory. When we surrender and turn our lives over to the Lord, our past doesn't get to define nor control us any longer. Where we once were lost, we are now given clear and precise direction. We also have access to an eternal guide that will always go before us and who will never forsake us.

Whom the Son sets free is unquestionably free through and through. It's time to walk in our liberty!!

Suggested Song of Meditation: "Set Me Free" by Myron Butler & Levi

Psalm 37:5 (The Voice/VOICE)

⁵ Commit your path to the Eternal; let Him direct you. Put your confidence in Him, and He will follow through with you.

The word journey has always been a special one for me. After graduating from college, I launched my clothing line called AMJ: A Mother's Journey. When I became certified as an Association of Bridal Consultants wedding planner a few years ago, the name of my wedding and event planning business was A Memorable Journey. And when the time came for me to start the blogs of inspiration that the Lord had been stirring up in my spirit, I decided that it should be called Encouragement for Your Journey.

In each instance, whether in the phrases that were screen printed on my apparel, in the experiences I gained as a wedding planner or in the messages that have been shared through my daily blog posts, when I look back I can see how the Lord was directing me because I chose to commit my path to Him.

Long ago, I realized that this race that I am running, although I was a sprinter all through elementary, junior and high school, is not a sprint at all. It is a journey and comparable to a marathon.

Like a marathon, the path that is set before me requires me to be prepared and to have the endurance to last the distance. In every season of my life, I have witnessed what happens when I commit my path to the Lord. When we depend on the Lord and trust Him, He directs and instructs us on how to use what has already been placed within us to be triumphant.

It is when we put our confidence in the Lord, that we can proclaim that we will make it. No matter come what may, we know that God's Word is the truth and that He will follow through and take care of us. Getting to a place where we are able to open up before the Lord, holding nothing back and reposing each of our cares upon Him, positions us to observe God acting on our behalf and doing whatever needs to be done to make a way, even when the path appears to be nowhere in sight.

Suggested Song of Meditation: "I'll Make It" by Hezekiah Walker & The LFCC featuring John P. Kee

Proverbs 18:21 (International Standard Version/ISV)

²¹ The power of the tongue is life and death—those who love to talk will eat what it produces.

All throughout last night and into this morning, I was thinking about words and the power of them. I am part of the generation where we would chant at the playground, "Sticks and stones may break my bones, but words will never hurt me." Good grief, that whole statement was grammatically incorrect and definitely inaccurate. Words have a way of penetrating and cutting deeper than most care to admit at times. Words also have a way of leaving us in a paralyzing state if we grant them the access to.

On the other side of the coin, words have the way to encourage, uplift and empower. Sometimes just hearing an encouraging word or being able to encourage yourself with the words you utilize in the midst of your situations makes all the difference.

As I continue along this journey of mine, I recognize that what I speak is based off what I have gained knowledge of and my own personal beliefs. If our mindsets and beliefs aren't rooted in the Lord, what comes out of our mouths will do more harm and detriment to us than anyone else ever could.

At times, I believe that we sleep on the power that our words possess. No truer statement has been spoken than the one that states, "Our words create our reality." If our trust and confidence is in the Lord, then we can speak those things that are not as if they already were and not allow a single shred of doubt to creep in. Not only do our words have power to speak to life and prosperity, but God has given us the authority and those same words have the power to defeat the enemy. We have to be able to speak it before we see it!!

Like most things in life, the choice is ours on which path we take with the words we use. Our destiny depends on us. Sometimes we have to take some inventory on the words that we utilize and anything that is associated with a toxic mindset, immediately replace it with those words that are linked to the fruitful mindset that we adopt when God is our source for it all.

I don't know what words you have been speaking or are currently declaring, but it is my prayer that those words are speaking into existence blessings, miracles, enlargement of territories, abundance, healing and restoration. There is no room for words associated with worry, fear and doubt. The smallest amount of toxicity that comes from our mouths can have catastrophic effects.

We have to make the choice to speak life. When we choose our words wisely and nurture them, we are then positioned to receive the fruits that are produced from them. We've got the power!! Let it be used to decree God's favor over our lives!!

Suggested Song of Meditation: "My Words Have Power" by Karen Clark Sheard

Psalm 32:8 (New International Version/NIV)

⁸ I will instruct you and teach you in the way you should go; I will counsel you with my loving eye on you.

The Lord has done so much for me that I couldn't even possibly express everything if I tried. I will tell you that it has been through the daily blog that I have created and my dedication to utilize it as God directs me to, that it has become so clear to me the path in which this ministry is supposed to go. My relationship with the Lord has strengthened immensely and I am walking in what He has had for me from the start.

There is a sense of freedom that resides inside of me that I didn't even know was possible. The areas of my life that I thought were shattered beyond repair, the Lord gathered up each and every single piece and put it all back together again. I have been released from the strongholds that had me bound.

The Lord has supplied me with everything I could ask for and so much more. He continues to guide, instruct and counsel me with His loving eye watching over me. I can see it all coming together, since I've made the decision to give the Lord my all.

He's made ways when there seemed to be no way at all. Knowing all that the Lord has done for me is part of the reason that praising, worshiping and exalting His name has become and will remain a part of my daily routine.

When I think about how good God has been, I rejoice knowing that every day He keeps looking out for me.

Suggested Song of Meditation: "That's What He's Done for Me" by Anita Wilson

Psalm 33:4 (Easy-to-Read Version/ERV)

4 The Lord's Word is true, and he is faithful in everything he does.

In God's Word, we are told that His love, grace and mercy are never-ending and that God will never leave us nor forsake us. My son walking across the platform to not only obtain his diploma but also his Science and Technology certificate was just one more illustration of God knowing the plans that He has for us and that we can always trust everything that He does because He can never fail and with Him all things are possible.

I realize that my life is a compilation of some unbelievable stories of how God's love, grace and mercy has kept my family and me. I am so grateful for the opportunity to be a storyteller in the name of the Lord.

See growing up, I was raised where we used the word, "storyteller" instead of calling someone a "liar". So being a storyteller wasn't ever a good thing. But God will take something that was intended for one thing and turn it completely around for His glory.

With each day that I live, the Lord opens my eyes to so much. I gain insight and grow wiser in the knowledge that I receive because of who God is and who He continues to be in my life. As I review the pages from the story of my life, with each one that I turn, I see nothing but the evidence of God's faithfulness.

I know that I will always have a story to tell because it is God who is the head of my life. Every day, He moves in and through my circumstances and all that I learn and experience, I desire to share, with the hopes of encouraging and motivating others to become acquainted or to develop an even deeper relationship with the Lord.

Suggested Song of Meditation: "Storyteller" by Morgan Harper Nichols (with Jamie Grace)

Psalm 66:9 (New English Translation/NET Bible)

⁹ He preserves our lives and does not allow our feet to slip.

Today, I spent most of the day really thanking the Lord and appreciating not just the extremely huge moves that He makes on my behalf, but also the little ones that matter just as much. The past few days have been so hectic, that even the times that I normally post my blogs have been affected. It is my desire to share them so much earlier than I have over the past week, but I also know that some adjustments had to be made as my family and I were taking the next steps in the moving process.

I believe that is why I was clothed in such a garment of thankfulness today. Trust and believe that I am thankful for the way the Lord loves me and expresses that love each day. But today, it was different and I just kept thanking Him over and over. And as I was driving off the base today and was observing those individuals in uniform walking to work, I thanked God for blessing my family and me in ways I didn't know to ask for or even consider.

When I was discharged from the Air Force in December 2002, I thought that my interaction and access to the military and its benefits had ceased forever. At that time, I had no idea that there was more that the Lord had in store for me and in turn, my family.

I'm here to tell you that I have witnessed and continue to see in my own life that when we surrender to the Lord's will, He will answer prayers that we were too closed-minded and limited in our thinking to even request. Because our lives are in His hands, we have the assurance that God will keep us from falling by holding our feet to the path that He has set before us.

I have absolutely no reason to be afraid of what is to come because the Lord did not give us a spirit of fear. With God, I know that I will always be taken care of and that He won't ever let me go.

Suggested Song of Meditation: "You Hold My World" by Israel Houghton

Colossians 1:10 (Amplified Bible/AMP)

¹⁰ That you may walk (live and conduct yourselves) in a manner worthy of the Lord, fully pleasing to Him and desiring to please Him in all things, bearing fruit in every good work and steadily growing and increasing in and by the knowledge of God [with fuller, deeper, and clearer insight, acquaintance, and recognition].

No matter how optimistic and filled with encouragement I strive to be, there are some days when I have to step back, spend some serious one-on-one with the Lord and regroup. That is what I have had to do over the past couple of days. Have you ever been so close to obtaining what you have envisioned (that which God has promised) and it seems the closer you get, the further it appears to be from within your grasp?

When I tell you that the spiritual warfare is real, please believe, **that's a fact, jack!!!** Now more than ever, I know that I must walk, talk and interact in a manner that is worthy of the Lord and pleasing in His sight. I realize that by constantly growing and increasing in and by acquiring a fuller, deeper and clearer insight into the Lord and who He has called me to be, I can obtain those things that He has destined for me.

Lately, the enemy has attempted to use both the past and all that I do not know regarding the future, as distractions and potential setbacks. I had to tell the enemy that I may not know all the specifics, but I do know that my future is exceptionally bright because I know who is in charge of it. I also had to remind the enemy that his reminders of my past only make me stronger. What he meant to break or destroy me, actually caused me to seek the Lord and lean on Him in ways I never knew I could. The end result has been a **radical**, **impermeable faith**; an airtight belief and trust in the Lord.

I have come too far and am learning far too much about life as a child of God, to turn back now. I am here to be, to have and to achieve everything that the Lord has spoken over my life.

In order to accomplish that, I must continuously work on improving myself; along with taking the time to recognize and learn more about the Lord and who He desires for me to be. As my knowledge in the Lord increases, the effect of the enemy's attacks decreases.

I am able to proclaim what I will be, what I will have, and what I will achieve because of the life worthy of the Lord that I strive to lead.

Suggested Song of Meditation: "I Will Be" by Anthony Brown and group therAPy featuring Vashawn Mitchell

Psalm 18:30 (GOD'S WORD Translation/GW)

30 God's way is perfect! The promise of the Lord has proven to be true. He is a shield to all those who take refuge in him.

Over the past few months, something that has really resonated deep within me is the importance of me not getting attached to how I think things should occur or the way I believe that everything should happen or play out in the end.

One very real and undisputed truth is that the Lord's way is perfect; it is absolute and complete. His Word is pure. His promises have been tested and proven to be true; they are flawless.

Possessing this knowledge, why would I ever desire to travel a path that is not of the Lord? Simple enough question, right? But one that I have ended up asking myself more times than I care to remember. I have truly learned to appreciate God's way because, through life experiences, I have seen that it is the only way we can ever possibly make it and be victorious as God aspires us to be.

In those seasons of my life when I opted to do things my way, yes, the Lord still received the glory, but in retrospect, I could have done without a few of those twists and turns. The importance of surrendering every area of my life became that much more apparent. I needed anything and everything removed that was preventing me from standing solely on His Word and nothing else.

I was reminded that I was created not for my own purposes or for my will to be done. I was created specifically for the Lord's glory and His purpose.

Therefore, whatever arises, I am encouraged and filled with hope, peace and joy because I undoubtedly recognize the God I serve. I know that His road stretches out straight and is smooth. I rejoice in knowing that every God-direction is road-tested and that when I run towards Him, I have the assurance that I will make it.

When we submit to God's perfect will and way for our lives, we position ourselves to receive His interminable love, with it permeating our souls to such a level that it overflows. With less of ourselves and more of God as the premise for all that we seek to accomplish, the end result is God having His way in our lives.

Suggested Song of Meditation: "Have Your Way" by Casey J featuring Jason Nelson

Psalm 16:2 (The Message/MSG)

² *I say to God, "Be my Lord!" Without you, nothing makes sense.*

I woke up with my heart filled with so much gratitude and joy. Every sentiment that I was feeling was taken to the next level when I viewed a snippet from a service that was held at a church in the local area.

The speaker wanted everyone to be encouraged and remember that the storm doesn't last always and that God is turning it around. I took some quiet time to just rest in the words that the Lord had laid upon the speaker's heart to minister to those within the congregation and to other individuals such as myself, who were blessed to receive her message over the Internet.

Something that the speaker said, which truly resonated down to the core of my being was when she stated we should thank God for providence. I hadn't ever heard that expressed before and although I knew what providence meant, I went to the dictionary for the precise definition. I found the word providence defined as "the protective or spiritual care of God."

When I sat back and thought about the protective and spiritual care that has kept me through circumstances and situations that I thought there was no way I could make it through, all I could do was hum, as tears rolled down my face. I began to think, "Where would I be without the Lord?" Those tears were met with chills and with much clarity; I recognized that through God's boundless love, grace and mercy, I had been given access to providence.

Through the topsy-turvy and unexpected twists and turns that I have experienced in my life, one thing has been made clearly evident and that is that without the Lord, I have nothing good. Without Him, absolutely nothing makes sense.

When you know that the Lord is with you and not just on but by your side; and you have that assurance that He has gone before you in all things and won't ever leave you or forsake you, you are able to endure and face trials rejoicing every step of the way because there are no doubts that it's all working together for your good.

I belong to the Lord and would be so very lost without Him. Not being divinely connected to the Lord is not even an option. It is required for my survival and that is not up for negotiation or discussion. Therefore, thanking God for providence has become a mantra that I intend to repeat on a very frequent basis.

Suggested Song of Meditation: "Without You" by Tasha Cobbs

Proverbs 16:3 (Expanded Bible/EXB)

> ³ ·Depend on the Lord in whatever you do [Commit your acts/deeds to the Lord], and your plans will ·succeed [be established].

Since yesterday, I have continued to reflect on the messages that were provided from the teachings by Bishop T.D. Jakes. As I converse and have dissected what I have learned with others, I have begun to pull back more layers of the onion regarding life lessons that the Lord has desired for me to acquire and then apply to my daily routine.

In this life that I am very fortunate and grateful to live, I want to be brought to the very place where God has need for me. I know that in order for that to occur, for me to obtain the destiny that He has for me, I must depend on the Lord in everything that I do; knowing that in doing so, my plans will be established and successful.

I have been redeemed and bought with a price. Therefore, nothing is more important to me than doing everything in my power to please the Lord. When I commit and entrust all that I do to the Lord, He will cause my thoughts to become agreeable to His will. Having my thoughts lined up with God's perfect plan means that I can move forward without any doubts because the source of my direction is coming from above.

I know what is like to plan things out in my own head, without consulting God. What ended up happening was a lot of chaos and confusion which resulted in me eventually running to the Lord to help bring me out of it anyway. Well, I have resolved that; I desire less chaos and more order; less confusion and more certainty. Our God is a God of order and there is nothing that I am more certain of than His sovereignty.

I am currently in a season of transitioning and am in between places. But I am encouraged and empowered because it's His will, and not my own, that I am focused on. In a particular message, Bishop T.D. Jakes compared transitioning to childbirth and what a great analogy that was.

As I was transitioning from being a young woman to a mother, it took some time, some tests, some work and some pain. But all those elements brought me to the moment of delivery and thus, experiencing the greatest joy ever; of becoming a mom. I am incorporating those same applications into my spiritual walk and realizing that as I press toward the destiny that God has for me, it requires some time, some tests and trials, some work and some pain; but every last component is working together to bring me to where God wants me to be and who He needs me to be.

Therefore, because I want my destiny, I will keep surrendering and entrusting every aspect of my life, as I look to the hills which is where my help comes from.

Suggested Song of Meditation: "I Want My Destiny" by Fred Hammond

Romans 8:15 (Common English Bible/CEB)

15 You didn't receive a spirit of slavery to lead you back again into fear, but you received a Spirit that shows you are adopted as his children. With this Spirit, we cry, "Abba, Father."

I was having a conversation with a dear sister in Christ yesterday. We are both preparing and waiting with expectancy for what the Lord has for our families and for us. While we were conversing, a theme that we recognized is how people tend to disappear, become distant or disconnect during those times in which we need them the most.

Over time, it has appeared as if the total dynamic of my relationships began to shift as soon as I was no longer needed to provide assistance or a service to them. And that has always been a hard pill for me to swallow. I will give my last and will do all I can to assist others. In most cases, it has been a very one-sided relationship, with that common courtesy or concern for my well-being not being reciprocated.

All my life, I have just wanted to belong and be loved by everyone, because growing up, I didn't fit in anywhere and those around me had no problem telling and showing me that. Trying to fit in and that longing to belong, according to the world's standards, caused so much heartache for me.

I remember learning in church that oftentimes, people who oppose or don't like us are individuals whom we have loved, have bent over backwards to help, have served and prayed for continuously. Another point that was shared was that we show others that we belong to the Lord when we are able to love those who do not express that same sentiment to us. Because we are God's children, Christ is within us and we are able to follow the lead of His Spirit, which gives us the capacity and ability to love those who have dissed, discounted and disconnected from us.

Because my life is not my own and I belong to the Lord, I strive to live it in a way that is most pleasing in the Lord's sight. I haven't always hit the mark. I have made some terrible choices, which in turn landed me in some horrible situations. And the Lord still loved me, forgave me, protected me, and turned my situations around to get me back on the right path toward my destiny.

We all yearn to be loved and that search for me hasn't always been pretty or reciprocated with the love that I eagerly desired to give. Even when others have hurt me, I wouldn't ever wish hurt or hard times to fall upon any of them. I love the example of Joseph, because even though he didn't expect his brothers to treat him the way they did, he still loved them, he forgave them and God placed Joseph in the position to be a blessing to them.

Jesus was born and knew the purpose His life would serve. He knew who would despise, reject and betray Him (and some of those individuals walked right alongside Him until the last day) and He still loved them, forgave them, served them and even washed their feet.

Now, keeping it 100% real with all of you, I don't know about washing the feet, but forgiving, serving and still loving others, even when they don't mean me any good and would prefer to see me fall, I will definitely do that!!

I belong to the Lord and have been captured by a love that cannot be defined or explained by words accurately. Because of His love, I'm forever changed and am no longer bound by a spirit of slavery which, in turn, leads to fear. I have abandoned everything that has prevented me from being who He has called me to be. I have surrendered my life to the Lord because I know that greater is He that is in me, than he that is in the world.

When our children leave the house, my husband and I always tell them to be cognizant of who they are representing when they walk out the door. Doesn't the same hold true for us?

A question that I constantly ask myself is when people meet or see me, can they tell that I have been adopted into the family circle of God and that I belong to Him?

My answer to that question lets me know how to proceed. How about you?

Suggested Song of Meditation: "I Belong to You" by William McDowell

Matthew 7:14 (Easy-to-Read Version/ERV)

¹⁴ But the gate that opens the way to true life is narrow. And the road that leads there is hard to follow. Only a few people find it.

As we navigate the course that is set before us, there are so many detours and side streets that we can be tempted to travel down because they appear to be less challenging and vigorous. Sometimes we look for the shortcuts, easygoing formulas, and cliff notes as our means for obtaining information on how to proceed in life.

I learned early on that nothing good comes from trying to rush, attempting to take the easy way out or deciding to follow the path of others instead of embarking on the road less traveled; the road that has been selected specifically for you.

What am I able to accomplish without the Lord? Absolutely nothing!!! He is the Vine and we are the branches. Whoever lives in Him and Him in them bears much (abundant) fruit. However, apart from Him [cut off from vital union with Him] they will be unable to do anything (John 15:5). The importance of having that divine connection with the Lord is illustrated so well in the above verse.

Recognizing that I can't live or make it without the Lord, I surrender my heart, my mind and my soul to Him because I am in need of the Lord taking complete control of my life. History has shown that when I have tried things on my own, I have done nothing but distance and separate myself further from what God has designed for my life.

In the days that I am fortunate to live, I want to be able to say that I found that path to true life. And not only did I find it, but upon uncovering it, I was committed to following the road by remaining focused on the Lord and giving Him my complete and total attention. The verse states that only a few find that path. I desire to be one of the few.

How successful I am in this life is not and will not be determined by the templates or blueprints set by man. It is the Lord's will that every need be supplied; therefore, my success comes from knowing that when I depend on the Lord in all that I do, my plans will succeed and be established (Proverbs 16:3).

My life is not my own and I, willingly and cheerfully, give myself to the Lord because I can't live or make it without Him. Forever and ever, I will trust in the Lord, because without Him, I can do nothing.

Suggested Song of Meditation: "What Can I Do" by Tye Tribbett

Ephesians 5:8 (New Century Version/NCV)

⁸ In the past you were full of darkness, but now you are full of light in the Lord. So live like children who belong to the light.

If there was one place that I needed to be today, it was in church. With all that has transpired lately, I couldn't wait for Sunday to get here.

Even though I have been praying and have been taking the time to fellowship with the Lord one-on-one, there is something about being in the Lord's house with other believers who desire to be in His presence like I do, that helps to bring everything back into focus for me.

Recently, the word that the Holy Spirit has kept before me is the word "light".

From observing a firefly to re-reading a couple of quotes from Dr. Martin Luther King, Jr., I was reminded of the importance of letting my light shine and taking the opportunities that the Lord places before me to do kingdom work.

When I went to church today here in Long Island and the subject of the message was "Ambassadors for Christ," (with the main scripture reading coming from 2 Corinthians 5:11-21), I knew that there was more that the Lord desired for me to know and to apply to my life and the assignment He has for me, as a child of God.

What was so interesting about the topic for today's message was that just before going to church this morning, I had read the following quote by Maya Angelou and had it added to my list of favorites.

The quote read, *"I found that I knew not only that there was God, but that I was a child of God. When I understood that, when I comprehended that, more than that, when I internalized that, ingested that, I became courageous. I dared to do anything that was a good thing. I dared to do things as distant from what seemed to be in my future. If God loves me, if God made everything from leaves to seals and oak trees, then what is it I can't do?"*

I thought about the above quote again as I began to listen to the message at church. By definition, an ambassador is an accredited diplomat sent by a country as its official representative to a foreign country.

These are undoubtedly some dark times we are living in, but I know that there was a time when I also was in darkness. But because of who the Lord is and all that He has been and has done for me, not only am I a recipient of His light, but I am also called to be a reflector of it as well.

We are ambassadors for Christ. We are expected to live our lives in a way that reflects and represents God and His kingdom each and every day. Because I have been reconciled to God through Christ, I am also tasked with the ministry of reconciliation; the privilege of telling others that they can be reconciled to God as well (2 Corinthians 5:18).

In keeping my focus on the Lord and the realities of heaven, just hours later after returning home from church, the Lord presented me with an opportunity to be that ambassador for Him that He has called me to be. Conversations began to take place with individuals who didn't even desire to utter a greeting in my direction in the past. In that moment, it wasn't about reciprocating what I had been on the receiving end of previously, but instead, it was a divine opportunity to reflect the God that is in me.

It is my heartfelt desire that each of us will choose to be ambassadors for Christ and that we will fill up the spaces around us with light.

As the Word of God reminds us, "The light shines in the darkness and the darkness has not overcome or overpowered it."(John 1:5)

Therefore, when we are filled and led by the Holy Spirit and are reflecting God's light, is there anything that we can't do as we strive to advance the interests of God's kingdom?

Suggested Song of Meditation: "Let There Be Light" by Bryan & Katie Torwalt

Psalm 73:28 (The Living Bible/TLB)

²⁸ But as for me, I get as close to him as I can! I have chosen him, and I will tell everyone about the wonderful ways he rescues me.

Most days, I feel free and as if I am soaring so high. It's as if there is an untouchable forcefield around me. On days like those, nothing can distract me or veer me off course. The enemy doesn't get a chance to infiltrate the camp. Nor does he get the opportunity to make me second guess any of the decisions that I have made or circumstances that are surrounding me.

But then there are a few days I encounter when I feel like I'm losing the fight. The pressures are too many to count and the setbacks come bundled up in mass quantities like items purchased at B.J.'s or Sam's Club. To make matters more trying, the number of mountains to climb increases exponentially right before my eyes.

It is at times such as these that I seek to be in the presence of the Lord and on the receiving end of the comfort and compassion that can only come from above. I desire to be as close as I can to the Lord because I know that drawing near to God is the absolute best for me and the best place to be.

It's easy to trust and believe in the Lord when everything is falling into place. But for me, placing my trust in the Lord and Him being my refuge during periods like these, lifts me out of my defeat; because through Him I am complete. I believe with my whole heart that I require the Lord in my life every day, because with the Lord I have everything I will ever need.

Nothing else matters than seeking out the One who reigns over my life and being able to lay it all at His feet and hear His voice speak ever so clearly to me. These days, so many things are being said and at the same time, so many things are not being spoken. I feel so lost and overwhelmed at the same time. To obtain that clarity and discernment, I have made God my place of safety and protection.

There is so much that I question and so much still left to be revealed. If I make the decision to focus on what I don't know, I give the spirit of defeat the opportunity to usher in. But I am making the choice to focus on what and who I do know; and that is our Heavenly Father.

The closer that I am to the Lord, the better. The Eternal One keeps me safe. And no matter how overwhelming my circumstances may appear, the Lord always shows up and rescues me.

I will continue to share with others all the wonderful ways that the Lord rescues me. I am reminded that nothing else matters than being in the presence of the Lord.

Suggested Song of Meditation: "Nothing Else Matters" by Israel and New Breed

Psalm 40:8 (New Living Translation/NLT)

⁸ I take joy in doing your will, my God, for your instructions are written on my heart."

If I haven't learned anything else over these past few months, I have recognized and acknowledged that the Lord's way is what is absolutely best for me.

Not only do I strive to accomplish things in the way that God expects me to, but I take joy in doing His will. His teachings are deep within me and have been written on my heart; which means I don't have to search far for the instructions and the guidance when it comes to making decisions in my life.

All the blessings and breakthroughs that have occurred lately have reminded me what happens when it is God's will and His direction that is ordering and guiding my steps and not some plan that I have created on my own. I rejoice and am so thankful that the Lord's ways are not my ways.

If the seasons of my life had navigated the courses that I had charted, oh my goodness, I don't know where I would be; but I know it wouldn't be where I should have been. I am so grateful and give the Lord my greatest praise because of a faithfulness and goodness that can only be associated with Him.

I don't have to understand it all. But, I'm making the choice to do things God's way. As I continue to just live life and mature in my spiritual walk, the importance of doing what God says to do, going where God says to go and being all that He has instructed me to be, resonates more and more within me. The absolute best is what I desire and I know that can only be obtained by having God's will as the center and focal point for all that I do. I choose to do it the Lord's way; no other way will suffice.

Suggested Song of Meditation: "Your Way" by Anthony Brown and group therAPy

1 Peter 3:15 (Contemporary English Version/CEV)

¹⁵ Honor Christ and let him be the Lord of your life. Always be ready to give an answer when someone asks you about your hope.

Earlier today, I thought of a song we used to sing in church when I was younger. The lyrics of the song state, "Lord I'm available to you, my will I give to you, I'll do what you say do, use me Lord, to show someone the way and enable me to say; my storage is empty and I am available to you."

With my whole heart and through my actions, I desire for the Lord to know and for others to see that I honor His sovereignty and holiness in my life. Without Him, where would I be? I don't ever wish to know. What I do know is that with the Lord on my side, my faith grows stronger and I possess a hope in Him that cannot and will not falter.

All I am is available to the Lord. I want the whole world to see how grateful I am for the faithfulness, truthfulness and goodness that can only come from the Lord. With the Lord, I am provided the protection, direction and guidance needed to live my life according to His will and not my own.

Just as the song from my childhood echoes, "My storage is empty and I am available to the Lord." I want to be filled up by the Lord with there being less of me and more of Him.

As I journey through life and my path crosses with others, it is my prayer that they see the hope that is within me which then affords me the opportunity to share with them, who is the one and only source of that hope. I welcome the chance to speak of God's boundless love and the perfect plan that He has for each of our lives.

I also embrace having the occasions to express why I worship and praise the Lord the way I do. Why is there always a song of praise on the tip of my lips? Why do I raise my hands in worship and tears of joy continuously fall from my eyes? I desire for those whom I come into contact with to have the opportunity to get to know the great I AM; just as I have. This life I live is not my own.

In honoring the Lord, I surrender my heart, my availability and my everything to the One who reigns above every name!!!

Suggested Song of Meditation" "All I Am" by Kierra "Kiki" Sheard

Ephesians 5:17 (The Message/MSG)

¹⁷ Don't live carelessly, unthinkingly. Make sure you understand what the Master wants.

I believe that one of the greatest gifts that we have is the gift of learning and obtaining knowledge in the areas that will prove most beneficial for us to live out the plans and walk into the destiny that the Lord has set before us.

Throughout my life, education has played such a significant role in what has mattered to me. I have always had a desire to know more. I didn't just want to know a multitude of things, I wanted to be educated on what was right and what was true. Being someone who is very black and white and who searches for the facts before making an informed decision, my decision-making process has always had to be one based on truths and not lies, facts and not opinions.

As I have journeyed and been educated in various institutions, I have learned that my greatest teaching has come from the Lord and the Bible. I have had some awesome professors in college and have kept quite a few of my textbooks from those days. No matter what degrees I may possess, they are concentrated in one or maybe two particular areas.

Whereas, taking the time to establish and develop an even deeper and stronger relationship with the Lord has provided me with an ever-evolving edification experience that covers every aspect and applies to every area in my life. I do not desire to represent the Lord, my family, my community or myself in a foolish, thoughtless or ignorant manner. For that reason, I study God's Word, His principles and teachings so that I may understand and fully grasp what the will of the Lord is for my life.

By understanding and learning what the Lord wants me to do, I'm able to hold on, remain steadfast and go where the Lord tells me to go, without wondering or questioning; because I have chosen to depend completely and confidently in Him. I won't give up or give in.

Staying in His will is a must if I desire to be all that the Lord has created me to be and if I wish to see His promises come to pass in my life. I am thankful for the education that I have received and for all that I continue to learn because as I tell my children, "School is in session every day!!" But most importantly, I am eternally grateful for the opportunity to learn about the Lord and what it is that He says. Each day, I petition, "Lord, let your will and not mine, be done."

Suggested Song of Meditation: "In Your Will" by Men of Standard

Proverbs 26:17 (New English Translation/NET Bible)

17 Like one who grabs a wild dog by the ears, so is the person passing by who becomes furious over a quarrel not his own.

One of the hardest principles for me to grasp growing up and very much into my adulthood was that everything that concerned everybody around me wasn't necessarily my business nor my cross to bear.

I was always told that being the oldest sibling and the oldest grandchild, it was my job to be the protector, the role model and everything else in between. For me, that meant that anything that pertained to those close to me in my family was also my responsibility to tend to as well.

Always making myself readily available to people also put me in the position to get pulled into quarrels, drama and nonsense that had absolutely nothing to do with me. But because I was always looking for validation from others and desired that feeling of inclusion, I took on the task of wanting to be the one to "save the day."

Looking back, I know good and well that the Lord did not task me with inserting myself into anyone else's messes or situations, especially when I had my own stuff to work through. I truly had to learn to pick my battles and how not to allow myself to be stressed, overwhelmed and weighed down by circumstances that didn't pertain to me and weren't worth my energy or time.

I had to grasp how to keep it moving. But there was something even more than that. I had to get to a place where I understood that it was okay not to know everything or to be included in everything. My need for inclusion took me down some very dark and hurtful paths.

Like one who grabs a wild dog by the ears (and why would we ever choose to knowingly do that), I have been bitten and barked at so ferociously more times than I care to remember. But I recognize that was because I involved myself in situations that shouldn't have had the opportunity to even catch my attention.

But I am so thankful that there was a lesson for me to receive in each one of those instances. By stepping back and learning the importance of being able to keep it moving, I was no longer overwhelmed by what was going on with others and was able to focus on those things that pleased the Lord and not what man desired from me.

Seeking to please the Lord, but desiring to please man and receive approval from others at the same time was a recipe for disaster and an example of what it means to serve two masters; which is something I need to avoid doing at all costs.

Our God is so awesome and doesn't make us jump through hoops for His approval, nor is His love conditional or fair-weather. We can't sweat the small stuff, other people's stuff nor the stuff that we have no control over.

To keep it moving doesn't mean we are selfish, heartless or insincere. It means that everything that comes our way is not meant for us to take on and there is nothing wrong with that.

Getting to a place where I could accept and own that wasn't easy, but I have been blessed with more stress-free days and more time dedicated and allotted to what is important; like spending that much-needed time with the Lord, praising and honoring Him for who He is, for the unparalleled and boundless love He shows me and the endless access that I have to His grace and mercy.

Suggested Song of Meditation: "Keep It Moving" by Jessica Reedy

Luke 6:46 (Disciples' Literal New Testament/DLNT)

⁴⁶ "And why are you calling Me 'Lord, Lord, and you are not doing the things which I say?

As I came across the song for my next post, I realized that I probably could have grouped my last few blog posts together and had them under the header of, "My Confession Series".

Each of the songs reminded me of just how misguided and misdirected I was and how I had to endure some really intense life lessons to not only learn more about the Lord and develop a relationship with Him, but I also had to learn about myself and get to the core of who I was, why I thought the way I did, did the things in the manner to which I would and ended up in some of the situations that I found myself in.

By no means has the journey been easy, but I appreciate every last step that I have taken in it. I had to learn the hard way that you can't plead and call on the name of the Lord, seeking direction and guidance, and then once He answers, you ignore the instructions given or you try to negotiate another way for a resolution because what God is telling you to do is either not the answer you desire to hear or will take you outside your comfort zone, where your fear of the unknown and being vulnerable outweighs your trust in the Lord.

I've had my seasons of being hard-headed and disobedient but what I took away from those periods in my life was that, regardless of what the Lord is requiring of me; because of the faith that I have in Him, I will be ready, willing and able to obey His will and to be a doer of His Words and commands.

The Lord has thoughts and plans for our lives that, I guarantee you, surpass and are infinitely beyond anything we could dare to hope or ask for. But we can't call on Him and not be ready to do as He says. That's like going to the doctor when you are ill and being given strict instructions on what you must do to get well and you ignore them. Now a doctor tends to a specific aspect of your life, whereas the Lord is in control of all areas.

Why call on Him in our times of need if we are not willing to submit to His will and authority? It may not always be easy and it may result in us being led down unknown paths, but I have made the decision that I shall do whatever He wants me to do.

Suggested Song of Meditation: "I Shall Do" by John P. Kee

Luke 9:23 (New Century Version/NCV)

²³ Jesus said to all of them, "If people want to follow me, they must give up the things they want. They must be willing to give up their lives daily to follow me.

As always, the Lord speaks to me through song and the first song that I heard on Pandora this evening described exactly where I am in my spiritual walk. It was a song I hadn't ever heard before but it reminded me of a sister song that has been sung time and time again. As I sat here in my dining room, all I could do was lift my voice to sing, "Yes Lord, yes Lord, from the bottom of my heart; to the depths of my soul, yes Lord; completely yes; my soul says yes. Not my will, but Thy will be done, no more I but it's you, Christ that lives inside. Lord, I give my everything, my everything to You, and I'm yielded completely through and through".

More than ever, the importance of doing all that needs to be done so that we are closer to the Lord, becomes that much more evident. I learned a long time ago that if I didn't give up the things I wanted or how I felt things should be done and instead trust the Lord completely, I was like a dog chasing my own tail; getting nowhere quick.

To be in the Lord's presence and to have His guidance is what matters. I don't want to move unless He has instructed me to go; I don't dare speak without hearing a clear word from Him and His stamp of approval is needed when it comes to the things that I do. I know what it's like to try things my way and that hasn't ever fared well for me.

That is why I have made the commitment to disown, forget and lose sight of myself and my own interests thus, taking up my cross daily and cleaving steadfastly to the Lord, conforming wholly to His example.

No more I, but it is Him that lives inside. I've surrendered completely through and through.

Suggested Song of Meditation: "Closer" by Aaron Sledge

1 Thessalonians 5:19 (Amplified Bible/AMP)

¹⁹ Do not quench [subdue, or be unresponsive to the working and guidance of] the [Holy] Spirit.

Free-range is defined as, "kept in natural conditions, with freedom of movement; not being confined." As the song for today ministered to my soul, I really thought about that definition and what it meant in regards to the role that I have allowed the Holy Spirit to have within my life.

Honestly, I have to admit that there have been seasons in my life where I have quenched and stifled the work of the Holy Spirit. But because I know that I cannot make it without the Lord's presence in my life, it was imperative that I seek forgiveness from the Lord for all those times when I didn't allow the Holy Spirit to not just move, but flow inside of me and throughout every area of my life.

Instead of compartmentalizing and restricting the Holy Spirit's access to me, I have adopted a "free-range" mentality. I will no longer take responsibility for extinguishing the Spirit's fire. There will be no more confinement or limitations.

By stifling the Holy Spirit, I, in turn, prevent the Holy Spirit from operating in the capacity that He was sent to me. In John 14:26, the Word states, "But the Helper (Comforter, Advocate, Intercessor—Counselor, Strengthener, Standby), the Holy Spirit, whom the Father will send in My name [in My place, to represent Me and act on My behalf], He will teach you all things. And He will help you remember everything that I have told you."

By making the decision to move myself out of the way, I am shown more, taught more and given an advocate on my behalf who promises to help, comfort, intercede, counsel and strengthen me.

I patiently wait for you, Holy Spirit. You have free range to flow in my life.

Suggested Song of Meditation: "Flow" by Jessica Reedy

2 Corinthians 2:9 (Amplified Bible/AMP)

⁹ For this was my purpose in writing, to see if you would stand the test, whether you are obedient and committed to following my instruction in all things.

For so long, something that I found extremely difficult to do was to say, "No." I thought it was my duty and responsibility to come to the rescue and be who others needed me to be, when they needed me. Spending so much time pleasing others meant I wasn't spending the necessary time doing what pleased the Lord.

But I was so entangled in a web that consisted of seeking acceptance and attempting to please everyone else, that I couldn't even see the forest for the trees. It wasn't until certain circumstances occurred where I should have said, "No" instead of "Yes" and I ended up in situations that I never dreamed I'd be in a million years, that I began to see what needed to be changed and purged from my life.

My obedience and commitment must be to the Lord, first and foremost and above all else. For so long, I had lost sight of who I was and whose I was. But I know that each trial that came my way had a specific purpose and helped to work toward my breakthrough, healing and restoration. Everything has actually come full circle because I went from saying, "Yes" to everyone and everything to regrouping which, in turn, led to me yielding and surrendering myself so that the "Yes" that I was giving went to the Lord first and without any hesitation.

In the past, I knew on numerous occasions what the Lord was asking me to do, but I was hesitant to commit and say, "Yes" for fear of where I would end up. But that was a tactic of the enemy because our Heavenly Father operates within the realm of faith; unlike the enemy who operates out of fear. Yielding, examining and surrendering myself were the vital components needed for my thought process to be altered and thus, the obstacles to my obedience and commitment to the Lord being diminished. I am determined to say, "Yes," to the Lord's will, His way and His Word, each and every day.

As I thought about all of this, it reminded me of a song we used to sing in the choir, when I was younger. That song is, "I'll Say Yes, Lord Yes." I couldn't help but sing the first few lines of the song that states, "I'll say yes, Lord, yes, to your will and to your way. I'll say yes, Lord, yes, I will trust you and obey. When your Spirit speaks to me, with my whole heart I'll agree and my answer will be yes, Lord, yes." In trusting the Lord and being obedient, I am able to simply say Y.E.S. (Yield myself, Examine myself and Surrender myself) to God.

Suggested Song of Meditation: "Simply Yes" by Byron Cage

Psalm 119:32 (World English Bible/WEB)

³² I run in the path of your commandments, for you have set my heart free.

Because I am fully aware of who I am and how I am intricately woven, each day I strive to be cognizant of what I allow my eyes to observe and my ears to apprehend. I can't be bogged down by constant sarcasm, cruelty and negativity on a daily basis.

That is why inspirational and motivational blogs, phrases and songs carry so much weight with me because they speak to my soul. And it never fails, that through one of those mediums, I am ministered to in some area and the Lord communicates with me in the way that I need Him to do.

While I was correcting an error link that was generated after my blog post was published one evening, I read a post that spoke to the depth of God's love for us being so much, that sometimes He has to remove people and things from our lives for our own protection.

Upon reading that, all I could do was smile because I truly could say that I fully comprehended what that meant. There was a time when I didn't. If someone walked out of my life or if a relationship became so toxic and unhealthy that I had to disassociate myself from it, I thought I was being punished.

Looking back now, I realize that I was trying to be everything to everyone else and my relationship with the Lord was being slighted and neglected. I wanted to be the one everyone else could run to, but when the storms of life would rage so ferociously that I couldn't tell my up from my down, I had no one to run to. That is, I had no one, but the One I should have been running to first and foremost.

I had the bad habit of discussing my circumstances and attempting to get advice from everyone else first, instead of taking it to our Heavenly Father, who has always proven to be my strong tower and refuge. After everyone else's suggestions didn't work, then I would fall on my knees, overwhelmed with tears, begging the Lord for forgiveness and guidance.

For my own protection and so that my heart could be free, the Lord had to remove some people from my life. They were hurdles and road blocks that were getting in the way of me running in the path of His commandments and eagerly pursuing His will. What I observed was that once those distractions were removed, I was free to focus on what was important; and that was, is and will always be the Lord and living my life according to His purpose.

It doesn't have to be the months of March, April or May for the Lord to perform some spring cleaning in our lives. When it happens, I no longer feel like a child being punished. To the contrary, I thank the Lord for loving me enough to do what I haven't been able to do in my own strength. I used to think I was being rejected. The Lord had to school me and say, "No my dear daughter, this is not happening because you are being rejected or punished. It is occurring because I love you that much."

The Lord is my everything. He continues to increase my understanding; therefore, I am going to continue to seek Him first and run to Him no matter come what way.

Suggested Song of Meditation: "Running to You" by Cheryl Fortune

John 3:30 (The Message/MSG)

³⁰ "This is the assigned moment for him to move into the center, while I slip off to the sidelines.

What a beautiful autumn day it was today. It was made even more special because my husband, children and I were all home together and able to get out of the house for a while to run some family errands.

It's amazing how dramatically the seasons change in what seems to be a matter of moments. Less than two weeks ago, we still had 80-degree weather and sun rays so strong that I couldn't even test being outside more than five minutes in them. But over the past few days, the vibrant colors on the leaves have taken over, a cooler air has ushered in and outside of our windows has been transformed into a picturesque autumn landscape like you would find on a postcard.

I am always intrigued by transformations that take place and because of the blog that I publish each day and all that I am encouraged to share, I have recognized the transformations within myself and the significant impact they have had on every aspect of my life.

One of the greatest life lessons I have received, has been understanding the importance of surrendering. Surrendering to Jesus is not seasonal or cyclical like the weather may be. It is a lifestyle that we must adopt each day.

I am a very hands-on person and have always had the mindset that if I wanted something to get done right, I just needed to do it myself. I have also always been one to initiate, plan and budget for everything. So, when unexpected circumstances and situations caught me by surprise, they affected me greatly.

In order for my circumstances to change, I had to change my way of thinking and surrender my all to the Lord. Surrendering meant that I was acknowledging that it wasn't about me, but completely about the Lord. I stepped back and put myself on the sidelines so that the decisions I made, the directions I adhered to and the paths I now took were coming from the Lord.

I have learned many mathematical equations over the course of the years, but less of me and more of Him ranks the highest of them all.

In order to receive all that the Lord has for me, I have to do my part. Faith without works is dead. Surrendering is part of what I must do. It's not always easy, but when I know that from it, I grow closer to the Lord and am made better, wiser and stronger so that His will may be done, why would I dare not?

I seek the Lord's presence daily and strive to do what He wants me to do. The seasons may change, but the role that surrendering has in my life, will not.

Suggested Song of Meditation: "I Surrender All" by Ruben Studdard

Ezekiel 36:26 (Expanded Bible/EXB)

²⁶ Also, I will give you a new heart, and I will put a new ·way of thinking [spirit] inside you. I will ·take out [remove from you] ·the stubborn hearts of stone from your bodies [your heart of stone], and I will give you ·obedient hearts [a heart] of flesh.

Regularly, as I watch the news from various outlets and read different articles online from the major news websites, I have witnessed more and more the effects that depression had and continues to have on people living here in the United States and all across the world.

When I was younger, my mom would watch the Oprah Winfrey show religiously. But there was one episode that stuck with me over the years. On this one particular segment, Oprah was interviewing women who were dealing with various bouts of depression. I remembered that each of these women seemed so sad and overwhelmed with grief.

As I was finishing up my homework that afternoon, I wondered what could happen that would cause a person to experience so much pain and be overcome with so much emotion.

And then, for me, life happened.

There were negative and indescribable painful situations that I encountered, along with circumstances that were so unforeseen and unfair that I didn't know which way to turn. My heart was shattered and my spirit was broken and, in those moments, my first thought was, "Now I know what could cause a person to hit rock bottom."

Because of the view I had on accountability, I blamed myself for everything; even things I had no way of predicting or preventing. I felt I should be punished for where I found myself and so my heart hardened toward myself.

I felt I wasn't worthy of the Lord's forgiveness or love and so, I ran away from it. That was until I realized that the Lord was all I had to run to.

Regardless of the pain I felt or how broken I was, I knew that I wanted and needed to change and that change could not happen without the Lord.

Although I had been baptized as a child, it was imperative that I rededicate myself; accepting Jesus as my Lord and Savior. In doing so, I was given a new heart and a new spirit and from that moment I have never been the same.

My way of speaking, thinking and acting all changed. Because Jesus died for my sins, I no longer had to be shackled or bound by past hurts, shame, fear, rejection, depression or any other generational stronghold.

I remember it being said that once we are saved we are no longer subject to our earthly heritage but to our heavenly one. That spoke to the innermost layers of my soul and I realized that because I had been given a new heart and spirit, nothing could prevent me from stepping into the destiny that the Lord declared specifically for me.

Suggested Song of Meditation: "Never Be the Same" by DeWayne Woods

Mark 11:25 (Amplified Bible, Classic Edition/AMPC)

> *25 And whenever you stand praying, if you have anything against anyone, forgive him and let it drop (leave it, let it go), in order that your Father Who is in heaven may also forgive you your [own] failings and shortcomings and let them drop.*

Forgiveness is a necessity!! For so long, I believed that forgiveness meant that those who I had been wounded by were excused of the behavior that caused the hurt, disappointment, mistreatment and betrayal that I had been subjected to.

I believed that by forgiving them, my pain wasn't valid and that I appeared weak not just to myself, but to everyone else as well. That was until I realized that the purpose of me forgiving them wasn't to free them, but it was to free me. It was the first step in the healing process for me.

Forgiving others wasn't necessarily the hard part for me. I constantly found myself struggling because I had an inability to forgive myself for the role I played in granting access to certain behaviors in my life.

Whether it was forgiving someone else or myself, I needed to be set free and I knew that forgiveness was the key to me moving forward and no longer being held captive. It didn't excuse others of their actions, but it meant that I was making the decision to trust the Lord with every aspect of my life, so that my heart wasn't destroyed by their behavior.

We don't want anything to hinder our relationship with God and unforgiveness will cause a barrier to be constructed between us and the Lord.

Unforgiveness is venomous and cannot be allowed to permeate us or the relationships that we have with the Lord and others. That is why it is so important to ask the Lord to search our hearts for any unforgiveness that may be present.

When we are able to view our circumstances through eyes of grace and are able to walk down the path of forgiveness, barriers and yokes are destroyed and we are brought that much closer to the Lord and all that He has planned for us.

To forgive means to drop it, leave it and not revisit it again. My prayers are vital to my communication with the Lord. Therefore, I cannot be the reason that my prayers go unanswered because unforgiveness has taken residency inside of me.

In this life, there are times when I must interact with those who have harmed me deeply, but I always want to make sure there aren't any remnants of unforgiveness still lodged, like undiscovered shrapnel from those previous battles in my heart.

Forgiveness allows us to let go, so that we can continue to grow, mature and obtain the bountiful life that the Lord has for us.

Suggested Song of Meditation: "Forgiveness" by Matthew West

2 Timothy 2:15 (The Living Bible/TLB)

15 Work hard so God can say to you, "Well done." Be a good workman, one who does not need to be ashamed when God examines your work. Know what his Word says and means.

What a milestone, my "Encouragement for Your Journey" blog celebrated on October 29, 2015. That day marked the 365th post that I had created and shared with my followers. Literally, there were enough posts to read a different one, that provided a new song, verse and thought each day of the year.

When I began to reflect on the road that had been traveled to get me to that very moment, I then thought about how close I was to not ever accomplishing this goal. As I have shared previously, my blog started off as a weekly, Monday Morning Motivational email from my Gmail account back on July 29, 2013. It was sent to a few family and friends but then after completing Dr. Celeste Owens' 40-Day Surrender Fast, I finally decided to take the big step to create my Encouragement for Your Journey blog.

On Monday, November 4, 2013, my weekly Monday blogs began. During the time that my blog began, I knew the Lord was calling me to do more, to learn and study more and, therefore, dedicate myself more to this ministry I had decided to move forward in.

I kept trying to ignore what the Lord was instructing me to do because I was still dealing with the strongholds of acceptance, validation, and rejection. I believed that I wasn't the right choice for what I was being asked to do. And although transparency is my best form of communication, I didn't want to offend anyone, I didn't want what I would be led to share to be judged or thrown back in my face at a later time. Plain and simple, I was so afraid.

But the Lord knew the purging, sharpening, sifting and molding I needed to succumb to in order to be ready.

Between November 4, 2013 and December 29, 2014, I composed and published 61 Monday morning blogs. During the days that connected those 61 Mondays, I participated in two Surrender fasts; cycle 7 and cycle 8. By the conclusion of cycle 7, generational strongholds and curses had been revealed and broken. My faith in the Lord grew deeper and my confidence in who He had called me to be grew stronger. At the completion of cycle 8, I was no longer afraid. I felt thoroughly prepared and ready to be catapulted into the new season that the Lord had for me.

And so, on December 30, 2014, I began my journey of utilizing the Encouragement for Your Journey blog that I had created so that I could begin publishing daily posts. I was very excited but the enemy still tried to prevent me from moving forward because it was quite a responsibility I had decided to take on.

There were times when the enemy went out of his way to try and get me to view posting the blogs daily as a daunting task, but the complete opposite happened. Each daily post became an accountability partner, of sorts, for me. By studying the Word of the Lord and allowing the Holy Spirit to guide me, I had the resources that I needed to navigate through whatever life would throw at me.

From November 4, 2013 to December 29, 2014, I created 61 Monday morning posts. And from December 30, 2014 until October 29, 2015, I created and published an additional 304 daily posts.

Not only was I able to share five times as many blogs in less time, but the Lord enlarged my territory, expanded my audience to include those who I have known throughout various seasons of my life and others I have yet to meet face-to-face here in the United States and abroad in areas like Germany, Belgium, Indonesia, the Caribbean and Russia.

Through these past 365 blogs, I have grown, matured and been given insight in ways I couldn't even imagine. I have become a new creation and am dedicated to showing the Lord that my life is not my own and that I am an ambassador for Him.

The first 365 blogs were just the beginning, I know that there is more that I am called to do and I look forward to sharing that with each of you what happens when we give ourselves away, so that we can be used by the Lord.

I will continue to stay in the Word because I know that in it, I can find protection, correction and direction. As great as I feel about all that the Lord has shown me up until this moment, I know that the best is yet to come!!

I thank the Lord for never giving up on me, even when I didn't believe I had the qualifications to proceed in the way He wanted me to. I have placed my life in His hands and truly long for His desires to be revealed in me.

Suggested Song of Meditation: "I Give Myself Away" by William McDowell

Galatians 5:25 (The Voice/VOICE)

²⁵ Now since we have chosen to walk with the Spirit, let's keep each step in perfect sync with God's Spirit.

Often, I have been told that I am a very fast walker. I never perceived myself to be until a few years back and I realized where it originated. I actually could attribute that to two things. First, being a child walking around in NYC, I had to keep up because it seemed as if I took three steps to every one step that my father took. If you ever try to Sunday stroll on the blocks in New York, you will probably hear some choice words from other pedestrians as your slow pace hinders them from trying to get from Point A to Point B. Therefore, keeping up was and still is the only option.

I also realized that another culprit to my accelerated pace could be traced back to when I first entered the Air Force and was in basic training. Anytime we lined up for formation, I was always in the front because, at 5'5", I was still one of the shortest females in my flight.

Because our formation went from shortest to tallest, that meant I had to be mindful of the importance of keeping in step because if I didn't, I would slow up others or cause them to misstep. It was nerve-wracking because I didn't want to be the cause of anyone or myself not being in step. To make sure that never happened, I focused and listened to that internal cadence that I had playing over and over in my head so that I wasn't the one who ended up being roasted and chastised by my training instructor (T.I.).

I think back to those times when I reflect on the importance of keeping in step with the Spirit, since it is through the Spirit that we have life. Day by day, I am reminded that if I don't take a delicate appreciation in the Spirit, I will become disconnected and nonaligned with God.

By being in perfect sync with the Spirit of the Lord, I don't question the direction I am given because I know that it is coming from above. Even if where I am being guided is in the complete opposite direction of where I believe my path should be routed, I continue to trust and believe because I know that any instruction that I receive from the Spirit will always align with the Word of God.

As we continue to encounter situations and circumstances that are far beyond our comprehension, the necessity to keep in step with the Spirit and to be obedient to the guidance we receive from the Lord is conveyed more and more.

I have learned many things by various means and through numerous individuals and outlets. But my greatest instruction continues to come from the Holy Spirit.

Day by day, I acknowledge that there is so much more for me to learn and that is why I choose for the Spirit to be my guide.

Suggested Song of Meditation: "Day by Day" by Yolanda Adams

Psalm 18:6 (Modern English Version/MEV)

⁶ In my distress I called on the Lord, and cried for help to my God; He heard my voice from His temple, and my cry for help came before Him to His ears.

I am so grateful for the way that the Lord utilizes songs to minister to my spirit. It's always the right song, at the absolute right time. Just when I think I know the direction that a particular blog post is going to go in, the Lord will redirect my route like the GPS navigation that some of us have in our vehicles or that most of us have downloaded on our phones.

Each morning, I am filled with such thankfulness for the opportunity that my family and I have to see another day. All throughout the day, I am constantly having conversations with the Lord. A lot of times, I communicate with the Lord through songs. I have songs for every situation and circumstance. Although I have no problem sharing my thoughts with the Lord; it is more personal for me when I express my thoughts and my feelings to Him through a melody or hymn.

So much has happened, so much is happening and there is more that has yet to happen. Therefore, I seek out the Lord for the clarity, guidance and strength to face any and everything. I believe that is why late in the evening holds a very special place for me. It's late in the evening that all dinner is cooked and eaten, dishes are loaded in the dishwasher, homework is completed and everyone is present, accounted for and asleep. During that time, I am able to go to the Lord and just call on Him, not stopping or letting go until a word from Him is delivered.

Everything that could be weighing on me, I release and surrender to the Lord knowing that, in times of distress, He hears my cry and will bless my soul. As much as I love singing, sometimes what I'm feeling leaves me so weary and heavy-laden that all I can muster up is a hum or murmur to accompany the tears that are falling down my face. But I know that, in those moments, as long as I continue to seek the Lord, my cries for help will reach His ears and be heard.

Suggested Song of Meditation: "All Night" by Alvin Darling and Celebration

1 Peter 3:4 (The Voice/VOICE)

⁴ let your adornment be what's inside—the real you, the lasting beauty of a gracious and quiet spirit, in which God delights.

With my birthday not too far off, I have been thinking about many of the life lessons that I have learned throughout the years.

I would have to say that over 90% of my life, I have been preoccupied with who I felt I needed to be for everyone else and how I was viewed by them. Because each person had their own needs and expectations, that meant there was a different hat I was expected to wear, depending on the person and purpose I was expected to fulfill.

Even though I stated there were different hats I was expected to wear, it felt more like a different mask I chose to cover myself up with. My heart was broken and my guard was up to a degree but I still desired to be a people-pleaser. It was easier to focus on who everyone else wanted me to be instead of who I was supposed to be.

With each heartache came the pain from the realization that I was involved in very one-sided relationships. In the midst of the hurt and confusion, when I looked around and saw that I was alone, I knew something had to give. I had gotten so consumed in focusing on who everybody wanted me to be, I had lost myself.

It was at that moment that I recognized that in putting others before the Lord, I had accumulated all these masks and I no longer desired to have myself covered up. I wanted the real me to shine through and I knew that by putting God first, no longer hiding from Him and making the choice to worship Him in spirit and in truth; I would be reintroduced to who the Lord had created me to be.

Where my heart was once closed from being shattered more times than I care to remember, it was now open to receive the fullness of the Lord. My defenses were down and I was in the most vulnerable place, waiting to hear from Him. I surrendered my will, thoughts and beliefs to the Lord, asking Him to use me as He pleased.

In that time, I learned things about myself that I never knew. Characteristics and attributes that I was led to believe were weaknesses, I actually learned were areas of strength and potential that I had not begun to scratch the surface of. I truly began to love the person I was.

My beauty, strength, importance and value were not tied to my external appearance; as I was led to believe time and time again. Who I am, the real me, is connected to the relationship I have with the Lord and the gracious and quiet spirit that is located inside of me.

I have been unmasked and it is the Word and direction that I receive from the Lord that guides my every step.

The beauty of it all is that now when I interact with others, it is the real me that they are getting. No masks, just me, on this journey to live my life on purpose and do the kingdom work that I have been called to do; and it's a beautiful thing.

Suggested Song of Meditation: "The Real Me" by Anita Wilson

Psalm 119:133 (Amplified Bible/AMP)

¹³³ Establish my footsteps in [the way of] Your word; Do not let any human weakness have power over me [causing me to be separated from You].

Since moving back to New York, I am finally beginning to feel like we have truly begun to settle into our new home and the area that we live in. With getting adjusted to the day-to-day responsibilities that I now have, I have been given ample quiet time to just meditate and ponder on what is next for me.

So many questions constantly run through my mind and I recognize that I am at a very critical place in my spiritual walk and that is why I need every word that I speak, every move that I make and every step that I take to be ordered by the Word of the Lord.

Creating this blog was a baby that I carried for quite some time before I actually gave birth to it. I knew the timing had to be perfect. I didn't want to jump the gun prematurely and not be spiritually and emotionally ready for the commitment that this required. I also didn't want to go past the due date of its release and miss the opportunity to share what the Lord had stirred up in my Spirit.

In looking back over my journey with my blog, I see where my vision and plans for the blog began to evolve as my relationship with the Lord intensified and became more intimate. The more I have learned about the Lord, the more I have come to learn and love about myself. The revelations and testimonies that I have acquired were never meant to be kept to myself.

But now I find myself at a crossroads. I have this tugging feeling inside of me and what it's screaming is that there is so much more left for me to do and that is why I am in need of the Lord's leadership and guidance, every day, as I wait for Him to reveal and instruct me on what I must do next.

I feel like I'm in a holding pattern and in this vulnerable time, I ask that the Lord take charge over my thoughts all throughout the day and night. I realize that the enemy is busy and I do not want to grant him access to infiltrate my views or feelings. We are reminded in Proverbs 16:9, "A man's mind plans his way [as he journeys through life], but the Lord directs his steps and establishes them." Instead of allowing human weakness to have power over me, which causes me to be separated from the Lord; the steps I take are steps of faith, trust and confidence as I move toward the plan that God has for my life. I know that in seeking the Lord first, He will usher me down the passage of His favor.

Suggested Song of Meditation: "Order My Steps" by GMWA Women of Worship

Proverbs 19:8 (Complete Jewish Bible/CJB)

⁸ To acquire good sense is to love oneself; to treasure discernment is to prosper.

Growing up, one of my favorite songs to sing in the children's choir was, "This Little Light of Mine." I would sing the song as if I composed the melody personally. As I grew older, the song still remained a special one to me, though I never realized that I was a walking contradiction when I would stand with my eyes closed and my hands waved in the air, belting out the words.

There were so many external circumstances happening around me, I didn't even realize that I was smothering the light that was placed within me to shine. I got to thinking about that in my early twenties when I was in the sanctuary listening to another children's choir sing that song and the words seemed to smack me all upside my head. I was so critical of myself growing up and when things bothered me, instead of talking about it, I kept everything bottled up inside and it ended up manifesting into a hair-pulling disorder called trichotillomania.

I remember being about 14-15 years of age when I first noticed that the majority of the hair located at the crown my head was gone. I realized that when I was stressed or bothered by something I would pull my hair but until that moment when I was looking in the mirror and with my head bent forward and I could see my scalp, I became so ashamed and made it a point of always wearing a bun, so no one ever knew my secret. As an impressionable teenage girl, realizing I was the cause of not having any hair, made me even more critical of myself. I did whatever I had to make sure my hands were nowhere near my head. And it worked because most people who have known me all my life, were unaware I was struggling with this.

As I got older, my hair became my indicator that I was carrying way too much, because I would notice my hair beginning to disappear in that same area. I knew then that I needed the Lord to help me conquer my troubles and anxieties. It was bigger than the presence of a significant bald spot on my head. The hair-pulling disorder was a symptom of a larger problem.

Ironically, and I have shared in the past, that it was the book, "A Jewel in His Crown" by Priscilla Shirer that helped in facilitating the breakthrough that I was in need of. And being someone who is very visual, the thought that I could allow all the temporal situations that I must face to cause me to damage the crown of my head, when I am viewed by God as a jewel in His crown, was so profound to me. That one book, which when coupled with the Bible, helped to teach me how to love me, because I was able to gain a deeper knowledge and understanding

Surrendering Must Be Adopted As A Lifestyle

into God's love for me. That truth trumped any and everything and assisted in reversing the mindset I had at that time.

I no longer desired anyone else's life because I knew that the one I was living was more than I could ever ask for. Trials and tribulations no longer were viewed as punishment, but as necessary tools of love utilized by my Heavenly Father to make me the best me I could be. I became excited about the endless possibilities that were ahead for me because our God is always there going before me.

Trichotillomania is something that I have to be mindful of. It's no longer a struggle like it was because I keep my eyes and my efforts on being that jewel in the Lord's crown. Adversities don't get to pull me in like they did; which would immediately result in me pulling my own hair. Recently, my journey with trichotillomania was brought full circle as I sat in my hair stylist's chair. As she combed through my curly hair and prepared to flat iron it, with excitement and a red nose I rejoiced. She and I discussed how there was a time when I wouldn't have been able to wear my hair all down or for it to have been healthy enough to withstand the chemicals that she uses to keep my tresses blonde.

My hair stylist also commented that the strength she sees in my hair each time I come back surprises her. And I told her, that is nothing but an example of the mighty hand of God. Going to the hair salon may seem like something so routine and trivial to some. But when you have had seasons where you've had to cover your scalp because of the shame, today for me was another victory in Jesus' name. That triumph and so many others are why I am so happy being me.

Suggested Song of Meditation: "Happy Being Me" by Anita Wilson

Psalm 118:5 (Expanded Bible/EXB)

5 I was in trouble [distress], so I called [prayed] to the Lord. The Lord answered me and set me free [in a broad place].

As I have continued to emphasize the importance of being thankful in all situations and circumstances, I have begun to observe the tactics and feel the attacks of the enemy in my life.

There was a rhema word that I was in need of this morning and that was what I prayed for. As I accessed the live broadcast from the church we attended in Maryland, I couldn't wait to receive what the pastor was going to share with the congregation. To my surprise, I learned that Dr. Tony Evans would be delivering the message today.

In some way, throughout various seasons of my life; the ministries associated with Dr. Tony Evans and his family have assisted in my spiritual growth and maturity. On this day, I needed a precious word from the Lord that spoke individually and specifically to where I was.

In his message, Dr. Evans' topic was pertaining to spiritual warfare and the giants that we face. His message came from 1 Samuel 17, where we find the well-known story about David and Goliath. At that moment, I knew that the message Dr. Evans was about to deliver was exactly what I needed to hear.

I found myself in a tight space, where it appeared as if giants that had been sleeping, had all been awakened at the same time.

Knowing that nothing that we face is greater than the Lord, I was reminded that while in distress and when facing the giants that are placed before us, it's imperative that we are in alignment with God. When this occurs, He will overturn situations that look impossible.

Today, I also learned the importance of being able to see the spiritual deficiencies behind the physical obstacles we encounter. Something else that resonated with me was when Dr. Evans stated, "Everything physical and visible is preceded by invisible and spiritual." By addressing the invisible and spiritual first, we are given the authority to approach the physical and visible.

The mindset and perspective we have are key when waging spiritual warfare and confronting our giants.

When we recognize the divine covering (covenant) that we are connected to and focus on being aligned with God's covenant; we can stand strong, boldly call on the name of the Lord and praise Him in advance, as we wait for Him to deliver us.

Lastly, I was reminded that our faith is about doing what God has placed in our hands to do and believing Him to do the rest. I have a totally different perspective on the giants I must face and rejoice in the freedom and wide-open spaces that are set before me.

Suggested Song of Meditation: "I Wanna Be Free" by Jessica Reedy

Matthew 18:21-22 (Amplified Bible, Classic Edition/AMPC)

²¹ Then Peter came up to Him and said, Lord, how many times may my brother sin against me and I forgive him and let it go? [As many as] up to seven times?
²² Jesus answered him, I tell you, not up to seven times, but seventy times seven!

What a testimony I have to share with you today and this is just the beginning!!

As most of you know, my family and I relocated back to New York. The whole preparation to move felt like an out-of-body experience because if you had told me three or four years ago that I would be back here, I would have laughed and said, "Stop playing, that's not ever going to happen."

That would have been my response because NYC has always represented two completely conflicting images for me. One image was my life as it originated and how I believed it would unfold, compared to the harsh reality of what life unveiled itself to be for me.

Moving to Long Island, just minutes from the city, but an area I was unfamiliar with, meant I was relocating to uncharted territory. But I knew that to be so close to where my heart beat for the first time and eventually where it suffered its greatest heartbreak meant there was so much work, from the inside out, that I needed the Lord to take the reins on.

I have been dealing with the task of trying to find a church for my family and me. That is not an easy feat on any day; let alone when you are in a new area and striving to move forward to live your life on purpose as God has called you to.

A few days ago, I was speaking to one of my childhood friends; that when we were growing up, we were like sister-cousins and although we were not related by blood, you couldn't tell us we weren't family. I called her mother Auntie and the memories that we shared at her grandmother's in the Bronx and then over at her house during the summertime were never to be forgotten.

Well, about four years ago, when I was still living in Maryland, I decided to search for her on Facebook and because of her uniquely beautiful name, it didn't take long to find my partner from back in the day. Throughout these past few years, we have remained in contact.

Because she still lived in Brooklyn, when we made the decision to move back to New York, I informed her and we promised to reconnect once I got back.

Fast forward to a few days ago, I was feeling a little lonely; not having that sister connection that I had fostered in Maryland and seriously needing to have that spiritual interaction with others. I was talking to my "sister-cousin" and she reminded me that her mother was now a pastor of her own church and invited us to come.

I was so excited and then when she provided me the address and I discovered that it was only 1.2 miles from my house, all I could do was cry. Because no one truly knows, except for the Lord, my husband and children, how where we currently live shouldn't have even been an option for us; but God (those two words incite miracles and change lives).

This morning as we were getting ready for church, the Holy Spirit made sure that I knew that there was a word that I needed to hear today and that it would be delivered by someone whom I have always loved and respected and who always opened her home and heart to me when I was young and at such an impressionable age.

The reunion that we experienced that morning was amazing, especially since she hadn't seen me since I was 13 years old and here I was standing in front of her as a grown woman, 39 years of age now, with my three children in tow.

Being at her church felt like home from the moment we entered it. After the initial shock wore off and we took part in praise and worship and prepared for the word to be delivered, I knew from the second she announced that the topic for today's message was, "The Power of Forgiveness", this message was just for me; and the tears just began to fall.

If there was ever any question, I will tell you that there definitely isn't any now. There is a healing that the Lord is orchestrating in my life and the tool being utilized is forgiveness.

The word that I received today at church confirmed that forgiveness is not a moment, but a process. It isn't required just once, but needs to be done continuously and as many times as needed for us to be released and unshackled from the weight that unforgiveness bears.

Whether it's forgiving a spouse, a parent(s), a child(ren), a sibling(s), a family member, a friend, a coworker, an additional authority figure(s), etc., we have to remember that there is no limit to the forgiveness we must be willing to give; especially since we acknowledge the unlimited access to forgiveness that we have through the Lord.

Forgiving doesn't mean forgetting, but it means engaging in the intentional and voluntary process of freeing yourself from the hurtful words, actions and intentions of others, so that barriers are not constructed between you and your relationship with the Lord.

Unforgiveness prevents us from moving forward and receiving the blessings and favor that the Lord has specifically for us.

Today, I feasted on the spiritual manna that provides me with the nourishment that will be converted into the energy needed for me to endure the Path of Forgiveness, Restoration and Reconciliation that is before me.

I have never been one to believe in luck or happenstance. So, know that residing just one mile from someone who I harbor nothing but the warmest and fondest memories of from my childhood and her being anointed and a vessel for the Lord is no coincidence at all.

Suggested Song of Meditation: "7X70" by Chris August

Luke 7:47 (New International Reader's Version/NIRV)

⁴⁷ So I tell you this. Her many sins have been forgiven. She has shown that she understands this by her great acts of love. But whoever has been forgiven only a little loves only a little."

As the word "Forgiveness" continues to permeate into every crevice of my thought and prayer life, I have come to acknowledge and own what has been the hardest part for me as I have attempted to embark down the essential "Path of Forgiveness."

When it comes to Brandi Nicole Jefferson-Motley (I know, I'm talking about myself in the third person and I can't stand when people do that), the truth is, it's not difficult at all for me to forgive others when they have hurt me, taken advantage, been untruthful or have had little regard for my well-being. What has been the most difficult for me was believing that I deserved any type of forgiveness, when it was I who made the decision to "love hard" in the first place.

Having a connection, desiring to be accepted and wanting to feel loved has always been at the core of my decision-making process. My whole life, I have shown love, loyalty and devotion, but it was for all the wrong reasons and was rooted and became rotted in brokenness.

When people and situations would reveal themselves to be toxic and in no way, shape, fashion or form in my best interest, I couldn't and didn't walk away. When my life then began to spiral out of control, I wasn't upset with the other parties involved; regardless of the lies, manipulations and deceit I was exposed to. I became ashamed and disgusted with myself, because people do show who they are and like some, I thought I could make them or the situation better. That was the furthest thing from the truth.

Therefore, the first layer of unforgiveness I harbored toward myself was because I was so broken I couldn't see the forest for the trees and I thought trying to save the day or being everything to everyone else was more important than taking care of myself first. But that layer of unforgiveness was no match for the resentment and emotional imprisonment I charged myself with because I knew I had not only let the Lord down, but I recognized that I didn't just put others before myself, but before the Lord as well.

In my head, how could God forgive me when I couldn't forgive myself?

The shame I carried, the scars that I just knew were visible for all to see and the consequences that at times, I observed had now left an unimaginable impact on my most precious blessings, my babies, was way too much to bear at times.

But God....His love, His Word and the people that He placed in my life to help me uncover those areas of brokenness, surrender those mindsets and patterns of behavior and then begin to heal and live a life according to His ways and thoughts; which thank goodness are not like mine, assisted in breaking me free and obliterating the access that the enemy had to persuade me to believe I wasn't worthy of forgiveness.

No matter how far I would try to progress in life, it always seemed that something was preventing me from going further. That something was me.

Unforgiveness is venomous and cannot be allowed to permeate us or the relationships that we have with the Lord or one another. I would always ask the Lord to search my heart for any unforgiveness that I was harboring toward anyone else. The majority of the time, the unforgiveness that was present in my heart was toward myself.

I didn't need anyone else to pick up stones to throw at me when I had my own satchel that I was hurtling at myself.

And that was a hard truth that I didn't have to just swallow, I had to ingest and digest that joker. But with God's help, I learned the truth, His truth, which has now become my truth.

My spiritual vision has been corrected and enhanced and I now view through eyes of grace; which makes it that much easier to walk down the path of forgiveness. Barriers and yokes have been destroyed and I have been brought that much closer to the Lord and all that He has planned for me.

God's Word has given me the clarity to recognize that all that has occurred in my life, a lot of it may have come as a surprise to me, but not to the Lord. And even with the sins and poor choices that I made, He still thought I was worth it.

I never have been nor will I ever be greater than our Heavenly Father and if He has forgiven me, the only choice I have is to forgive myself so that I can continue to grow, mature and obtain the abundant life that the Lord has for me.

Jesus' blood cancels it all and, therefore, we are not required to be cloaked in a garment of shame. That also means we must release those stones and cast them no more upon ourselves.

Suggested Song of Meditation: "Forgive Yourself" by Downhere

1 Corinthians 13:5 (Easy-to-Read Version/ERV)

⁵ Love is not rude, it is not selfish, and it cannot be made angry easily. Love does not remember wrongs done against it.

I pray that as I share the various antics and tactics that construct a barrier between us and our ability to let past mistakes and situations go, much needed conversations with the Lord and a lifestyle of surrendering are taking place.

When my two oldest children were younger, I had a plaque on my wall that was immediately visible the moment anyone walked through the front door. That plaque had 1 Corinthians 13:4-8 inscribed on it, where it read: "Love is patient and kind. Love is not jealous, it does not brag, and it is not proud. Love is not rude, it is not selfish, and it cannot be made angry easily. Love does not remember wrongs done against it. Love is never happy when others do wrong, but it is always happy with the truth. Love never gives up on people. It never stops trusting, never loses hope, and never quits. Love will never end."

I would look at the plaque every day and although all the adjectives used to describe "Love" had a special meaning to me, because of who I am, how I process things and the difficulty I had in forgiving myself for the former things; verse 5, where it stated, "Love keeps no record of wrong," always stuck out to me.

I knew that verse represented something I was very guilty of, which was keeping record of my wrong-doings. I am a very visual person and so I actually had a "list of shame" which archived the mistakes and wrong turns I had taken in my life. I initially believed that the purpose for that list was to hold me accountable and assist in making sure I didn't make those same decisions again.

But in all actuality, that list kept me shackled and left me feeling like I couldn't ever be freed from my past.

As much as I love to write, I realized I was transcribing and focusing on the wrong things. Instead of allowing myself to continue to be a prisoner to my past, I stood in front of that plaque in my hallway on a day that I was off from work and my children were at school and something happened.

As many times as I had looked at the plaque and read the words that were placed on it, this was the first time I was actually absorbing what I was reading and, right then, I began to meditate on what the Lord was saying to me.

His limitless love for me meant I was forgiven and didn't have to be held captive to the wrongs that had occurred in my yesterdays. I was reminded that my debt had been paid and by having that list in my possession, I was not being loyal to the faith and trust that I had in Jesus Christ; which was never my intention.

In every instance, I have repented and sought forgiveness from the Lord and although I knew that the Lord granted that forgiveness, I never felt I was worthy of it because of the choices I had made or the situations I had found myself in.

Instead of basing the definition of forgiveness by my standards, I called on the Lord and He heard my cry. I looked over that "list of shame" one last time, said goodbye and then I shredded it into hundreds of itty bitty pieces, making the promise to not allow history to repeat itself again because I no longer had the desire to go back there anymore.

That one moment taught me so much about the love that the Lord has for us, the forgiveness we must be willing to give and receive and the importance of refraining from keeping record of wrongs that have occurred.

Suggested Song of Meditation: "The List" by Matthew West

2 Corinthians 3:17 (Amplified Bible/AMP)

¹⁷ Now the Lord is the Spirit, and where the Spirit of the Lord is, there is liberty [emancipation from bondage, true freedom].

While taking time to examine the "Path to Forgiveness", something became clearly evident to me. Not only am I no longer bound by the shackles of unforgiveness, but I have been freed in ways that could only be associated with the Spirit of the Lord.

A total renovation has taken place; from the inside out. Every situation, every circumstance, every wrong turn and every sin that the enemy just knew he could manipulate and keep me bound by, the Lord has loosed me from.

I believe that one of the greatest modifications that has occurred in my life has been the result of my mindset shifting. Where my focus used to be on the unforgiveness that I once harbored; it is because of the victory that I uncovered I had through Christ Jesus, that my focus became and continues to remain on the Lord and setting my mind on those things above, and no longer on those things from my past.

The negative titles and judgments that once influenced my every thought and action and that were my drive to prove those who assigned them wrong, don't even get the opportunity to permeate or penetrate my forcefield of faith.

I am not ashamed to proclaim that I am a new creation and the Lord has given me a new name. I have been emancipated from bondage and am unquestionably free. Therefore, I choose to declare nothing but the goodness that is over my life.

Most people only associate imprisonment with the physical incarceration that individuals face when they break the law. But for some of us, we walk around trying to pretend everything is alright, all the while we are spiritually and emotionally confined and held captive by some type of stronghold(s).

At least, that is part of my journey. And it wasn't until I decided to make surrendering a lifestyle, so that I could continue to mature in my spiritual walk and thus, continue fostering a deeper and stronger relationship with the Lord, that I am finally free to soar.

I have been liberated and now have the freedom to be reconnected, renewed and restored in every facet of my life. I am eternally grateful for the yokes and strongholds that have been broken. The Lord has taken control and has changed my heart and soul. He has made me whole.

The chains of unforgiveness are no longer binding me. Because the Son has set me free, I am free indeed (John 8:36)!! And that freedom is manifesting in ways that I didn't even know to dream for.

Suggested Song of Meditation: "I'm Free Indeed" by Kim Burrell

Hebrews 4:12 (Complete Jewish Bible/CJB)

¹² See, the Word of God is alive! It is at work and is sharper than any double-edged sword—it cuts right through to where soul meets spirit and joints meet marrow, and it is quick to judge the inner reflections and attitudes of the heart.

I was so excited for the blog post that I thought I was going to share this evening and within a matter of seconds from just one phone call, everything changed and I was left feeling so hurt and confused.

This whole week, I have focused on the power of forgiveness and the path I have encountered on this road to forgiveness. As much as I would like to say that every situation has resulted in that happy-fairy-tale-ending, that is not the truth.

In just the past couple of hours, I've had to come out of the disappointment, hurt and pain I have been experiencing so that I could focus on what the Lord was saying and desiring to reveal to me.

This evening, I was reminded that forgiveness has to be the only option, even if the end result does not come to fruition as you hoped it would.

While meditating on that sentiment, I came across three quotes online that really expressed the state I currently find myself in.

1. "Forgiveness is not always easy. At times, it feels more painful than the wound we suffered to forgive the one who inflicted it. And yet, there is no peace without forgiveness."
2. "Forgiveness doesn't excuse their behavior; forgiveness prevents their behavior from destroying your heart."
3. "Forgiveness does not change the past, but it does enlarge the future."

With there being so much that I don't understand, I still will not allow the enemy to convince me that operating within the realm of unforgiveness is the best place for me.

I have no doubt about how much the Lord loves me and I know that my journey down the path of forgiveness has brought me that much closer to Him, has set me free and has brought peace to my life on levels that I couldn't even imagine before because I was held captive by the shackles of unforgiveness.

I will continue to keep my focus on the Lord and, in all things, I will give thanks as He speaks into my life. Because I know that the Word of the Lord is alive and full of power, it will serve as my guide. It penetrates deep and I know that it is capable of discerning the thoughts and intentions of a person's heart (an area where I definitely am weak).

Since I believe and trust in God's Word, I am less inclined to keep my eye on the problem. In His Word, the Lord has already declared that all things are working together for my good. What we go through may not always look or feel good, but through the tears, I am rejoicing knowing that everything that the enemy meant for evil, God is turning it around for us.

Suggested Song of Meditation: "Speak into My Life" by Micah Stampley

Psalm 62:1 (New International Version/NIV)

⁶²¹ Truly my soul finds rest in God; my salvation comes from him.

In just living life and experiencing the highs and lows associated with each of my days, there is one undisputed and undeniable fact that remains constant and that is, "There is truly something about the name Jesus. It is the sweetest name I know."

When I call upon the Lord, my soul finds rest knowing that when we invite Jesus into our situations, just the mention of His name causes changes to occur.

I have observed how just calling on the name of Jesus brings out a peacefulness, even while in the midst of the turbulent storm fronts in my life. The name of Jesus represents a loving presence that I don't ever have to search for or be afraid will reject me or walk away.

I can't ever think about Jesus without thinking about His birth, His life and His death; which illustrates the most amazing unconditional love we could ever know.

I give the Lord all the honor, glory and praise because I know that through Him, I have the truest and greatest friend, counselor, comforter, protector, deliverer and provider. He is Alpha and Omega, the first and the last; the beginning and the end. He is God and God alone.

I am able to rest and find peace while I am going through because I know that when I call on the name of Jesus, I have released my circumstances to the best and only problem solver there is. In Him we have the victory.

Suggested Song of Meditation: "You Are God" by Brandon Mitchell and S.W.A.P

Psalm 139:23-24 (Complete Jewish Bible/CJB)

²³ Examine me, God, and know my heart; test me, and know my thoughts.
²⁴ See if there is in me any hurtful way, and lead me along the eternal way.

For the majority of my life, my identity was tied to my past, my connection to others, to the decisions that I had made and the situations I found myself in. Instead of my identity being rooted in my desire to find my purpose in the Lord, during many seasons of my life, I was more concerned about finding that purpose that I could fulfill in the lives of others first.

When you operate, whether knowingly or unbeknownst to yourself, from a victim mindset, most of your decisions come from a place of brokenness and disconnection from Christ. And even though the choices we make disappoint and hurt the Lord, He never gives up us on.

There will come a moment when we have to take a stand and not give away anymore of the precious time that is not promised to us. We cannot allow the wrong mindset to keep us in a place where we continue to waste our destiny and lose our identity.

When I was younger, I used to assist my teachers with proofreading some of the classwork and homework that was submitted. When I was in the Air Force, one of the responsibilities I had was as a QC'er; a quality control analyst. I was expected to review reports and see if anything was missing, needed to be included or revised. As a wife and mother, anything that my husband and children would like for me to review for them, I gladly do in a second.

In each one of those instances, I would search to see if anything was missing, placed where it shouldn't be or needed to be removed. In surrendering to the Lord, I am releasing it all and trusting and believing in Him to be responsible for the quality control of my life.

Because I desire for my identity to reflect the Lord, first and foremost, I continuously ask Him to search my heart and my entire being. If there is anything that is unlike Him; any pattern of behavior or thought process that is getting in the way of me being more like Him, then it needs to be removed.

My mind is stayed on Jesus and my eyes are focused on those realities of heaven. Because I have decided to live a surrendered life, I am able to live freely with a champion and conqueror mindset.

My identity will not ever be tied to those former things again. When people see me, it will be the God in me that will be reflected; not my flaws, my regrets, my disappointments or the shame I once held.

Suggested Song of Meditation: "Identity" by James Fortune and FIYA

1 Timothy 4:16 (Contemporary English Version/CEV)

¹⁶ Be careful about the way you live and about what you teach. Keep on doing this, and you will save not only yourself, but the people who hear you.

A sentiment that I have always had and have shared with my family and others is that we need to be very cognizant of how we act and portray ourselves and the words that we allow to come out of our mouths, especially as children of God, because for some people we may be the only Bible that they ever read.

As I was reviewing my Bible plans for today, I read another quote which paralleled the above sentiment and drilled that point in for me even deeper. The devotional content stated, "How we reflect God's truth in our actions every day is often more important than what we say about God's truth."

Just like we observe the actions of others on a daily basis, we are also being observed constantly whether we ever come into direct contact or have one-on-one dialogue with individuals.

That thought is always in the forefront of my mind. It serves as an accountability tool for me and makes me ask myself daily, "When people see you, from your actions and how you conduct yourself, what are they reading from the pages of your life?"

"Are they observing a child of God who strives to live her life on purpose?" One who, even when she misses the mark and stumbles, provides a transparency and authenticity that reflects a woman who is committed to living a surrendered life; trusting, believing and praising God in ALL circumstances? Or is what is being presented illustrating hypocrisy or that of being a walking contradiction?

I grew up hearing "Do as I say not as I do," and that was frustrating, but I also observed and learned a lot. So, when I became a mother at 20 years of age, so much was unknown to me and I needed the Lord to guide me in this new and most important role and I worked so hard to lead my children by example; God's example. It is imperative for them to witness how important the Lord is in my life and then, in turn, should be in their lives.

It is a must that we be careful about the way we live and what we speak and teach. That is why before I open my mouth, I seek and wait for the Lord to speak to me first. Before I can teach and guide anyone, I must be instructed and directed by the Lord myself. How can I lead or show anyone anything, if I don't know?

In the Bible, we see how God used the underdogs; those whom others rejected and ones who most considered the most unlikely choices, to bring deliverance, slay giants, perform miracles, win battles, etc.

Many may never pick up a physical Bible or download a Bible app and we may be the only reference to God's Word that they may read. What an amazing opportunity to be a blessing to others by reflecting the countless ways that God has and continues to bless us; even when WE are deemed the most unlikely candidates.

Our tests were never meant to be kept to ourselves; they become our testimonies. And from the messes we have been delivered from, come the most personal messages of God's love, grace and mercy that we could ever share.

Suggested Song of Meditation: "Before I Tell Them" by Yolanda Adams

Psalm 46:10 (Amplified Bible, Classic Edition/AMPC)

¹⁰ Let be and be still, and know (recognize and understand) that I am God. I will be exalted among the nations! I will be exalted in the earth!

I can't remember when the last time was that I actually had a good night's sleep. It's not that I don't desire to, but for a while I have been bombarded by various personal situations that have conjured up such a kaleidoscope of emotions; it hasn't been until everyone in the house has fallen asleep that I could even begin to sift through each one.

So, when you couple all of that with being prescribed a medication by my doctor last month where one of the possible side effects is insomnia, you are now looking at a sleep-depriving cocktail that I never had any intentions of consuming.

With all the responsibilities that I am tasked with each day (and you'll never hear any complaints because I am thankful that God chose me to assume those roles), I recognize the importance of letting go of my concerns and knowing He is God; that way, I can obtain the physical, spiritual, emotional and mental rest that I require so that I can be who God has called me to be.

Last month, when I was informed of how all the stress, hurt and pain I have been carrying was beginning to affect my heart, that didn't just cause me to slow down, it made me stop where I was and all I could do was be still and redirect my focus back onto God. He is the One who is exalted among the nations, supreme over the world and above everything.

We are given one life to live physically and I am so grateful for the sacrifice that Jesus made on our behalf, so that we could be born again and have that sacred connection with the Lord.

Just like we only have one life, we also only have one heart. I am learning that in being still and letting go of my concerns, the Lord is able to speak to this heart of mine uninterrupted. When I shift my focus, I am able to recognize and feel God's presence and experience that boundless and steadfast love that can only come from Him.

I also am able to receive the wisdom that assists in circumventing any chance of me dwelling in a place of complacency. Instead, I hold tight to the grace, strength, safety, peace and hope that He has provided me with to press forward.

I used to be one of the first ones to say a phrase that I have heard thousands of times before and that phrase is, "If I want it done right, I have to do it myself." I'm shaking my head as I type those words now. I have come to learn that "my way" of doing things hasn't always been right.

When we are successful and have victory, it is not because of any of our own works or actions. It is because of the Lord. Our best is in His hands and our success is in His plans.

Contrary to popular belief, the Lord does not need our assistance regarding one single detail of our lives. Remember, He is supreme and above everything!!

I release such a deep sigh when I think about all the heartache and heart breaks I could have saved myself from if I had just trusted in Him first, instead of keeping my hands on the wheel. I guess that's why it's called hindsight.

They say hindsight is 20/20 but I believe it's when our spiritual senses are finely tuned and no longer distorted that we are given that clarity and discernment to understand how we arrived where we have and what actions and mindsets must be in place for us to truly live our lives according to God's purpose.

We have to slow down, release all our worries to Him and leave them there. We must also be still long enough to develop that intimate relationship with God so that we can obtain that guidance and direction, which will lead to us seeing the Lord's hand of victory in every area of our lives.

After finally falling asleep sometime around 4:00 this morning, I woke up a few short hours later to make sure my oldest daughter was up and getting ready to head out the door. Before I opened my eyes, in my sleep, I was singing the suggested song of meditation that I have chosen. And when I woke up, I just kept singing it and I knew exactly what the Lord was saying to me.

Suggested Song of Meditation" "Be Still" by Yolanda Adams

James 4:8 (New Life Version/NLV)

⁸ Come close to God and He will come close to you. Wash your hands, you sinners. Clean up your hearts, you who want to follow the sinful ways of the world and God at the same time.

Here at home, one of my youngest daughter's favorite games to play is hide and seek. Whether all of us in the family know we're playing or not, she looks for any opportunity to hide and yell for us to come and find her. I thought about that last night when she decided to hide from me before putting on her pajamas. It is the cutest thing and we have actually come to expect her to do it.

As much fun as playing hide and seek is with her, I recognize that nothing cute, funny, entertaining or beneficial comes from me hiding or separating myself from the Lord. To the contrary, my seasons of trying to hide from the Lord (as if we actually can; it's about as effective for me as it was for Adam and Eve) are no longer. More and more, I find myself seeking that one-on-one time with God.

In His Word and through life experiences, I have learned that when I draw close to God, He draws close to me. It's when I am in the presence of the Lord that I receive the truth!! The necessary cleansing and purging of any and all methods of thinking and patterns of behavior that have caused me to end up in a place where I find myself trying to follow God and please the world at the same time, also takes place.

I do not desire to be a walking contradiction or a hypocritical believer. That is why having that personal, set-aside time with God every day is paramount. Without any interruptions, I first and most importantly seek the kingdom of God and His way of doing and being right and all those attributes that pertain to the attitude and character of God.

There are so many questions that I have and I know that if I continuously seek the Lord and wait on Him, He will provide the answers that will give me the insight to stay on course and to live my life as He wants me to. I desire the kind of closeness with the Lord that cannot be paralleled nor compared to anything else. And that is why we must commune one-on-one with the Lord regularly.

Suggested Song of Meditation: "One on One" by Zacardi Cortez

John 17:3 (Contemporary English Version/CEV)

³ Eternal life is to know you, the only true God, and to know Jesus Christ, the one you sent.

What an amazing day we had celebrating my husband's birthday. I thank God that He allowed my husband to see another year and that as a family we were together to recognize this special day.

As much fun as we had clowning and cutting up like we normally do, once we got home, all it took was for me to be reminded of some of the broken and disconnected relationships that I have in my life for me to become overwhelmed with so much sadness and just break down in tears.

I felt so guilty that I allowed myself to be overcome by so much sorrow on a day that was not about me and that had been on such a high note. But what a wake-up call it ended up being because I recognized that as much as I think I may know people, I really don't.

Because I have always made myself available to others, I automatically equated that with a mutual and reciprocal relationship of caring and concern for one another's well-being. I thought that I knew where others were coming from because of the viewpoint and convictions I possessed.

Boy, was I wrong. I spent so much time trying to acquaint myself with and understand the world, that I now see that it took the Lord separating me from certain individuals and relationships so that the focus on who I needed to know shifted back to God and His Word.

As Galatians 2:20 tells us, "We have been crucified with Christ and we no longer live, but Christ lives in us. The life we now live in the body, we live by faith in the Son of God, who loved us and gave Himself for us."

My life is no longer my own. It is not concerned with the things of this world and what I do or do not know about others. Each day, the importance of knowing God and having that personal relationship with Him resonates more and more. I desire to obtain that crown of life (which is eternal life) that God promised to those who love Him and remain faithful to Him throughout all obstacles and trials they may face.

My devotions and pursuits are no longer dictated by the value systems of this world nor the thoughts or actions of man. I desire to obtain that maturity in faith that comes when I direct my energy to the pursuit of God and His righteousness in every aspect of my life.

Seeking the Lord and making His Word my primary reference means that through God's Word, the Lord reveals His character, love, holiness, power, compassion, righteousness and judgment to me. I am given insight to the purpose that the Lord has for my life instead of who I believe others expect me to be for them.

Knowing God and His Word allows me to see the Lord, to inquire of Him and gain that spirit of wisdom and discernment. I am provided a more intimate and in-depth understanding of the only true and real God we serve and the anointed Messiah that He sent to earth.

Taking the time to know the Lord reminds me that there is no way that I would be able to live without Him. My decisions are no longer self-guided but, instead, are Spirit-directed.

As I began writing, I was in a very melancholy state, but as I began to think about all that I have grown to know about the Lord and all that there is still for me to learn, I began to find joy and peace in knowing that "greater is He that is in me, than he that is in the world."

To receive the rewards that the Lord has purposed for our lives, knowing Him better must be adopted into the lifestyle that we live.

Suggested Song of Meditation: "Know Him" by J. Moss featuring Karen Clark-Sheard

Philippians 4:8 (Tree of Life Version/TLV)

> *⁸ Finally, brothers and sisters, whatever is true, whatever is honorable, whatever is just, whatever is pure, whatever is lovely, whatever is commendable—if there is any virtue and if there is anything worthy of praise—dwell on these things.*

I love having that quiet time with the Lord each day. Some days, I just need that one-on-one time to be able to express to the One who already knows what I'm going to say before the words ever have the opportunity to form and leave my lips.

And then on days like today, I am humbled and truly cherish when what the Lord has spoken to me is confirmed as I meditate on His Word. Even if it's not what I necessarily want to hear, I am thankful because I know that anything that God has assigned to me is, both, for my good and for His glory.

My desire to know the Lord better and more intimately has become such an integral part of my life and in taking the steps to do so, I have realized that there have been some situations that have been hindering me from progressing.

I remember reading from one of Joel Osteen's daily devotionals where he said, "What we think about the most determines the quality and direction of our lives."

In my mind, I believed that if I thought about a situation too long, I was giving the situation and the people involved too much power and so, I would just push everything into the background, or so I thought.

Over the past few weeks, the Lord has been revealing to me the importance of mending that way of thinking. I shy away from confrontation at all costs, but the Lord has been calling me to step outside of my comfort zone because in order to live my life according to His purpose, I've had to come to grips with the fact that there are indeed times when we must examine those unhealthy habits, behaviors and mindsets and confront the past hurts, defective ways of thinking, abuse, fear, unforgiveness, bitterness, disappointment and/or betrayal we have encountered and release them to the Lord so that we can be free and blessed!!

How can God pour into me until I overflow, if I'm still filled with issues that are holding me back in one way or another?

With the mending of my mindset comes a clarity that assists me in guarding my heart and causes me to empty all that has been a hindrance up to this point. Instead of me living my life in distress, I am free to focus on those things which are holy, just, pure, honorable, beautiful, good and worthy of praise.

My tomorrow will not be like my yesterday. Standing in the faith that I have in the Lord, I know that if I trust and obey Him, He will supply the answers and work it all out for me, but I must do my part as well.

I desire for everything to be blessed (my assignment, my family, my life, my finances, etc). I will continue to follow the Lord's direction and instruction.

God's Word repairs and restores my mind so that I am able to bid adieu to the negativity and, in turn, open the door and my heart to God's plans for my life.

Suggested Song of Meditation: "Be Blessed" by Yolanda Adams

Jeremiah 10:23 (Lexham English Bible/LEB)

²³ I know, O Yahweh, that to the human is not his own way, nor to a person is the walking and the directing of his own step.

Being someone who spent so much of my life looking to others to give me all that only the Lord could provide me with, opened my eyes to see that who I had become, where I was and all that I had been able to accomplish had only occurred not because of me but because of the Lord who directs my steps.

Proverbs 16:9 reminds us that, "A man's mind, plans his way, but it is the Lord, who directs his steps and makes them sure."

We can have all the strategies and well-thought out plans in the world, but none of us is in charge of our own destiny and it is not in our power to determine what will happen to us.

That is why it is so important that we remain connected and rooted in the Lord. The Word of God is the strongest foundation that we have to stand on.

In those times when we may go astray, the Lord will come our way, meet us where we are and help see us through. He will save us and be our ever-present help.

When we make mistakes and fall short, it is because of His never-ending mercy and grace that directs, inspects, corrects, protects and perfects us; that we are made whole and not consumed.

So many of us have been placed in a position of authority and leadership in one way or another. May we never make the mistake of thinking that anything that we have obtained or will obtain is because of our own doing.

Sometimes people get caught up in who they see standing in front of them, presently. They have no idea all that the Lord has done and been in your life, for you to still be here and to be able to interact and communicate with such a joy, peace, love and excitement for the Lord.

We all, to some degree, have experienced what happens when we try to walk and establish our own steps. It's not possible and we end up learning that firsthand. But we also are given a testimony of how it all does work out for us in the end, when it is the Lord who is guiding and directing us.

If we think about where we were, compared to how far the Lord has brought us, recognizing that there is still more that He intends to do; we can proclaim that we know without a doubt that we would be nothing without the Lord.

Suggested Song of Meditation: "Nothing" by J. Moss

Luke 9:62 (Disciples' Literal New Testament/DLNT)

⁶² But Jesus said to him, "No one having put his hand on the plow and looking to the things behind is fit for the kingdom of God".

I remember when I lived in Maryland, our pastor told us that there would be times when the Lord would allow us to come back to a similar situation that we have once encountered, as a way of testing our character and faith to see if we really have been changed; being adamant in bidding farewell to that old man we once were and forgetting those former things.

Not only am I a "words" person, but I'm also an "actions" person as well. I'm not here to say one thing and do the complete opposite.

Because it is the Spirit that now leads me and the decisions I make and no longer that sinful nature I was once enslaved to, I make the vow each day not to allow myself to be distracted from doing the work God has called me to do. As my pastor encouraged us to do last night at bible study, I am yielding my days, my nights and all that they include to the Holy Spirit.

If we harp or dwell on those things of the past too long, those old feelings of shame, rejection and disappointment will creep up and take residency within us all over again. There is absolutely no room for all that; especially since we have been redeemed and bought with a price.

Jesus paid my sin debt and now it is the Holy Spirit that is the constant operating system in my life. The enemy will try to distract me and get me to veer off the path that God has for me, but that's not an option. Because I am one who constantly says that it's not possible to go both backwards and forwards at the same time, Luke 9:62 really spoke to me.

When Jesus spoke about putting a hand to the plow, He was referring to engaging in a task; which for us is serving the Kingdom of God. When you are looking back, it definitely makes it difficult for one to plow straight furrows.

If we are constantly looking behind ourselves and being distracted by those things from our past, our commitment to the Lord and the work that He has prepared for us will be severely impacted. And those are two things we do not want to happen.

As I think about the price that we end up paying when we don't forget what lies behind and instead straining toward what is ahead, I think about Lot's wife. The Lord being merciful, gave a direct command to Lot and his family to escape and not look back and linger as God was destroying Sodom and Gomorrah. But Lot's wife, who was reluctant to leave in the first place, disobeyed, looked back and became a pillar of salt.

I am excited and eagerly awaiting all that the Lord has for me to do. There is nothing from my past that is worth getting hung up on, where I would then be viewed as unfit for the Kingdom of God.

I have been changed, healed, delivered and freed to walk as a new creation through Christ and I won't go back.

Suggested Song of Meditation: "I Won't Go Back" by William McDowell

1 Thessalonians 4:1 (Tree of Life Version/TLV)

> *4 Finally then, brothers and sisters, we ask you and appeal in the Lord Yeshua—just as you received from us the way you ought to walk and please God (as in fact you are walking)—that you keep progressing more and more.*

I sit before my laptop this evening filled with so much joy as I observe both the individual and collective decisions that the members of my family and I are making regarding our walk with the Lord.

Watching my husband and our 19-year-old son walking out the front door this morning at 6:30 a.m., to meet up with the other men from our church to attend an all-day Men's Fellowship had me filled with so much gratitude, that I couldn't even go back to sleep right after they left. I needed some time just to say, "Thank you Lord," and to exalt Him for all that He is doing in the lives of each of us.

As Joshua 24:15 states, "But if serving the Lord seems undesirable to you, then choose for yourselves this day whom you will serve, whether the gods your ancestors served beyond the Euphrates, or the gods of the Amorites, in whose land you are living. But as for me and my household, we will serve the Lord."

I don't take one word that I type on this keyboard, one word that I speak with those I encounter or one word that I sing whether here at home, church or elsewhere lightly.

The life I used to live was focused on pleasing the world, but those days are long gone. I strive not to be a walking contradiction or hypocrite.

I can't say that I'm a Christian who walks with a dependency on God, but then when someone sees me, I am behaving or carrying myself in a way that is unpleasing to the Lord.

Every day, I strive to acknowledge the Lord in all my ways. I stand on the faith that I have in Him and am grateful that no matter what it is that concerns me, I can take it to the Lord in prayer. I desire to not just learn His Word but to keep that truth which is life to me and apply it daily.

I seek the Lord, surrendering it all, so that my mind, thoughts and heart can all be on one accord. As I behold the glory of the Lord, that is what I strive to reflect. It's my desire that nothing gets in the way of my light shining before others, so that they may see my good deeds and glorify my Father in heaven (Matthew 5:16)

What a blessing it is to know that I am not alone. This is a family affair. The girls and I thoroughly enjoyed listening to my husband and son share with us, later in the evening, all that they learned today at their Men's Fellowship.

We are choosing to follow the instruction that we have received, pursuing a life of purpose and living in a way that expresses gratitude to God for our salvation.

That is the life that we strive to live.

Suggested Song of Meditation: "Life I Live" by Marvin Sapp

Psalm 28:7 (New English Translation/NET Bible)

⁷ The Lord strengthens and protects me; I trust in him with all my heart. I am rescued and my heart is full of joy; I will sing to him in gratitude.

Every day, I have felt so blessed and fortunate to have the opportunity to use my blog as a means of expressing God's goodness and faithfulness to the world.

I remember for so long I dragged my feet when it came to taking on the responsibility of doing a daily motivational and inspirational blog. If it wasn't me questioning my own qualifications to take on such an endeavor, the enemy was right there waiting to dredge up my past that had already been redeemed and forgiven, as a means of trying to attach me, once again, to that old man that was now dead and gone.

As much as I hope that what the Spirit has led me to share, ministers to and serves as a source of encouragement to all those who read it, I can tell you that not a day goes by that I do not remain inspired by all that the Lord reveals to me.

But even with all of that, lately, I have just felt stuck; like I'm in a stalemate. I continue to strive to live right, to have the right mindset and to present myself in ways that are pleasing in the Lord's sight, but the enemy is continuously trying to use various aspects of my life and my past to render the steps I desire to take forward, useless.

I was sharing these sentiments with my husband while we were in Barnes & Noble with our children, purchasing books. We were in the Christian Life section looking for books to read and I was disclosing just how stuck I had been feeling and how I was in need of some reading material to encourage me as I sought the Lord's help to take me beyond where I presently was and to where He desired for me to be.

Not two seconds after saying that, I glanced down to the second to last shelf at a book cover that caught my attention because it had a pair of pink boots, with a piece of pink gum stuck to the bottom of one of the shoes; along with a pink Gerbera daisy next to the shoe and the title read, "Life UNSTUCK—Finding PEACE with Your Past, PURPOSE in Your Present, PASSION for Your Future," written by Pat Layton, who is also the author of the book, "A Surrendered Life."

As soon as I saw the title, I knew that God had led me to that particular book on that specific shelf. It was the last copy too and that was all the confirmation that I needed to purchase that book.

I am thankful that the God I serve, "Has searched me and knows me. He knows when I sit and when I rise; He perceives my thoughts from afar. He discerns my going out and my lying down and is familiar with ALL my ways. Before a word is on my tongue, the Lord, knows it completely. He hems me in behind and before and lays His hand upon me. Such knowledge is too wonderful for me, too lofty for me to attain (Psalm 139:1-6)."

So much of where I feel stuck is tied to the numerous relationships in my life. It appears as if it doesn't matter if forgiveness, grace, mercy or love is shown; or if record is not kept of wrongdoings or if revenge is never being taken. These relationships never seem to get better and so I know I must move on and I can't allow anyone or anything to get in the way of me living according to God's will for my life; but at the same time when you have a connection to someone, it's hard to let go and move forward; even if it is the best thing for you to do.

And that is why I am filled with so much gratitude because no one knows me better the Lord. He knew me before I was a sparkle in either of my parent's eyes. He knows the intricate way that my mind and heart have been designed and so it is Him that I defer to. The Eternal One is the source of my strength and the shield that guards me. I trust in Him with all my heart and I am rescued and will always have a song of gratitude to sing.

In just reading the beginning pages of the Introduction and the Manifesto for the book, "Life Unstuck", I knew that this book would be an invaluable resource and another weapon that would be added to my arsenal.

As the book reminded me at the end of the Unstuck Manifesto section, "Though my enemy surrounds me, God surrounds my enemy. My God has all authority over my life. Therefore, I will stand under the impenetrable covering of the blood of Jesus—because greater is He that is in me, than he who is in the world."

Those are just a few of the words I will repeat and speak over myself each day because I know it is the Lord's desire for me not to remain stuck, but to move beyond and find peace with my past, the purpose in my present and the passion for my future.

Suggested Song of Meditation: "Beyond" by JoAnn Rosario

Ezekiel 36:27 (Lexham English Bible/LEB)

²⁷ And I will give my spirit into your inner parts, and I will make it so that you will go in my rules, and my regulations you will remember, and you will do them.

With so much happening in the world today, it is that much more imperative that we seek the Lord in every situation. All that we say and do needs to be rooted in the statutes and laws that the Lord has provided us with.

It seems as if, each day, a new test or trial is just waiting for the opportunity to make its presence known. But I am so grateful that even before the first hint of adversity is able to come my way, God's enduring love and His constant mercies are made new every single morning. Great is His faithfulness!!

It wasn't until I got to know the Lord for myself that my life began to change. He gave me a new heart and placed a new spirit within me (Ezekiel 36:26). I now know what it truly means to have unspeakable joy; and that is because of the unfailing love that can only come from the Lord.

Regardless of what the world may try to make me think, it is the Lord, His Word and His laws that I choose to stand on and use as my guide for any and all decisions that I must make in life. Day by day, with His Spirit inside of me, I have no desire to be conformed to the ways of this world; but through the renewal of my mind, I am inspired to live by His statutes and to follow His laws. In John 14:15-17, Jesus reminds us that:

"If we love Him, we will keep His commandments. And that He will ask the Father, and He will give us another Advocate, in order that He may be with us forever—the Spirit of truth, whom the world is not able to receive, because it does not see Him or know Him. But we know Him, because He resides with us and will be in us."

What has been placed within me comes from above and I will never let it go. I intend to keep His Spirit in my heart. I will let it show and take it everywhere that I go.

Suggested Song of Meditation: "Day by Day" by Yolanda Adams

Proverbs 31:27-28 (GOD'S WORD Translation/GW)

²⁷ She keeps a close eye on the conduct of her family, and she does not eat the bread of idleness.
²⁸ Her children and her husband stand up and bless her. In addition, he sings her praises.

For me, there is no greater honor than God choosing us women, to be on the receiving end of the gift of bearing a child. And although I enjoy celebrating Mother's Day; for me, every day is Mother's Day.

I have always thought that on Mother's Day the emphasis should be my children because they are the reason that I am able to celebrate Mother's Day in the first place. What a privilege it is.

I haven't and won't ever take the role of being a mom lightly. As a mother, I have been through so much. It has been more than my children could ever truly know, but never more than I could handle. And that is because it has been the Lord who has been by my side from the moment I have conceived each one of them and throughout every step of my journey through motherhood.

When it comes to my responsibility as a mother, I always tell my children how blessed I am that out of all the mothers in the world—past, present and still yet to be born; the fact that the Lord chose me for them means more than I could ever formulate words to express.

It was almost 20 years ago, that I gave birth to my firstborn, my son. For so much of my life, I fought so hard to try and fit in, to be loved and accepted and it seemed as if it was all to no avail. That was until I learned that I was going to be a mother.

Even though I wasn't married at that time nor when I had my other two children, I realized that I served a God of order and that even though I had done some things out of order, I knew God was blessing me far more than I could ever see or begin to comprehend at that time.

I felt that I was born to be a mother and that changed everything. Becoming a mom actually brought me closer to the Lord. Although I have always known that God loves me, in so many ways I was so lost. It has been through the unconditional love that I have received from and reciprocated back to my three amazing children that I have come to gain some insight into just how much the Lord loves me.

There was just something about looking into my own eyes, that incited me to want to emulate the qualities and attributes that I have read about for so long; as they pertain to the

Surrendering Must Be Adopted As A Lifestyle

Proverbs 31 woman. I knew that I had to be better and do better than I ever had in the past. I knew that I had to walk in truth and lead by example because I had been chosen to be our Heavenly Father's representative for my children.

In His Word, God provided me the instruction, guidance, encouragement and the examples of the type of mother I should be and also should not be. As time has progressed, I have not only learned what it takes to be a Proverbs 31 mother but also a Proverbs 31 wife and those are two gifts that keep on giving; and that is why Proverbs 31:10-31 stays close to my heart. I make it a point to keep a close eye on the conduct of my family; not wasting any time or eating the bread of idleness. I am here to nurture, encourage, support, instruct, guide with wisdom and speak with kindness as the rule for everything.

It is when my children and husband stand up, bless me and sing my praises that I feel most loved and like I am doing and being all God has called me to be for Him and my family. There isn't any price tag that can be placed on that feeling. During a time when it appears as if taking responsibility and accountability for one's actions seems like an endangered species, I know that God holds me accountable for every last one of my actions; along with how I instruct, guide and direct my children.

Failing is not an option when I have the greatest instructor and am a recipient of the greatest love we could ever know. The truth and love that the Lord leads and covers me with is what I desire to share with my children. Mothers are a special breed. And I am just blessed to be in the number.

Suggested Song of Meditation: "Mothers Are Special" by The Chicago Mass Choir

Ephesians 4:24 (The Voice/VOICE)

²⁴ Then you are ready to put on your new self, modeled after the very likeness of God: truthful, righteous, and holy.

Lately, I have noticed more and more commercials and public service announcements on television pertaining to depression and other mental health disorders that millions in this country suffer from.

I think that sometimes we forget just how powerful our minds can be. What we think about ourselves has a direct and profound impact on every other aspect of our lives.

That is why it is so important that we do not allow our identities to be defined by any of the things that may have taken place in our past. Nor should we define who we are or what we are worth by the interactions or relationships we do or do not have with others.

There have been seasons in my life when I hit such an emotionally low place; I couldn't even find a way to articulate the sadness that I was feeling. All I knew was that the storms within and around me were raging and I could not handle them on my own.

I am one who has always loved so very hard. Whether it was familial relationships, friendships or personal relationships with men; how I saw myself was based on the dynamics associated with each individual relationship.

Where I thought the bond that was being shared was a mutual one rooted in love and concern for one another; the connection that actually linked me to the other person was brokenness. But back then I couldn't see that.

So, when those relationships that I loved so hard in and fought so hard for, came to an end, I felt like a failure. And that was a very hard pill to swallow when I have always pushed and challenged myself to never give up or give in.

Those were very turbulent times in my life and it became evidently clear there was only one person who could calm those waves for me. There was only one person who could show me the person He had created me to be and not the person; who through lies, guilt and shame, the enemy wanted to make me believe I was.

Only the Lord could reintroduce me to Himself and, in turn, to myself. The process wasn't easy and didn't happen overnight. Many tears were shed as the truth began to surface and I realized that each of those relationships that I had placed before my connection with the Lord were all one-sided and being used by the enemy to keep me further separated from the Lord.

Surrendering Must Be Adopted As A Lifestyle

The gloominess that I felt came from the weight of trying to find in others what could only be found in the Lord.

I am so thankful that through His Word and through the aid of some really awesome spiritual mentors that He placed in my path, my mind was renewed and my identity was changed to who He said I was.

For each shackle of rejection, doubt, regret or shame that the enemy attempts to reattach to me, I defend myself with the Word of God.

That doesn't mean that I'm not saddened when I'm blindsided by unexpected circumstances in life. It just means that before, I tried to figure everything out on my own, which only made things harder for me. But now, because I live a life surrendered to Christ, I know who to turn to in my times of need.

Instead of trying to please everyone else, I now focus on displaying that new nature/identity and living the new life that God's grace and mercy have provided me with. In doing so, I strive to be an imitator of Christ; modeled after the very likeness of God.

I have learned to surrender it all to the Lord because He is most definitely concerned about all that concerns me. He has never given up on me, nor has He ever abandoned me; even when I have fallen short and done things that have not been pleasing in His sight. And because my identity is rooted in Christ, my sadness has been transformed into joy. I know He will guide me and that "trouble don't last always."

T.D. Jakes shared a message today that contained some of those sentiments. In a few of the lines he stated, "Pretending to be okay when you're not does nothing to help you. There is growth when you admit that you could use some support. God knows all your feelings. Be transparent with God and allow Him to guide you."

We can see and speak to people on a regular basis, never knowing all that someone else is carrying and vice versa. We can get so good at wearing masks that we don't even want to admit to ourselves that everything is not okay.

Nothing that we encounter is a surprise to the Lord and if He allows us to endure it, that means that He's already made the provisions for us to get through it.

Because I have been made new, I take my cue from the Lord and wait to receive instruction from Him. Masks are no longer needed because I know who I am and whose I am. For the longest time, that was the hardest thing for me to distinguish.

Suggested Song of Meditation: "Identity" by Israel and New Breed

Psalm 86:11 (The Living Bible/TLB)

¹¹ Tell me where you want me to go and I will go there. May every fiber of my being unite in reverence to your name.

What a rough few days it has been for me. There have been days when I have pondered on whether I should continue doing my blog on a daily basis. But I was reminded that my inspirational blog has been an accountability partner of mine since the day I created it.

It keeps me going and reminds me, on a daily basis, of just how much the Lord loves me; especially on days like today when my heart is so divided. It also inspires and motivates me to share with others about the goodness of the Lord; regardless of what I am going through.

The words and thoughts that I share in each blog post is so sincere and honest. So, when I say that I know that God won't give me anything that He can't handle, I believe that wholeheartedly.

What has become the most difficult part for me is realizing that something that I desire so badly just may not be God's will for my life. And that hurts so much. There have been so many things that I have felt robbed of throughout my life. At the time when I was going through it, I couldn't understand why it was happening to me.

Now when I look back, I can see the blessings that were birthed from the life lessons I have endured.

But what I am facing now is tied to the greatest heartbreak that I ever experienced and that is connected to the relationship that I haven't had with my father since I was the age of 12.

"Daddy pain" has a way of cutting down through to the marrow and leaving lasting effects that most don't even realize. One day, Lord willing, I will speak more in depth about that. But on this evening I can tell you that there is nothing that I desire more than a relationship with my father.

And where I think it should be so seamless, it is anything but. If I had my way, everything would have been reconciled and restored by now.

I was reminded that I was not created for my own purposes or for my will to be done. I was created specifically for the Lord's glory and His purpose.

That has to be the foundation of who I am so that how I act, the words I speak and the decisions I make are, in turn, divinely connected to the Lord because I am constantly relying and depending on His perfect ways to guide me.

Therefore, in this most emotional and personal situation and with whatever else that arises, it is because of my faith in the Lord that I am able to remain encouraged and filled with hope, peace and joy.

I rejoice in knowing that every God-direction is road-tested and that when I run towards Him, I have the assurance that I will make it.

While I don't know what lies ahead for my biological father and me, I do know that by submitting to my Heavenly Father's perfect will and way for my life, I am positioned to receive His interminable love, which permeates my soul to such a level that it overflows and my heart is no longer divided.

With less of myself and more of God as the premise for all that I seek to accomplish, the end result is God having His way in every area of my life.

Suggested Song of Meditation: "Have Your Way" by Casey J featuring Jason Nelson

Romans 6:14 (The Living Bible/TLB)

¹⁴ Sin need never again be your master, for now you are no longer tied to the law where sin enslaves you, but you are free under God's favor and mercy.

I just got home a little over two hours ago from another powerful and truly insightful bible study session. As I have shared before, I always look forward to Wednesday evenings, where I have the opportunity to dive further into the Word of God and obtain a deeper understanding of the Lord's principles and teachings with my church family.

The undeniable theme for tonight's session was God's grace and the importance of us understanding that we are no longer tied to the law where sin enslaves us, but we have been freed under God's grace and mercy.

There is no disputing that John Newton's, *Amazing Grace*, is probably one of the most widely known and sung hymns. Every time I hear the beginning chords to that song and my lips part to begin singing, "Amazing grace, how sweet the sound, that saved a wretch like me. I once was lost, but now I'm found; was blind, but now I see," I am continuously reminded of just how lost I would be if it wasn't for the grace of God.

God's grace loves me, adores me, watches over me, saves me and gives me more than I could ever deserve. And that is why I seek the Lord's face every day, so that I am able to walk in the power of His grace which is sufficient.

I know what it is like to lose your way, but it has been God's grace that has raised me, freed me and gotten me back on course to living my life the only way I should; and that is on purpose and with the Lord's will, not my own, being accomplished.

Nothing but gratitude continues to flow from my heart when I think about the Lord's grace that has kept me.

Where would we be if it wasn't for His unmerited favor which we have access to through Christ?

Suggested Song of Meditation: "God's Grace" by Luther Barnes

TESTS AND TRIALS COME TO MAKE US BETTER, WISER AND STRONGER

Isaiah 64:8 (The Voice/VOICE)

> ⁸ *Still, Eternal One, You are our Father. We are just clay, and You are the potter. We are the product of Your creative action, shaped and formed into something of worth.*

One of the things that I love most about the Lord is that He is an omniscient God, meaning He knows all. Because God knows all about me, including my past, my present and what has yet to come, I can rejoice in knowing that any areas that need to be changed and refined in me, who better to mold and reshape me than the one who knows the path and purpose that He had sanctioned for my life long before I was ever placed in my mother's womb?

Why would we entrust that to anyone else?

I love going to stores like Ikea because they have some really awesome pottery on display. Anytime I see a piece of pottery, I think about the intricate and delicate process that occurs from conception to completion, making the item ready for display. When a potter is molding the clay, he/she must be careful when shaping it so that the clay obtains the desired form that the potter had in mind.

Once that step is completed, then the clay must go into the fire and it takes a trained eye and gifted potter to know the right amount of time that each piece must endure in that heat. Timing is everything; firing clay too high can cause it to deform or even melt, too low and it will not be durable. If the process is so precise for a piece of clay, why would we not expect that and so much more for ourselves?

There is no greater potter than our Heavenly Father and I rejoice knowing that He desires to reshape our lives and change us from who we were into who He wants us to be.

So when you feel yourself going "through the fire", remember two things: (a) when you're going through the fire, the Lord knows just how much we can bear and will not allow us to feel the heat any longer than we need to; and (b) it's when we're in the fire, that like clay, we are rid of the imperfections and impurities that are blocking, hindering and distracting us from the path and course that God has for our lives.

The end result is a transformed person with a shine and brilliance for all the world to see. You become a walking testimony of not only how great our God is, but just how much He loves us.

Suggested Song of Meditation: "The Potter's Hand" by Hillsong

Ecclesiastes 7:8 (New Life Version/NLV)

⁸ The end of something is better than its beginning. Not giving up in spirit is better than being proud in spirit.

It's days like today, when I find myself in a tight space or pressed on all sides, that I need to be able to encourage myself first; before I even attempt to encourage anyone else.

I thank the Lord for the daily blog that He called me to create, because it has always led me right to His Word; which is where I need to be anyway and where I am always able to find the truth, teachings and guidance that are essential for me to keep moving forward.

Because I know that nothing that I face is greater than the Lord, I continue to surrender my all and seek discernment from the One who is the author and finisher of my faith.

Not only am I thankful for the daily blog that has been created, I am most grateful for the book that you are now reading, that has been completed.

This book was a dream, placed inside of me, way back when I was a young girl in elementary school. At that time, I didn't know how it would all happen nor did I have any inclination of all that would transpire in my life in the days ahead. But I am here to tell you that every detail and encounter has played a pivotal role in bringing God's assignment for my life to fruition.

I had one interpretation of Ecclesiastes 7:8 when I first began preparing for this book. But as I finished the final pages and submitted the manuscript to my publisher, I had a greater understanding of why this verse states that it's better to finish something than to start it and that it's also better to be gentle and patient thank to be proud and impatient.

When I reflect on past situations and circumstances and how they began, I am so thankful that how they started, weren't a clear indication of how they would conclude. I am also grateful that the Lord has always placed that drive and determination in me to finish the assignments, tasks, roles and responsibilities that I have begun.

That is why, these days, no matter what is taking place in front of or around me, I know that the end will be better than the beginning. Sticking it out and not giving up in spirit is better than being proud and arrogant.

When we can trust, and believe in the Lord and not rely on our own understanding; but live our lives patiently and according to the faith that we have in Him, we will see that it can only get better for us because our Heavenly Father is that good and that faithful.

Suggested Song of Mediation: "Better" by Hezekiah Walker

Psalm 46:1 (New Century Version/NCV)

¹ God is our protection and our strength. He always helps in times of trouble.

It's a given that we cannot live our lives without encountering tests and trials. Some challenges we may see coming but often we are blindsided by what we are brought up against.

I've come to realize that the more you desire and strive to live your life on purpose and work for the advancement of our Heavenly Father's kingdom, the stronger the attacks become. It's great to have those who you can confide in, but what I have learned is the best person to run to, where you are the safest against any battle you are up against, is God (Elohim).

Psalm 46 reminds us that God is the refuge for all His people. In my study bible which is translated into the New King James Version, Psalm 46:1 states, "God is our refuge and strength, a very present help in trouble." In the study notes, my bible commenced to explain that the phrase "our refuge and strength" could be rephrased as "our impenetrable defense". Impenetrable is defined as impossible to pass through or enter.

What an accurate descriptive phrase to illustrate who God is for us and the fact that He is a sure defense against battle.

When we hope and trust in the Lord, we are reminded that the Lord is indeed our all in all. If we take refuge or place our hope in anyone or anything else, we will surely fail because all power belongs to God. God is constantly our help and His presence is stronger than any other that we could seek from man.

I know that there are answers that I need that only God can provide. And when there is so much happening around me, I need the covering and assistance of the One who wouldn't ever give me more than I can bear. No matter how uncomfortable or (oftentimes) painful the situation is, I am filled with peace knowing that God has been tried and proven to be a very present help in trouble. He never leaves us nor forsakes us and is close by our side as the storms of life continue to rage.

There is no one greater than God and so I will abide in Him each and every day of my life.

Suggested Song of Meditation: "Psalm 46" by Jenny & Tyler

Isaiah 40:29 (Amplified Bible, Classic Edition/AMPC)

²⁹ He gives power to the faint and weary, and to him who has no might He increases strength [causing it to multiply and making it to abound].

After the eventful day that I had earlier today, I was reminded that the Lord never promised that the road would be easy.

But what He did promise us was that He would never fail or abandon us and that if we didn't give up and called out to Him in our time of need, He would give power to us when we were weak and increase our strength in those times when we didn't have any might.

As I thought about Isaiah 40:29, it reminded me of one of the songs I always looked forward to singing when I was in the choir as an adolescent. That song was called, "We're Gonna Make It." I always felt encouraged and like there wasn't anything I couldn't endure every time we began to sing, "I know somehow and I know some way, we're gonna make it. No matter what the test, whatever comes our way, We're gonna make it. With Jesus on our side, things will work out fine. We're gonna make it!!"

And that's why on this day, I am encouraged and want to encourage and remind each of you that there is not one obstacle or hurdle that we have or will encounter that is greater than God.

When it is the Lord's power and strength that we are filled with, there is absolutely nothing that we cannot overcome or withstand. It's when we are able to keep trusting and doing what the Lord instructs us to, that we position ourselves to have the Lord's "super" meet our "natural".

When that occurs, we are able to believe without wavering and wait without fainting, with the confidence that we're going to make it and have victory in every area of our lives.

Suggested Song of Meditation: "You're Gonna Make It" by Meaghan Williams

Isaiah 38:17 (The Voice/VOICE)

17 Paradoxically, my bitter experience was pushing me toward wholeness. For You, God, have put behind all my shortcomings and wrongdoings. You have rescued me from death. You pulled me from a black hole of nothingness and held me close to You.

Because I am very much a visual person, I try to keep my time on social media to a minimum, because words and images penetrate my thoughts easily. In three separate instances, yesterday, one via a generated email from one particular social network, another which suggested an individual I may know and may want to add as a friend and another email listing upcoming events; one which takes places less than five minutes from where I spent my first years as a young girl here in NYC, reminded me of several relationships with family members that are severely disconnected in a way I would have never predicted.

After some tears were shed, I just had to let it go and remind myself that, YES, most of the tests and obstacles I have encountered have been trials of the heart. But I have come to accept these trials as part of God's good plan for my life. Lord knows it hasn't been easy.

The disconnection with these relationships and others have cut down to the marrow and, in turn, caused me to step back to allow the Lord to show me, me; which in turn has pushed me toward that wholeness that He desires for me.

I am someone who needs the truth to survive. So being surrounded by people who love me enough to always speak the truth and be a source of encouragement but also to check me if, I'm all the way to the left, has been imperative to me.

But I have learned that you can have the best intentions in the world; that doesn't mean people want you telling them what is right or wrong or what they should do in their lives. I've also come to realize that when you place everyone else's worth, value and needs above your own, THAT my friend, is a Molotov cocktail recipe for disaster.

Yesterday, I was reminded of areas of my life that still bring me pain, but like Isaiah 43:18 reminds me, I can't "dwell on past events and brood on times gone by." Sometimes, if you wait on someone else to give you closure in a situation, you will end up waiting forever and carrying so much resentment.

We cannot hold onto the events of the past or we will become so bitter and end up the ones getting in the way of what God has for us. Those former things have helped to shape us into the people we are today. When given to God, the most painful and devastating experiences will be used by Him to do something new and miraculous in our lives. He will clear a way for us in the desert lands and make streams of water in the dry and empty areas of our lives (Isaiah 43:19).

Holding onto the past fosters bitterness. As much as we may like to at times, we cannot change the past. Our focus should be on learning from our past and using that knowledge, along with God's guidance, to move forward and be victorious. We are unable to receive that when our focus and attention are on the wrong things.

Find peace in knowing that surely it has been for our benefit that we have suffered. Our bitter experiences have been pushing us toward the wholeness that can only be obtained through the love that God has for us. He has put behind Him all our shortcomings and wrongdoings. God has rescued and pulled us from a black hole of nothingness and has held us close to Him.

When I think about the word bitter versus better, the difference between the two words is one letter and that letter is the letter "I". Therefore, when I see and hear that word, I am automatically reminded that bitterness is a byproduct of what happens when the focus is on us.

If you allow it to, life can leave you so bitter. But when you remind yourself of that and that He who has begun a good work in you, will complete it until the day of Christ Jesus (Philippians 1:6); you can be confident and believe that regardless of how it all appears, it will get better!!

Suggested Song of Meditation: "Better" by Jessica Reedy

Joel 2:25-26 (The Voice/VOICE)

> ²⁵ *Eternal One: I will compensate you for the years that the locusts have eaten—the swarming locusts, The creeping locusts, the stripping locusts, and the cutting locusts— My great army that I unleashed against you.*
> ²⁶ *In that day, you will eat plenty of food and always have enough, so you will praise My name, The Eternal One, your God who is merciful to you. Never again will My people be shamed among the nations.*

Music means so much to me. There are times when nothing but a sweet ballad with the most encouraging words is the answer to soothing my soul. Then there are times when I need my "battle cry" songs. Songs that get me pumped and revved up with the distinguished sounds of the percussion and keyboard and a strong voice singing the words of praise and motivation that get me in the mindset to tackle any and everything that may come my way. That, is the kind of morning that I am having today.

Along with having a love for music, I have said time and time again that I am a very visual person. I write down everything and need to see how things look on paper when assessing a situation. Now, I believe that is a good thing at times, but I have to know how to reel that in, because what I come up with in my natural state and put down on paper, is nothing compared to what God will do when His "super" becomes attached to my "natural". That right there is enough reason to rejoice. Where it looks impossible to my natural eyes, I am reminded that all things are possible through Christ.

That whole premise has become so much clearer for me. I have a habit at times of beating myself up for the poor decisions I have made thus far in my journey and the environments I found myself in. The times when I wasn't aligned with the Lord the way I should have been—consuming, digesting and then being a steward of His Word—left me so lost. I look back and think about the many twists and turns and areas of my life where I gave the enemy so much access to cause pure and utter chaos. Feeling so ashamed of myself, I have wanted nothing more than to make it up those years to God and make amends for being disobedient.

I have lived the majority of my life feeling robbed of so much, when that wasn't at all the case. The realization that each attack that has occurred, although a surprise to me at times, wasn't ever a surprise to God has been monumental for me. What have appeared to be the hardest seasons in my life were actually tools used for my betterment to sharpen me. I felt as if I was losing it all with no way of getting it back. And no matter how much I desired to repay God for the time I wasted, I knew that I couldn't repay Him, but if I turned away from my sins and those acts of disobedience, He would turn my disobedience into usefulness.

I can tell you firsthand that the Lord will compensate for all that has been lost. Not only will He restore, but the restoration will be plentiful.

Knowing that we serve the God of the overflow, the One who will give us a double portion and who can do infinitely beyond in our lives, I am here to take it all back. Everything that the enemy has stolen, I know God will give it back to me. My joy, peace and faith are not up for grabs. All the blessings that I may have missed in the past were stored up and kept by the Lord.

Suggested Song of Meditation: "Take it Back" by Dorinda Clark-Cole

John 16:33 (The Living Bible/TLB)

³³ I have told you all this so that you will have peace of heart and mind. Here on earth you will have many trials and sorrows; but cheer up, for I have overcome the world."

God has been working miracles for my family and me. Our family continuously remains in awe of Him. Please believe me when I say that if you just wait on the Lord and do not faint, in due season (in God's appointed time), it shall come to pass. And boy, God's timing is better than any date on the calendar or time on the clock that we "think" we need something completed or received by. Our timing short-changes us. God's timing produces abundance.

It's so important that we recognize that with the blessings will come the trials. That is par for the course. No matter what you face, let the enemy know that you are encouraged. We must stay strong because regardless of what we are facing, God will work it all out and bring resolution to your situation if you just believe.

For me, in these past few days, that is what I have had to continue to remind myself. In one moment, I am elated and crying tears of joy and thankfulness and then I turn around and I am met with circumstances that have me feeling like I am being pressed on all sides. Through it all, I am encouraged and recognize how imperative it is to praise God, not just when my family and me are being blessed beyond what our minds can comprehend, but also through every last trial, knowing that through Him, I have peace of mind and heart because I am more than a conqueror.

There is no victory over the Lord. With each and every obstacle that we face (because they will come), my encouragement comes from knowing that troubles will not last forever and that God has overcome the world. Nothing and no one is greater than Him! Be encouraged knowing that through Christ, we have already overcome!!

Suggested Song of Meditation: "Be Encouraged" by William Becton

2 Corinthians 4:8-9 (Amplified Bible/AMP)

⁸ We are hedged in (pressed) on every side [troubled and oppressed in every way], but not cramped or crushed; we suffer embarrassments and are perplexed and unable to find a way out, but not driven to despair;
⁹ We are pursued (persecuted and hard driven), but not deserted [to stand alone]; we are struck down to the ground, but never struck out and destroyed.

Have you ever had times in your life when it felt like the walls were closing in on you? I know I have. I believe that if we all looked back, we would recollect those seasons in our lives when we felt so much constraint being placed on us. At the same time, we can also recall all that we learned during that time and the amount of growth and transformation that occurred within us.

No one ever said that the molding, shaping or pressing process would always be fun or feel good. But when I think about all the areas where God has and continues to bring restoration in my life, I know that none of that would have been possible if I hadn't been put through the "presser".

In order to get that "greater" that God has for our lives, there are some processes we must succumb to. As the suggested song of meditation states, "An olive must go through three stages in order for its oil to run—the shaking, the beating and the pressing."

In Romans 11:16, it states that Jesus is our olive root, supporting every olive branch and also every olive in the tree. When God puts that needed pressure on us, it is so that our oil can flow. It is used as a preparation tool for our "greater" that is coming.

There was a time when I viewed any degree of shaking, beating or pressing in the Spirit as a punishment. What I once perceived as a punishment, I realize has just been another example of God's limitless love for me and His desire to want the best of me by bringing out the best in me.

Even we are hard pressed, perplexed, pursued and struck down, we are not crushed, driven to despair, deserted or destroyed. We are being prepared for "greater". Our greater anointing, power and destiny is coming; get ready and press on.

Suggested Song of Meditation: "Greater is Coming" by Jekalyn Carr

James 1:3 (Amplified Bible/AMP)

³ Be assured and understand that the trial and proving of your faith bring out endurance and steadfastness and patience.

For each of us, God desires to bring a replenishment, renewal and restoration in the various facets and areas of our lives. None of that can be accomplished if we do not do our part and activate our faith.

The other night, I was having a discussion with my two oldest children about the importance of knowing which factors should influence their decision-making processes because those will be life lessons that will assist them in pressing ahead and persevering in this race called life. I was telling them that life is more like a marathon than a sprint and, therefore, we have to rely on our faith to build up the endurance (patience) we need to finish strong.

I shared with them that not only is our faith fueled by reading and meditating on the Word of God and by taking that one-on-one time with Him, but what will also power us through those rough times will be recalling all the previous tests that we have had to endure and the remarkable testimonies that were birthed from each one of them.

I always tell my family that we may be the only Bible that some people will ever read and we never know who may be watching us.

Through our tests come the testimonies that are meant for us to share with others. No one can tell yours like you!!

Suggested Song of Meditation: "My Testimony" by Marvin Sapp. May it minister to you as it does to me.

James 1:12 (Good News Translation/GNT)

¹² Happy are those who remain faithful under trials, because when they succeed in passing such a test, they will receive as their reward the life which God has promised to those who love him.

How great and mighty is the Lord. He is so worthy to be praised. I was having a discussion with one of my children about some of the life lessons that I have experienced thus far. When we are going through, it can be so easy to get distracted by the temporal intensity of what currently is occurring that we forget to keep our eyes on the One who allowed those trials to come our way; the One who knows what we are able to handle and all the areas where we need to be sharpened.

Growing up, I used to hear people around me say, "What doesn't kill you makes you stronger." If I happened to do something I wasn't supposed to and was punished, I was told that one day, I would understand why disciplining me was for my own good. In church, I learned that the Lord wouldn't ever give me more than I could handle and that no matter how we're persecuted, tested, tempted and tried, if we keep our mind stayed on God, He will reward us with the life that He promised us in His Word. The disappointments, hard trials and various situations we go through all happen for a reason.

When I think about where my life would be if God hadn't allowed those trials to surface and for me to come through each of those situations, I am eternally grateful and rejoice knowing He loves me that much.

When it's all said and done, what decides whether or not we view what we endure as being a blessing is the mindset that we have adopted and what we speak over ourselves and our situations while we are in the midst of our storms. We have to be able to encourage ourselves.

Words of affirmation is my primary love language, which means that the manner in which words are utilized truly matters to me. When I know that God's grace and mercy are made afresh each morning, I am able to recognize that there is a blessing that is being birthed from each lesson that the Lord has allowed me to experience; and having that knowledge, makes the storms seem not as turbulent and the attacks not as penetrable.

The mindset that I now possess reassures me that even when being pressed on all sides and when I don't know how I will get through, because of the faith and trust that I have in the Lord who is my way-maker, I am thankful to Him for not only the trials but the blessings that will be the result of the pressing.

Through all trials, I will remain faithful to the Lord. Each day, I remind myself that there isn't any need for stressing when I know, without a shadow of a doubt, that there are blessings in each lesson that I've gone through and will go through in my life.

Suggested Song of Meditation: "Blessin' In Your Lesson" by Isaac Carree featuring Le'Andria Johnson

Habakkuk 3:19 (Amplified Bible/AMP)

¹⁹ The Lord God is my Strength, my personal bravery, and my invincible army; He makes my feet like hinds' feet and will make me to walk [not to stand still in terror, but to walk] and make [spiritual] progress upon my high places [of trouble, suffering, or responsibility]!

"Who opens doors that we cannot see and who makes all of our decisions for us? Jesus will, Jesus will." The song, "Jesus Will" by Anita Wilson has been my new praise and worship song for a while. That song gets me revved up and my mind right as I prepare for whatever lies ahead for me throughout the course of the day. We always have to remember that the Lord will fight our battles, if we keep still.

One of the wonderful things about the seasons changing is watching all the new life that emerges. Whether it is the flowers that sprout from the ground or the lush trees and greenery that surround where I live, it is in complete contrast of what was observed in the same area just a couple of months prior.

Another observation that I have made is that with the seasons changing, it appears as if the number of deer in our area continue to increase. Although I stay on alert when I see deer, especially having totaled a car in the past upon unexpectedly hitting one, I think that deer are beautiful and very graceful creatures.

When I was younger and was in school, I was taught the importance of the feet of deer and how the way their feet are constructed allows them to be very swift and agile, but also permits them to climb very steep and what would be appear to be very dangerous altitudes without stumbling. I found that to be very fascinating then and even more so now, given the verse that was chosen today.

I acknowledge and rejoice in knowing that my strength and bravery comes from the Lord. Regardless of the obstacles, I have the assurance that I am equipped with all that I could possibly need to not just climb, but to walk without stumbling to reach the high places that God has set for me. Standing in fear is not an option when I have been granted the ability to be surefooted like a deer. I am stronger and wiser than I have ever been and that comes from who God is in my life and all that He has revealed to me.

Because of our knowledge and faith in the Lord, we are able to ascend to new heights and through His grace, we have the ability to rise above our circumstances. Diligently focused on God's Word, we can make it through the trying times we encounter.

To look at a mountain and make the decision to climb it could be a very fearful one, especially if we spend too much time trying to analyze the daunting task ahead. God has assured us that when we put all our trust in Him, He will not only cause our feet not to stumble but He will lead us safely through our circumstances and to our mountaintop destinations.

Suggested Song of Meditation: "For Every Mountain" by The Kurt Carr Singers

1 Corinthians 10:13 (The Message/MSG)

¹³ No test or temptation that comes your way is beyond the course of what others have had to face. All you need to remember is that God will never let you down; he'll never let you be pushed past your limit; he'll always be there to help you come through it.

Day after day, I see just how great God's mercy and loving-kindness is toward me. I believe that as a child of God, one of the hardest things for us to grasp while in the midst of a storm or trial is that whatever we are facing truly is not more than we can bear.

I know that I have been through some things. Earlier on in my walk, I felt that the trying times I had to endure were punishment for my past thoughts or actions. It wasn't until I took the time to read and study the Word that I learned that even when I am going through the fire, none of it has the ability or opportunity to be that breaking point for me.

Upon the realization that nothing can come my way without God's approval, my feelings and mindset shifted from that of feeling punished to feeling empowered. I recognized that we serve a faithful God. The trust and belief that I have in Him outweighs the temporal uneasiness and discomfort of my tests. Having the Bible as my primary tool of reference, I have been able to observe numerous examples of others that have been in similar situations as the ones I have faced. Their faith, trust and obedience in the Lord brought about changes in their lives.

When I think about the Lord never giving us more than we can handle, I always find myself back at the book of Job. With all that Job encountered, he still remained faithful and believed that God wouldn't ever push him past his limit and that God would always be there to help him get through.

I thank God for knowing me better than I know myself. I am grateful that even when I don't have the strength to muster up, through the Lord who strengthens me, I am able to do all things. I believe that everything that I face is working together for my good and that it won't ever be more than I can bear because God has declared so in His Word.

With joy and gladness, I can say that I know for a fact, that if God has allowed certain trials to enter my life, then the provisions have already been established to help me endure and eventually get through it.

Suggested Song of Meditation: "More Than I Can Bear" by God's Property from Kirk Franklin's Nu Nation

Deuteronomy 20:4 (The Living Bible/TLB)

⁴ For the Lord your God is going with you! He will fight for you against your enemies, and he will give you the victory!'

In recent days, there has been a sound that I have been hearing; it has been a feeling that has taken residence deep within me. Everything that is being communicated through my natural and spiritual senses is imparting that my victory is on its way. That victory begins in the way that I praise the Lord.

I am praising the Lord knowing that I have already won because in every instance, the Lord our God goes with me, fights on my behalf against my enemies and grants me victory. Therefore, the louder that victorious sound becomes and the deeper that victorious feeling gets, the louder and deeper my praise becomes, in turn. No matter how hard it gets, my praise gets that much harder and when everything around me intensifies, my praise is multiplied.

I am here to make and share a victorious sound everywhere I go because I know that I have already overcome and that I don't ever have to fight because I have already won. Yes, in this world that we live in, we shall have trials and tribulations but we should be confident and of good cheer because the Lord has overcome the world (John 16:33)!!

There isn't any room for a victim mentality here because we were born to be victorious. I don't need to see it to know that things are changing in my favor and that my victory is on the horizon. My faith and trust in the Lord fuels my praise and that is what I desire to express.

Whether I am experiencing a pinnacle or valley moment, I will praise the Lord and continue to claim the victory that He has already declared I will receive through Him. It is victory that I hear, how about you?

Suggested Song of Meditation: "I Hear the Sound (Of Victory)" by Maurette Brown Clark

James 1:2 (Expanded Bible/EXB)

> ² *My brothers and sisters [fellow believers], when you have many kinds of ·troubles [trials; testing], ·you should be full of joy [consider it all/pure joy].*

There used to be a time when I believed that the reason that I faced the multitude of trials that I did was because I was being punished. Part of my reason for believing that was because that was what I was told by others and being immature in my spiritual walk, I didn't understand the purpose for the tests that I found myself encountering; and I made the mistake of not seeking God first for guidance.

I remember one blessed morning; honestly, it was a very rough morning during one of the lowest moments in my life, I had a revelation. I realized that the purpose of tribulations was actually to make me better. Even though I felt broken and at the point of no return, I felt a warmth and a fullness grow inside of me that caused my entire mindset to change. God had been trying to reveal so many things to me, but I wasn't ready to receive what He had for me. I learned awhile back that God will not force Himself upon us. He will wait until we come to our senses, until we seek Him out and surrender it all to Him.

The moment my mindset shifted, the way I responded to being in the midst of tribulations shifted as well. No longer did I complain or beat myself up. I learned the importance of when troubles came my way, allowing them to be an opportunity or occasion for me to express joy. My entire countenance changed and instead of hurt, frustration and disappointment being splashed all across my face, I began stepping out with smiles, boasting and bragging about the God I serve, while still going through.

One may ask, how can you have joy, smile and brag about the Lord when chaos appears to be coming from every corner? I am capable of doing so because no matter how weak a situation may try to render me, I know that my strength comes from the Lord and if I were not able to handle it, God would have prevented it from occurring, as His approval is required for anything that happens in my life.

I count it all joy knowing that tribulations are used to get us to where God needs us to be. We are unable to go where God desires to takes us until He removes whatever is in us that is preventing us from moving forward. Trials allow God to separate what is useful in us from what is unproductive and causing a disconnect in our walk with Him. I am able to go through the sifting and molding process praising Him in advance, because I know that the same God, who brought me through past tribulations, will bring me through my current and future tribulations.

Each of us is going through something that is challenging us to some magnitude. God wants to take us to the next level; but that requires Him to purge us of some patterns of behavior and ways of thinking first. It's time to stop complaining and pointing fingers. What we need to do is dance, smile and shout through our tribulations because the God we serve is always looking out for us and when He does move in the midst of our situations, there won't be any doubt that God did it!!

Through tribulations, perseverance is produced, which, in turn, produces character and from character, hope is built.

Therefore, our challenge is while we are in the midst of our tribulations, smile through it and boast about it, that God's got it!!"

Suggested Song of Meditation: "Just Smile" by James Fortune and Fiya, featuring Carvena Jones and D'shondra Rideout

James 5:11 (Easy-to-Read Version/ERV)

¹¹ And we say that those who accepted their troubles with patience now have God's blessing. You have heard about Job's patience. You know that after all his troubles, the Lord helped him. This shows that the Lord is full of mercy and is kind.

One of the things that I loved most about creating the daily blog posts, is the accountability tool that it continues to be for me. It never fails that what the Lord stirs up in my spirit to share via a song, a verse and words, then becomes something that I am called to apply to my life right away.

It's one thing to compose these blogs on a daily basis. It's something totally different to not just talk the talk but to also walk the walk. I have spoken about exercising radical faith, believing and trusting God even when you don't see the end result in sight and having that confidence in Him to speak those things that are not as if they already were.

Today was a very trying day for me and one where I needed to apply all that I encourage each of you to. As many know, my family and I are in the process of buying a new home and relocating. In a perfect world, everything would be seamless. But as we know, we don't live in a perfect world, but we do serve a God whose thoughts and ways are. I am human, so yes, when unexpected hiccups arise, they catch me off guard momentarily and a few tears may fall, but those tears of frustration are immediately converted to tears of joy as I am reminded that my life is in the Lord's hands. I know that if I endure and am patient while dealing with the temporal troubles that come my way, I will be blessed.

And that is why on this day and each day to come, I have chosen to rise above the trials I face, which have an expiration date, and praise and rejoice in the Lord knowing that through His tenderness and mercy, it will all be brought together for me.

While going through, I will proclaim that, "It is well," because no matter what I face, I know that if I couldn't handle it, God wouldn't allow it. When I think of that principle, I think of Job. In learning about Job, I have come to understand what it means to truly trust the Lord, even when it appears that all odds are stacked against you.

Job also serves as a reminder to me that, through it all it will be well, if I continue to trust, believe and rest in the Lord. What ends up being a surprise or an unexpected turn for me is far from being a surprise to God. And so, when I take a moment to just remember that He who has begun a good work in me will complete and accomplish it, I can persevere with joy knowing that it's all working together for my good.

I will count it all joy when trials and tests come my way, because blessed are those who have endured.

Suggested Song of Meditation: "It Is Well" by Mary Mary

John 14:27 (Jubilee Bible 2000/JUB)

²⁷ Peace I leave with you, my peace I give unto you; not as the world gives, give I unto you. Let not your heart be troubled, neither let it be afraid.

Wouldn't it be wonderful if every day was met without any trials, hardships or troubles? But as children of God, we know that is very unrealistic wishing and thinking on our part.

No matter how much the Lord loves us, He never said that the path that was set in front of each of us would be without trials or roadblocks. There are some things that we must encounter, but we should rejoice in knowing that through it all, the Lord is right there with us and He won't ever let us down.

It is so important that I keep those words embedded in my head and close to my heart, especially on days when things do not go the way that I hoped they would. When I continue to remind myself that the Lord is the source of my strength, I am able to experience the peace that Jesus has given me; a peace that encourages me not to let my heart be troubled or afraid while going through.

The combination of His strength and peace gives me the reassurance that everything is already alright and working towards getting better, regardless of what my current situations may reflect.

How quickly we can become discouraged, frustrated and disappointed. I have made a promise to myself that when those feelings creep up, I cannot allow them to take over. I turn to the Lord and grab hold of that peace that surpasses all understanding and a strength that holds me together when I would otherwise fall apart into a million pieces.

No complaints shall you hear from me, because in the midst of it all, I know everything is all good and working as it should. I will overcome and be victorious in the end.

Suggested Song of Meditation: "Alright Ok" by J. Moss

Job 23:10 (Amplified Bible/AMP)

¹⁰ But He knows the way that I take [He has concern for it, appreciates, and pays attention to it]. When He has tried me, I shall come forth as refined gold [pure and luminous].

I remember being at such a crossroads and in need of discernment on a level that I haven't ever required before. To say that I felt lost and utterly confused was a complete understatement.

When I was younger, one of the TV game shows that I would love to watch was, "Let's Make a Deal." I couldn't wait until the contestant had to choose between the different doors to see which prize was awaiting them and if they had chosen wisely. Now when I would watch the show, I would always pick a door before the contestant did and I have to tell you that I had a knack for picking the door with the most rewarding prize. The complete opposite would have probably occurred had I been on live television and a contestant myself.

Life is imitating TV, because here I am with two doors in front of me and I am perplexed at the thought of making a decision that would disappoint the Lord. These two doors are in reference to decisions that I must make in this ever-spiraling home-buying process I have been submerged in. As the days continue to pass by, the enemy remains adamant in his efforts to make me feel like my back is up against the wall and that I need to make a decision ASAP based on the timeline that is before me.

I can't voice my dependence, trust and belief in the Lord and attempt to take the wheel back at the same time. I know that the two doors that are set before me represent two totally different paths. One door leads down the path of me walking according to God's will for my life; whereas the other door represents what my future would hold according to my own preferences. It is that door, which I am striving to avoid completely.

I am opening my heart in full surrender and crying out to the Lord because I need His guidance like never before. I am aware that nothing about what has transpired in my life is a surprise to the Lord and that He pays attention and is concerned about me and the steps I take. My heart's desire is just to have a home to call my own so that my family and I can begin this new season that is upon us reunited and back under one roof again.

My mind, my world, everything just seems so cloudy and that is why hearing just one single word from the Lord is imperative at this present time. My desire is to do things the Lord's way; according to His will and not my own. I've made the mistake before of getting so close to what God had for me and out of fear, grabbing the wheel and making the arrival to where I should have been that much longer unnecessarily. I don't want to make that mistake again; especially because I know that the Lord did not give us a spirit of fear. Operating in fear is a tactic of the enemy.

On this day, another scripture that I am standing on is James 1:5 which states, "But anyone who needs wisdom should ask God, whose very nature is to give to everyone without a second thought, without keeping score. Wisdom will certainly be given to those who ask." I am seeking godly wisdom for decisions that do not just affect me but my family as well.

I am being tried and pressed on all sides and all I want is to live my life on purpose without any doubts in the decisions that I make. I want to emerge as refined gold with a testimony to share with each and every one of you.

I know that the same Lord that brought me through my trials in the past will do it again. That is why I am opening up my heart because I believe that He will guide me through and that I will be even better once on the other side of it; having obtained what He has for me, which is the most rewarding prize of them all.

Suggested Song of Meditation: "Open My Heart" by Yolanda Adams

2 Corinthians 12:10 (Lexham English Bible/LEB)

¹⁰ Therefore I delight in weaknesses, in insults, in calamities, in persecutions and difficulties for the sake of Christ, for whenever I am weak, then I am strong.

I am praising and rejoicing in the name of the Lord because He is so worthy to be praised!!! I am also so grateful that He always knows what I need to hear and when I need to hear it.

The message that my pastor delivered was so on time, that there was absolutely no way that I couldn't take what God desired for me to hear and not share it with each of you. I was already pumped up by the praise and worship that was conducted by guest worship leader, Israel Houghton. He sang so many songs that ministered to my soul and that spoke to exactly where I was.

By the time the verses that the message would be coming from and the title of the message were revealed, you could have stuck a fork in me because I was already done. The message was entitled, "Count It All Joy" and it came from James 1: 2-4, which instructs us, "My brethren, count it all joy when you fall into various trials, knowing that the testing of your faith produces patience. But let patience have its perfect work, that you may be perfect and complete, lacking nothing."

James 1: 2-4 is actually one of my favorite passages. There is no way we can live our lives without enduring some trials, struggles, hardships or drama.

I was reminded just how much we profit from the trials we endure. As our pastor shared with the congregation, most of us put the situations and circumstances of our lives into two categories, the "good" category and the "bad" category. But it is when we have matured in our spiritual walk, that we are able to recognize that everything we encounter belongs in one category, the "count it all joy" category.

Regardless of whether it's good, bad or indifferent, we should consider them with a positive attitude knowing that troubles and difficulties are tools which God uses to refine and purify our faith; thus, producing the patience and endurance needed to be able to continue our walk and obey God regardless of what our temporal circumstances may reflect.

There have been situations in my life that left me so heartbroken and confused. They included places where I thought I was supposed to be, relationships that I thought I was supposed to have, etc. But those very things that I thought were bad, God brought so much good from it.

In each situation, my faith was tested. And as our pastor made it so evidently clear, "We don't know if our faith is legit until it has been tested." Something else that he said that hit so close to home was when he relayed that until our faith is tested, we don't know if we truly believe God will do it, until we find ourselves in a situation that we know, hands down, if God doesn't cause things to change and happen, it won't get done.

And that is exactly where I am right now. It's a situation in which the only way it will all come together the way we need it to, is if God does it!!!

Therefore, no more claiming things as good or bad; they will only be recognized as those things that I will consider and count as a delight in my life, knowing that all of it is working for my good.

God won't ever allow anything to come into our lives that we do NOT have the capability to handle. I find joy and strength in knowing that. No matter what it is, count it all joy!!!

Suggested Song of Meditation: "Count It All Joy" by Tarralyn Ramsey

Isaiah 43:2 (The Living Bible/TLB)

> ² When you go through deep waters and great trouble, I will be with you. When you go through rivers of difficulty, you will not drown! When you walk through the fire of oppression, you will not be burned up—the flames will not consume you.

Earlier today, my youngest daughter, who is very independent, was in need of some serious "Mommy and Me" time. She wanted nothing more than to climb up in my lap and for me to wrap my arms around her and hold her tight. As I was looking over at her older brother and sister, I wished I could go back to the days when I was able to just hold them in my arms and keep them safe from the rest of the world.

But the reality is that we all will endure tests, trials and obstacles. And as much as I do not desire that for my children, because I don't ever want them to be hurt, disappointed or left questioning themselves; I know that tests and trials come to make us stronger.

What I also know and strive to show them each day is that no matter what we face in life, God is with us. He knows what we are going to encounter long before we ever see it coming. And because of that, we are able to overcome because in His arms we are safe.

When the storms of life begin to rage, it is the Lord who calms the elements and circumstances around us. All we have to do is call on the name of Jesus as we pass through the waters. And like Peter, during those "walk on water" moments we encounter, we have the reassurance of knowing that we will not drown; because our focus is on the Lord, knowing He is by our side.

In the same respect, when we are going through the fire, like the three Hebrew boys—Shadrach, Meshach and Abednego, we will not be burned nor will the flames harm us. And that is because the Lord is with us and closer to us than we could ever possibly imagine.

Even when we can't decipher or decode what is happening around us, none of it is a surprise to the Lord. He has already prepared us and made provisions for us. In Him, we are covered and have protection.

As a parent, I know how much protecting, shielding, guiding and being there for my children means to me. In no way am I able to see what is ahead for them, but I stay committed to doing my best and imparting God's principles and commandments into them.

Because of the love that our Heavenly Father has for us, His children, we can find peace and safety in His arms, regardless of the circumstances we face, because the Lord is always with us.

Suggested Song of Meditation: "Safe in His Arms" by Lucinda Moore

1 Peter 4:12-13 (Easy-to-Read Version/ERV)

> *¹² My friends, don't be surprised at the painful things that you are now suffering, which are testing your faith. Don't think that something strange is happening to you.*
> *¹³ But you should be happy that you are sharing in Christ's sufferings. You will be happy and full of joy when Christ shows his glory.*

Since I was a youngster, music has played such an integral part in my life. No matter what I have gone through or experienced, good, bad or indifferent; you can best believe that I can name you the song that was popular at that time, or the group of songs that I depended on to get me through.

One of my favorite groups I listened to growing up was Rufus; and so, when Chaka Khan became a solo artist, I continued to follow her career and remained a huge fan. One of my favorite songs by Chaka Khan is, "Through the Fire." When I was younger, I would just sing the lyrics because Chaka Khan did. But as I got older and matured, some of the obstacles and trials that I encountered appeared to be so fiery that I would immediately think of the song.

That song crossed my mind again recently because the trials I am currently facing are so intense and consuming. I truly needed a word from the Lord to remind me that these sufferings should not come as a surprise or be viewed as something strange.

It's during trying times such as these that I am reminded that all of this is a spiritual refining process with glory just around the corner. When I am able to have faith while going through the fire, I can rejoice exultantly because I will have the wonderful joy of seeing Christ's splendor and radiance revealed.

During some much needed quiet time, I began to reflect on what it means to be a child of God and a follower of Christ. God never said that we wouldn't suffer and endure trials, but He did instruct us to count it all joy when we meet trials of various kinds (James 1:2). He also promised that after we have suffered a little while, the God of all grace, who has called us to His eternal glory in Christ will Himself restore, confirm, strengthen, and establish us (1 Peter 5:10).

And that is why I keep the Lord's Word treasured in my heart. Because if I focused on the temporary external circumstances that I encounter, I wouldn't have anything to rejoice about. But, while in the midst of my trials, I am able to praise God and rejoice in Him because our Heavenly Father is the God of all grace and mercy.

While in The Midst, I will continuously praise His name!!!

Suggested Song of Meditation: "In The Midst" by Byron Cage featuring Tye Tribbett

Isaiah 54:17 (Good News Translation/GNT)

17 But no weapon will be able to hurt you; you will have an answer for all who accuse you. I will defend my servants and give them victory." The Lord has spoken.

When the storms of life begin to intensify, it's so important that we be able to encourage ourselves. Sometimes we won't be able to get anyone on the phone to speak words of motivation to us. That is why it is imperative to have God's Word stored up and ready to speak and stand on.

In times when we are distressed and overwhelmed, we can rest on the promises that He has spoken and provided in His Word. God is able to raise up the provisions and assistance that is required in our time of need. The Lord's fullness is infinite and through the ultimate price that was paid by His Son for our sins, we as believers and followers of His Word will be on the receiving end of the favor, grace and glory that God releases.

When you believe that the same God who created the heavens and the earth, who gave children to the barren, provided food in times of famine and performed so many other miracles is the same God who is working in the midst of your situation and is protecting you; you have that assurance that no weapon that is formed against you, nor any judgment or accusation that is made shall be effective; it won't work. All the power is in the Lord's hands and He will stand by His Word and come through.

I know for myself and continue to see what happens when you put your trust and faith in God first and allow Him to direct your path and order your steps. I have found myself able to sleep more peacefully and less inclined to adopt a spirit of worry or fear. When we know who is defending us and fighting our battles for us, in those instances when we are being tried, tested and attacked, the impact doesn't feel as overwhelming as it used to.

I rejoice because what I endure sharpens and makes me that much stronger. As a servant of the Lord, I have inherited the privilege and blessing of the Lord defending me, which means I am and will continue to be more than a conqueror!!

When we strive to live our lives for Christ, that doesn't do anything but upset the enemy. Therefore, expect the attacks, the accusations and that he will try to do whatever he can to plant doubt and make you question what our Heavenly Father has already declared.

Since we are covered by the blood of Jesus Christ, we can rest on God's promises knowing that no weapon formed against us shall prosper.

Suggested Song of Meditation: "No Weapon" by Fred Hammond

Psalm 66:10 Expanded Bible/EXB

God, you have tested [examined] us; you have purified [refined] us like silver [removing the dross].

As my family and I began our journey back down to Maryland to get the last of our things from storage, so much was going through my head. This was the final step to closing this chapter and beginning our new season in our new home in a new city in New York.

As we crossed over into Maryland and I was listening to Praise 104.1, I began to think about a song that I heard a few weeks back but a video for it hadn't been released on YouTube yet, so I was unable to use it for one of my daily blog posts.

Just as I was thinking about that song, it played on the radio and to my surprise when I checked YouTube, I discovered that a video for the song was just uploaded the day previous.

The song speaks to not being that easy to break and when I think about my total of over 14 years spent here in Maryland that is exactly how I feel. There have been so many unexpected and emotionally crippling tests and trials that I have endured while living in Maryland but through it all, I recognize that God was examining me and taking me through a refinement process.

I am grateful for every trial and obstacle that I have encountered because the end result has been a deeper relationship with the Lord, a faith that cannot be taken away or diminished and the reality that I have become so much stronger and wiser through the tests that I have faced. I have an untouchable confidence that is rooted in my Heavenly Father.

I can boldly declare that I am not that easy to break when I have the reassurance that all things are working together for my good and that the tests and trials are tools used by the Lord to mold me into who He desires me to be.

Suggested Song of Meditation: "Not That Easy" by Trinity Dawson

Psalm 119:50 (International Children's Bible/ICB)

⁵⁰ When I suffer, this comforts me: Your promise gives me life.

One thing that we all have to come to terms with is that there will be trying times and tests that each and every one of us must encounter.

For so long, I thought that the obstacles and challenges that I faced were a punishment from God for some of the things I had done that I shouldn't have, along with those things I should have done that I hadn't gotten to yet.

That was my misguided perception of how everything transpired, until I took the much-needed time to develop my relationship with the Lord. During that time, I learned the truth (by way of His Word and the teachings that ministered to my soul and spoke to me right where I was). My comprehension and grasp of the meaning of trials and afflictions were no longer connected to what had been relayed to me in the past or what I had conjured up in my own mind.

Not only did I learn and begin to appreciate that tests and trials come to make me strong, it became that much easier to hold on and press forward when I realized that the Lord is always in my corner and vows to be there to catch me when I fall.

Through each problem, situation and circumstance, I am able to find comfort because the Lord's promises revive me. Through each storm, across every uncharted territory I must encounter and with every mountain that I must climb, the Lord has instructed me to be strong and courageous, because it is the Lord my God, who goes with me; and who has promised to never leave me nor abandon me (Deuteronomy 31:6).

When I call on the name of the Lord, I have no doubt that He hears me. Therefore, because I know that the Lord is in my corner, I no longer feel as if my back is up against the wall or like all the odds are stacked against me when I face adversity. Instead, I praise the Lord in advance and thank Him because each obstacle that comes my way is working together for my good.

In times of trouble, I am comforted by the promises that come from the Lord. I am given the strength to hold on because I trust and believe that in each situation, the Lord will see me through.

Suggested Song of Meditation: "In Your Corner" by Tamela Mann

Proverbs 24:10 (Contemporary English Version/CEV)

¹⁰ Don't give up and be helpless in times of trouble.

As I was reading a few different blog posts that included inspirational quotes, I came across one that really spoke to where I currently found myself, as I attempted to sift through the plethora of emotions that I was dealing with.

The quote read, "Faith in God includes faith in His timing."

I originally had to re-read the quote because I needed time to take in each word individually before swallowing and digesting the entire sentiment.

Lately, I have had nothing but my faith in the Lord to rely on, as doors that only He could open have begun to come ajar. As much as I trust and believe in the Lord, one area where I have been weak has regarded the timing to which circumstances have transpired in my life.

We can sing songs about the Lord being an "On Time God" and then part our lips to say, "He may not come when you want Him, but He's always right on time." Those words are really easy to proclaim and belt out when things occur sooner then we may expect or in such a manner infinitely beyond how we thought they would.

In those moments as we're waiting on the Lord to fulfill His promises, there may be times when we encounter adversity; but the key is to never give up and to keep our faith not just in the Lord, but in His timing.

The Lord holds our lives in His hands. He's all-knowing and everything that He does is perfect. It took a while for me to fully grasp that no matter how soon I desired resolution and answers to a particular situation, it was God who was in control. He is well aware of what I can and cannot handle and will not allow any situation to get the best of me.

When my perspective shifted and I was reminded to associate my faith with the Lord AND His perfect timing, I embraced each situation with a different mindset, knowing that I would overcome, regardless of what the current circumstances reflected.

In the past, as I faced adversity and hard times, I believed that the longer that it took me to get through equated to the amount of time the Lord was punishing me. Constantly maturing and continuing to grow spiritually, I realize that I was not being punished, but having those things purged that were creating roadblocks and obstacles in my relationship with the Lord. In hindsight, I can attest to the fact that if things had happened or concluded according to the timetable I had established, my life would have been short-changed tremendously.

I would have never known what I could overcome if I hadn't ever been in the fight. I also wouldn't have had the opportunity to see the hands of God at work, all in and through my circumstances, if He had operated on anyone else's time other than His own.

Today, I was reminded of the importance of never losing faith in the Lord or His timing. When we are able to keep our trust and belief in the One who has the ability to do the impossible, we will not hesitate to believe that we shall overcome.

Suggested Song of Meditation: "Overcomer" by Mandisa

Job 8:7 (New American Bible (Revised Edition)/NABRE)

⁷ Though your beginning was small, your future will flourish indeed.

What an absolutely beautiful winter day it has been. After the past two days of bone-chilling temperatures, I gladly welcomed an almost 40-degree sunny winter afternoon.

As I ran out the house to run errands, as soon as I hopped in my van, my daily automobile dialogues with the Lord commenced. I have had so much on my mind lately and it seems as if as soon as I attempt to address one issue another one unexpectedly pops up that catches me off guard and causes me to regroup.

While in the midst of sharing my thoughts and concerns, I stopped at a red light and observed the most beautiful image. Although it was partly cloudy outside, there was this one area of the sky where the sun had broken through the clouds and its rays were just illuminating the sky.

In that moment, it got me to thinking about the clouds and storms that are associated with the trials and obstacles of life that we can expect to encounter as children of God. Even though the storms of life may rage, because of the Son who was born, died, and then rose again so that we could have everlasting life, we can expect and claim those better days that are ahead for us.

As all of this was occurring, my Pandora station played the song which I have included as the suggested song of meditation and it conveyed everything that I was feeling and reminded me of what the Lord has promised, all of which has been provided in His Word.

I am so grateful that we serve a God who not only hears us, but who answers our prayers. He's a God that meets us right where we are and communicates to us in a way that we can comprehend.

The book of Job has always been one of my favorite books in the Bible because it keeps me focused, humbled and encouraged as I go through the tests and trials that had to get the Lord's permission before they could ever be brought to me. I'm not saying that anything that I have experienced has come even close to all that Job encountered, but there is a lot that can be learned from Job and the manner to which he continued to honor the Lord and remain obedient; even as he endured such catastrophic hardships and losses.

But in the end, Job's latter was greater than his former days and that is something that we need to remain mindful of.

Regardless of how small, insignificant or unimportant we may have viewed our beginnings or lives to be thus far, the best is yet to come and everything that we are experiencing is working together for our good; just as the Lord said it would.

As I think about all that has occurred in my life up 'til this moment, I rejoice because where I am is far better than where I started and being a work in progress, I still have further to go; but Oh happy day, there is still "greater" waiting in my latter days.

Speak victory over your life. Rebuke fear and worry. Instead of being consumed and overwhelmed by how "big" you may think your problems may be, remind your problems that you serve a God who is bigger, greater and Almighty!!

Give your problems and circumstances their walking papers and eviction notices as you wait with expectancy for that "greater" that is coming.

Suggested Song of Meditation: "Better Days" by Anthony Brown and group therAPy

1 Peter 1:6-7 (J.B. Phillips New Testament/PHILLIPS)

⁶⁻⁷ This means tremendous joy to you, I know, even though you are temporarily harassed by all kinds of trials and temptations. This is no accident—it happens to prove your faith, which is infinitely more valuable than gold, and gold, as you know, even though it is ultimately perishable, must be purified by fire. This proving of your faith is planned to bring you praise and honour and glory in the day when Jesus Christ reveals himself.

Now that the storm has come and gone, I have just been sitting here looking at the huge banks of snow that I haven't had the pleasure of seeing in quite a while. My youngest daughter was so captivated watching all the snow fall from the sky throughout the day yesterday. She couldn't believe how much snow was outside on the ground.

Because she is young and was born in Northern Virginia and lived in Maryland the first four years of her life, she really didn't get to observe a significant amount of snow. To be able to view life and the simplest things through the eyes of a child is such a blessing.

Yesterday, as the snowflakes increased in size and intensified in accumulation, I was very thankful that my family and I were all under one roof; safe and sound. Because of the blizzard, we were all confined to the house and that was a great thing. We were given a break from the hustle and bustle of our daily routines and could just put everything on pause and just be.

It's interesting because I observed a number of people complaining and commenting on how much of an inconvenience the storm has been. I actually had the complete opposite perspective. Whether it's a rainstorm, snowstorm, hailstorm or any storm, I know that each happens for a reason and serves a purpose.

Instead of complaining or looking at things negatively, I look for God in every situation and seek to uncover what He desires for me to learn from every circumstance that I face.

Watching what was occurring in the natural immediately made me rejoice in what I have already learned in the spiritual. And that is there is a blessing in our storms. We may be tossed to and fro, but we serve a Master who has control and power over all the elements and every last thing that we could ever come up against.

It's when we are going through and in the midst of the storm that the Lord will show up in ways man could never and He'll provide on a level that only He can!! Just as some of the lyrics from the suggested song of meditation states, "Some of us wouldn't pray if we never went through anything." That's real talk, all day!!

That is why I choose to rejoice and have joy, even when being temporarily harassed by all kinds of trials and temptations and that is because I know that the storms come to test the genuineness of my faith.

A quote that I came across also reiterated another reason that I count it all joy (even my storms). Charles Caleb Colton stated, "Times of great calamity and confusion have been productive for the greatest minds. The purest ore is produced from the hottest furnace. The brightest thunder-bolt is elicited from the darkest storm."

I have applied this quote to my spiritual walk and it reminds me that through the greatest of trials and tribulations, our minds are made stronger as we take our focus off the issue and shift it completely onto the Lord. And just like the brightest thunder-bolt that is elicited from the darkest storm, when we go through the fire, all those flaws and impurities that have hindered our walk are burnt off and removed so that nothing can get in the way of us letting our LIGHT SHINE before others so that they may see our good deeds and give glory to our Father who is in heaven.

The more ferocious the storm, the hotter the fire and the harder the pressing means that from our tests and trials, a triumphant testimony and a mighty message will be birthed. It is through that faith and trust that the Lord will receive the praise, honor and glory that He most righteously deserves!!!

Suggested Song of Meditation: "Blessing In The Storm" by Kirk Franklin

Luke 8:39 (J.B. Phillips New Testament/PHILLIPS)

39 "Go back home and tell them all what wonderful things God has done for you." So the man went away and told the marvellous story of what Jesus had done for him, all over the town.

For the past week, the recurring theme that I have come across at church, bible study, in my bible study plans and in just reading my Bible is transparency.

Being transparent is something I strive to do at all times, regardless of where I am and who I am speaking to. Both individually and collectively, my family and I have had numerous conversations on why transparency is so important to me.

I'm a very honest and matter-of-fact kind of person. I love to communicate with others on different levels and by way of whatever means the Lord deems fit. Any opportunity that I have to tell those in earshot just how marvelous and amazing the Lord has been in my life, you can best believe that I am sharing that good news.

After church on Sunday, my son and I were discussing what we had taken away from the church service and it led to us reflecting on just some of what the Lord has done for our family.

Being 19, my son and I have endured some turbulent and at times heartbreaking circumstances. In those moments, I knew that the only way we would get through would be because God said so. They were situations that if God didn't step in and make a way, no way would have been provided.

All I had was my faith and during those times, all I could muster up the strength to do was pray, cry, believe that the Lord would come through and pray some more. And that was what my son had a front row seat to observing.

All of it took a significant toll on me mentally, emotionally and spiritually. Nothing meant more to me than being a mom, but I was broken and I placed my trust and the life of my child(ren) and myself in the hands of the wrong individuals and I never dreamed for a second that we would be dealt the cards we were.

The shackles of pain, shame, regret and disappointment had me so bound, I felt like I was moving at the pace of a slug. But God delivered us. He healed and restored me in a way that anyone who knew what I had gone through, had no doubt that the only reason that I was still here and able to smile and continue on was because of the faith that I had in my Heavenly Father.

As my son and I continued talking, we recalled the car accident we were in almost five years ago. At the time, we still lived in Maryland and were heading to NY for Labor Day weekend. My husband, my son, my oldest daughter, my youngest daughter (who was only six months old) and I were all in the car.

It was rainy and due to the reckless driving of another person, trying to prevent them from hitting us, our car spun out of control and ended up facing the oncoming traffic as it slid across the road to an upcoming embankment that was located in front of a steep grassy hill that led down to a farmhouse in the distance.

For all intents and purposes, when our car hit that embankment and went up in the air, it should have flipped over and rolled down the hill, but right at that moment when our car was elevated in the air, the Lord dropped it right back down where it was.

It was an experience that none of us can talk about without our eyes watering in gratitude because we know it was only because of God that we are still here. What could have been a very tragic incident for all of us at one time, became a moment of extreme thankfulness, praise and honor to the Most High who covered, protected and saved us.

That is why I love the verse that was chosen today because it speaks to one of my favorite accounts of God's grace, mercy and deliverance in the Bible.

The man that Jesus instructs to go back to where he was from and be a witness to those in his community of all God has done was once possessed by multiple demons for a long time. What I love about this particular instance is that when Jesus commanded the unclean spirits to come out of the man, the spirits asked to enter the bodies of the herd of swine that were feeding nearby. When the same demons that were in one man were cast into a herd of swine, they immediately ran down a steep hill into the sea, where they drowned.

What a herd of swine could not handle, this man was able to carry within himself for years, until the appointed time when Jesus would deliver him. Isn't that how God works? The things in our lives that would be too much or unbearable for someone else, God's grace and mercy covers us and upon deliverance, we are blessed with a testimony that wasn't ever meant for us to keep to ourselves.

By returning home and to our communities, those who knew us when we were bound by the yokes and strongholds of our situations will marvel in what they now observe in us; knowing that it could only be because of the blood of Jesus and the role that God has in our lives that we have been saved.

Our testimonies are birthed from the tests and trials that we encounter. No one can tell your testimony for you or like you. In that same respect, no one can praise God like you, nor can they praise Him for you. That redemption from the hand of the enemy is worth shouting about and sharing with those whom you come in contact with. We never know what someone else may be enduring or struggling with at any given moment. And what God just did for you in your life could be utilized to encourage that staying power in someone else, for them to continue on, keeping their faith in the Lord.

Suggested Song of Meditation: "I Testify" by ADA

Philippians 2:14 (Amplified Bible, Classic Edition/AMPC)

¹⁴ Do all things without grumbling and fault finding and complaining [against God] and questioning and doubting [among yourselves].

Because of Ash Wednesday, many of my friends have been posting on social media what they are giving up for Lent. As I was reading the various responses, I began pondering on patterns of behavior that we exhibit that we should be giving up permanently, especially being children of God, and one of the first ones that came to mind was complaining.

One of the things that I love most about the Bible is that it provides me with the truth, the whole truth and nothing but the truth (so help me God)!!

If we take the time to open the Word of God and not just skim the pages, but consume each word that is inscribed in it, we have the opportunity to learn about the favor, blessings and miracles that happened in the lives of countless individuals because they believed in God and remained faithful to His Word.

We are able to find that encouragement and inspiration in our daily journeys when we have the names and details documented of how God continuously used the unlikely, overlooked and rejected to accomplish His will.

As much as I love reading about the underdog, who, because of God, becomes the victor in the end, I also appreciate and am thankful that God also provides us with the knowledge of what happens when we disobey and go against His Word.

Depending on the situation I am encountering, there are specific areas of the Bible that I turn to. When I started thinking about the detriment that complaining is to us, our spiritual walk and the opportunity we have to obtain what God has for us, I began to think about the Israelites and how, at times, we often display mannerisms that parallel how they acted after being freed from captivity from Egypt and were making their way to the Promised Land.

We can be freed from the bondage of strongholds and encompassed by blessings and God's unmerited favor happening all around us and we'll still find a reason to complain. Listen, God never said that every day would be "sunshiny-happy-go-lucky". He told us tests and trials should be expected and that they come to make us stronger; which, in turn, produces a deeper and closer relationship with Him.

Honestly, in order for there to be a victory doesn't a trial, attack or battle have to occur first? But the wonderful thing is that the battle is already won because it isn't ever ours to fight in the first place; it is the Lord's. And He has promised to never leave us nor forsake us.

So, if we know all of these things, why do we complain?

I want to share a couple of reasons that I am choosing to be grateful instead of second-guessing God and complaining. First of all, there is always someone else who is worse off than you. While in the midst, what we endure seems so unbearable, but no matter how trying it may be, best believe, there is someone out there who would gladly step into your shoes instead of where they currently find themselves. And if we know that God doesn't give us more than we can bear, that means that whatever we are facing, He had to approve and, through Him, we already have everything that we need to be victorious.

Secondly, I am reminded of what happened to the Israelites because of their complaining. God used Moses and Aaron to lead the Israelites out of captivity and not only did God deliver them but He provided for every last one of their needs and protected them from some of the most treacherous circumstances. But because everything wasn't happening in the manner they felt it should and within the time frame they expected, instead of remaining thankful and focusing on God; they defaulted back to their old ways and began grumbling against the Lord and complaining with the end result being them wandering the wilderness for 40 years.

I don't know about you, but I do not want to be what is getting in the way of all that God has for me. That is why I meditate on the Word of God, so that I may know the truth and be reminded of the blessings that we receive when we are grateful and remain faithful to the Lord; along with what happens when we don't.

What occurs day-to-day may surprise or catch me off guard, but it doesn't surprise the Lord. He saw our unformed bodies and all the days ordained for us were written in His book before any one of them came to be (Psalm 139:16). That is why we must remain grateful and not complain. Because no matter what it is, the Lord has the final say. As we continue to move forward, may we always know that God will provide for us and protect us from those hazardous things, both seen and unseen.

Suggested Song of Meditation: "Be Grateful" by The Love Center Choir/Walter Hawkins

Isaiah 48:10 (New International Reader's Version/NIRV)

¹⁰ I have tested you in the furnace of suffering. I have tried to make you pure. But I did not use as much heat as it takes to make silver pure.

You would think that with living back in NY, along with the snow and unbelievably cold temperatures we have been hit with due to the past couple of storm fronts that have come through, I would be focused on that.

But the complete opposite has been occurring. For the past few weeks, my mind has been consumed with thoughts of going through the fire and being burned. I believe what initiated these thoughts were two separate events that impacted me personally but that are all tied to me spiritually.

My oldest daughter and I have been wanting to take part in a 5K Color Run since we were in Maryland. We recently learned that one will be taking place here in a few months; and not even two miles from where we live. To say that we became extremely excited is an understatement.

At the same time that I was researching all the registration information for the 5K, I also had begun researching hotels for the vacation our family will be taking in a few months as well. But as I sat back and looked at both the tabs I had up regarding these two upcoming events, a harsh reality stuck a pin in my balloon of enthusiasm and brought me back to ground level.

For those who don't know, I have a skin condition called polymorphous light eruption (PMLE). During the spring and summer months, if I am in the sun more than 5 minutes, I not only burn severely but every exposed area of skin that ends up getting burned becomes covered with (what appears to be) millions of red bumps that itch and sting at the same time.

What is so frustrating about this condition is that I'm always on the go and love the warm weather and this condition hinders and sometimes prevents me from taking part in activities that I would love to share in with my family and friends. Another reason for my frustration is because I didn't always have this condition.

Growing up and all the way up until the age of 24, I was that one person you could always find running track, outside double-dutching and hop-scotching, playing in the water coming from the fire hydrants, swimming in every pool all day long that was open, in attendance at every BBQ and block party; and taking part in every outdoor activity known to man.

But all of that came to an abrupt end in 2000 when I took a trip to Jamaica and learned about this condition that had laid dormant for all those years prior until I was exposed to the intensity of the rays associated with that most beautiful tropical sun.

From that moment on, the relationship between the sun and I had changed.

Ironically, at that same time, I was in the worst place personally and spiritually but wouldn't allow myself to really acknowledge it. My relationship with the Lord was disconnected. So, not only was I dealing with trying to wrap my mind around this recurrent and abnormal reaction to sunlight that I didn't even fit the criteria to be susceptible to, the Lord was also taking me through His refining furnace at the same time.

Back then, I felt like I was being punished on every level. When I was first diagnosed with the skin condition, I only had my son, but enjoyed taking part in everything that we could do outdoors and now I couldn't. I didn't understand why this was happening to me and I actually ignored the severity of the condition because nothing was going to stop me from being the mom I desired to be. But the pain from the burnt skin and the bumps that seemed to appear instantaneously was excruciating.

I was feeling the heat externally from the physical sun and because of the disconnection between the Lord and me, the Lord was bringing the heat to me internally as well.

Not too long after that trip, I experienced one of the most traumatic personal times ever and it altered the direction my life took in what appeared to be a matter of seconds. Like silver, I felt like I was being held in the middle of the fire where the flames are the hottest. It was at that moment I truly recognized that the current state of my life was not where God desired me to be. I was in a valley so low, that it took the furnace of affliction that I was being tested in to find my way back to the Lord.

It didn't feel good, I didn't know what my future held, but what I did know was that the way I was doing things was not working for me and that in putting my trust and my future in the hands of others, I had lost my way.

I realized that the fiery trials I was enduring were not intended to destroy me. They were being used to transform my life and to conform my character to resemble that of Jesus; along with getting my focus back to the One who holds my future and knows every day (good, bad and indifferent), that I have awaiting me before they ever come to fruition.

From all that I have endured and all that was revealed to me during that season of my life, I rededicated my life back to Jesus and my relationship with Him changed forever.

I did some research regarding the process that occurs when silver is refined. And this is what I learned. A silversmith holds a piece of silver over the fire and lets it heat up. When silver is refined, the silversmith needs to hold the silver in the middle of the fire where the flames are hottest to burn away all the impurities. The silversmith sits there in front of the fire the whole time the silver is being refined. He has to keep his eyes on the silver the entire time it is in the fire because if the silver is left too long in the flames, it could be destroyed or if the silver absorbs the oxygen it will become unworkable.

One of the last things that I found interesting was that a silversmith knows when the silver is completely refined when the silver shines with a mirror-like quality to it and the silversmith can see his image in it (Wow).

I actually watched the silver refining process on YouTube and it brought new meaning to "going through the fire."

Through the afflictions that I go through and the flames from the fiery furnace that may surround me, I am reminded in Malachi 3:3 that, "He will sit as a refiner and purifier of silver." Therefore, when I'm going through, I have the assurance that the Lord keeps His eye on me, knows just how much I can bear and will not allow me to endure the heat any longer than I need to. When we're in the fire, we are being rid of the imperfections and impurities that are blocking, hindering and distracting us from the path that God has for our lives.

I have come to understand and appreciate that I am being refined and purified by our God and that I will remain in the fire until the Lord sees His image in me.

Whether I'm speaking of my physical condition or the testing of my faith, in both cases, I will trust and obey the Lord and seek His covering. I know that His refining fire continues to transform me and set me apart so that I can bring honor and glory to His most precious name.

Suggested Song of Meditation: "Refiner's Fire" by Passion. May it minister to you as it does to me.

2 Chronicles 20:17 (New Living Translation/NLT)

17 But you will not even need to fight. Take your positions; then stand still and watch the Lord's victory. He is with you, O people of Judah and Jerusalem. Do not be afraid or discouraged. Go out against them tomorrow, for the Lord is with you!"

There is a song that was my praise and worship song every morning at the beginning of last year. It's also one of my aunt's favorites. As my seasons change, the songs that minister to where I am at the moment, also evolve.

But over the past three days, the Lord has had that original song constantly on my heart and playing in my head.

Yesterday, my oldest daughter and I were having a very in-depth conversation about trusting God, His direction for our lives and recognizing that the battle is not ours.

So many of the tests and trials that she's facing parallel many that I also had to face at her age. As I listened to her express her thoughts and feelings, I was just so grateful for the opportunity that the Lord was providing me with at that moment.

I couldn't be the mother God has called me to be if I didn't trust and believe in Him in every area of their lives and mine. From the moment I got pregnant with my son, 20 years ago, I had to learn the importance of seeking the Lord in every situation so that the position I took would come from Him and not my emotions or the temporal circumstances that I was facing.

Being one who is always on the go, who likes to get things done and done in the most effective and efficient way; learning to keep still, when the enemy seems to be so relentless and coming from all sides, was quite a feat for me. It wasn't that I didn't trust the Lord to fight my battles, but I felt the longer I remained quiet and didn't move in the situation the way I thought I should; I believed that made me look weak and gave others the upper hand.

That way of thinking caused a disconnect between the Lord and me. I had to be reminded that He makes the decisions in my life; not me. If I just stepped aside and stood still, I would have that front seat to witnessing that incredible rescue operation that only God could perform for me and in a way that promises to work together for my good.

More importantly, I know that His grace is sufficient for me. His power is made perfect in weakness which, in turn, makes me stronger because I know who the source of my strength is and where my deliverance comes from.

I was sharing with my daughter that no matter what she may face in life, if she surrenders it all to the Lord, she will observe the victory that the Lord has for her and will not have to fear or be discouraged because He is with her at all times.

Exodus 14:14 ties into this perfectly, as it states, "The Lord will fight for you, and you only have to be still/silent" (in some translations).

Sometimes we need that reminder that we don't need to fight because the battle is not ours but the Lord's. He is Jehovah Jireh, the Lord Our Provider and Jehovah Nissi, the Lord Our Banner.

If we just keep still and trust Him, the Lord will fight our battles, He'll open doors that no one can close, but will also shut doors that are not ours to walk through.

A little while ago, Chrystal Evans Hurst shared on social media a quote that said, "If God shuts a door, stop banging on it! Trust that whatever is behind it, is not meant for you."

Continue to trust that our God can provide for absolutely any need that we have and no matter what we may come up against, He desires to give us the victory!!

Suggested Song of Meditation: "Jesus Will" by Anita Wilson

James 1:4 (The Living Bible/TLB)

⁴ So let it grow, and don't try to squirm out of your problems. For when your patience is finally in full bloom, then you will be ready for anything, strong in character, full and complete.

I will be the first one to tell you that there is so much going on in this world that I do not understand. But it's not so much about what I am able to process through my own natural eyes or human mind; it's more importantly about knowing where and who to turn to in times of heartache, strife, confusion, disappointment and hardships.

This is not the time to lean unto my own understanding. To the contrary, I must have the ability and patience to endure with a trust in the Lord that supersedes and overrides anything that I may be confronting.

I have learned not to try to squirm out of the problems, tests and trials that may come my way. Instead, I am to rejoice and press forward with a smile on my face as my perseverance/patience has its perfect work; which in the end, results in me maturing, being made whole and having everything I need; lacking nothing.

Before the trials conclude and we are able to say, "It's over," we are to praise the Lord in advance, because we know that everything that we are encountering is working together for our good and to strengthen our character. Recently, I read a quote by Rick Warren which stated, "God changes caterpillars into butterflies, sand into pearls and coal into diamonds, using time and pressure. He's working on you too."

Our turnaround is coming. When our tests and hardships are over, we'll know it. We should not attempt to get out of anything prematurely. We have to let it do its work, so that we can become mature and well-developed; not deficient in any way!!

Suggested Song of Meditation: "And It's Over" by Bryan Andrew Wilson

Psalm 71:20 (New International Version/NIV)

²⁰ Though you have made me see troubles, many and bitter, you will restore my life again; from the depths of the earth you will again bring me up.

With each day that I am blessed to see, I am continuously reminded that we must put all our trust in the name of the Lord.

One of my favorite songs by Fred Hammond is, "I Will Trust." The lyrics in the first verse resonate so profoundly within me as they state, "There was a time when I truly believed that I could do it on my own. But all that I found at the end of that road is, that concept for me was all wrong. But I found a Savior who turned me around and placed His love on me. And I will trust in you until my last heartbeat."

It is because I have come to know the Lord and trust in His name that I no longer lean unto my own understanding. Instead, the belief that I have in Him has shown me that even though the Lord has made me endure trouble and hardship, He has also restored me back to life again.

Those areas of my life that seemed so unproductive and unfruitful; the Lord has brought restoration in a way that only He is capable of doing. All that the swarming locusts have eaten throughout the years, the Lord has reinstated (Joel 2:25). Where there once was lack, because of my relationship that I now have with the Lord, I am living in the overflow.

I have been redeemed and reconnected by the blood of Jesus. There is no more guilt, shame or rejection. Those former things are done and have passed away. Shackles and chains have been loosed and I am released from bondage.

I am free, protected, covered, healed, changed, rebuilt, wiser, recommitted and stronger.

As I have come to trust in the name of the Lord, I realize that there are things that the Lord allows us to go through, so that He and only He, can bring us out and back from the depths of the earth.

Suggested Song of Meditation: "Restored" by J. Moss

Psalm 61:2-3 (New Life Version/NLV)

² I call to You from the end of the earth when my heart is weak. Lead me to the rock that is higher than I.
³ For You have been a safe place for me, a tower of strength where I am safe from those who fight against me.

How encouraging it is to know that the name of Jesus is higher than all other names. There is no other name like His. He is our strong tower and our strength. It doesn't matter what each day may bring, He remains the same.

Time and time again, it has been proven that there is not a friend like the lowly Jesus. He knows about every last one of our struggles and will guide us until the day is done.

When I need assistance and my heart feels overwhelmed, I call on Jesus and nobody else. I have learned how important it is for us not to take advice and guidance from the wrong sources.

Where God speaks to us in truth, the enemy utilizes lies and deception when communicating. God provides a pathway and a means of progression for us. The Lord never said that our lives would be without tests and trials or that suffering wouldn't ever be a part of the equation. As a matter of fact, He said the complete opposite.

The Lord has told us, "Dear brothers and sisters, when troubles of any kind come your way, consider it an opportunity for great joy. For you know that when you are tested, your endurance has a chance to grow (James 1:2-3)."

And during those times of suffering, the Lord instructs us, "To this you were called, because Christ suffered for you, leaving you an example, that you should follow in his steps (1 Peter 2:21)."

We have to remember that when we endure trials, they build and develop our character and strengthen our faith in the Lord. That is why I seek Jesus to lead me to that rock that is higher than me. It is there that I find my refuge where I am kept and protected.

As we navigate through the twists and turns in life and discern what is of God and what isn't, how blessed we are to know that He is our rock and our safe place. In Him, I find the strength that I need to make it through. He is the source of my hope and future. Not only does He know the thoughts and plans that He has for us, but all that He has begun, He will complete.

I will continue to call on the name of Jesus because He is our Savior, our keeper and our friend.

Suggested Song of Meditation: "Keep Me" by Patrick Dopson

Psalm 119:111 (Lexham English Bible/LEB)

¹¹¹ I have taken as my own your testimonies forever, for they are the joy of my heart.

Whenever I find myself in the midst of any trial or obstacle, I grasp tightly to the statutes and rules that the Lord has provided in His Word. They are the joy of my heart.

I learned a long time ago the difference between happiness and joy. Happiness is dictated by external circumstances, unlike joy, which comes from within and is rooted in the divine connection that we have with our Heavenly Father.

The rules and commandments that the Lord has provided me with, I have taken as a heritage forever. And that is why, even in those most trying of times, I have joy. His written instructions provide me with the guidance and answers that I seek in my times of need.

I don't care what the world attempts to make me believe or tries to accomplish; I know that I am a survivor and more than a conqueror because I have the Lord on my side ordering every last one of my steps.

The joy that I feel comes from God's presence in my life and His testimonies that remind me that when I am pressed, cracked and chipped from my afflictions on all sides, I will not be crushed by them. And when I am bewildered at times, I am not to give in to despair. Although I may be persecuted, the Lord has not and will not abandon me. And in those instances where I get knocked down, I will not be destroyed (2 Corinthians 4:8-9).

There have been so many times when the enemy thought he had me but in each situation and through every circumstance, my joy remained in place and could not be moved.

Because I apply His decrees to my life every day, I have joy for my sorrows and hope for my tomorrows. Regardless of what I encounter, I know that the world did not give it to me, therefore, the world cannot take my joy away.

Suggested Song of Meditation: "You Can't Take My Joy" by Dorinda Clark-Cole

Isaiah 41:13 (The Voice/VOICE)

¹³ After all, it is I, the Eternal One your God, who has hold of your right hand, Who whispers in your ear, "Don't be afraid. I will help you."

No matter where we go, like clockwork, my youngest daughter knows to automatically grab my hand, as we navigate from one point to another. As she takes hold of my hand, she trusts that I am going to keep our fingers interlocked and that we will arrive to our destination safely.

I thought about that as I read the verse for this evening's blog. Sometimes when my daughter and I hop in the car to run errands, she doesn't always know where we have to travel to, but she trusts me to get us there.

That is what Isaiah 41:13 reminded me of. The type of blind faith and trust that children exercise... that is what I desire to demonstrate to the Lord on a daily basis.

There is a lot we could learn from children. Just as Jesus stated in Matthew 18:3, "I assure you and most solemnly say to you, unless you repent [that is, change your inner self—your old way of thinking, live changed lives] and become like children [trusting, humble, and forgiving], you will never enter the kingdom of heaven."

Like my daughter, I don't always need to know where I'm going when I know that it is the Lord who has taken hold of my right hand and is guiding me along the way.

There is also no need to fear when the One that we serve is so faithful and promises to help us.

No matter who we are or where we are located, each of us has some test or trial that we are facing. While reflecting on all that I have learned and the knowledge that I continue to gain about the Lord and His love for me, coupled with the testimonies that have been birthed from each test that I have encountered; it is with an unwavering hope and unswerving faith that I am able to be confident about what lies ahead for me because I know that He who promised is reliable, trustworthy and faithful to His Word (Hebrews 10:23).

The Lord did not give us a spirit of fear but of power, and of love, and of a sound mind (2 Timothy 1:7). I am able to hold on and keep my head up because the same God who has held my hand and brought me through before is the same yesterday, today and forevermore.

To stay guarded, I always chronicle the different seasons in my life when I needed the Lord in ways I hadn't ever needed Him before. These binders, notebooks and journals remain written sources of encouragement for me.

Each of the pages have captured my most intimate thoughts, inquiries, prayers, joys, hurts and dreams. They serve as an everyday reminder for me of just how faithful our God is.

They also reflect the mindsets and patterns of behavior that have been transformed, the yokes and strongholds that have been destroyed, the generational curses that have been broken and the breakthroughs and miracles that have taken place.

But even if I didn't have them, there isn't any possible way that I could ever forget all that the Lord has done for me. It is because I recognize that He has always been with me and has never left my side, that I will continue to hold on to God's unchanging hand.

Suggested Song of Meditation: "Hold On" by Spensha Baker

www.ingramcontent.com/pod-product-compliance
Lightning Source LLC
Chambersburg PA
CBHW080402300426
44113CB00015B/2385